MEN IN THE TROPICS

MEN
IN THE TROPICS

A Colonial Anthology

Compiled and Edited

by

HAROLD EVANS

With Maps and Illustrations

LONDON   EDINBURGH   GLASGOW
WILLIAM HODGE AND COMPANY LIMITED

First published 1949

PRINTED IN GREAT BRITAIN BY
EBENEZER BAYLIS AND SON, LTD., THE
TRINITY PRESS, WORCESTER, AND LONDON

PREFACE

THIS book, which is an ambitious kind of book and possibly has ideas above its station, aims at being both a piece of entertainment and a work of reference. As a piece of entertainment it has tried to bring together some of the more piquant, shrewd and illuminating things that have been written about people and places in the Tropics: and as a work of reference it has tried to shape all these things into a design which will give those who want it an introduction—though emphatically no more than an introduction—to the history, geography, topography, flora, fauna and anthropology of the British Colonial Empire.

This dual purpose explains the pattern of the book. It has five parts, each dealing with a geographical region, each self-contained, each introduced by a potted history, each ending with biographical notes about the selected authors, and each having in the middle anything from twenty to forty thousand words of extracts. If you already know your history, or don't want to know it anyhow, then you can skip the potted history. If you are not interested in the authors, but only in what they say, then you can skip the biographical notes. And if you could not care less about history, authors and colonial empires, then you can browse at will in the anthology proper and imbibe the sights, sounds and smells of the Tropics.

Also influencing the pattern of the book has been the necessity to impose some limits to the field of selection. In 500 years a quite remarkable number of people have written one or more books about what are now British dependent territories in the Tropics. So the starters had to be limited, and this was done in two ways. First, by deciding to quote only from British writers, and, among British writers, only from those who recorded on-the-spot experiences—the sailors and soldiers, the traders, the explorers, the missionaries and the administrators. It was done, secondly, by deciding not to draw on works published since the early years of this century. The anthology is not, therefore, an attempt to show the tropical colonies as they are at the moment, but an attempt to show the nature of the legacy left by the empire-builders. That it *is* a retrospective view should be remembered, especially when reading of habits and customs which are primitive and barbarous: the primitive still exists in many areas, and possibly the barbarous, but no Colonial people is to-day without its intelligentsia.

So much for the pattern. As to the imperfections, the regional treatment has meant exclusion of those territories not fitting easily into
one of the regions: Aden, Somaliland, Mauritius, Hong Kong, and—a
difficult decision—Northern Rhodesia and Nyasaland. These last
two could have been included only by dealing regionally with Central
Africa, as well as with East Africa, and this would have required in-
clusion of Southern Rhodesia, which does not qualify as a Crown
Colony. Since in addition there were problems of time and space, it
was reluctantly concluded that they would have to be omitted. Also
excluded, as clearly they had to be from the nature of the anthology,
are the non-tropical territories—the Mediterranean islands, Bermuda,
the Falkland Islands, and a few isolated islands such as St. Helena.
Since this sounds a formidable list, I should perhaps put it into perspective by saying that the anthology nevertheless manages to have reference to ninety per cent of the people of the Colonial Empire.

Gaps exist also in the list of authors. Even with the limits fixed in the
two ways I have mentioned, there remained several hundred "pos-
sibles" which it would have required prolonged research to comb
thoroughly. In eighteen months I have read perhaps 250 of them, including most of those considered important, and selections have been
made from ninety, ranging chronologically from Sir Walter Raleigh
to Mr. Winston Churchill. But the experts will have no difficulty in
spotting omissions, and for these I have no excuse except the physical
impossibility of covering the whole field in the time available.

That, indeed, must be my excuse for other evident shortcomings.
The work has had to be done during train journeys, week-ends and
holidays. Clearly it should have been undertaken by someone with
more time for research: but the need for a book of this kind has so long
existed, and so long gone unsatisfied, that perhaps a charitable view
will be taken of this spare-time effort.

Even as a spare-time effort it would have been impossible without
the help and inspiration of my wife who, during eighteen months,
has typed not less than half-a-million words, foregone all holidays,
endured much short temper, and condoned no backsliding.

Rottingdean, 1949.

CONTENTS

	PAGE
PREFACE	v
LIST OF ILLUSTRATIONS	viii
ACKNOWLEDGMENTS	x

PART ONE: WEST AFRICA 1

The Gambia, Gold Coast, Nigeria and Sierra Leone.

PART TWO: THE CARIBBEAN 103

British Guiana, British Honduras, Barbados, Jamaica, Trinidad, the Bahama Islands, the Leeward Islands, and the Windward Islands.

PART THREE: EAST AFRICA 177

Kenya, Tanganyika, Uganda and Zanzibar.

PART FOUR: THE MALAY ARCHIPELAGO . . 245

The Federation of Malaya, Singapore, Sarawak, North Borneo, and Brunei.

PART FIVE: PACIFIC ISLANDS 319

Fiji, Tonga, the Gilbert and Ellice Islands, and the Solomon Islands.

LIST OF ILLUSTRATIONS

Facing page

The Gold Coast 20

The Compound of a Northern Territories Chief . . . 21

Statesman and Warrior, The Waziri of the Sultan of Sokoto, Nigeria 36

The Age-old Look—An Agboabra Girl of Onitsha Province, Nigeria 37

The End of a Fish Drive by Men of the Konkomba Tribe, Northern Territories of the Gold Coast 68

Traditional Caparison of Northern Nigeria 69

Grandson of a Chief, B.Sc., A.M.I.—A Modern Citizen of Accra and his Children 69

Arrival of a Chief, Gold Coast 84

Courtesan in a robe of amber brocade, Sokoto Emirate . 85

Fulani girl with a bowl of milk to sell, Nigeria . . . 116

Grace and thirst, Barbados 117

Barbados Landscape, Parish of St. Joseph 132

Bathsheba, Barbados 133

River Road, Grenada 164

Basseterre, St. Kitts 165

Kaietur Waterfall, British Guiana 180

Black and Silver, the Symbol of Arab Influence on the East Coast of Africa 181

An Arab Shopkeeper from Pemba in his turban of yellow, acid pink and purple 196

Local Water Transport, Pemba, North-East of Zanzibar . 197

Uganda Landscape 212

The Redoubtable Masai 213

Johore Bahru, Malaya 260

Beach Scene near Malacca 261

Kuala Lipis, Pahang 276

Buddhist Idols in the Ayer Itam temple in Penang . . 277

Fishing in Sunlit Waters—East Coast of Malaya . . . 308

A Fijian Beach 309

A South Seas' Harbour 324

A Typical Fijian 325

A beautiful Lagoon 340

A Fisherman in the South Seas 341

Givutu, Solomon Islands 356

A Lone Coconut Islet in the Solomon Islands . . . 357

ACKNOWLEDGMENTS

My personal thanks are due to Sir Albert R. Cook for permission to quote from *Uganda Memories*, and to Mr. Walter W. Skeat for permission to quote from *Malay Magic*. To the Society of Authors, as Literary Representative of the Estate of the late Robert Louis Stevenson, I am indebted for permission to quote from the author's *In the South Seas*, and to Mr. W. G. Wallace for permission to quote from the late Alfred Russel Wallace's *The Malay Archipelago*.

My thanks are also due to the following publishers for permission to quote from the books named:

Odhams Press Ltd.: *My African Journey* by Winston S. Churchill.

Cambridge University Press: *Fables and Folk Tales from an Eastern Forest* by Walter W. Skeat, and *Twenty-five Years in East Africa* by John Roscoe.

William Blackwood & Sons, Ltd.: *The Rise of Our East African Empire* by Lord Lugard, and *At Home in Fiji* by C. F. Gordon Cumming.

Sampson Low, Marston & Co., Ltd.: *The Western Pacific* by Walter Coote, *Through the Dark Continent* by H. M. Stanley, *Two Kings of Uganda* by R. P. Ashe, *Twenty-five Years in British Guiana* by Henry Kirke, *Hausaland* by C. H. Robinson, and *Glimpses of a Governor's Life* by Sir Hesketh Bell.

Edward Arnold & Co.: *Eighteen Years in Uganda and East Africa* by Bishop Alfred Tucker, *Benin: City of Blood* by Commander R. H. Bacon, *Early Days in East Africa* by Sir Frederick Jackson, *Soldiering and Surveying in British East Africa* by Sir James Macdonald, *The East African Protectorate* by Sir Charles Eliot, and *Rise of our East African Empire* by F. D. Lugard.

John Lane The Bodley Head Ltd.: *The Real Malay* and *Malay Sketches* by Sir Frank Swettenham.

John Murray: *The Great Rift Valley* by J. W. Gregory (and the Author's Executors), and *Funafuti* by Mrs. E. David.

Wells Gardner, Darton & Co., Ltd.: *Ten Years in Melanesia* by Alfred Penny.

George Philip & Son, Ltd.: *A Naturalist Among the Head-Hunters* by C. M. Woodford.

ACKNOWLEDGMENTS

Richards Press Ltd.: *In Court and Campong* by Sir Hugh Clifford.

Routledge & Kegan Paul, Ltd.: *Among the Indians of Guiana* by Sir Everard im Thurn.

The Sheldon Press: *The Flame Tree* by Rosetta Baskerville.

Hutchinson & Co., Ltd.: *The Uganda Protectorate* by Sir Harry Johnston.

The Straits Times Press, Ltd.: *East Coast Etchings* by Sir Hugh Clifford.

In all instances I have endeavoured to trace copyright and to make correct acknowledgment of the sources of all extracts appearing in *Men in the Tropics*. If I have inadvertently been guilty of any error of omission or commission, I tender my apologies for that inadvertence.

H. E.

To
S. M. Evans and G. M. Evans.
Most selfless of parents.

PART ONE

WEST AFRICA

THE GAMBIA, GOLD COAST, NIGERIA AND SIERRA LEONE

Perspective

1. WHITE MAN'S GRAVE
2. THE WEST AFRICAN SCENE
3. DISPOSITION OF THE PEOPLE
4. FUN AND GAMES
5. "MAN IS THE NOBLER ANIMAL"
6. "THIS THEY CALL THEIR FITTISH"
7. POMP AND CIRCUMSTANCE
8. WARFARE
9. SLAVES
10. BEASTS, BIRDS AND CREEPING THINGS

Books and Authors: with biographical notes

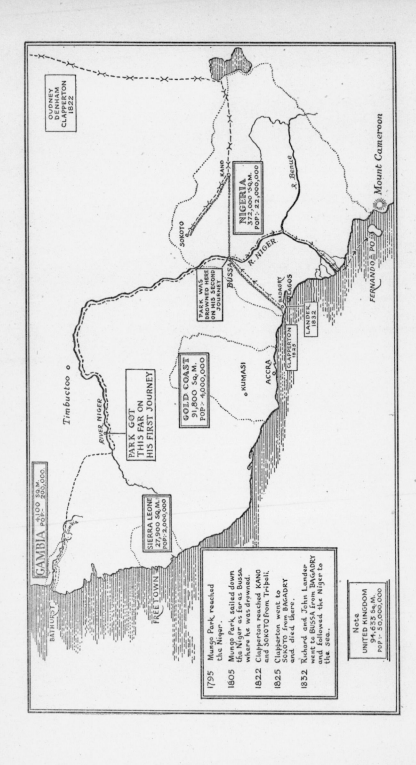

OUDNEY
DENHAM
CLAPPERTON
1822

Mount Cameroon

NIGERIA
372,000 SQ.M.
POP: 22,000,000

KANO

SOKOTO

R. Benue

R. NIGER

BUSSA

PARK WAS
DROWNED HERE
ON HIS SECOND
JOURNEY

BAGADRY

FERNANDO PO

LAGOS

LANDER
1832

CLAPPERTON
1825

ACCRA

PARK GOT
THIS FAR ON
HIS FIRST JOURNEY

GOLD COAST
91,800 SQ.M.
POP: 4,000,000

KUMASI

Timbuctoo

RIVER NIGER

GAMBIA
4,100 SQ.M.
POP: 200,000

SIERRA LEONE
27,900 SQ.M.
POP: 2,000,000

BATHURST

FREE TOWN

Note
UNITED KINGDOM
94,633 Sq.M.
POP: 50,000,000

1795   Mungo Park reached
       the Niger.

1805   Mungo Park sailed down
       the Niger as far as Bussa
       where he was drowned.

1822   Clapperton reached KANO
       and SOKOTO from Tripoli.

1825   Clapperton went to
       SOKOTO from BAGADRY
       and died there.

1832   Richard and John Lander
       went to BUSSA from BAGADRY
       and followed the Niger to
       the sea.

PERSPECTIVE

AT the risk of offending the French, who have other ideas, most authorities begin the story of Europe and West Africa with the Portuguese vessels which Prince Henry the Navigator sent to probe their way southwards along the African coast. Awareness of a Kingdom of the Blacks had, of course, existed in Europe long before. The peoples of North Africa had been trading across the Sahara from the beginning of recorded history, and Herodotus, writing in the fourth century B.C., pieced together a tolerable geography of Negroland. The Portuguese were not even the first people to find their way there by sea. A modest 1,700 years earlier the Carthaginians sent a gentleman named Hanno with sixty ships, each of fifty oars, to explore, colonise and trade with the Atlantic coast of Africa. Just how far he got is a matter of speculation, but from an interpretation of the records Mary Kingsley for one was prepared to believe he saw Mount Cameroon in eruption.

The fact remains that for all practical purposes it was the Portuguese who brought Europe and West Africa together, since Prince Henry's men not only showed that it was possible to get there by sea, but also came back with stories of gold and ivory and other riches, and this inevitably set the French, English, Dutch and Danes hard on their heels. Unhappily, the commodities on offer included slaves; and still more unhappily, developments on the other side of the Atlantic—the discovery of the New World and the carving out of plantations—conspired to make trade in slaves far and away the most lucrative. So it was that for the next 200 years Europeans made fat profits out of shipping black men to America.

The English took their full share in this trade though, like the rest, they started legitimately enough. Queen Elizabeth roundly rebuked Sir John Hawkins for being the first Englishman to carry a cargo of slaves. "If any of the negroes should be carried off without their free consent," she told him, "it would be detestable and call down the vengeance of heaven upon the undertakers." It must be added that later she lent him a ship for the purpose, knighted him, and allowed him to include in his coat of arms the bust of a negro in chains. Yet the English did in general hold back from the trade. Hawkins made his voyages in the 1560's. In 1618, when James I granted a Royal Charter to a group of citizens dubbing themselves, "The Company of Adventurers trading into Africa," one of the Company's captains,

Richard Jobson, records that in the Gambia River an African merchant offered him slaves for sale. "But," says Jobson, "I made answer, We were a people who did not deale in any such commodities, neither did we buy or sell one another, or any that had our owne shapes; he seemed to marvell much at it."

Alas, these high principles were then on their last legs. In the 1620's English planters settled in Barbados and other West Indian islands, and demanded that they, too, should be provided with slaves. Scruples went by the board. From then until the abolition of the trade in 1807 a succession of English trading companies dealt mainly with slaves— and did it so successfully that most European competitors were forced out of the business.

This trading association between Europe and Africa had peculiarly little influence on the life and thought of West Africans. From the European it required only that he should set up a number of trading depots at suitable points along the coast, with fortifications to protect them. He neither desired to penetrate into the hinterland, nor was he encouraged to do so by the Coast Africans who were anxious to retain their position as middlemen. To quote Lady Lugard: "Europe held the coast. Slaves were hunted for her in the far interior. Ivory was shot for her, gold was washed for her; but Europe herself, the civilisation, penetrated no farther than perhaps twenty miles inland." Mary Kingsley put it with characteristic pithiness: "The only radical change made on the majority of Africans by the presence of white men was made by exporting them to America."

The stirring of a new spirit did not come until the end of the eighteenth century. It found expression in two events of the greatest significance to West Africa. One, obviously, was abolition of the slave trade, and of this I shall say more later. The other was the founding in England in 1788 of an African Association, later to be incorporated into the Royal Geographical Society. Its founder members were ninety men of science who sought to know just what went on in the hinterland of West Africa and, in particular, where the River Niger began and ended its course.

Knowledge of the existence of the river had existed for centuries, but the knowledge was, at the best, third or fourth hand. Some said it flowed eastwards; some westwards; some thought it was really the River Gambia; others expounded theories which required it to flow into a great lake or, alternatively, into a great swamp; yet others were quite certain that it must flow into the sea somewhere along the coast of Guinea, and was therefore either the Volta or the Congo; there were even those who asserted that Niger and Nile were one and the same;

only very late in the day did the correct theory gain currency—that the innumerable river mouths between Lagos and Calabar together made up the Niger's outfall.

Well, there was the problem, and personal investigation seemed the only way of solving it. So the ninety men of science engaged in rapid succession three men who had distinguished themselves in various parts of the world as explorers. The three died in no less rapid succession, one at Cairo, one five days' journey south of Tripoli, and the third, the "gay and sanguine" Houghton, getting very close, well into the interior beyond the Gambia. With a fourth attempt came real progress. A young ship's surgeon named Mungo Park, son of a Scottish farmer, accepted the Association's invitation to go and look for the Niger. He made the Gambia River his line of entry and, travelling alone, followed up what clues he could find until on July 18th, 1795, he found himself standing on the banks of the river. It was "glittering to the morning sun," he wrote, "as broad as the Thames at Westminster, and flowing slowly to the *eastward.*"

In getting there Park suffered such privations and ill-treatment that, after following the course of the river for some distance on horseback, he had no alternative but to return. But his news greatly stirred distinguished opinion at home and in due course he was sent back again, this time at the head of an expedition financed from public funds and including thirty-nine white men besides himself. Park planned to take the expedition from the coast to the Niger very much along the route of his earlier journey, and then to build a boat and sail in it wherever the river went. Unhappily the party began its journey during the rains, and only ten of the white men lived to see the Niger. By the time the boat had been built five more were dead, and so Park set out with only four European companions, of whom one was mad. Just before embarking he wrote to his wife: "I do not intend to stop or land anywhere until we reach the coast." That was the last the world heard from the expedition.

News of Park's death came from a guide who had accompanied him much of the way. The guide said that Park sailed as far as the town of Bussa, some 1,000 miles from his starting point and 720 miles from the sea. There he in some way excited the hostility of the people, and was drowned when his boat capsized in the rapids during a fight.

It was not until nearly twenty years later that corroborative accounts were obtained. They were collected by Commander Hugh Clapperton. Like Park, Clapperton was a Lowland Scot for whom life at sea had led to a taste for exploration. Placed on half-pay after the Napoleonic Wars, Clapperton talked his way into an expedition organised by Dr. Oudney and Major Denham to cross the Sahara from Tripoli on a visit to the kingdom of Bornu, adjoining Lake Chad. Having reached Lake Chad, Denham explored to the south-east while Oudney and Clapperton set out to visit the Hausa States to the west. After only a few days' journey Oudney died, but Clapperton continued, and so became the first white man to visit the ancient city of Kano and the less ancient, but no less important, city of Sokoto. At Sokoto Clapperton not only obtained news of Park, but also pieced together information which tended to confirm theories that the Niger, having reached the Hausa States, turned south and had its outfall in the Bight of Benin.

Clapperton now held the limelight. In addition to his news about Park and the Niger, he came back to England in 1825 with the first authentic accounts of the existence in the interior of West Africa of a group of semi-civilised Mohammedan states, looking to the East for their traditions, ruled on feudal lines by powerful kings, and commanding an extensive commerce. What was more, Clapperton had put himself on very good terms with Sultan Bello of Sokoto, to whom all the other kings of the Hausa States paid tribute both as their religious and secular leader. Bello had declared his anxiety to establish friendly intercourse with England, to exchange articles of trade, and to have posted on his frontiers an English physician and an English consul with whom he might transact all matters of business; he had even declared his willingness to help the English in their campaign against the slave trade by forbidding any of his subjects to sell slaves to the Coast people.

The advantages of such an intercourse, if it could be established, were so apparent that Lord Bathurst, then Secretary of State for Colonies, quickly despatched Clapperton back to Africa. On this occasion he started his journey into the interior, not from Tripoli, but from the Guinea Coast at Badagry, a town a little to the west of Lagos. Things went wrong immediately. Clapperton had five white companions. His chief aides were Captain Pearce and Dr. Morrison; a young Cornishman named Richard Lander accompanied him as personal servant, and a seaman named Dawson acted in a similar capacity to Dr. Morrison; and finally there was a Mr. Houston, a British merchant resident in Benin, who had agreed to travel with the expedition part of the way into the interior. Within a few marches of the coast, Dr. Morrison, Captain Pearce and Dawson were all dead, and when Houston returned to the coast (where, incidentally, he died shortly afterwards), Clapperton was left with Richard Lander and a Hausa guide as his sole companions. Nor was the cup yet full. On arrival at Sokoto, Clapperton found Bello in a very different mood. Where before he had been eager, friendly and open-handed he was now sullen, reserved and suspicious. The change probably originated in the fact that Clapperton was carrying presents for the Sheikh of Bornu, a monarch whom he had met on his first journey, but with whom Bello was now at loggerheads. Whatever the cause, Bello virtually detained his visitor and caused him to live in conditions which aggravated the illness into which he had already fallen. As a result, Clapperton became rapidly worse and eventually died in the arms of the faithful Lander. In his journal Lander describes how he took Clapperton's body to a village five miles outside Sokoto, and buried it there with the help of a few slaves. Beside the grave he placed the Union Jack, which waved "slowly and mournfully" while he read the funeral service. "Not a single soul listened . . . for the slaves were quarrelling with each other the whole time it lasted."

Lander succeeded in making his way back to the coast, and was held to have acquitted himself so well that in 1830 the Government commissioned him to return and to "ascertain the course of the Great River" below the point at which Clapperton had seen it. With him went his brother John (without either salary or promise of reward), and the two young Cornishmen, sons of an innkeeper, did the job with the greatest thoroughness. Following the river down by canoe, they came at last to the sea by one of its many mouths, and so completed the task which the African Association had set itself forty years earlier.

These same forty years had seen very considerable changes in the affairs of the trading establishments on the coast. With the slave trade to America outlawed by most of the nations chiefly concerned, the companies found profits much harder to come by in legitimate trade, the outcome being a reduction in the number of establishments and a disposition to retire from the Coast altogether. As far as the British were concerned, the abolition had one particularly significant result. It brought official administration to the Coast for the first time. Three factors contributed to this development. Someone had to take administrative responsibility for the growing community of liberated slaves settled at Freetown; a base had to be provided from which the Royal Navy's anti-slavery patrol could operate; and finally the Company of Merchants Trading in Africa complained that it could not go on maintaining the security of the British establishments with the small subsidy it was now receiving. Accordingly, from January 1st, 1808, Sierra Leone became a Crown Colony.

Freetown's growth had been phenomenal. It started in 1788 with the purchase of land from a local chief to provide a home for emancipated negroes from Britain. Though this first settlement was mis-managed most grossly, it provided a nucleus. The emancipated negroes were followed by a batch of 1,100 "Nova Scotians", slaves who had deserted from American plantations during the American War of Independence, plus a sprinkling of free negroes from Virginia who had joined the Loyalists. Then came 550 "Maroons" from Jamaica, people of African extraction, but with Spanish and Carib blood in their veins, who were deported from the island following an unsuccessful revolt. Finally, with the abolition of the slave trade, the Royal Navy began to bring their prize vessels into Freetown, and to deposit ashore the rescued Africans, an astonishing miscellany of people from every tribe in West Africa. In a period of forty years something like 60,000 slaves were liberated in Freetown.

The town thus became the British Government's headquarters on the Coast, and as and when responsibility was assumed for other British establishments it seemed the logical thing to make them off-shoots of the Sierra Leone Government. This was done in the case of the settlement in the Gambia, and later, in 1821, when Parliament decided to assume direct administration of the Gold Coast establish-ments, these too were placed under the Sierra Leone Government.

First attempts at administration in the Gold Coast proved short-lived, however, chiefly because Government badly burned its fingers in its dealings with the King of Ashanti. Until the beginning of the century there had been little or no direct contact between Europeans and Ashantis. The merchants regarded the Ashantis as a "rude un-polished set of men, governed by a despotic tyrannical Prince", and were content that in trade with Ashanti the Fanti people of the Coast should act as middlemen. But in 1807 an Ashanti army invaded Fanti-land and came down to the coast. Apart from the very satisfactory plunder he collected in slaves and gold dust, the King saw that from his point of view there was much to commend direct contact with the Europeans. In any event, his monarchy was based on military power, and military power needed regular exercise. So he began to make a habit of descending on the Fantis, doing so in 1811 and again in 1816. "These invasions inflicted the greatest miseries on the Fantees," wrote Bowdich. "Few were slain in battle, for they rarely dared to encounter the invaders; but the butcheries in cold blood were incredible, and thousands were dragged into the interior to be sacrificed. . . . Famines, unmitigated by labour, succeeded the wide waste of Fanti territory, the wretched remnant of the population abandoning itself to despair."

As a result, the Committee of Merchants which in 1817 was still administering the affairs of the settlements, decided to send a mission to Kumasi, the King's capital, "to deprecate these repeated calamities, to conciliate so powerful a monarch, and to propitiate an extension of commerce." The mission was, in fact, most civilly received, as can be seen from the account which Bowdich gives of it, and a treaty of "perpetual peace and harmony" was signed. For some reason, in which personal intrigue was certainly not absent, the Government at home decided the following year to send a mission of its own, and assigned the task to Joseph Dupuis, whose chief qualification appears to have been a "long residence in Barbary". His instructions were to "cultivate the existing harmony with the king of Ashantee", with a view to fostering trade between Ashanti and the British (as distinct from the Dutch and the French). Dupuis, no less than Bowdich, had an amiable welcome, and also came back with a treaty which appeared to ensure satisfactory relations.

Misunderstandings in interpretation of the treaty nevertheless began to be evident, and it was at this point that the Gold Coast establishments were placed under the Government of Sierra Leone. By 1824 relations with Ashanti had become so strained that Sir Charles McCarthy, then "Governor-in-Chief of the British West African Possessions", came down from Sierra Leone with some military reinforcements. He appears to have acted somewhat impetuously, both in seeking the causes of the trouble and then engaging the Ashantis in battle without a proper appreciation of their numbers, skill and fanaticism. His little force of trained men was annihilated and he himself was killed and his head carried off.

Though the Government showed great energy in avenging this defeat and humiliation—the Ashantis were put to flight in a battle near Dodowah the following year—the expense and bitterness, added to the considerable mortality by disease among the troops, seems to have thoroughly sickened them, and in 1828, after only seven years administration, it was proposed to withdraw all official support from the British establishments. This proposal the merchants indignantly denounced, and fought their cause so stoutly that Government, though proceeding with its determination to have no more to do with direct administration, agreed to make a Parliamentary grant of £4,000 a year for maintenance of garrisons and fortifications, and to place control in the hands of a committee of three London merchants.

There followed a period of outstanding progress in the affairs of the Gold Coast establishments. "You will get nothing done in tropical Africa," wrote Mary Kingsley, "except under the influence of individual men." So it was now. As Governor the Committee of Merchants appointed Mr. George Maclean a man of exceptional character, ability and integrity. For twelve years he not only managed the affairs of the establishments most efficiently, but also exercised a remarkable influence over the people of Fantiland. With the King of Ashanti, too, he was on the best of terms. All this he achieved on the official grant of £4,000 a year. Sir James Alexander visited the Coast during this period, and subsequently described Mr. Maclean as "a tall and sparely made gentleman. . . . He had regular features and fair hair and was apparently in the prime of life". Sir James continued: "With the small and (I think) inadequate grant of £4,000 a year Mr. Maclean has done, and does more for his country, than when the Gold Coast establishments cost £30,000 annually. His own salary is only £700; his secretary, captain of the guard, and surgeon receive £200 each; the commandant of Accra has £100; and one hundred black regulars, acting as infantry and artillery, and dressed in red with blue facings, cost £12 a year each. . . . Besides the above expenses, there are paid out of the small grant—labourers at the rate of one dollar and a half per month, canoe-men, messengers, ammunition, presents, stationery, medicine, funerals, and non-commissioned officers, including the sergeant-major, Berryman, a valuable man, active, determined and sober. Lastly the agent at home receives £100; and the remainder of the grant is applied to the repair of the forts. Cape Coast and Accra alone appear on the books; but Annamboe and Dixcove are also maintained, as they are considered too valuable for the protection of the merchants to be given up."

Towards 1840, unhappily, innuendoes began to be whispered against Maclean at home, inspired partly by the sudden death of his wife, and they eventually reached such a pitch that the Government felt compelled to appoint a Select Committee to inquire into them. The Committee's conclusion was that Maclean had "acquired a very wholesome influence over a coast not much less than 150 miles in extent and to a considerable distance inland, preventing within that range external slave trade, maintaining peace and security, and exercising a useful, though irregular, jurisdiction among the neighbouring tribes". Nevertheless, the Committee thought that the time had come for the Government to resume direct control of the establishments, and this was done in 1842. A new governor was appointed and Maclean, characteristically, accepted the lesser post of Judicial Assessor. He died at Cape Coast five years later.

Contemporary with Maclean, and exercising an influence equally notable in the affairs of another part of the Coast, was Macgregor Laird, a Liverpool merchant, whose imagination had been fired by the possibilities of the Niger as a commercial highway into the interior. In 1832, only two years after Richard and John Lander had located the river's outfall, Laird fitted out an expedition comprising two steam vessels, which were to make their way up the river, and a sailing vessel which was to remain at the mouth and receive the cargoes brought down by the steam vessels. He described his project as one designed to interest two groups of people—"those who look upon the opening of Central Africa to the enterprise and capital of British merchandise as likely to create new and extensive markets for our manufactured goods, and fresh sources whence to draw our supplies; and those who, viewing mankind as one great family, consider it their duty to raise their fellow-creatures from their present degraded, denationalised and demoralised state, nearer to Him in whose image they were created". Here was a very early statement of the principles which Lugard later re-defined and gave currency as the "dual mandate".

As a commercial proposition, however, Laird's expedition failed dismally, and its loss of life was appalling, only nine of the forty-eight Europeans surviving. Laird himself came back, but among those lost was Richard Lander, who died at Fernando Po as the result of a bullet wound received during a brush with the people of the Delta. Yet Laird felt able to declare that it had proved "that any man with common sense and common ability may ascend and descend the main artery of Africa (provided he escapes the effects of the climate) with perfect safety, in moderate sized vessels, from the sea to Boussa".

For the next thirty years Laird persisted in his belief. An expedition organised by the Government in 1841 proved hardly less disastrous than his own, losing forty-eight of its 145 Europeans, but Laird was persuasive and in 1853 the Treasury subsidised an expedition, led by William Balfour Baikie, R.N. This time there were solid results. For the expedition Laird's brother built the *Pleiad*, the first exploring vessel to be fitted with a screw propeller. The *Pleiad* spent 122 days in the river, did not lose one of its forty-five Europeans, and went up the Benue tributary 200 miles beyond the farthest point hitherto reached. In part these results were achieved by the use of quinine as a prophylactic against malaria—a development of which one can say with hand on heart that it marked a new era in African exploration. With this success behind him, Laird advocated a regular service of steamers to ply up and down the Niger and develop trade. In 1856 the Government was so far convinced as to give him a subsidy, and he sent out a ship called the *Dayspring*. Three trading stations were established, but then the troubles started. The *Dayspring* was wrecked, two other vessels could balance only one successful trip against several which were financially disastrous, and then in 1861 Laird died. Without his faith and inspiration the venture promptly collapsed.

Setbacks such as this helped to explain the conclusions of the Parliamentary Select Committee which in 1864 began an inquiry into the state of the British establishments in West Africa. "All further extension of territory or assumption of government, or new treaties offering any protection to native tribes, would be inexpedient," decided the Committee. "The object of our policy should be to encourage in the natives the exercise of those qualities which may render it possible for us more and more to transfer to them the administration of all the Governments, with a view to our ultimate withdrawal from all except, probably, Sierra Leone."

Not, indeed, that the establishments commanded very much territory, for a map submitted to the Committee showed only dots here and there along the coast, accompanied by a few pink lines which, it was explained, represented influence extending not more than a mile inland. Only in the Gold Coast was there any indication of protected territory lying inland. Here an Agreement dated March 6th, 1844, had been signed with the chiefs of "countries and places . . . adjacent to the said forts and settlements", whereby the power and jurisdiction of the Queen was recognised. But a very firm distinction was drawn between this protection and the actual possession of territory. The Acting Chief Secretary of the Gold Coast establishments found this to his cost when, in 1865, he ventured to issue a notice declaring that territory within cannon shot (or five miles) of any of the forts was to be regarded as belonging to Great Britain. Ordering recall of this notice, the Secretary of State for the Colonies said sternly: "Whatever influence you may be able to exert in discouraging or repressing barbarous customs, leading to loss of life, will be very proper, and I shall be happy to approve your exercise of it; but the extension of British territory is a different matter, and cannot receive my sanction." Incidentally, it seems doubtful if a cannon *could* be fired from some of the forts, such was the condition into which they had been allowed to fall. A. B. Ellis, posted to Secondee, says cheerfully of the fort: "I learned that when a gun was about to be fired it was necessary to send out the garrison to lean against the walls of the fort to prop them up, or else the concussion would bring them down."

Here, as Lady Lugard commented, was the "lowest ebb of British sentiment with regard to the West African Colonies."

It was the French who, more than anyone else, induced a change of heart: the French and Sir George Goldie. Inspired by the foresight and drive of Gambetta, the French saw very quickly the possibilities opened up to them by the introduction of steam transport. It meant, they saw, that the barrier of the Sahara became very much less a barrier, and that there was now no real reason why their outposts in Morocco should not be linked with those in West Africa. Indeed, why should they not create a vast French Empire in Africa, stretching from the Mediterranean to the equator? Nor did they have any doubts about the value of the West African trade. The Niger Delta, in particular, was rich in palm oil; palm oil was important in the manufacture of both grease and soap, and for both commodities the Industrial Revolution had created a demand. So the French began to take a lively interest in the Lower Niger, and in a very short time their flag flew over some thirty trading stations on the banks of the river.

But Britain, too, had her man of vision, though for a long time he battled alone. At the end of 1877 Sir George Goldie (or plain Mr. Goldie-Taubman as he then was) had occasion to visit the Niger delta. His purpose was partly to inspect certain trading interests in which his family was interested, and partly to investigate the prospects of crossing Africa from the Niger to the Nile. What he saw and heard in the delta caused a concentration of his ideas. He saw that if British commercial interests were not to be squeezed out of the Niger region it was imperative that the several small companies at present trading there should amalgamate. They were at first a little coy about it, but by 1879 they had been persuaded, and an amalgamated company came into being. With Goldie's restless energy as the spur, the company pushed vessels up both the Niger and Benue, opened new stations, and entered into treaties with the chiefs and emirs. So successfully did the work proceed that by 1884 the French companies decided to call it a day and allowed themselves to bought out.

As it turned out, this development came not a moment too soon. Germany had now entered the field and the "scramble" for Africa had well and truly begun. In 1885 the Powers met in Berlin and agreed on rough-and-ready rules. It was agreed that where a Power could produce reasonable evidence that it had already established a predominant interest in a given region, that region should be recognised as its sphere of influence. Thanks to Goldie and the work of the British Consul in the delta, the British representative was able to claim that only British interests were now represented in the Lower Niger. He gained his point and a British protectorate was declared over the Niger Delta. The conference had cleared the course, and "steeplechases" into the hinterland began all along the coast, the object being to persuade chiefs in the interior to accept treaties of protection. By now the British Government saw that they must either compete in the race or abandon influence in Africa to France and Germany. They decided to compete, and in the Niger region gave the National African Company a Royal Charter which meant, in effect, that for international purposes the flag of the company, renamed the Royal Niger Company, was equivalent to the British flag. The company engaged men of the calibre of Joseph Thomson and Lugard, fresh from their achievements in East Africa, and they "steeplechased" to such good effect that French and German expeditions to the Hausa States were forestalled, and treaties obtained with all the States.

There was still a great deal of international bickering before the details were sorted out, but in 1898 an Anglo-French Agreement in Paris regulated boundaries, and the map of West Africa assumed the appearance which in the main it still has.

1. WHITE MAN'S GRAVE

As late as 1893, when the prophylactic value of quinine was well known, Mary Kingsley received this advice from a seasoned Coaster:

When you have made up your mind to go to West Africa the very best thing you can do is to get it unmade again and go to Scotland instead; but if your intelligence is not strong enough to do so, abstain from exposing yourself to the direct rays of the sun, take 4 grains of quinine every day for a fortnight before you reach the Rivers, and get some introductions to the Wesleyans; they are the only people on the Coast who have got a hearse with feathers.

KINGSLEY: *Travels in West Africa.* 1897.

Outward bound, conversation customarily had a horrific twist.

One of the Agents would look at the Captain during a meal-time, and say, "You remember J., Captain?" "Knew him well," says the Captain; "why, I brought him out his last time, poor chap!" then follows full details of the pegging-out of J., and his funeral, etc. Then a Government official who had been out before, would kindly turn to a colleague out for the first time, and say, "Brought any dress clothes with you?" The unfortunate new-comer, scenting an allusion to a more cheerful phase of Coast life, gladly answers in the affirmative. "That's right," says the interlocutor; "you want them to wear at funerals. Do you know," he remarks, turning to another old Coaster, "my dress trousers did not get mouldy once last wet season."

"Get along," says his friend, "you can't hang a thing up twenty-four hours without its being fit to graze a cow on."

"Do you get anything else but fever down there?" asks a newcomer, nervously.

"Haven't time as a general rule, but I have known some fellows get kraw kraw."

"And the Portuguese itch, abscesses, ulcers, the Guinea worm and the small pox," observe the chorus calmly.

"Well," says the first answerer, kindly but regretfully, as if it pained him to admit this wealth of disease was denied his particular locality; "they are mostly on the South-west Coast." And then a gentleman says parasites are, as far as he knows, everywhere on the Coast, and some of them several yards long. "Do you remember poor C.?" says he to the Captain, who gives his usual answer, "Knew him well. Ah! poor chap, there was quite a quantity of him eaten away, inside and out, with parasites, and a quieter, better living man than C. there never was." "Never," says the chorus, sweeping away the hope that by taking care you may keep clear of such things—the new Coaster's great hope.

KINGSLEY: West African Studies. 1899.

When Laird took his two steam vessels up the Niger in 1832 even the value of quinine was not appreciated. In one week in November this is what happened to the expedition.

On the 18th, Mr. Andrew Clark, a fine young gentleman about eighteen years of age, died. He had joined the expedition as a volunteer against my wishes, but with the full approbation of his friends, with whom I was intimately acquainted. Poor fellow! he expired with the utmost calmness, drinking a cup of coffee; and his amiable and obliging disposition having endeared him to the crew, his death threw an additional gloom of despondency over these ill-fated men. In the afternoon James Dunbar, one of the firemen, died.

On the 19th, my chief mate, Mr. Goldie, and my sailmaker, John Brien, followed; and on the morning of the 20th, our supercargo, Mr. Jordan, expired. I thought at the time that Dr. Briggs had died also; as, while he was endeavouring to revive Mr. Jordan, he swooned and remained insensible for a long time. In the evening of the 20th, Mr. Swinton also died—he was a most respectable man, and filled the situation of carpenter; he was a native of Grangemouth, and having been a resident many years in the Indian Archipelago, thought that no climate could affect him. A few hours after his death, Mr. Millar, our chief engineer, a young man of high promise and respectable connexions in the South of Scotland, followed him.

On the 21st November, we lost William Ramm, the steward; William Parry, an apprentice; and Gardner, a seaman. On the 22nd, these were followed by William Ellison, the second mate, and a fine lad about sixteen years old whom Captain Harries had picked up and adopted in Dublin: his name was George ——, and I believe he was respectably connected, and entitled to some property when of age. The 23rd of November was a day of respite; but on the 24th, Hugh Cosnahan, a seaman, died, and for another interval the mortality ceased.

LAIRD and OLDFIELD:
Narrative of an Expedition into the Interior of Africa. 1837.

The malignity of the climate was usually attributed to miasma rising from the swamps.

Every Morning a thick, stinking and sulphurous Damp or Mist riseth, especially near Rivers or Watry-places: Which Mist so spreads its self, and falls so thick on the Earth, that it is almost impossible to escape the Infection while we are fasting, and our Bodies more susceptible to it than the Natives. This Fog happeneth most frequently in the ill Season of the six Months, which we here call Winter, but more especially in July and August. Wherefore we are more seized with Sickness in that time, than in the good Season or Summer. The Stench of this unwholesome Mist is very much augmented by the Negroes' pernicious Custom of laying their Fish for five or six Days to putrify before they eat it, and their easing their Bodies round their Houses, and all over their Towns; and if this odious Mixture of noysome Stenches very much affects the State of Health here, it is not to be wondered, since 'tis next to impossibility, not only for new Comers, but those who have long continued here, to preserve themselves intirely from its Malign Effects. The great Difference betwixt the European Air and this, is so observable, that few come hither, who are not at first seized by a Sickness which carries off a great many, and that chiefly because we are so wretchedly unprovided with what should comfort and nourish these poor Men; for we have no help to have recourse to but corrupted Medicines, and unskilful Physicians, they being only ignorant Barbers, who bring several into the utmost danger of their Lives: Whereas Nature is strong enough, by the Assistance of good nourishing Diet and Restoratives, it might probably recover the Patient. But, alas! how should he be able to get them? For our Medicines, as I have before told you, are most of them spoiled; and for Food, what is here to be gotten for the common People besides Fish and a dry lean Hen? And, indeed, were he able to pay for better, here is nothing proper for a weak Stomach; for all the Oxen or Cows, Sheep and Hens, are dry, lean and tough: So that a sound Man, not to mention an infirm one, hath enough to do to eat them.

BOSMAN: *Description of the Coast of Guinea.* 1721.

Victorians said the same thing in their own Victorian way.

From the fact of the intervening valleys not admitting of free perflation, from whatever direction the wind prevails, the products of rapid tropical decomposition, aided as they are by the hygrometric state of the atmosphere, hang over particular spots like clouds, and poison, like so much mephitic gas, those who are exposed to their influence. So well understood is the poisonous character of those emanations that residents close the doors and windows against the land breeze, and usually burn the air in their bedrooms by placing in it a chauffer of lighted charcoal at a safe interval of time before they retire for the night.

GORDON: *Life on the Gold Coast.* 1881.

Bosman declared that the English contributed to their own undoing by an addiction to rum punch.

'Tis incredible how many are consumed by this damnable liquor (pardon the expression), which is not only confined to the soldiery, but some of the principal people are so bigotted to it, that I really believe for all the time I was upon the Coast, that at least one of their agents, and factors innumerable died yearly. So that if the state of health in Guinea be computed by the number of the English which dye here, certainly this country must have a much more unhealthful name in England, than with us; and to tell an Englishman that their illness proceeds from their debauches in this liquor, would signifie just as much as to inform them that the excessive eating of flesh (of which they are such great lovers) is very prejudicial to human bodies.

BOSMAN: *Description of the Coast of Guinea.* 1721.

Every newcomer commented on excessive eating by the residents.

Five full meals per diem appeared upon the table, and though this far exceeded the calibre of the governor, yet those, to whom habit had become nature, went through the process, with much credit to their digestive powers; why five meals are necessary in such a climate as Africa, when one often amply suffices elsewhere, no one can possibly imagine; at breakfast, roast ducks, savoury stews, and cutlettes, assist in filling, with their fumes, the already too loaded atmosphere; at luncheon, hot soups and stews; dinner is a compound of both, rendered more terrible by the addition of very second rate pastry; tea presents the half-cold meat of the former meal—and supper is a repetition of the luncheon; with each of these meals, porter, ale, wine, etc., is introduced freely; and now why wonder if Europeans hasten, if not originate, the causes of their death?

HUNTLEY: *Service on the Slave Coast.* 1850.

The doctors did their best: it was at least drastic.

An intelligent and very hospitable gentleman, Dr. Tibbs, told me that, six years ago, when he arrived at Bathurst, the colonial surgeons said to him, "In bilious fevers, you must not be surprised or annoyed if you lose one half of your patients. We consider ourselves lucky if we do not lose three-fourths." "What is your mode of treatment?" inquired Dr. Tibbs. "We bleed copiously, and throw in plenty of mercury." "Since bleeding and mercury have been attended with so little success," thought Dr. Tibbs, "I'll try what purgatives, and bark of quinine will do": and they have succeeded.

ALEXANDER: *Narrative of a Voyage of Observation.* 1837.

★

On Friday I became considerably worse, and on the following day my life was despaired of. In the evening I was bled in the temple; but the doctor, who was himself suffering from fever, being unable to hold the instrument steadily, inadvertently thrust it into my skull. This accident occasioned the most excruciating agony, and made me shriek with pain. I passed the night in a manner that cannot be described, but next morning felt much easier and better. On Monday, however, the fever returned with more violence than ever, attended by a severe headache that almost drove me distracted, and at my own suggestion Dr. Morrison ordered my head to be shaved. To perform this delicate operation a native barber was at length found, who came wielding a tremendous knife curved like a reap-hook, instead of a razor, and began his avocation in a most brutal manner, just like a clumsy English butcher shaving a slaughtered pig; insomuch, that when his labour was finished, my skull was scalped almost as effectually as if it had been done by the tomahawk of a North American Indian. Although my head was thus miserably excoriated, a large blister, covering the whole of it, was applied; and my suffering was heightened to the utmost degree of intensity; so that I lost my reason, and in the evening was completely delirious. In this state, as I subsequently learnt, I sprang from my couch, and being animated with the fury of a maniac, knocked down the doctor and my master, broke and destroyed every thing within my reach, and when in the act of escaping in my night-dress from the door, was forcibly dragged back to my bed by the united strength of the whole party, who had been alarmed with the noise I had made. Weakened and exhausted by this mad prank, the phrenzy left me, and reason returned, but with it came the loss of speech. About an hour afterwards a consultation was held by my bed-side; and the doctor having carefully felt my pulse, I was comforted by the expressed opinion, that it would be impossible for me to live throughout the night. Much to the astonishment of all, however, on Tuesday the disorder had abated so greatly, that I was enabled to sit up and converse rationally with those around me: my health, in fact, seemed to return almost as rapidly as I had lost it.

LANDER: *Records of Captain Clapperton's Last Expedition.* 1829.

THE GOLD COAST

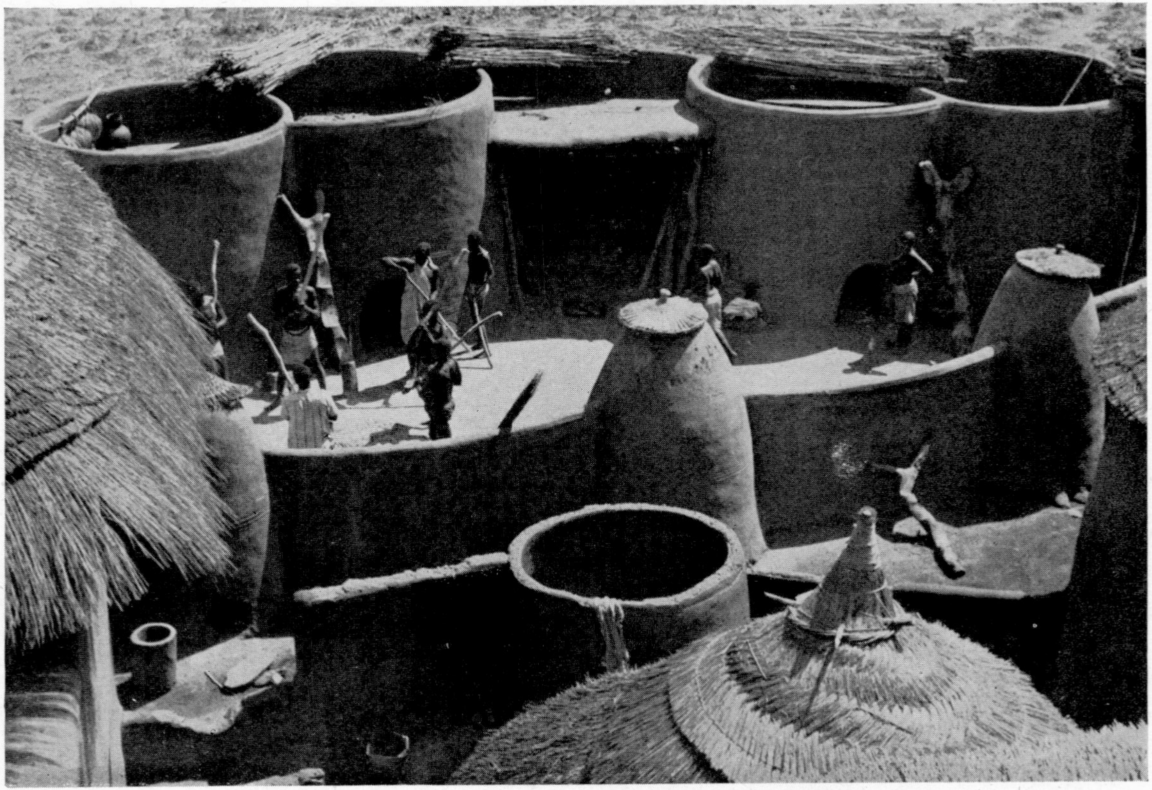

THE COMPOUND OF A NORTHERN TERRITORIES CHIEF

2. THE WEST AFRICAN SCENE

A tropical thunderstorm not infrequently heralded one's approach to the Coast.

At night, the electric fluid seemed to pervade all parts of the heavens: we appeared to be in the centre of destruction; blue, forked, butterfly, and sheet lightning flashed and glared round and over us; and the thunder cracked and crashed between our masts, as if artillery and musquetry had been fired close over us. Fortunately we were not struck, though the admiral saw a fireball fall hissing into the sea, like a hot iron in water, only a ship's length from us.

ALEXANDER: Narrative of a Voyage of Observation. 1837.

To land in the Gold Coast one had to brave the surf: at Accra one still does.

The Landing-Place here is so very dangerous that no Boat can venture ashore, but must wait for a Canoe to come off and fetch either Goods or Passengers ashore, and even the Canoes are often over-set and the Gentlemen well washed.

SMITH: A New Voyage to Guinea. 1745.

★

The canoe being just outside the breaking surf, the head was turned to the sea, and there it was held stationary by the paddles: the man steering now carefully regarded the appearance of each swell as it heavily but rapidly rolled on to hurl itself upon the beach, which it did with the noise of thunder, when on a sudden he noticed some change in the wave, which none of less experience could recognize, and instantly turning the head of the canoe to the shore, the song was raised again, and the paddles were lustily plied, when, mounted on the summit of the surge, the canoe was borne along with incredible velocity, and being flat was carried high upon the beach: the instant it touched the ground every black leaped out, and seizing its sides the force of the retreating wave was thus counteracted. The next operation was to seize the passengers, one of whom was taken possession of by a black respectively, and landed beyond the reach of the next surge, which by this time was close at his heels, roaring and foaming apparently in pursuit of him: all the passenger has to do is at first to

21

sit still, and indeed not move till the canoe-man fixes upon him as his burden, he then, to make his landing sure, must clasp the naked body of his carrier, lubricated with palm oil, to which he must cling, to the utter discomfiture of his white drill trowsers, and whatever the officer, unpractised in the humours of landing on an African beach, may have assumed in deference to dress and appearance.

HUNTLEY: *Service on the Slave Coast.* 1850.

On shore the outlook from the average trading factory was likely to be monotonous.

It consists of four different things in four long lines—lines that go away into eternity for as far as eye can see. There is the band of yellow sand on which your little factory is built. This band is walled to landwards by a wall of dark forest, mounted against the sky to seaward by a wall of white surf; beyond that there is the horizon-bounded ocean. Neither the forest wall nor surf wall changes enough to give any lively variety; they just run up and down a gamut on the same set of variations. In the light of brightest noon the forest wall stands dark against the dull blue sky, in the depth of the darkest night you can see it stand darker still, against the stars; on moonlight nights and on tornado nights, when you see the forest wall by the lightning light, it looks as if it had been done over with a coat of tar. The surf wall is equally consistent, it may be bad, or good as surf, but it's generally the former, which merely means it is a higher, broader wall, and more noisy, but it's the same sort of wall making the same sort of noise all the time. It is always white; in the sunlight, snowy white, suffused with a white mist wherein are little broken, quivering bits of rainbows. In the moonlight, it gleams with a whiteness there is in nothing else on earth. If you can imagine a non-transparent diamond wall, I think you will get some near idea to it, and even on the darkest of dark nights you can still see the surf wall clearly enough, for it shows like the ghost of its daylight self, seeming to have in it a light of its own, and you love or hate it. Night and day and season changes pass over these things, like reflections in a mirror, without altering the mirror frame; but nothing comes that ever stills for one half second the thunder of the surf-wall or makes it darker or makes the forest-wall brighter than the rest of your world. Mind you, it is intensely beautiful, intensely soothing, intensely interesting if you can read it and you like it, but life for a man who cannot and does not is a living death.

KINGSLEY: *West African Studies.* 1899.

Most of the West African coast is fringed by mangrove swamp.

It would be difficult to imagine a more depressing and gloomy region than that of the Delta of the Niger. On all sides, as far as the eye can reach, one sees nothing but swamp after swamp of countless mangroves, intersected in every direction by foul creeks of reeking and muddy water; while, when the tide is out, vast expanses of black, slimy mud, on which hideous crocodiles bask, are exposed to the sun. It is indeed a horrible and loathsome tract, and it is a matter for wonder that Europeans can be found willing to pass the best years of their lives in such a place. Yet such is the case, and though a large percentage of the white residents annually succumb to the pestilential climate, and all suffer more or less from its effects, the survivors jog along uncomplainingly, and some even seem in a measure to enjoy their existence—one can hardly call it life.

Wherever any dry land is found on the banks of these rivers, there are established native towns; and opposite these are moored the hulks in which the traders live. Some of these hulks have been fine vessels in their day, and all are very comfortably fitted up and roofed over: the finest is that of the African Steamship Company, the *Adriatic*, which formerly belonged to the White Star Company, and is now moored in Bonny river. Morning after morning the Europeans doomed to a wretched existence in these floating prisons wake up with a feeling of weariness and depression, and look out daily on the same muddy river with its banks of reeking ooze and interminable mangrove swamps. At night time the miasma creeps up from every creek and gradually enfolds all objects in a damp white shroud; while the croaking of the bull-frogs, the cry of a night-bird, and the lapping of the restless tide against the sides of the hulk, are the only sounds that break the oppressive silence.

ELLIS: *The Land of Fetish.* 1883.

It is only fair to say that Ellis' "damp white shroud" did not look the same to Mary Kingsley.

I don't think this sort of mist is healthy, but it is often supremely lovely and always fascinates me. I have seen it play the weirdest, wildest tricks many a time, in many a place in West Africa. I have, when benighted, walked hurriedly through it for miles in the forest while it has mischievously hidden the path at my feet from the helpful illumination of the moon, swishing and swirling round my moving skirts. I have seen it come out of the forests and gather on the creek before and round me when out o' nights in canoes, gradually as we

glided towards the breeze-swept river, forming itself into a great ball
which has rolled before us, alongside, or behind us, showing dimly
now in the shadow, ghostly white now in the moonshine, and bursting
into thousands of flakes if the river breeze when it met it was too strong
for it; if it were not, just melting away into the sheet of mist that lay
sleeping on the broad river itself. Now and again you will see it in the
forest stretch up a gradually lengthening arm, and wind it lazily round
and round some grand column of a tree-stem, to the height of ten or
twenty feet from the ground, spread out its top like a plume and then
fall back again to the mist-river from which it came. It has weird
ways, this mist of the West Coast. I have often, when no one has been
near to form opinions of my frivolity, played with it, scooping it up
in my hands and letting it fall again, or swished it about with a branch,
when it lay at a decent level of three or four feet from the ground.
When it comes higher and utterly befogs you, you don't feel much inclination to play with it. The worst of it is, you never quite know
how high it is coming.

KINGSLEY: Travels in West Africa. 1897.

*Also, of course, there is more to West Africa than mangrove swamp. "The
Gold Coast", says Brodie Cruickshank, "presents a wide field for curious and
varied speculation."*

Its sunny skies, but seldom disfigured by gloom or tempest; its
modulating sweep of hill and dale; its deep, impenetrable thickets;
its magnificent forest trees, the ever-verdant freshness of its luxurious
vegetation; the richness of its mineral wealth, still shrouded in the
mysterious recesses of its mountains, or in the depths of its dark and
muddy streams; its luscious fruits; the gorgeous plumage of its birds;
and the endless variety of animal and insect life, which inhabit its wild
jungle tracts; invest it with an indescribable charm of vague and wondering curiosity.

CRUICKSHANK: Eighteen Years on The Gold Coast. 1853.

Of Freetown estuary William Smith says this:

The next Morning, we found ourselves in a small pleasant Bay,
surrounded with exceeding high Hills, all covered with tall beautiful
Trees, swarming with various Kinds of Birds, which, as soon as Day
broke, made the Woods ring. Which Captain Crocker also did, for
as soon as he saw the Union-Flag at our Mast-Head, he saluted it with
Five Guns, and we returned him three. In this Bay is extraordinary

good fresh Water, which, gushing out of the Rocks on the Side of the Hill, comes down like a Spout, so that we could fill all our Casks without the Help of a Tundish. Here we watered. And the Bottom of the Bay being pretty clear of Rocks, we drew our Sain, or Net, and catched good Store of large Mullets, and other Fish: Also an Alligator, which the Negroes devoured greedily.

SMITH: *A New Voyage to Guinea.* 1745.

Beyond Nigeria's coastal swamps, Lander found scenes which moved him to rhapsodies.

The earth, clad in simple and lovely magnificence, was embellished with superb trees filled with singing birds—plots of Indian corn waved in the wind—a luxuriant vegetation sprung up at every step—every living thing revelled in enjoyment—happiness, peace, and plenty dwelt on the enchanting spot. It was evening when I took a stroll a little way into the country—a calm, cloudless, lovely evening. The earth had just before been refreshed by a shower, and the sun was setting in all his glory; the neatly-attired maidens of Eggebee, returning to the town with calabashes of milk, sang as they went along; birds of golden plumage fluttered on the branches of the noble trees; insects of dazzling brightness buzzed in the air; the stridulous notes of the grasshopper was heard from the ground; smoke ascended in circling volumes to the skies from the dwellings of the people; and the music of guitars and dulcimers swelled from the town—all was soothing, serene, heavenly.

LANDER: *Records of Captain Clapperton's Last Expedition.* 1829.

At its junction with the Benue (or Shary as it was then known), the Niger presents a spectacle which delighted Macgregor Laird.

An immense river, about three thousand yards wide, extending as far as the eye could reach, lay before us, flowing majestically between its banks, which rose gradually to a considerable height and were studded with clumps of trees and brushwood, giving them the appearance of a gentleman's park; while the smoke rising from different towns on its banks, and the number of canoes floating on its bosom, gave it an aspect of security and peace far beyond any African scene I had yet witnessed. The confluence of the Shary was just in sight, and a range of low hills on the northern bank trended east-north-east; while on the western bank of the Niger were two remarkable isolated table-lands of a romantic and beautiful appearance, giving a finish to a picture to which no description can do adequate justice.

LAIRD and OLDFIELD:
Narrative of an Expedition into the Interior of Africa. 1837.

Most spectacular natural feature in West Africa is Mount Cameroon, particularly when seen from the island of Fernando Po.

The view from the galleries of the Government House on a clear moonlight night, I never saw equalled, nor can I conceive it surpassed. To the north-east, the lofty peak of the Cameroons, rising to the immense height of fourteen thousand feet, throws its gigantic shadow half-way across the narrow strait that separates the island from the main land; while the numerous little promontories and beautiful coves that grace the shores of Goderich Bay, throw light and shadow so exquisitely upon the water, that one almost can imagine it a fairy land.

Ibid.

Behind the coastal swamp normally lies a belt of tropical forest.

The opacity of this forest communicated to the atmosphere and the surrounding scenery a semblance of twilight; no ray of sunshine penetrated the cheerless gloom, and we were indeed entombed in foliage of a character novel and fanciful. The death-like stillness that prevailed was soon interrupted by the occasional shouting of the negroes, to put to flight, as they termed it, the evil spirits of the forest. Now and then a flight of parrots and other gregarious birds interrupted the intervals of silence; but the richness of this vegetable canopy prevented the possibility of gaining even the most imperfect view of these feathered screechers, or indeed of anything but those objects by which we were immediately surrounded.

DUPUIS: *Journal of a Residence in Ashantee.* 1824.

★

On first entering the great grim twilight regions of the forest you hardly see anything but the vast column-like grey tree stems in their countless thousands around you, and the sparsely vegetated ground beneath. But day by day, as you get trained to your surroundings, you see more and more, and a whole world grows up gradually out of the gloom before your eyes. Snakes, beetles, bats and beasts, people the region that at first seemed lifeless.

It is the same with the better lit regions, where vegetation is many-formed and luxuriant. As you get used to it, what seemed at first to be an inextricable tangle ceases to be so. The separate sorts of plants stand out before your eyes with ever increasing clearness, until you can pick out the one particular one you may want; and daily you find it easier to make your way through what looked at first an impenetrable wall, for you have learnt that it is in the end easier to worm your way in among networks of creepers, than to shirk these, and go for the softer walls of climbing grasses and curtains of lycopodium; and not only is it easier, but safer, for in the grass and lycopodium there are nearly certain to be snakes galore, and the chances are you may force yourself into the privacy of a gigantic python's sleeping place.

There is the same difference also between night and day in the forest. You may have got fairly used to it by day, and then some catastrophe keeps you out in it all night, and again you see another world. To my taste there is nothing so fascinating as spending a night out in an African forest, or plantation; but I beg you to note I do not advise any one to follow the practice. Nor indeed do I recommend African forest life to any one. Unless you are interested in it and fall under its charm, it is the most awful life in death imaginable. It is like being shut up in a library whose books you cannot read, all the while tormented, terrified, and bored. And if you do fall under its spell, it takes all the colour out of other kinds of living. Still, it is good for a man to have an experience of it, whether he likes it or not, for it teaches you how very dependent you have been, during your previous life, on the familiarity of those conditions you have been brought up among, and on your fellow citizens; moreover it takes the conceit out of you pretty thoroughly during the days you spend stupidly stumbling about among your new surroundings.

When this first period passes there comes a sense of growing power. The proudest day in my life was the day on which an old Fan hunter said to me—"Ah! you see." Now he did not say this, I may remark, as a tribute to the hard work I had been doing in order to see, but regarded it as the consequence of a chief having given me a little ivory half-moon, whose special mission was "to make man see Bush", and when you have attained to that power in full, a state I do not pretend to have yet attained to, you can say, "Put me where you like in an African forest, and as far as the forest goes, starve me or kill me if you can."

KINGSLEY: *Travels in West Africa.* 1897.

3. DISPOSITION OF THE PEOPLE

Most Europeans remark that whatever the West African does he does noisily.

Neither are these drummes without dayly imployment, for this is their continuall custome every night after it seemes they have filled their bellies, they repaire to this Court of Guard, making fires both in the middle of the house, and in the open yard, about which they doe continue drumming, hooping, singing, and makeing a hethenish noyse, most commonly untill the day beginnes to breake, when as we conceive dead-sleepes take them, by which meanes sleeping one part of the day, it makes the other part seeme shorter, untill the time of feeding come againe, otherwise it is done to that purpose in the night, to feare and keepe away the Lyons, and ravening beasts from about their dwellings, who are at that season ranging and looking out.

JOBSON: *The Golden Trade.* 1623.

★

In Africa, whether one is ill or well, it is exactly the same, nothing like peace or quiet is anywhere to be found. Independent of the continual fluttering of pigeons, which roost close to our ears, the bleating of sheep and goats, and the barking of numerous half-starved dogs, we are still more seriously annoyed by the incessant clatter of women's tongues, which pursues us everywhere, and which I really believe nothing less than sickness or death on their part can effectually silence. The shrillness of their voices drowns the bleating of the sheep and the yellings of the canine race; and notwithstanding all my brother's exertions, seconded by those of our people, their noise in this town has constantly disturbed me during my illness. A person in England might be inclined to think lightly of the matter; but it is indeed a grievance which can ill be borne by an invalid languishing under a wasting disease, and who has equally as much need of rest and silence as of medicine. Besides these grievances, the shouts of the people outside the yard, and the perpetual squalling of children within it—the buzzing of beetles and drones—the perpetual attacks of mosquitoes and innumerable flies, form a host of irritating evils, to which a sick person is exposed, and to which he is obliged patiently to submit, until, by a relief from his disorder, he is enabled to stand upon his legs and once more take his own part.

RICHARD and JOHN LANDER: *An Expedition to the Niger.* 1832.

Bosman denounced the African without reservation. It should be added that he took a hardly better view of the English.

I design to treat of the Natural Temper of the Natives; and if this Letter doth not swell to an unusual Bulk, I shall be at a loss to do Justice to my Subject: Wherefore I must beg your excuse for crouding so many things into one Letter so immethodically, for you are presented with them as they occur to me; and so, Sir, be pleased to accept them.

To begin. The Negroes are all, without Exception, crafty, villainous and fraudulent, and very seldom to be trusted; being sure to slip no Opportunity of cheating an European, nor indeed one another. A Man of Integrity is as rare among them as a white Falcon, and their Fidelity seldom extends farther than to their Masters; and it would be very surprizing if upon a Scrutiny into their Lives we should find any of them whose perverse Nature would not break out sometimes; for they indeed seem to be born and bred Villains: All sorts of Baseness having got such sure-footing in them, that 'tis impossible to lie concealed; and herein they agree very well with what Authors tell us of the Muscovites. These degenerate Vices are accompanied with their Sisters, Sloth and Idleness; to which they are so prone that nothing but the utmost Necessity can force them to Labour: They are besides so incredibly careless and stupid, and are so little concerned at their Misfortunes, that 'tis hardly to be observed by any Change in them, whether they have met with any good or ill Success. An Instance of which is that when they have obtained a Victory over their Enemies, they return Home diverting themselves with leaping and dancing: But if on their side they are beaten out of the Field, and utterly routed, they yet feast and are merry, and dance, and can chearfully sport around a Grave. In short, Prosperity and Adversity are no otherwise distinguishable in them than in the cloathing and shaving of their Head.

BOSMAN: *Description of the Coast of Guinea.* 1721.

With this sweeping condemnation few other qualified observers agree.

Born beneath the rays of a tropical sun, with a clear and serene sky over his head, seldom ruffled by lowering storms, his character partakes largely of the gaiety of external nature, and his exuberant spirits are in unison with her bountiful profusion. Freely as the earth minis-

ters to his wants, supplying him with the necessaries of life almost
without the penalty of labour, as thoughtlessly and unstintingly does
he make use of her bounties. Fond of his ease, and loving to indulge a
quiet, voluptuous indolence of disposition, he can seldom be roused
to much bodily exertion, unless enticed by the prospect of obtaining
the means of festivity, to which he delivers himself up with the most
determined abandonment. Possessed of high physical qualities, and
patient in the prosecution of his object, when once his mind is fairly
bent upon it, he is capable of enduring the severest toil and the greatest
privations; but unless his affections are engaged in his work, he soon
relapses into inactivity and indifference, and leaves his task un-
finished. . . .

His memory is strong and retentive, and he dwells with a garrulous
minuteness upon the recollections of his youth. His lively imagination
delights to feed itself with pleasing reveries; but it is gross, sensual,
and unrefined. He is naturally eloquent, speaks with an easy and
fluent grace, with suitable and appropriate action, and clothes his
ideas with a simple and natural imagery. He has frequent recourse to
parables, and dark and enigmatical sayings, which he never deigns to
explain, taking an apparent delight in leaving the minds of his hearers
to puzzle out his hidden meaning. He is fond of repartee, dearly loves
a joke, the coarser the better, and has a most lively sense of the ridiculous. He delights in rude and barbarous merriment, and in noisy
and turbulent carousals. He is quick and irascible in his temper, but
easily appeased if the injury be unintentional or slight; but when deeply
offended, it is impossible to regain his favour without a peace-offering,
in the shape of a present of rum, or a sheep, with which he makes a
libation or a sacrifice to his Fetish "to give him a good heart".

In the excitement of the moment, he is sometimes perfectly blinded
by his passion, and commits acts which he deeply repents, and which
he would undo the very next instant. With all this, he is, in ordinary
intercourse, particularly observant of the courtesies of life, is slow to
give offence, often dignified in his deportment, regardful of another's
consequence, and tenacious of his own. Indignity and slight rankle
deeply in his heart, and are seldom forgiven. His affections are keen,
but not durable, and the impressions of sorrow are soon effaced. His
joys and his sorrows equally find vent in spontaneous song, and at
morn, noon, and night the streets re-echo with the loud catch of the
bacchanal, the impassioned lays of the lover, and the plaintive notes
of the mourner. He is slow to form friendships, but firm to retain
them, and will often sacrifice his money and his comfort to help a
friend in distress. He does not easily give his confidence to an Euro-

pean, although he may treat him with the greatest outward deference and respect. He is quick in discovering peculiarities of temper and conduct, and treasures up words and acts, to enable him to form a true estimate of character.

CRUICKSHANK: *Eighteen Years on the Gold Coast.* 1853.

*

These people of the Gold Coast are, perhaps, the most cleanly natives in the world. They take a bath in the morning, and another in the evening, washing themselves from head to foot with palm-oil soap of their own manufacture, and then rub lime-juice over the skin. At almost every hour of the day may be heard infantine shrieks and lamentations, which, when traced to their source, are found to proceed from children three years of age being washed by girls scarcely older than themselves. As for the boys, they are always in the water: the sea is their playground. Lying on pieces of board outside the surf, they let the breakers carry them in—a pleasure analogous to sliding.

READE: *The African Sketch-Book.* 1873.

With few exceptions the first Europeans were hospitably received. Mary Kingsley went among the Fans, a tribe of whom she had received the most ominous reports.

I saw at once he was a very superior man to any of the chiefs I had yet met with. It was not his attire, remarkable though that was for the district, for it consisted of a gentleman's black frock-coat such as is given in the ivory bundle, a bright blue felt sombrero hat, an ample cloth of Boma check; but his face and general bearing was distinctive, and very powerful and intelligent; and I knew that Egaja, for good or bad, owed its name to this man, and not to the mere sensual, brutal-looking one. He was exceedingly courteous, ordering his people to bring me a stool and one for himself, and then a fly-whisk to battle with the evening cloud of sandflies. I got Pagan to come and act as interpreter while the rest were stowing the baggage, etc. After compliments, "Tell the chief," I said, "that I hear this town of his is thief town."

"Better not, sir," says Pagan.

"Go on," said I, "or I'll tell him myself."

So Pagan did. It was a sad blow to the chief.

"Thief town, this highly respectable town of Egaja! a town whose moral conduct in all matters (Shedule) was an example to all towns, called a thief town! Oh, what a wicked world!"

I said it was; but I would reserve my opinion as to whether Egaja was a part of the wicked world or a star-like exception, until I had experienced it myself. We then discoursed on many matters, and I got a great deal of interesting fetish information out of the chief, which was valuable to me, because the whole of this district had not been in contact with white culture; and altogether I and the chief became great friends.

Just when I was going in to have my much-desired tea, he brought me his mother—an old lady, evidently very bright and able, but, poor woman, with the most disgusting hand and arm I have ever seen. I am ashamed to say I came very near being sympathetically sick in the African manner on the spot. I felt I could not attend to it, and have my tea afterwards, so I directed one of the canoe-shaped little tubs, used for beating up the manioc in, to be brought and filled with hot water, and then putting into it a heavy dose of Condy's fluid, I made her sit down and lay the whole arm in it, and went and had my tea. As soon as I had done I went outside, and getting some of the many surrounding ladies to hold bush-lights, I examined the case. The whole hand was a mass of yellow pus, streaked with sanies, large ulcers were burrowing into the fore-arm, while in the arm-pit was a big abscess. I opened the abscess at once, and then the old lady frightened me nearly out of my wits by gently subsiding, I thought dying, but I soon found out merely going to sleep. I then washed the abscess well out, and having got a lot of baked plantains, I made a big poultice of them, mixed with boiling water and more Condy in the tub, and laid her arm right in this; and propping her up all round and covering her over with cloths I requisitioned from her son, I left her to have her nap while I went into the history of the case, which was that some forty-eight hours ago she had been wading along the bank, catching crawfish, and had been stung by a "fish like a snake"; so I presume the ulcers were an old-standing palaver. The hand had been a good deal torn by the creature, and the pain and swelling had been so great she had not had a minute's sleep since. As soon as the poultice got chilled I took her arm out and cleaned it again, and wound it round with dressing, and had her lady-ship carried bodily, still asleep, into her hut, and after rousing her up, giving her a dose of that fine preparation, *pil. crotonis cum hydrargi*, saw her tucked up on her own plank bedstead for the night, sound asleep again. The chief was very anxious to have some pills too; so I gave him some, with firm injunctions only to take one at the first time. I knew that that one would teach him not to take more than one for ever after, better than I could do if I talked from June to January. Then all the afflicted Egaja turned up, and wanted medical advice.

There was evidently a good stiff epidemic of the yaws about; lots of cases of dum with the various symptoms; ulcers of course galore; a man with a bit of broken spear head in an abscess in the thigh; one which I believe a professional enthusiast would call a "lovely case" of filaria, the entire white of one eye being full of the active little worms and a ridge of surplus population migrating across the bridge of the nose into the other eye, under the skin, looking like the bridge of a pair of spectacles. It was past eleven before I had anything like done, and my men had long been sound asleep, but the chief had conscientiously sat up and seen the thing through. He then went and fetched some rolls of bark cloth to put on my plank, and I gave him a handsome cloth I happened to have with me, a couple of knives, and some heads of tobacco, and wished him good-night.

KINGSLEY: *Travels in West Africa.* 1897.

The black man's attitude to the white was reflected in his folk tales.

All the Natives of this Coast believe there is one true God, the Author of them and all Things: They say, that in the Beginning God created Black as well as White Men; that he having created these two Sorts of Men, offered two Kinds of Gifts, viz., Gold, and the Knowledge of Art, Reading, and Writing, giving the Blacks the first Election, who chose Gold, and the Whites was obliged to take the Knowledge of Letters; that God granted their Request, but being incensed at their Avarice, resolved, that the Whites should for ever be their Masters, and they their Slaves.

SMITH: *A New Voyage to Guinea.* 1745.

★

Others, who waver between the Mahomedan religion and the ancient faith, believe that at the end of the world a voice will sound from heaven to invite all black men to the world of bliss, but that these will be too much unconcerned and too lazy to embrace the offer— a second voice will then proclaim the same invitation to white men, who will spring up with alacrity and transport, and enter the celestial regions before them with books in their hands.

RICHARD and JOHN LANDER: *An Expedition to the Niger.* 1832.

Africa has adopted the Oriental proverb which says: "Haste is of the devil, and tardiness from the All-Merciful."

The natives, perhaps twenty or thirty, would enter the town, each bringing a little gold dust, often under half an ounce; they sent to in-

form Mr. Bannerman of their arrival, he returned some answer sufficient to convey an invitation to barter, but expressive of no exact
desire for it; a day or two passed, and they sent to say that they would
come to look at the goods he had; at the appointed time, the whole
body came in procession, some carrying a little bit of rag tied up, and
containing the gold; the goods were displayed, and after a time food
was given to them, so far they were gainers; they made an offer,
Mr. Bannerman all this time was walking backwards and forwards on
his veranda above, apparently indifferent to the whole proceeding, and
refusing or acquiescing but by a simple monosyllable, he said nothing
more; all day the country traders were crouching about the yard, nor
left till sunset; this scene was repeated for days, the object of the
African being to weary out the patience of the Englishman, an attempt
utterly futile as it applied to Mr. Bannerman; at length the respective
parties agreed, the gold dust was weighed and tested, a very necessary
precaution, the merchandize chosen, the traders fed, and by the
evening they were on their journey to their own homes, having possibly wasted weeks in endeavouring to obtain a trifling advance in
favour of their gold dust; time is valuable only where industry prevails, consequently it is no where less esteemed than in western Africa.

HUNTLEY: *Service on the Slave Coast.*   1850.

★

One of the inducements urged by this monarch for our longer stay
with him, is rather whimsical. He has made us a present of a quantity
of worthless feathers, which he had caused to be plucked from the
body of a live ostrich; and because he entertained an opinion that if
others were added to them, they would altogether form a very acceptable present to our gracious sovereign, he informed us that it would
be necessary we should wait till such time as the ostrich should regain
its plumage, in order for that part of its body which had not been
previously plucked to undergo a similar operation; for the weather,
he asserted, was much too cold for the bird to lose all its feathers at
one and the same time. And further, to encourage their growth, he
would order that two thousand cowries' worth of butter (about
twelve pounds weight) should be diligently rubbed into the skin of
the animal. This money has actually been deducted by the sultan, for
this express purpose, from the sum which he was indebted to us, because he said he did not approve of paying for the butter from his own
pocket.

RICHARD and JOHN LANDER: *An Expedition to the Niger.*   1832.

★

At first, when I was left by myself in the fort, I felt rather lonely and at a loss for society, so I ransacked my imagination to invent occupations to pass the time. The town of Secondee was in ruins, and the people were living in holes and corners of the tottering houses, so I determined to have it rebuilt in a proper manner, with some regularity, and with broad roads between the houses. I became enthusiastic, and thought I would make a model settlement. I sent for the king, told him my intentions, and requested that he would order all his able-bodied men to meet me in the morning, when I would plan the roads and mark out the plots for houses.

I awoke next morning full of confidence, dressed, and rushed down to the town. It was time for the king to be there with his following, but I saw nobody. I sent a messenger, and after an interval of some fifteen minutes, his majesty came along, placidly gnawing a banana. I inquired where the men were, and he said they had gone to the bush to cut sticks. I then told him to be sure and have then there at five p.m., at which time I judged it would be cool enough to work.

At five nobody turned up; they had gone to wash, or to cook, or something or other, so I proceeded to cut poles and stake out the roads myself. Next morning the king had some other excuse for the absence of his subjects, and I began to feel annoyed. At the end of the second day I had recourse to extreme measures. I took two or three men from the garrison of the fort, went into all the houses in the town, regardless of odours, and turned the inhabitants out to work for their own good. By this means I succeeded in getting together some thirty workmen, who did each day, on an average, the work of two English labourers. They would dig and pick for about five minutes, and then one would sit down to rest and smoke, or scratch himself, or catch fleas; and then another and another would drop off, until the whole lot would be basking in the sun and snoring. There is no being in the world so incorrigibly lazy as your negro; he will never work unless he is compelled to by force or hunger.

On the evening of the first day on which they worked, a deputation of the natives came and waited upon me at the fort. They said they had come to be paid for their work. I said:

"What? Do you mean to say you expect to be paid for doing your own work—for making roads through your own town, and building your own houses?"

They replied it was true they were doing it for their own benefit, but, as Europeans did everything for them, they thought I might pay them too. I wished them good-evening then.

Every day I had to go and hunt up my labourers, and then I had to stand by them all the time they were at work to prevent them from going to sleep; and they did everything in their power to defeat my proposed improvements. They said they did not want roads more than three feet broad; that was quite enough; to have them broader would only be a waste of ground. They liked to live herded together like brutes, with their fowls and pigs, amongst the dirt and distemper around. They did not care if in the rainy season the rains did come down and flood their huts, and wash down two or three of them; they would rather that should happen than have the trouble of digging ditches to drain off the water. And every day some of them had fresh excuses for getting off work; they wanted to go to the bush to see their grandmothers, or buy corn, or settle a palaver, or something. After about three weeks of this my patience wore out. I do not think Job's would have lasted more than a month under the aggravating circumstances. My model settlement was a failure.

ELLIS: *West African Sketches.* 1881.

Yet there are plentiful signs of industry.

On all the borders of the numerous branches of the river, as well as on its small islands, vast quantities of corn were growing; and it being near the time of harvest, it was nearly ripe, and waved over the water's edge very prettily. Platforms were everywhere erected to the height of, or rather above the corn, which grows as high as ten or twelve feet. People were stationed on these to scare away the numerous flights of small birds, which do great mischief, and would, without this precaution, destroy the hopes of the cultivator. A boy or girl, and in many cases a woman with a child at her breast, and even a whole family together, we observed on the platforms, amusing themselves in this manner, without the slightest shade or covering of any kind to shelter them from the fierceness of the sunbeams. Standing erect and motionless, many of them looked like statues of black marble rather than living human beings; but others, particularly the women, disregarding their duty, were industriously employed in plaiting straw, supplying the wants of their children, manufacturing mats, dressing provisions, etc. In order the more effectually to frighten away the birds, several of the watchers were furnished with slings and stones, in the use of which they seem to be very skilful; besides these, pieces of rope were fastened from the platform to a tree at some distance, to which large calabashes were suspended, with holes in them, through

STATESMAN AND WARRIOR
THE WAZIRI OF THE SULTAN OF SOKOTO, NIGERIA

THE AGE-OLD LOOK
AN AGBOABRA GIRL OF ONITSHA PROVINCE, NIGERIA

which sticks were passed, so that when the rope is pulled they make a loud clattering noise.

RICHARD and JOHN LANDER: *An Expedition to the Niger.* 1832.

★

All which indeed are imployed chiefly in the making of Wooden or Earthen Cups, Troughs, matting of Chairs, making of Copper Ointment Boxes, and Arm-Rings of Gold, Silver or Ivory, with some other Trash. Their chief Handicraft, with which they are best acquainted being the Smithery; for with their sorry Tools they can make all sorts of War-Arms that they want, Guns only excepted; as well as whatever is required in their Agriculture and House-keeping. They have no Notion of Steel, and yet they make their Sabres and all cutting Instruments; Their principal Tools are a kind of hard Stone instead of an Anvil; a pair of Tongs, and a small pair of Bellows, with three or more Pipes; which blow very strong, and are an Invention of their own. These are most of their Arts, besides that of making of Fetiche's; which I have before informed you of: But their most artful Works are the fine Gold and Silver Hat-banks which they made for us; the Thread and Contexture of which is so fine, that I question whether our European Artists would not be put to it to imitate them: And indeed if they could, and were no better paid than the Negroes, they would be obliged to live on dry Bread.

BOSMAN: *Description of the Coast of Guinea.* 1721.

Most Europeans were favourably impressed by the character of the people of the hinterland.

The general character of the people is much superior to that of the inhabitants of the swampy country between them and the coast. They are shrewd, intelligent and quick in their perception, milder in their dispositions, and more peaceable in their habits. The security of life and property is evidently greater among them; though it is still sufficiently precarious to prevent the inhabitants from living in isolated situations, nor will any of them venture upon the river after sunset in small canoes. Agriculture is extensively followed, and Indian corn and other grain are raised with little labour and less skill on the part of the cultivators. Tobacco is grown sparingly, and when dried and made up for sale, costs one hundred cowries, or one penny per pound. It has a mild, pleasant flavour, and is made up in rolls in the Turkish

4

fashion. The natives are greatly addicted to smoking, and use the long reed pipe common in the Levant. The bowls of these pipes are neatly manufactured of clay.

LAIRD and OLDFIELD: *An Expedition into the Interior of Africa.* 1837.

The Fulani are the herdsmen of West Africa, though one section settled in the Hausa states and established ruling houses there early last century.

These are called Fulbies, being a Tawny people, and have a resemblance right unto those we call Egiptians: the women amongst them, are streight, upright, and excellently well bodied, having very good features, with a long blacke haire, much more loose than the blacke women have, wherewith they attire themselves very neatly, but in their apparell they goe clothed and weare the same habite, the blacke woemen do; the men are not in their kinds, so generally handsome as the women are, which may be imputed to their course of lives, whereof I proceede to tell you; Their profession is keeping of Cattle, some Goats they have, but the Heards they tend are Beefes, whereof they are aboundantly stored: In some places they have settled Townes, but for the most part they are still wandering, uniting themselves in kindred and families, and so drive their heards together; where they find the ground and soyle most fitte for their Cattle, there, with the Kings allowance of the Country, they sit downe, building themselves houses, as the season of the yeare serves, and in such places as lies most convenient, for preservation of their Heards they looke unto; during the times of the raines, they retire to the mountaines, and higher grounds, and againe as they grow drie, and barraine to the low plaines and bottomes, even to the River side; that in the times of our chiefest Trade, their cattle are feeding by us, and the women with their commodities daily customers to us. These mens labour and toyle is continuall, for in the day time, they watch and keepe them together, from straying, and especially from comming to neare the River, where the Crocodile doth haunt, and in the night time, they bring them home about their howses, and parting them in severall Heards, they make fires round about them, and likewise in the middle of them, about which they lie themselves, ready uppon any occasion to defend them from their roring enemies, which are Lyons, Ounces, and such devouring beasts, whereof the Country is full.

JOBSON: *The Golden Trade.* 1623.

The Kroos, a seafaring people living on the coast of Liberia, won golden opinions. They formed an indispensable part of the crews of ships working up and down the Coast, and also figured largely in the Niger expeditions.

You can go and live in West Africa without seeing a crocodile or a hippopotamus or a mountain, but no white man can go there without seeing and experiencing a Kruboy, and Kruboys are one of the main tribes here. Kruboys are, indeed, the backbone of white effort in West Africa. . . .

They have devoted themselves to us English, and they have suffered, laboured, fought, been massacred, and so on with us for generation after generation. Many a time Krumen have come to me when we have been together in foreign possessions and said, 'Help us, we are Englishmen.' They have never asked in vain of me or any Englishman in West Africa, but recognition of their services by our Government at home is—well, about as much recognition as most men get from it who do good work in West Africa.

KINGSLEY: West African Studies. 1899

4. FUN AND GAMES

Africa has a parlour game peculiarly its own.

In the heat of the day, the men will come forth, and sit themselves in companies, under the shady trees, to receive the fresh aire, and there passe the time in communication, having only one kind of game to recreate themselves withall, and that is in a peece of wood, certaine great holes cut, which they set upon the ground betwixt two of them, and with a number of some thirtie pibble stones, after a manner of counting, they take one from the other, untill one is possessed of all whereat some of them are wondrous nimble.

JOBSON: *The Golden Trade.* 1623.

From the oil palm comes Africa's wine.

In some places there are whole grounds or groves of them, the use whereof is to draw from them a most sweete and pleasant drinke, which wee call Palmeta Wine, and as wee approve and like of it to bee tooth-some, so likewise in operation, wee find it wholesome; the manner whereof is this, they do cut into the body of the tree holes, in some more, in some lesse, as the tree is in substance, to which holes, they place a hollow cane cut sloping to goe the neatlier in, into which the juyce of the tree distilleth and is conveid, as in pipes, unto goudes set handsomely into the ground reddy to receive it, which is in lesse then twenty foure houres taken away, and as they please disposed of: now this is of that esteeme, that the vulgar sort may not meddle with, but the principall persons, and therefore they will send of this unto us, foure or five miles distance, as a curteous present; the tast whereof, doth truely resemble white Wine when it comes first over into England, having the same sweetnes of tast, and in colour, if they were together, not to be distinguished; onely this is the misery, it will not keepe above one day, for if you reserve of it untill the morning it will grow sowre, notwithstanding any dilligence that can be used.

Ibid.

The kola nut, no less than palm wine, is a symbol of African hospitality.

The nut is easily divided into several, generally four sections, of which one is eaten at a time. The taste is a pleasant bitter, and somewhat astringent. Water drunk "upon it", as the phrase is, becomes, even if before offensive, exceptionally sweet. It must be a fine tonic in these relaxing climates. I am not aware of an extract having been made from it: if not, it would be as well to try. Travellers use it to quiet the sensation of hunger and to obviate thirst. In native courts eating kola nuts forms part of the ceremony of welcoming strangers, and the Yorubas have a proverb: "Anger draweth arrows from the quiver: good words draw kolas from the bag."

BURTON: *Wanderings in West Africa.* 1863.

No people have a keener ear for rhythm, or take a greater delight in dancing.

Of all the amusements of the Africans, none can equal their song and dance in the still, clear hours of night, when the moon, walking in beauty in the heavens, awakens all the milder affections of their nature, and invites them to gladness and mirth. As soon as this splendid luminary appears above the horizon, every individual, both slave and free, is on the alert—some to fetch wood from a neighbouring forest, and others to procure provisions in the village; and forming themselves in a circle, generally round a venerable tree, they prepare large fires, in order to frighten away any wild beasts that may be prowling near the spot, and begin their country dance, which does not differ from one extremity of the continent to the other. I have often been a party to these innocent entertainments, which are frequently kept up with inconceivable spirit and agility, till the approach of morning; and as often been delighted with the perfect harmony and kindly feeling that prevailed amongst the dancers. It produces a pleasing and romantic effect, to observe the silvery light of the moon, blending with the radiance of the flames, and thrown upon the sable countenances of the happy group—as well as the lengthened reflection of the majestic tree cast along the ground, and the moving figures, gliding like shadows across it.

LANDER: *Records of Captain Clapperton's Last Expedition.* 1829.

The rhythm of the tom-tom is irresistible.

He had no sooner struck the instrument, than the master of the house left his occupation, came into the garden and began to shake himself, striking up the dust with his feet, and working the muscles of his loins and shoulders. A neighbour ran to join him; and the pair, face to face, strove to excel in excess the shaking and wriggling. The young people of the family caught the infection and forsook their rice and oil, but not without a rebuke from the mother; who, with a miserable child yellow with the craw-craw at her back, came forth to recall the piccaninies to their dinner. Yet, even whilst scolding them, her own frame grew restive, her shoulders were shrugged, her hands rose and fell, and in a moment all was over with her matronly sedateness. Each instant she became more energetic, to the discomfiture of the unhappy little son tied behind her, who lay there in no easy bed, and had not health to enjoy such rough pleasure. By degrees young and old dropped in, until the garden was filled with mothers loaded with babes, and children with food in their hands which they ate as they danced, and labourers holding their implements of industry, all vibrating from side to side like pendulums. As their mode of dancing hardly demanded the use of feet, and chiefly required movements of the head, arms, and chest, although upon horseback I imitated the rest to their abundant amusement.

RANKIN: The White Man's Grave. 1836.

★

Africans are passionately fond of music, and have an excellent ear for it. The native airs are very simple, consisting merely of detached bars. Their songs are chiefly a species of recitative or chaunt, with a short chorus. They are often improvised, the principal performer giving out a line, and a band of choristers joining in the refrain. He stands up while the others are seated around him, and turns from one to another, while he pours forth his unpremeditated lay. As one gets wearied, or his invention fails him, another takes his place, and continues the amusement, which frequently lasts for hours. They are very expert in adapting the subjects of these songs to current events, and indulge in mocking ridicule, in biting sarcasm, in fulsome flattery, or in just praise of men and things, according as circumstances seem to demand. The bravery of a chief, the beauty of a young girl, the liberality of a friend, the avarice of a miser, the poltroonery of a coward, the affection of a mother, and the disappointments of a lover, form indiscriminately the themes of these extemporaneous effusions.

If a white man were to pass these songsters, while thus employed, they would quickly seize upon some peculiarity of his character, whether good or bad, and celebrate it aloud, amidst the unrestrained merriment of the by-standers. Even a passing stranger whom they had never seen before, would come in for a share of their notice, and some eccentricity of look, of gait, or of apparel be quickly fastened upon as worthy of praise, or of ridicule. This habit of publishing the praise or shame of individuals in spontaneous song, exercises no little influence upon conduct; for the African is most sensitive to public opinion, and dreads being held up to ridicule, while the incense of flattery incites him to actions which will gain for him the admiration of his country-men. In this way these singing men and women become the organs of public opinion, and supply the place of our journals and gazettes.

CRUICKSHANK: *Eighteen Years on The Gold Coast.* 1853.

*

Each minstrel has a song-net—a strongly made net of a fishing net sort. On to this net are tied all manner and sorts of things, pythons' back bones, tobacco pipes, bits of china, feathers, bits of hide, birds' heads, reptiles' heads, bones, etc., etc., and to every one of these objects hangs a tale. You see your minstrel's net, you select an object and say how much that song. He names an exorbitant price; you haggle; no good. He won't be reasonable, say over the python bone, so you price the tobacco pipe—more haggle; finally you settle on some object and its price, and sit down on your heels and listen with rapt attention to the song, or, rather, chant. You usually have another. You sort of dissipate in novels, in fact. I do not say it's quiet reading, because un-principled people will come headlong and listen when you have got your minstrel started, without paying their subscription. Hence a row, unless you are, like me, indifferent to other people having a little pleasure. . . .

The most impressive song-net that I saw was the one at Buana. Its owner I called Homer on the spot, because his works were a terrific two. Tied on to his small net were a human hand and a human jaw bone. They were his own songs. I heard them both regardless of ex-pense. I did not understand them, because I did not know his language; but they were fascinating things, and the human hand one had a pas-sage in it which caused the singer to crawl on his hands and knees, round and round, stealthily looking this side and that, giving the peculiar leopard questing cough, and making the leopard mark on the earth with his doubled-up fist. Ah! that was something like a song! It would have roused a rock to enthusiasm; a civilised audience would have smothered its singer with bouquets. I—well, the headman with me had to interfere and counsel moderation in heads of tobacco.

KINGSLEY: *West African Studies.* 1899.

A display of tumbling and dancing was arranged in Clapperton's honour by the King of Yoruba.

The actors having retired to some distance in the back ground, one of them was left in the centre, whose sack falling gradually down, exposed a white head, at which all the crowd gave a shout, that rent the air; they appeared indeed to enjoy this sight, as the perfection of the actor's art. The whole body was at last cleared of the incumbrance of the sack, when it exhibited the appearance of a human figure cast in white wax, of the middle size, miserably thin, and starved with cold. It frequently went through the motion of taking snuff, and rubbing its hands; when it walked, it was with the most awkward gait, treading as the most tender-footed white man would do in walking bare-footed, for the first time, over new frozen ground. The spectators often appealed to us, as to the excellence of the performance, and entreated I would look and be attentive to what was going on. I pretended to be fully as much pleased with this caricature of a white man as they could be, and certainly the actor burlesqued the part to admiration.

CLAPPERTON: *Journal of a Second Expedition.* 1829.

The King of Kiama invited the Landers to a race meeting.

The distant sound of drums gave notice of the king's approach, and every eye was immediately directed to the quarter from whence he was expected. The cavalcade shortly appeared, and four horsemen first drew up in front of the chief's house, which was near the centre of the course, and close to the spot where his wives and children and ourselves were sitting. Several men bearing on their heads an immense quantity of arrows in huge quivers of leopard's skin came next, followed by two persons who, by their extraordinary antics and gestures, we concluded to be buffoons. These two last were employed in throwing sticks into the air as they went on, and adroitly catching them in falling, besides performing many whimsical and ridiculous feats. Behind these, and immediately preceding the king, a group of little boys, nearly naked, came dancing merrily along, flourishing cows' tails over their heads in all directions. The king rode onwards, followed by a number of fine-looking men, on handsome steeds; and the motley cavalcade all drew up in front of his house, where they awaited his further orders without dismounting. This we thought was the proper time to give the first salute, so we accordingly fired three rounds; and our example was immediately followed by two soldiers, with muskets which were made at least a century and a half ago.

Preparations in the meantime had been going on for the race, and the horses with their riders made their appearance. The men were dressed in caps and loose robes and trowsers of every colour; boots of red morocco leather, and turbans of white and blue cotton. The horses were gaily caparisoned; strings of little brass bells covered their heads; their breasts were ornamented with bright red cloth and tassels of silk and cotton; a large quilted pad of neat embroidered patchwork was placed under the saddle of each; and little charms, inclosed in red and yellow cloth, were attached to the bridle with bits of tinsel. The Arab saddle and stirrup were in common use; and the whole group presented an imposing appearance.

The signal for starting was made, and the impatient animals sprung forward and set off at a full gallop. The riders brandished their spears, the little boys flourished their cows' tails, the buffoons performed their antics, muskets were discharged, and the chief himself, mounted on the finest horse on the ground, watched the progress of the race, while tears of delight were starting from his eyes. The sun shone gloriously on the tobes of green, white, yellow, blue, and crimson, as they fluttered in the breeze; and with the fanciful caps, the glittering spears, the jingling of the horses' bells, the animated looks and war-like bearing of their riders, presented one of the most extraordinary and pleasing sights that we have ever witnessed. The race was well contested, and terminated only by the horses being fatigued and out of breath; but though every one was emulous to outstrip his companion, honour and fame were the only reward of the competitors.

A few naked boys, on ponies without saddles, then rode over the course, after which the second and last heat commenced. This was not by any means so good as the first, owing to the greater anxiety which the horsemen evinced to display their skill in the use of the spear and the management of their animals. The king maintained his seat on horseback during these amusements, without even once dismounting to converse with his wives and children who were sitting on the ground on each side of him. His dress was showy rather than rich, consisting of a red cap, enveloped in the large folds of a white muslin turban; two under tobes of blue and scarlet cloth, and an outer one of white muslin; red trowsers, and boots of scarlet and yellow leather. His horse seemed distressed by the weight of his rider, and the various ornaments and trappings with which his head, breast, and body, were bedecked. The chief's eldest and youngest sons were near his women and other children, mounted on two noble looking horses. The eldest of these youths was about eleven years of age. The youngest being not more than three, was held on the back of his animal by a male attendant, as he was unable to sit upright in the saddle without this assistance. . . . Young virgins, according to custom, appeared in a state of nudity; many of them had wild flowers stuck behind their ears, and strings of beads, etc., round their loins; but want of clothing did not seem to damp their pleasure in the entertainment, for they appeared to enter into it with as much zest as any of their companions. Of the different coloured tobes worn by the men, none looked so well as those of a deep crimson colour on some of the horsemen; but the clean white tobes of the Mohammedan priests, of whom not less than a hundred were present on the occasion, were extremely neat and becoming. The sport terminated without the slightest accident, and the king's dismounting was a signal for the people to disperse.

RICHARD and JOHN LANDER: *An Expedition to the Niger.* . 1832.

The Kroos are noted sportsmen.

They delight in wrestling matches, and in the display of vigour, skill, and perseverance. Their strength is almost superhuman. The Kroos will not submit to the heavy idleness with which the other races show their reverence for the sabbath-day, but being released from the harsher duties of service to their white masters, devote hours to the indulgence of their favourite passion for wrestling; and rival parties or factions meet on the sands of the little bay called Kroo Creek, to gratify ambition or to maintain acknowledged pre-eminence. Far and wide may be heard the shout of victory as a champion hurls his antagonist to the earth. The process is not unlike that with which we are familiar, but is introduced with more ceremony. A clean circle of spectators, well kept by strong fellows armed with ropes' ends or short staves, incloses a space of a dozen yards in diameter.

A brawny hero, perfectly naked, steps forth and vaunts with preposterous gestures, leaping and dancing, and spurning the dust with his feet in all directions, like a bull proud and in wrath. He thus springs backwards and forwards, and singles out by turns for his disdain all the finest-looking men in the assemblage, inviting them contemptuously to certain destruction; and, as his insult is disregarded, turning on his heel, and flirting up the dust at them behind him with his toe. But his vaunting excites the ambition of some noted wrestler, who cannot endure to see the challenger thus glory in his superiority undisturbed. The challenge is accepted; and the rival, entering the arena, capers round the first boaster, snaps his fingers at him in scorn, and dashes the dust over his person. Each now acts the same part, leaping round his antagonist, sometimes with a prodigious bound, then stooping in a sitting posture upon the ground, and kicking up the earth; a prelude in which considerable time is spent. This introduction to the more serious contest was inexpressibly ludicrous to me; yet it always extorted long and fervent applauses from the bystanders, who repaid every excessive demonstration of vigour or contempt on either side by tumultuous cheers. Having sufficiently shown their confidence in their own superiority, and their perfect disdain for each other, they approach slowly and cautiously, endeavouring by every wily means to win an advantageous close; eyeing each other intently and scornfully, advancing a hand or a foot as an offer; speedily withdrawing it, however, when in an unfavourable position. At length the hand is seized, and the combatants are in an instant locked in iron embrace. The struggle for mastery is terrific but short. Upon the slightest inequality of advantage, the lucky Kroo summons his whole energy, makes a strong grasp upon the leg and shoulder of his gigantic opponent, lifts him off his feet, and dashes him to the earth. I have more than once seen the victor hurl the vanquished with amazing violence over his head.

The issue of the contest never appeared to disturb the amicable feelings of the parties engaged. Sometimes the successful hero encounters a series of emulous Kroos, until he himself falls, or departs amidst the plaudits of the assemblage, full of honour. Sometimes the unfortunate in one encounter burns to retrieve his character, and springs forth as challenger. The sport is always welcome to them.

RANKIN: *The White Man's Grave.* 1836.

The Hausas have Queensberry rules of their own.

Having heard a great deal of the boxers of Haussa, I was anxious to witness their performance. According I sent one of my servants last night to offer 2000 whydah for a pugilistic exhibition in the morning. As the death of one of the combatants is almost certain before a battle is over, I expressly prohibited all fighting in earnest; for it would have been disgraceful, both to myself and my country, to hire men to kill one another for the gratification of idle curiosity. About half an hour after the massi dubu were gone, the boxers arrived, attended by two drums, and the whole body of butchers, who here compose "the fancy". A ring was soon formed, by the master of the ceremonies throwing dust on the spectators to make them stand back. The drummers entered the ring, and began to drum lustily. One of the boxers followed, quite naked, except a skin round the middle. He placed himself in an attitude as if to oppose an antagonist, and wrought his muscles into action, seemingly to find out that every sinew was in full force for the approaching combat; then coming from time to time to the side of the ring, and presenting his right arm to the bystanders, he said, "I am a hyena;" "I am a lion;" "I am able to kill all that oppose me." The spectators, to whom he presented himself, laid their hands on his shoulder, repeating, "The blessing of God be upon thee;" "Thou art a hyena;" "Thou art a lion." He then abandoned the ring to another, who showed off in the same manner. The right hand and arm of the pugilists were now bound with narrow country cloth, beginning with a fold round the middle finger, when, the hand being first clinched with the thumb between the fore and mid fingers, the cloth was passed in many turns round the fist, the wrist, and the fore arm. After about twenty had separately gone through the attitudes of defiance, and appeals to the bystanders, they were next brought forward by pairs. If they happened to be friends, they laid their left breasts together twice, and exclaimed, "We are lions;" "We are friends." One then left the ring, and another was brought forward. If the two did not recognise one another as friends, the set-to immediately commenced. On taking their stations, the two pugilists first stood at some distance, parrying with the left hand open, and, whenever opportunity offered, striking with the right. They generally aimed at the pit of the stomach, and under the ribs. Whenever they closed, one seized the other's head under his arm, and beat it with his fist, at the same time striking with his knee between his antagonist's thighs. In this position, with the head in chancery, they are said sometimes to attempt to gouge or scoop out one of the eyes. When they break loose, they never fail to give a swinging blow with the heel under the ribs, or sometimes under the left ear. It is these blows which are so often fatal. The combatants were repeatedly separated by my orders, as they were beginning to lose their temper. When this spectacle was heard of, girls left their pitchers at the wells, the market people threw down their baskets, and all ran to see the fight. The whole square before my house was crowded to excess. After six pairs had gone through several rounds, I ordered them, to their great satisfaction, the promised reward, and the multitude quietly dispersed.

CLAPPERTON:
Travels and Discoveries in Northern and Central Africa.   1826.

5. "MAN IS THE NOBLER ANIMAL"

From Jobson onwards travellers commented on the "wonderful great subjection" of African women, in part a natural consequence of the practice of polygamy.

Yarro entertains the whimsical notion, that as females came into the world naked, naked they ought to live in it till their death, he does not, however, extend the same opinion to his own sex. "Man," said the king, "is the nobler animal, and wears clothing in token of his superiority over the weaker part of the creation"; and in accordance with this singular doctrine, none of his wives ever dare to approach his presence with any other dress than that which nature has supplied them with.

LANDER: *Records of Captain Clapperton's Last Expedition.* 1829.

*

I had retired to rest rather earlier than usual one evening, being greatly fatigued, when about the midnight hour a loud, long, and piercing shriek awoke me with a start, and springing hastily from my couch, I turned aside the slight mat which served instead of glass for my window, to ascertain the cause of it. The moon shone in the heavens with peculiar lustre and beauty, rivalling in splendour the brilliant orb whence she receives her light, so that I was enabled to distinguish clearly every object for some distance from the hut. Another fearful scream at the moment arrested my undivided attention upon a group of persons about ten or twelve yards from my window, in the midst of whom I could perceive two females struggling violently to get loose from the iron gripe with which they were held by their merciless guardians. I called as loudly as I could to the fellows, (who, as well as the perturbation of my mind, and the confusion of the scene would allow me to discern, were eight in number), to demand the reason of their ill-treatment of the defenceless women at that unseasonable hour, when one of them answered with the greatest unconcern, that the females whom I saw were the King's wives, who, having spoken their mind with too much frankness in the royal presence an hour before, had been ordered by their husband to make expiation for the offence by having their throats cut—that being considered as the mildest punishment which could be inflicted for the consummation of so heinous a crime, by the laws of Badagry; a punishment which none

49

but Adolee's favourites ever underwent. Whilst the man was yet speaking, the trembling criminals shrieked long and bitterly; but from exhaustion their struggles were less vehement than before. At length I saw their hands bound, next their feet; and lastly their heads, bent forcibly backwards, by four of the ruffians, were held tightly by the hair in that painful position. I then heard the poor creatures utter their last thrilling cry of anguish, which caused my blood to run cold in my veins, and a shudder to creep over every limb; and at that moment, the gleam of the uplifted daggers shot across my vision, and as quick as lightning the poinards were buried in the throat and bosom of each, severing the windpipe in their course. A faint gargling sound like water issuing from the mouth of a bottle, was the only noise produced; the ruthless assassins glided like spectres from before my window, trailing their bleeding victims along the earth; and all was as still and solemn as the grave.

LANDER: *Records of Captain Clapperton's Last Expedition.* 1829.

Yet for all this "wonderfull great subjection", feminine influence is strong in African affairs, particularly in commerce.

Having arrived at the bank of the river, the old woman directed all the yams to be placed in a row before our people, and in distinct and separate bundles, and the owners to retire to a short distance, which order was implicitly obeyed. The purchaser now inspected the bundles, and having selected one to his satisfaction, which might contain the finest yams, placed what he considered to be its value by the side of it, consisting of cloth, flints, etc. The old lady looking on all the time, if in her opinion it was sufficient to give, takes up the cloth and gives it to the owner of the bundle, and the purchaser likewise takes away the yams. But on the contrary, if the cloth, or whatever was thus offered by the purchaser, is not considered sufficient by the old woman, she allows it to remain a short time to give him an opportunity of adding something else to his offer. If this were not done, the owner of the yams was directed by the old woman to take them and move them back out of the way, leaving what had been offered for them to be taken away also. All this was carried on without a word passing between the parties, and the purchase of a sufficient number of yams by our people occupied three hours.

RICHARD and JOHN LANDER: *An Expedition to the Niger.*   1832.

★

Among my visitors on this day was the largest woman I ever beheld
—and a jolly good-tempered dame she was. On thanking her and
making her a small present for the attention which she had shown my
men while on shore, she assured me that "her belly had long been
hungry to see white men and their houses", and that she had come
alongside to see the interior of mine. I would very willingly have got
the old lady on board, had the foreyard been strong enough—as it was,
she was obliged to content herself with a peep through the cabin
windows. She certainly could not have weighed less than twenty-
five stone, and she informed me that she was mistress of more than
two hundred slaves, whom she employed in collecting palm-oil, cultivating yams, etc. Her personal charms were set off by a straw-hat
nearly five feet in diameter, about a dozen brass bracelets, two ivory
leglets ten inches wide by about six deep, and necklaces innumerable.

LAIRD and OLDFIELD: *An Expedition into the Interior of Africa.* 1837.

*

Mrs. Carew, or "Betsy Crew", was brought to Freetown some years
ago, a wretched slave captured in a slave-ship. Without the faintest
dream of civilised society, without connexions, without knowledge of
the English tongue, and possessing no resources but her own industry
and talent, this remarkable woman has risen to opulence, owning
landed and house property, and having a considerable interest in
shipping; and even takes the whole army and navy contracts for pro-
visioning the troops and the men-of-war, giving ample security
doubtless. Feeling in her own case the disadvantage of want of education, she has placed her son in a school of high respectability in London.
I was informed that she had suffered a severe loss by the sinking of a
vessel, whose cargo, her property, was uninsured; but that she bore the
reverse cheerfully, preferring to comfort herself with the good which
she retained, rather than to grieve for what she had lost. . . .
Her beauty is all of internal quality. Externally is beheld a very obese
and a very smiling woman, round wherever rotundity in the human
figure is possible; the gibbous jet face, large and shining, is surmounted
by the lace of a smart cap; the head is further adorned with a red kerchief; and perched aloft, to crown the whole, is a sky-blue beaver
Welsh hat. Her ear is loaded with many pendants of various dimensions, dragging that useful appendage towards the shoulder as to a
resting-place, and stretching the originally small perforation to a wide
chasm. Her gown is of a tasteful pattern; and from beneath it peeps
the wonted skirt of bright yellow "duckas", or dorcas, an under-

garment of woollen considered so ornamental that a portion is always
allowed to show itself as if by accident. The heavy cotton umbrella,
whose weight is more oppressive than the heat which it may ward off, is
of course in Betsy's hand; and, as she grasps it, rings are perceived
glancing upon her fingers. If this interesting woman has vanity, it is
in her earrings; an ornament worshipped in perfect consistency by
the savage, who makes an incision or bores a hole through the flesh of
the ear from which to suspend it, upon precisely the same principle as
that which prompts her to gash her face, and tear her back, shoulders,
and bosom, with a thousand beautiful wounds.

RANKIN: *The White Man's Grave.* 1836

★

I once overheard a long discussion between two ladies: "I always
clay my rubber up well," says number one. "I think," says number
two, "a bit of yam is better, with just a coat of rubber outside, then he
hop good too much when Mr. —— frows him for floor." They did
not convince each other as to the superiority of their individual
methods, but became very friendly over the foolishness of a mutual
friend, who both clayed and yammed her rubber to such an extent
that when Mr. —— "frowed him for floor he done squat." Mr. ——
then cut him open and "frowed" both the pieces at her head—a performance that raised Mr. —— in their esteem, as it demonstrated
commercial intelligence, a thing universally admired down here.

KINGSLEY: *Travels in West Africa.* 1897.

Africa has its own standards of feminine beauty.

Before breakfast, Addizetta was employed above an hour in cleaning
and polishing her teeth, by rubbing them with the fibrous roots of a
certain shrub or tree, which are much esteemed and generally used for
the purpose in her own country, as well as in the more interior parts.
Great part of the day is consumed by many thousands of individuals
in this amusing occupation, and to this cause the brilliant whiteness of
their teeth, for which Africans, generally speaking, are remarkable,
may be attributed.

RICHARD and JOHN LANDER: *An Expedition to the Niger.* 1832.

★

I saw two girls tattooed at Katunga, in the following manner:
The hands and feet of each being first bound, the head was held by the

father, and the operator began his work by making five incisions on the forehead with the instrument above described; the little sufferer uttering the most piercing screams, till from hoarseness she was unable longer to cry aloud, or speak so as to be understood. This being done, the man cut eight other deep gashes on the left cheek; and the only means by which one could then judge of the child's distress was by observing a large pool of mingled blood and tears on the ground, fed by a copious stream flowing from the face of the little innocent.

The patients are invariably left to bleed till they become insensible; and death frequently occurs in weakly cases. After some days, when their strength is in a measure restored, they are privileged to beg in the streets till their wounds completely heal; and this does not take place oftentimes for four or five months after the operation, the children, during that long period, carry slender branches of trees in their hands, in order to scare away flies, which, on alighting upon the lacerated face, cause considerable pain, and occasion it to swell prodigiously. This imparts to the countenance an unsightly appearance; one than which nothing can be more truly disgusting; and many of these pitiable objects we observed in the deepest misery, wandering through the streets of Katunga, and other cities, and almost starving from want of food.

LANDER: *Records of Captain Clapperton's Last Expedition.* 1829.

*

The Felatah ladies are very particular in adorning and ornamenting their persons; their toilet occupies them several hours, and preparations for it are commenced the night before, by laying the leaves of henna, moistened, to the toes and finger-nails, and hands; on the following morning the leaves are removed, the parts being stained a beautiful purple colour. They have an extraordinary practice of staining the teeth with the acid of the Goora nut and indigo, by which a blue colour is produced: a yellow dye is produced by mixing the Goora nut with a small shrub; the four front teeth of the upper and lower jaw are dyed, one of a blue, the next its natural colour—white; the next purple, the next yellow. The eyelids then take up great attention; they are pencilled with the sulphuret of antimony, which, contrasted with their ebony countenances, and the conjuctiva, or white of the eye, gives them an expressive appearance. Their hair (or wool) is another important part: seven or eight attendants are employed moistening the indigo for it. The hair is plaited in perpendicular knots of four or five inches along, and then bedaubed all over with the moistened indigo; after which the hair resembles a helmet in appearance. Several mornings in the week, they besmear themselves all over, from head to foot, with a red pigment, prepared from red wood brought from the Eboe country: it is supposed to possess a tonic quality, and also to lighten the colour of the skin and correct the fetor of perspiration. They are clean in their persons, and perform their ablutions twice a day in the river. The lobes of the ears are bored very large, and studs are worn, made of small stones and pieces of cornelian: a few of the females wore bells and buttons, which we had given them.

LAIRD and OLDFIELD: *An Expedition into the Interior of Africa.* 1837.

★

The interpreter was directed to advance the looking-glass, the effect of which was conclusive and sudden; in an instant the king was left, as it were, a monument, solitary, but for those who lounged or played at its base; the queens rushed forward, like the masses at a Vauxhall exhibition, from sight to sight, and now to view faces and charms they probably had never before had an opportunity of contemplating; the struggle to occupy a front position of the glass was severe, which the king observing, he very unceremoniously pushed the ladies aside, placed a minister of state on each side the looking-glass, then calling the queens up in succession, allowed each a glance of herself as she passed by.

HUNTLEY: *Service on the Slave Coast.* 1850.

Lander paid this tribute to African women:

I take this opportunity of expressing my high admiration of the amiable conduct of the African females toward me; in sickness and in health; in prosperity and in adversity—their kindness and affection were ever the same. They have danced and sung with me in health, grieved with me in sorrow, and shed tears of compassion at the recital of my misfortunes. When quite a boy, and suffering from fever in the West Indies, women of the same race used to take me in their arms, or on their knees, sing and weep over me, and tell me not to die, for that my mother would break her heart to hear the news; and pointing to the ocean, they cheered my spirits, by saying that it laved the shores of England, and would shortly bear me on its bosom to my distant home. In fine, through whatever region I have wandered, whether slave or free, I have invariably found a chord of tenderness and trembling pity to vibrate in the breast of an African woman; a spirit ever alive to soothe my sorrows and compassionate my afflictions;—and I never in my life knew one of them to bestow on me a single unpleasant look or angry word.

LANDER: *Records of Captain Clapperton's Last Expedition.* 1829.

6. "THIS THEY CALL THEIR FITTISH"

*Those Africans not recognisably Christian or Muslim were customarily
dubbed "pagans". But the pagans usually believed in a Great Spirit.*

To this unknown God they pay divine adoration, through the
medium of insignificant and inanimate objects, by the offering up of
sacrifices to the latter, under the belief that the Great Spirit exists at so
immeasurable a distance from them, and his time is so much employed
in other and more important matters, that he cannot listen to the
prayers of every individual. In consequence of this he appoints innumerable subordinate agents and machines, who aid and assist him,
and minister to the affairs of mankind.

LANDER: *Records of Captain Clapperton's Last Expedition.* 1829.

★

The most numerous Sect are the Pagans, who trouble themselves
about no Religion at all; yet every one of them have some Trifle or
other, to which they pay a particular Respect, or Kind of Adoration,
believing it can defend them from all Dangers: Some have a Lion's
Tail; some a Bird's Feather, some a Pebble, a Bit of Rag, a Dog's Leg;
or, in a short, any Thing they fancy: And this they call their Fittish,
which Word not only signifies the Thing worshipped, but sometimes a
Spell, Charm, or Inchantment. To take the Fittish, is, to take an Oath;
which Ceremony is variously performed in several Parts of Guinea.
In some Places, they drink a large Draught of Water, and wish their
Fittish may kill them, if what they attest be not true: And, generally
speaking, a Negro's taking the Fittish in Guinea may as sincerely be
relied on as the Oath of a Christian in Europe. To make Fittish, is to
perform Divine Worship; Fittish-men, are the Pagan Priests. In short,
they all commonly wear their Fittish about them, which is so sacred
that they care not to let any Body touch it, but themselves.

SMITH: *A New Voyage to Guinea.* 1745.

★

Charms are made for every occupation and desire in life—loving,
hating, buying, selling, fishing, planting, travelling, hunting, etc., and
although they are usually in the form of things filled with a mixture in
which the spirit nestles, yet there are other kinds; for example, a

great love charm is made of the water the lover has washed in, and this, mingled with the drink of the loved one, is held to soften the hardest heart. Of a similar nature is the friendship-compelling charm I know of on the Ivory Coast, which I have been told is used also in the Batanga regions. This is obtained on the death of a person you know really cared for you—like your father or mother, for example—by cutting off the head and suspending it over a heap of chalk, as the white earth that you find in river beds is called here, then letting it drip as long as it will and using this saturated chalk to mix in among the food of any one you wish should think kindly of you and trust you. This charm, a Bassa man said to me, "was good too much for the white trader," and made him give you "good price too much" for palm oil, etc., and that statement revived my sympathy for a friend who once said to me that when he used first to come to the Coast he had "pretty well had the inside raked up out of him" from the sickness caused by the charms that his local cook administered to him in the interest of the cook's friends.

KINGSLEY: *Travels in West Africa.* 1897.

★

A circumstance occurred to this poor woman which is strongly characteristic of the blind superstition of the natives in this part of Africa. This poor creature imagined that she possessed a maghony (charm) which rendered her invulnerable to all edge-tools and cutting instruments. So positive and convinced was she of the efficacy of her charm, that she voluntarily assented to hold her leg whilst some person should strike it with an axe. The king (or chief) of her town, on hearing this, determined to try the power of her charm, and desired a man to take an axe, and see whether this wonderful maghony would protect her from its effects; considering that if it did so, such a charm would be of great advantage in war. Her leg was laid on a block, and a powerful blow given below the knee, the result of which was as might have been expected. To the poor woman's great horror, and the terror of all present, her leg flew to the other side of the room. But she survived it, and now crawled about on her knees. I determined on making application at Fernando Po for a wooden one for the poor creature, as soon as we returned.

LAIRD and OLDFIELD: *An Expedition into the Interior of Africa.* 1837.

★

That is the worst of charms and prayers. The thing you wish of them may, and frequently does, happen in a strikingly direct way, but other times it does not. In Africa this is held to arise from the bad character of the spirits; their gross ingratitude and fickleness. You may have taken every care of a spirit for years, given it food and other offerings that you wanted for yourself, wrapped it up in your cloth on chilly nights and gone cold, put it in the only dry spot in the canoe, and so on, and yet after all this, the wretched thing will be capable of being got at by your rival or enemy and lured away, leaving you only the case it once lived in.

Finding, we will say, that you have been upset and half-drowned, and your canoe-load of goods lost three times in a week, that your paddles are always breaking, and the amount of snags in the river and so on is abnormal, you judge that your canoe-charm has stopped. Then you go to the medicine man who supplied you with it and complain. He says it was a perfectly good charm when he sold it you and he never had any complaints before, but he will investigate the affair; when he has done so, he either says the spirit has been lured away from the home he prepared for it by incantations and presents from other people, or that he finds the spirit is dead; it has been killed by a more powerful spirit of its class, which is in the pay of some enemy of yours. In all cases the little thing you kept the spirit in is no use now, and only fit to sell to a white man as "a big curio!" and the sooner you let him have sufficient money to procure you a fresh and still more powerful spirit—necessarily more expensive—the safer it will be for you, particularly as your misfortunes distinctly point to someone being desirous of your death. You of course grumble, but seeing the thing in his light you pay up, and the medicine man goes busily to work with incantations, dances, looking into mirrors or basins of still water, and concoctions of messes to make you a new protecting charm.

KINGSLEY: Travels in West Africa. 1897.

In addition to dispensing charms, the witch doctor was expected to "smell out" witches, and to conduct trials of innocence. Richard Lander was subjected to one such trial.

The news of the white man's arrest, and approaching trial, spread like wild-fire through the town, and the inhabitants, assembling from all parts, armed with axes, spears, clubs, and bows and arrows, followed the procession to the dismal spot. On entering the hut, I beheld a number of priests and elders of the people, seated in a circle, who desired me to stand in the midst of them. When I had complied with their request, one of the priests arose and presenting me with a bowl, containing about a quart of a clear liquid, scarcely distinguishable from water, cried out in a loud voice, and with much emphasis, "You are accused, white man, of designs against our king and his government, and are therefore desired to drink the contents of this vessel, which, if the reports to your prejudice be true, will surely destroy you; whereas, if they be without foundation, you need not fear, Christian; the fetish will do you no injury, for our gods will do that which is right."

I took the bowl in my trembling hand, and gazed for a moment on the sable countenances of my judges; but not a single look of compassion shone upon any of them; a dead silence prevailed in the gloomy sanctuary of skulls; every eye was intently fixed upon me; and seeing no possibility of escape, or of evading the piercing glance of the priests and elders, I offered up internally, a short prayer to the Throne of Mercy—to the God of Christians—and hastily swallowed the fetish, dashing the poison-chalice to the ground. A low murmur ran through the assembly; they all thought I should instantly have expired, or at least have discovered symptoms of severe agony, but detecting no such tokens, they arose simultaneously, and made way for me to leave the hut. On getting into the open air, I found my poor slaves in tears; they had come, they said, to catch a last glimpse of their master; but when they saw me alive and at liberty, they leaped and danced for joy, and prepared a path for me through the dense mass of armed people. These set up an astounding shout at my unexpected appearance, and seemed greatly pleased (if I might be allowed to judge), that I had not fallen a victim to the influence of their fearful fetish. On arriving at my dwelling, I took instant and powerful means to eject the venomous potion from my stomach, and happily succeeded in the attempt.

I was told that the liquid I had swallowed was a decoction of the bark of a tree abounding in the neighbourhood, and that I was the only individual who, for a long season, had escaped its poisonous qualities. It had a disagreeably bitter taste, but I experienced no other ill effects from it than a slight dizziness, which wore off completely a few hours after the conclusion of the trial.

LANDER: *Records of Captain Clapperton's Last Expedition.* 1829.

Mary Kingsley's studies led her to the conclusion that witch doctors based their work on the belief that a human being has four souls—the soul that survives, the soul that lives in an animal, the shadow cast by the body, and the soul that acts in dreams.

The dream-soul is the cause of woes unnumbered to our African friend, and the thing that most frequently converts him into that desirable state, from a witch doctor's point of view of a patient. It is this way. The dream-soul is, to put it very mildly, a silly flighty thing. Off it goes when its owner is taking a nap, and gets so taken up with sky-larking, fighting, or gossiping with other dream-souls that sometimes it does not come home to its owner when he is waking up. So, if any one has to wake a man up great care must always be taken that it is done softly—softly, namely gradually and quietly, so as to give the dream-soul time to come home. For if either of the four souls of a man have their intercommunication broken, the human being possessing them gets very ill. We will take an example. A man has been suddenly roused by some cause or other before the dream-soul has had time to get into quarters. That human being feels very ill, and sends for the Witch Doctor. The medical man diagnoses the case as one of absence of dream-soul, instantly claps a cloth over the mouth and nose, and gets his assistant to hold it there until the patient gets hard on suffocated; but no matter, its the proper course of treatment to pursue. The witch doctor himself gets ready as rapidly as possible another dream-soul, which if he is a careful medical man, he has brought with him in a basket. Then the patient is laid on his back and the cloths removed from the mouth and nose, and the witch doctor holds over them his hands containing the fresh soul, blowing hard at it so as to get it well into the patient. If this is successfully accomplished, the patient recovers. Occasionally, however, this fresh soul slips through the medical man's fingers, and before you can say "Knife" is on top of some 100-feet-high or more silk cotton tree, where it chirrups gaily and distinctly. This is a great nuisance. The patient has to be promptly covered up again. If the doctor has an assistant with him, that unfortunate individual has to go up the tree and catch the dream-soul. If he has no assistant, he has to send his power up the tree after the truant; doctors who are in full practice have generally passed the time of life when climbing up trees personally is agreeable. When, however, the thing has been re-captured and a second attempt to insert it is about to be made, it is held advisable to get the patient's friends and relatives to stand round him in a ring and howl lustily, while your assistant also howling lustily, but in a professional manner, beats a drum. This prevents the soul from bolting again, and tends to frighten it into the patient.

In some obstinate cases of loss of dream-soul, however, the most experienced medical man will fail to get the fresh soul inserted. It clings to his fingers, it whisks back into the basket or into his hair or clothes, and it chirrups dismally, and the patient becomes convulsed. This is a grave symptom, but the diagnosis is quite clear. The patient has got a sisa in him, so there is no room for the fresh soul.

Now, a sisa is a dreadful bad thing for a man to have in him, and an expensive thing to get out. It is the surviving soul of a person who has not been properly buried—not had his devil made, in fact. And as every human surviving soul has a certain allotted time of existence in a human body before it can learn the dark and difficult way down to Srahmandazi, if by mischance the body gets killed off before the time is up, that soul, unless properly buried and sent on the way to Srahmandazi, or any other Hades, under expert instruction given as to the path for the dead, becomes a sisa, and has to hang about for the remaining years of its term of bodily life.

These ensisa are held to be so wretchedly uncomfortable in this state that their tempers become perfect wrecks, and they grow utterly malignant, continually trying to get into a human body, so as to finish their term more comfortably. Now, a sisa's chief chance of getting into a body is in whipping in when there is a hole in a man's soul chamber, from the absence of his own dream-soul. If a sisa were a quiet, respectable soul that would settle down, it would not matter much, for the dream-soul it supplants is not of much account. But a sisa is not. At the best, it would only live out its remaining term, and then go off the moment that term was up, and most likely kill the souls it had been sheltering with by bolting at an inconvenient moment. This was the verdict given on the death of a man I knew who, from what you would call faintness, fell down in a swamp and was suffocated. Inconvenient as this is, the far greater danger you are exposed to by having a sisa in you lies in the chance being 10 to 1 that it is stained with blood, for, without being hard on these unfortunate unburied souls, I may remark that respectable souls usually get respectably buried, and so don't become ensisa. This blood which is upon it the devils that are around smell and go for, as is the nature of devils; and these devils whip in after the sisa soul into his host in squads, and the man with such a set inside him is naturally very ill—convulsions, delirium, high temperature, etc., and the indications to your true witch doctor are that that sisa must be extracted before a new dream-soul can be inserted and the man recover.

But getting out a sisa is a most trying operation. Not only does it necessitate a witch doctor sending in his power to fetch it *vi et armis*, it also places the medical man in a position of grave responsibility regarding its disposal when secured. The methods he employs to meet this may be regarded as akin to those of antiseptic surgery. All the people in the village, particularly babies and old people—people whose souls are delicate—must be kept awake during the operation, and have a piece of cloth over the nose and mouth, and every one must howl so as to scare the sisa off them, if by mischance it should escape from the witch doctor. An efficient practitioner, I may remark, thinks it a great disgrace to allow a sisa to escape from him; and such an accident would be a grave blow to his practice, for people would not care to call in a man who was liable to have this occur. However, our present medical man having got the sisa out, he has still to deal with the question of its disposal before he can do anything more. The assistant blows a new dream soul into the patient, and his women see to him; but the witch doctor just holds on to the sisa like a bull dog.

Sometimes the disposal of the sisa has been decided on prior to its extraction. If the patient's family are sufficiently well off, they agree to pay the doctor enough to enable him to teach the sisa the way to Hades. Indeed, this is the course respectable medical men always insist on, although it is expensive to the patient's family. But there are, I regret to say, a good many unprincipled witch doctors about who will undertake a case cheap.

They will carry off with them the extracted sisa for a small fee, then shortly afterwards a baby in the village goes off in tetanic convulsions. No one takes much notice of that, because its a way babies have. Soon another baby is born in the same family—polygamy being prevalent, the event may occur after a short interval—well, after giving the usual anxiety and expense, that baby goes off in convulsions. Suspicion is aroused. Presently yet another baby appears in the family, keeps all right for a week may be, and then also goes off in convulsions. Suspicions are confirmed. The worm—the father, I mean—turns, and he takes the body of that third baby and smashes one of its leg bones before it is thrown away into the bush; for he knows he has got a wanderer soul—namely, a sisa which some unprincipled practitioner has sent into his family. He just breaks the leg so as to warn the soul he is not a man to be trifled with, and will not have his family kept in a state of perpetual uproar and expense. It sometimes happens, however, in spite of this that, when his fourth baby arrives, that too goes off in convulsions. Thoroughly roused now, paterfamilias sternly takes a chopper and chops that infant's remains up extremely small, and it is scattered broadcast. Then he holds he has eliminated that sisa from his family finally.

I am informed, however, that the fourth baby to arrive in a family afflicted by a sisa does not usually go off in convulsions, but that fairly frequently it is born lame, which shows that it is that wanderer soul back with its damaged leg. It is not treated unkindly but not taken much care of and so rarely lives many years—from the fetish point of view, of course, only those years remaining of its term of bodily life out of which some witchcraft of man or some vengeance of a god cheated it.

If I mention the facts that when a man wakes up in the morning feeling very stiff and with "that tired feeling" you see mentioned in advertisements in the newspapers, he holds that it arises from his own dream-soul having been out fighting and got itself bruised; and that if he wakes up in a fright, he will jump up and fire off his gun, holding that a pack of rag-tag devils have been chasing his soul home and wishing to scare them off, I think I may leave the complaints of the dream-soul connected with physic and pass on to those connected with surgery.

Now, devoted as I am to my West African friends, I am bound in the interests of Truth to say that many of them are sadly unprincipled. There are many witches, not witch doctors, remember, who make it a constant practice to set traps for dream-souls. Witches you will find from Sierra Leone to Cameroons, but they are extra prevalent on the Gold Coast and in Calabar.

These traps are usually pots containing something attractive to the soul, and in this bait are concealed knives or fish-hooks—fish-hooks when the witch wants to catch the soul to keep, knives when the desire is just to injure it.

In the case of the lacerated dream-soul, when it returns to its owner, it makes him feel very unwell; but the symptoms are quite different from those arising from loss of dream-soul or from a sisa.

The reason for catching dream-souls with hooks is usually a low mercenary one. You see, many patients insist on having their own dream-soul put back into them—they don't want a substitute from the doctor's store—so of course the soul has to be bought from the witch who has got it. Sometimes, however, the witch is the hireling of someone intent on injuring a particular person and keen on capturing the soul for this purpose, though too frightened to kill his enemy outright. So the soul is not only caught and kept, but tortured, hung up over the canoe fire and so on, and thus, even if the patient has another dream-soul put in, so long as his original soul is in the hands of a torturer, he is uncomfortable.

On one occasion, for example, I heard one of the Kru boys who were with me making more row in his sleep, more resounding slaps and snores and grunts than even a normal Kru boy does, and resolving in my mind that what that young man really required was one of my pet pills, I went to see him. I found him asleep under a thick blanket and with a handkerchief tied over his face. It was a hot night, and the man and his blanket were as wet with sweat as if they had been dragged through a river. I suggested to the head-man that the handkerchief muzzle should come off, and was informed by him that for several nights previously the man had dreamt of that savoury dish, crawfish seasoned with red pepper. He had become anxious, and consulted the head-man, who decided that undoubtedly some witch was setting a trap for his dream-soul with this bait, with intent, etc. Care was now being taken to, as it were, keep the dream-soul at home. I of course did not interfere and the patient completely recovered.

We will now pass on to diseases arising from disorders in the other three souls of a man. The immortal or surviving soul is liable to a disease that its body suffered from during its previous time on earth, born again with it. Such diseases are quite incurable, and I only personally know of them in the Calabar and Niger Delta, where reincarnation is strongly believed in.

Then come the diseases that arise from injury to the shadow-soul. It strikes one as strange at first to see men who have been walking, say, through forest or grass land on a blazing hot morning quite happily, on arrival at a piece of clear ground or a village square, most carefully go round it, not across, and you will soon notice that they only do this at noontime, and learn that they fear losing their shadow. I asked some Bakwiri I once came across who were particularly careful in this matter why they were not anxious about losing their shadows when night came down and they disappeared in the surrounding darkness, and was told that that was all right, because at night all shadows lay down in the shadow of the Great God, and so got stronger. Had I not seen how strong and long a shadow, be it of man or tree or of the great mountain itself, was in the early morning time? Ah me! I said, the proverb is true that says the turtle can teach the spider. I never thought of that.

Murders are sometimes committed by secretly driving a nail or knife into a man's shadow, and so on; but if the murderer be caught red-handed at it, he or she would be forthwith killed, for all diseases arising from the shadow-soul are incurable. No man's shadow is like that of his own brother, says the proverb.

Now we come to that very grave class of diseases which arise from disorders of the bush-soul These diseases are not all incurable, nevertheless they are very intractable and expensive to cure. This bush-soul is, as I have said, resident in some wild animal in the forest. It may be in only an earth pig, or it may be in a leopard, and, quite providentially for the medical profession no layman can see his own soul—it is not as if it were connected with all earth pigs, or all leopards, as the case may be, but it is in one particular earth pig or leopard or other animal—so recourse must be had to medical aid when anything goes wrong with it. It is usually in the temper that the bush-soul suffers.

It is liable to get a sort of aggrieved neglected feeling, and want things given it. When you wander about the wild gloomy forests of the Calabar region, you will now and again come across, far away from all human habitation or plantations, tiny huts, under whose shelter lies some offering or its remains Those are offerings administered by direction of a witch doctor to appease a bush-soul. For not only can a witch doctor see what particular animal a man's bush-soul is in, but he can also see whereabouts in the forest that animal is. Still, these bush-souls are not easily appeased. The worst of it is that a man may be himself a quiet steady man, careful of his diet and devoted to a whole skin, and yet his bush-soul be a reckless blade, scorning danger, and thereby getting itself shot by some hunter or killed in a trap or pit; and if his bush-soul dies, the man it is connected with dies. Therefore if the hunter who has killed it can be found out—a thing a witch doctor cannot do unless he happens by chance to have had his professional eye on that bush-soul at the time of the catastrophe; because, as it were, at death the bush-soul ceases to exist—that hunter has to pay compensation to the family of the deceased. On the other hand, if the man belonging to the bush-soul dies, the bush-soul animal has to die too. It rushes to and fro in the forest—"can no longer find a good place". If it sees a fire, it rushes into that; if it sees a lot of hunters, it rushes among them—anyhow, it gets itself killed off.

KINGSLEY: *West African Studies.* 1899.

Human sacrifice was customary, particularly as part of the funeral rites of chiefs, in the belief that chiefs must be fittingly attended in the other world.

'Tis a most deplorable Spectacle to see these miserable Creatures killed in the most barbarous Manner in the World; what with Hacking, Piercing, Tormenting, etc. they endure a Thousand Deaths.

'Twas not without the utmost Horrour that I saw eleven Persons killed in this manner; amongst which there was one, who after having endured a great deal of exquisite Torture, was delivered to a Child of six Years of Age who was to cut of his Head, which it was about an Hour in doing, not being strong enough to wield the Sabre.

These Human Sacrifices are in use amongst those Negroes who are not fully subject to our Government, and live very distant from our Forts: But where we have any Authority we don't suffer it, though they will privately remove to other places in order to perpetrate this Villany.

BOSMAN: *Description of the Coast of Guinea.* 1721.

*

Waking up again I noticed the smell in the hut was violent, from being shut up I suppose, and it had an unmistakably organic origin. Knocking the ash end off the smouldering bush-light that lay burning on the floor, I investigated, and tracked it to those bags, so I took down the biggest one, and carefully noted exactly how the tie had been put round its mouth; for these things are important and often mean a lot. I then shook its contents out in my hat, for fear of losing anything of value. They were a human hand, three big toes, four eyes, two ears, and other portions of the human frame. The hand was fresh, the others only so-so, and shrivelled.

Replacing them I tied the bag up, and hung it up again. I subsequently learnt that although the Fans will eat their fellow friendly tribesfolk, yet they like to keep a little something belonging to them as a memento. This touching trait in their character I learnt from Wiki; and, though it's to their credit, under the circumstances, still it's an unpleasant practice when they hang the remains in the bedroom you occupy, particularly if the bereavement in your host's family has been recent.

KINGSLEY: *Travels in West Africa.* 1897.

Horror reached its peak at Benin at the end of the last century. Following the murder of the British Vice-Consul on his way to visit the Oba, a punitive expedition fought its way to the city.

Following this road for about two hundred yards, we came upon the first evidence that we were approaching Benin in the shape of a human sacrifice. Laid on the grass where two paths met was a young woman horribly mutilated, a rough wooden gag tied in her mouth was clenched tightly by her teeth, which, with the expression of her face, told of the agony of her murder. At her feet lay a goat with its knees broken. I asked the guide what it meant, and he said it was to prevent the white man coming farther; a queer idea! A few yards farther brought us to another; this time a man, with his arms tied behind him, lying on his face in the path, but for some reason not decapitated, which as a rule is the second form of sacifice.

BACON: *Benin, The City of Blood.* 1897.

⋆

It was in these Juju compounds that the main sacrifices were carried out. To describe one of these Juju places will be to describe all of them, as they only differed in position and size.

These spaces were about a hundred and fifty yards long, and about sixty broad, surrounded by a high wall, and covered with a short brown grass. At one end was a long shed running the whole breadth of the enclosure, and under this was the altar. The altar was made by three steps running the whole length under the shelter of the shed; slightly raised for some distance in the centre, on which raised portion were handsomely-carved ivory tusks placed on the top of very antique bronze heads. Near these tusks were carved clubs, undoubtedly for use upon the victims of the sacrifice. The altar was deluged in blood, the smell of which was too overpowering for many of us. This same awful smell seemed to pervade the whole compound, as if the grass had been watered with blood.

In the centre of several of these Juju places was an iron erection like a huge candelabra with sharp hooks. Its purpose was not known, but it is probable that it was some instrument of torture, or for hanging portions of the victims on. In most of the Juju compounds was a well for the reception of the bodies.

The one lasting remembrance of Benin in my mind is its smells. Crucifixions, human sacrifices, and every horror the eye could get accustomed to, to a large extent, but the smells no white man's internal economy could stand. Four times in one day I was practically sick from them, and many more times on the point of being so. Every person who was able, I should say, indulged in a human sacrifice, and those who could not, sacrificed some animal and left the remains in front of his house. After a day or so the whole town seemed one huge pest-house.

And these pits! who could describe them; out of one a Jakri boy was pulled with drag-ropes from under several corpses; he said he had been in five days.

Ibid.

7. POMP AND CIRCUMSTANCE

Chiefs, kings, sheikhs, sultans greeted the traveller wherever he went in West Africa. The greater among them maintained an impressive panoply of state.

He came mounted on a beautiful red roan, attended by a number of armed men, on horseback and on foot; and six young female slaves, naked as they were born, except a stripe of narrow white cloth tied round their heads, about six inches of the ends flying out behind; each carrying a light spear in the right hand. He was dressed in a red silk damask tobe, and booted. He dismounted, and came into my house, attended by the six girls, who laid down their spears, and put a blue cloth round their waists before they entered the door. . . . On his leaving me, I attended him to the door. He mounted his horse, the young ladies undressed, and away went the most extraordinary cavalcade I ever saw in my life.

CLAPPERTON: *Journal of a Second Expedition.* 1829.

*

The eunuchs and other individuals who were present at the interview prostrated themselves before their prince, agreeably to the custom of the country, and rubbed their heads with earth two separate times, retreating at some distance to perform this humiliating and degrading ceremony, and then drawing near the royal person, to lie again with their faces in the dust. They saluted the ground also near which he was sitting, by kissing it fervently and repeatedly, and by placing each cheek on it. Then, and not till then, with their heads, and faces, and lips, and breasts, stained with the damp red soil, which still clung to them, they were allowed to seat themselves near their monarch, and to join in the conversation. Two or three of the inferior eunuchs, not satisfied with this servile prostration, began to sport and roll themselves about on the ground; but this could not be effected without immense labour and difficulty, and panting and straining, for, like Sir John Falstaff, they could be compared to nothing so appropriately as huge hills of flesh. There they lay wallowing in the mire, like immense turtles floundering in the sea, till Ebo desired them to rise.

RICHARD and JOHN LANDER: *An Expedition to the Niger.* 1832.

THE END OF A FISH DRIVE BY MEN OF THE KONKOMBA TRIBE,
NORTHERN TERRITORIES OF THE GOLD COAST

TRADITIONAL CAPARISON OF NORTHERN NIGERIA

GRANDSON OF A CHIEF, B.SC., A.M.I.
—A MODERN CITIZEN OF ACCRA AND HIS CHILDREN

Monarchy was nowhere more absolute than in the interior of Nigeria where the ruling houses had accepted Islam. To the west were the Hausa states and to the east the kingdom of Bornu.

Soon after daylight we were summoned to attend the Sultan of Bornou. He received us in an open space in front of the royal residence: we were kept at a considerable distance while his people approached to within about 100 yards, passing first on horseback; and after dismounting then prostrating themselves before him, they took their places on the ground in front, but with their backs to the royal person, which is the custom of the country. He was seated in a sort of cage of cane or wood, near the door of his garden, on a seat which at the distance appeared to be covered with silk or satin, and through the railing looked upon the assembly before him, who formed a sort of semi-circle extending from his seat to nearly where we were waiting. . . . Large bellies and large heads are indispensable for those who serve the court of Bornou; and those who unfortunately possess not the former by nature, or on whom lustiness will not be forced by cramming, make up the deficiency of protuberance by a wadding, which, as they sit on the horse, gives the belly the curious appearance of hanging over the pummel of the saddle. The eight, ten, and twelve shirts, of different colours, that they wear one over the other, help a little to increase this greatness of person; the head is enveloped in folds of muslin or linen of various colours, though mostly white, so as to deform it as much as possible; and those whose turban seemed to be the most studied had the effect of making the head appear completely on one side. Besides this they are hung all over with charms, inclosed in little red leather parcels, strung together; the horse, also, has them round his neck, in front of his head, and about the saddle.

When these courtiers, to the number of about two hundred and sixty or three hundred, had taken their seats in front of the sultan, we were allowed to approach to within about pistol-shot of the spot where he was sitting, and desired to sit down ourselves, when the ugliest black that can be imagined, his chief eunuch, the only person who approached the sultan's seat, asked for the presents. Boo-Khaloom's were produced, inclosed in a large shawl, and were carried unopened to the presence. Our glimpse was but a faint one of the sultan, through the lattice-work of his pavilion, sufficient however to see that his turban was larger than any of his subjects', and that his face, from the nose downwards, was completely covered. A little to our left, and nearly in front of the sultan, was an extempore declaimer shouting forth praises of his master with his pedigree; and near him one who

6

bore the long wooden frumfrum, on which he ever and anon blew a blast, loud and unmusical. Nothing could be more ridiculous than the appearance of these people squatting down in their places, tottering under the weight and magnitude of their turbans and their bellies, while the thin legs that appeared underneath but ill accorded with the bulk of the other parts.

DENHAM: *Travels and Discoveries in North and Central Africa.* 1826.

But the travellers also found powerful "pagan" kingdoms, in particular those of Ashanti, Dahomey and Benin.

We entered Coomassie at two o'clock, passing under a fetish, or sacrifice of a dead sheep, wrapped up in red silk, and suspended between two lofty poles. Upwards of 5,000 people, the greater part warriors, met us with awful bursts of martial music, discordant only in its mixture, for horns, drums, rattles, and gong-gongs were all exerted with a zeal bordering on phrenzy, to subdue us by the first impression. The smoke which encircled us from the incessant discharges of musquetry, confined our glimpses to the foreground; and we were halted whilst the captains performed their Pyrrhic dance, in the centre of a circle formed by their warriors; where a confusion of flags, English, Dutch, and Danish, were waved and flourished in all directions; the bearers plunging and springing from side to side, with a passion of enthusiasm only equalled by the captains, who followed them, discharging their shining blunderbusses so close, that the flags now and then were in a blaze; and emerging from the smoke with all the gesture and distortion of maniacs. . . .

This exhibition continued about half an hour, when we were allowed to proceed, encircled by the warriors, whose numbers, with the crowds of people, made our movement as gradual as if it had taken place in Cheapside; the several streets branching off to the right, presented long vistas crammed with people, and those on the left hand being on an acclivity, innumerable rows of heads rose one above another; the large open porches of the houses, like the fronts of stages in small theatres, were filled with the better sort of females and children, all impatient to behold white men for the first time; their exclamations were drowned in the firing and music, but their gestures were in character with the scene. When we reached the palace, about half a mile from the place where we entered, we were again halted, and an open file was made, through which the bearers were passed, to deposit the presents and baggage in the house assigned to us. Here we were gratified by observing several of the caboceers pass by with their trains, the novel splendour of which astonished us. The bands, principally composed of horns and flutes, trained to play in concert, seemed to soothe our hearing into its natural tone again by their wild melodies; whilst the immense umbrellas, made to sink and rise from the jerkings of the bearers, and the large fans waving around, refreshed us with small currents of air, under a burning sun, clouds of dust, and a density of atmosphere almost suffocating. We were then squeezed, at the same funeral pace, up a long street, to an open-fronted house, where we were desired by a royal messenger to wait a further invitation from the king. Here our attention was forced from the astonishment of the crowd to a most inhuman spectacle, which was paraded before us for some minutes; it was a man whom they were tormenting previous to sacrifice; his hands were pinioned behind him, a knife was passed through his cheeks, to which his lips were noosed like the figure of 8; one ear was cut off and carried before him, the other hung to his head by a small bit of skin; there were several gashes in his back, and a knife was thrust under each shoulder blade; he was led with a cord passed through his nose, by men disfigured with immense caps of shaggy black skins, and drums beat before him; the feeling this horrid barbarity excited must be imagined. We were soon released by permission to proceed to the king, and passed through a very broad street, about a quarter of a mile long, to the market place.

Our observations *en passant* had taught us to conceive a spectacle far exceeding our original expectations; but they had not prepared us for the extent and display of the scene which here burst upon us: an area of nearly a mile in circumference was crowded with magnificence and novelty. The king, his tributaries, and captains, were resplendent in the distance, surrounded by attendants of every description, fronted by a mass of warriors which seemed to make our approach impervious. The sun was reflected, with a glare scarcely more supportable than the heat, from the massy gold ornaments, which glistened in every direction. More than a hundred bands burst at once on our arrival, with the peculiar airs of their several chiefs; the horns flourished their defiances, with the beating of innumerable drums and metal instruments, and then yielded for a while to the soft breathing of their long flutes, which were truly harmonious; and a pleasing instrument, like a bagpipe without the drone, was happily blended. At least a hundred large umbrellas, or canopies, which could shelter thirty persons, were sprung up and down by the bearers with brilliant effect, being made of scarlet, yellow, and the most shewy cloths and silks, and crowned on the top with crescents, pelicans, elephants, barrels, and arms and swords of gold; they were of various shapes, but mostly dome; the valances (in some of which small looking glasses were inserted) fantastically scalloped and fringed; from the fronts of some, the proboscis and small teeth of elephants projected, and a few were roofed with leopard skin, and crowned with various animals naturally stuffed. The state hammocks, like long cradles, were raised in the rear, the poles on the heads of the bearers: the cushions and pillows were covered with crimson taffeta, and the richest cloths hung over the sides. Innumerable small umbrellas, of various coloured stripes, were crowded in the intervals, whilst several large trees heightened the glare, by contrasting the sober colouring of nature.

"Discolour unde auri per ramos aura refulsit."

The king's messengers, with gold breast plates, made way for us, and we commenced our round, preceded by the canes and the English flag. We stopped to take the hand of every caboceer, which, as their household suites occupied several spaces in advance, delayed us long enough to distinguish some of the ornaments in the general blaze of splendour and ostentation. . . .

The prolonged flourishes of the horns, a deafening tumult of drums, and the fuller concert of the intervals, announced that we were approaching the king: we were already passing the principal officers of his household; the chamberlain, the gold horn blower, the captain of the messengers, the captain for royal executions, the captain of the market, the keeper of the royal burial ground, and the master of the bands, sat surrounded by a retinue and splendour which bespoke the dignity and importance of their offices. The cook had a number of small services covered with leopard's skin held behind him, and a large quantity of massy silver plate was displayed before him, punch bowls, waiters, coffee pots, tankards, and a very large vessel with heavy handles and clawed feet, which seem to have been made to hold incense; I observed a Portuguese inscription on one piece, and they seemed generally of that manufacture. The executioner, a man of an immense size, wore a massy gold hatchet on his breast; and the execution stool was held before him, clotted in blood, and partly covered with a cawl of fat. The king's four linguists were encircled by a splendour inferior to none, and their peculiar insignia, gold canes, were elevated in all directions, tied in bundles like fasces. The keeper of the treasury added to his own magnificence by the ostentatious display of his service; the blow pan, boxes, scales and weights, were of solid gold.

A delay of some minutes whilst we severally approached to receive the king's hand, afforded us a thorough view of him; his deportment first excited my attention; native dignity in princes we are pleased to call barbarous was a curious spectacle: his manners were majestic, yet courteous; and he did not allow his surprise to beguile him for a moment of the composure of the monarch; he appeared to be about thirty-eight years of age, inclined to corpulence, and of a benevolent countenance; he wore a fillet of aggry beads round his temples, a necklace of gold cockspur shells strung by their largest ends, and over his right shoulder a red silk cord, suspending three saphies cased in gold; his bracelets were the richest mixtures of beads and gold, and his fingers covered with rings; his cloth was of a dark green silk; a pointed diadem was elegantly painted in white on his forehead; also a pattern resembling an epaulette on each shoulder, and an ornament like a full blown rose, one leaf rising above another until it covered his whole breast; his knee-bands were of aggry beads, and his ancle strings of gold ornaments of the most delicate workmanship, small drums, sankos, stools, swords, guns, and birds, clustered together; his sandals, of a soft white leather, were embossed across the instep band with small gold and silver cases of saphies; he was seated in a low chair, richly ornamented with gold; he wore a pair of gold castanets on his finger and thumb, which he clapped to enforce silence. The belts of the guards behind his chair were cased in gold, and covered with small jaw bones of the same metal; the elephants tails, waving like a small cloud before him, were spangled with gold, and large plumes of feathers were flourished amid them. His eunuch presided over these attendants, wearing only one massy piece of gold about his neck; the royal stool, entirely cased in gold, was displayed under a splendid umbrella, with drums, sankos, horns, and various musical instruments, cased in gold, about the thickness of cartridge paper: large circles of gold hung by scarlet cloth from the swords of state, the sheaths as well as the handles of which were also cased; hatchets of the same were intermixed with them: the breasts of the Ocrahs, and various attendants, were adorned with large stars, stools, crescents, and gossamer wings of solid gold.

We pursued our course through this blazing circle, which afforded to the last a variety exceeding description and memory; so many splendid novelties diverting the fatigue, heat, and pressure we were labouring under; we were almost exhausted, however, by the time we reached the end; when, instead of being conducted to our residence, we were desired to seat ourselves under a tree at some distance, to receive the compliments of the whole in our turn. . . .

The king's messengers who were posted near us, with their long hair hanging in twists like a thrum mop, used little ceremony in hurrying by this transient procession; yet it was nearly eight o'clock before the king approached.

It was a beautiful star-light night, and the torches which preceded him displayed the splendour of his regalia with a chastened lustre, and made the human trophies of the soldiers more awfully imposing. The skulls of three Banda caboceers, who had been his most obstinate enemies, adorned the largest drum: the vessels in which the boys dipped their torches were of gold. . . . He stopped to enquire our names a second time, and to wish us good night; his address was mild and deliberate; he was followed by his aunts, sisters, and others of his family, with rows of fine gold chains around their necks. Numerous chiefs succeeded; and it was long before we were at liberty to retire. We agreed in estimating the number of warriors at 30,000.

BOWDICH: *Mission to Ashantee.* 1819.

Not all monarchies were absolute.

The king did not look altogether as pacific as could have been desired, but again he appealed to the people, "Tubabl-Mansa has spoken—is he right," an old man rose from nearly the centre of the crescent, and throwing his mantle from his right shoulder, a mark of respect equivalent to lifting the hat in Europe, leaning upon his spear, against the stick of which his grey-bearded chin rested, while the iron point gleamed above his head, and said, "the king has spoken the law truly—he has a right to the property of his people dying as this man did—all Mandingoes know it—we do not like to see our king insulted, nor do we like the laws to be kicked—I am an old man—I have seen too much of war—my house was broken—my boys were killed—I am left by myself—war is bad, and it makes bad men worse than they were before—every one rushes to fight—the ground dies—trade is stopped —this is war;—the 'Tubabl-Mansa' has spoken—I counsel my king to hear him—if he trust the 'Tubabl-Mansa' he will have justice," then turning to the right and left, he said to those on each side—"I have spoken; am I right?"   A murmur of approbation ran through the crowd, and a loud expressed "ah" decided the case of peace or war, at least for the time; the king said he was glad to be at peace, that he willingly put his case in the hands of the white king, and that now the war palaver was done with, they must talk together with "fun".

HUNTLEY: *Service on the Slave Coast.* 1850.

8. WARFARE

Most famous fighting people of the West Coast were the Ashantis.

The Ashantees never undertake any national concerns without invocations to the deities, conjurations, incantations, and a variety of
customs which occupy incredible time, as these mysteries can only
be practised on particular days of the week or month, the others being
deemed ominous and portending evil, are days of grief and tribulation. Out of the 365, the proportion of good or lucky days, the Bashaw
says, is no more than 150 or 160. During the evil days, councils
cannot be holden, nor can troops either march or engage the enemy,
unless in self-defence. An Ashantee army, in proportion to the rank of
its commander, and certainly if the king was at its head, could not
march to Cape Coast or to the seaside in less than three or four months,
for there are various other causes (independent also of circumspection,
rank, and dignity) to impede the march, such as divinations from the
flight of birds, track of particular beetles and insects, screechings of the
turkey buzzard, dreams, predictions, celebration of customs, etc., etc.
In short, the Ashantees are slow, and I believe, cautious in the cabinet;
they are slower, however, in warlike movements, and, for those very
reasons, more to be dreaded by those who do not know them; and
certainly no man had a just conception of this nation during my residence on the Gold Coast. The Ashantees are energetic in the field on
days when they can act; and, as the Bashaw and the Moslems in general
relate, are more justly dreaded than any other tribe of Negroes. When
the army takes the field, it usually pushes forward a body of two or
three thousand men to the distance of a day or two in advance of the
main army, covering the enemy's towns and frontiers by little detached corps of observation, who prosecute their march during the
silence of night, in the most intricate parts of the forest, only seeking
refuge as occasion may require, in the loftiest boughs of the trees,
where they sustain life for many days, if necessary, upon a sort of
soluble gum, pounded grain, and "war nuts," called by them Boesie,
which they never travel without. As the main body advances, so do
these detachments, and when the king and priesthood deem the
opportunity a fit one for battle, these corps of observation, strengthened by others, concentrate themselves within a compass adequate
to support the war with a most deadly effect from ambush and intrenched positions, or from the canopy which conceals their comrades;

for during the attack, these elevated warriors pour incessantly upon the foe a tempest of musquet-shot, and poisoned missiles, javelins, and arrows.

DUPUIS: *Journal of a Residence in Ashantee.* 1824.

★

No effort of our sailors could move the enemy, who had fixed themselves in a dense corner of jungle. It really seemed as if nothing but the failure of their ammunition would drive them out. Now at one point, now at another, along the hill-crest, they poured down crushing volleys. Life they counted no price, if only a white man could be killed. It was the same desperate obstinacy we had seen at Abrakrampa. They climbed trees to fire with more deadly effect, but the mass just lay down, and shot, and shot, till shot themselves or short of ammunition.

BOYLE: *Through Fanteeland to Coomassie.* 1874.

First encounter between the English and the Ashantis took place in 1807, *when the Ashantis invaded Fanteeland and became embroiled with the garrison of Annamaboe fort. The Ashantis suffered very heavy losses, but the garrison was glad to call a truce. Ten years later Bowdich had an opportunity to discuss the engagement with the general who commanded the Ashanti army.*

I called on Odumata, whom I found well charged with palm wine: his usual discourse of the greatness of the King and the manner of the Ashantees fighting took up his time: he said that when white men wished to fight, they sent a book to the other party, telling them they would meet them on such a day, but the Ashantees took their enemies by surprise, which shortened their wars. I told him he had repeated the same story about fifty times in two months, and wished to know if the English did so at Annamaboe, where fifteen white men killed thousands of Ashantees; this put him on the fidget, as I knew it would, and he said that it was on him the English fired first, and he fought them without the King's leave, who was angry when he heard that they had returned the fire of the fort; I told him it was a fine excuse to cover their defeat. He enquired if I thought they could not have taken the fort? I told him if they could have done it they would. He said, if the King says we must do any thing, we must do it. I asked him, if the King told them to pull down the moon, if they could do it? He then got up from his chair and began to manœuvre how he and Apokoo were to have made a breach in Annamaboe fort, to the no small enjoyment of several of his wives, captains, and slaves, who were present; they were to have burned the gates, and with axes to have cut through the walls. He said they had Dutch and Danish flags, which they had taken from forts; why, I enquired, did they not show the English trophies? They had none, he said; and the King had told them, that were he to kill white men from England, he might as well kill all the cocks in the kingdom; the one told the hour, and when to rise in the morning; the other brought them good things from England, and learned them sense; besides, if any of their slaves did ill, they told them they would sell them to the whites which made them better. I told him black men had the eyes of a thief, the paws of a tiger, and the belly of a hog, for they were never satisfied; he said I was right, for they were now going to war, and would take whatever they could find; he thought 30,000 Ashantees would be killed, but that was nothing. He then locked up his wives because I put evil in their heads, by saying that Englishmen allowed every one a husband. I then took my leave.

BOWDICH: Mission to Ashantee.   1819.

Hardly less famous than the Ashantis were the Amazons of Dahomey.

Abbeokuta, the capital of the Egbas, a town with a population of over fifty thousand, is the usual point of attack of the Dahomans. It is situated on the left bank of the Ogu river, and is enclosed with thick mud walls some twenty-five feet high, loop-holed for musketry, strengthened with flanking bastions, and further protected by a broad and deep ditch.

The King of Dahomey suffered a rather severe repulse at his attack on this town in 1851. For some months he had been threatening to destroy Abbeokuta, being only restrained by the remonstrances of the British consul; and, though at last diplomacy was found to be of no avail, the Egbas had benefited by the respite which had been obtained for them, and had been enabled to prepare for a vigorous defence. The van of the Dahoman army, consisting of Amazons, arrived at the ford on the river Ogu on the morning of March 3rd, 1851. The Egbas, who had received ample intelligence concerning the movements of the Dahomans, had mustered in force to dispute the passage of the river, and the Amazons found themselves confronted by a body of some 12,000 or 15,000 men. Forming up in a dense column, they crossed the river with a rush, cutting the Egba line in two and scattering the enemy like chaff. Had they then followed up their first success it is probable that they would have succeeded in entering the town with the rabble of fugitives, but the male corps of the Dahoman army was some miles behind, having been outmarched by the Amazons, and the commander of the latter did not consider it advisable to enter a town containing 50,000 enemies with a force of but 3,000 disciplined troops. The Amazons consequently extended beyond the ford and remained halted until the male corps was close at hand, when they advanced to the attack.

In the meantime every man, woman, and child in the town capable of holding a musket had crowded to the walls, which were, in the words of an eye-witness, "black with people, swarming like ants." The Amazons advanced across the plain, which was utterly destitute of cover, in a species of column of companies; and, under a most furious discharge of musketry, deployed into line; then, after firing rapidly for a few moments, rushed madly on to the assault. Such a merciless shower of balls and slugs met them from the walls that, notwithstanding the most conspicuous gallantry and a wonderful contempt of death, they were repulsed with considerable loss, and, retiring beyond musket-shot, formed up in line facing the town. The Egbas did not venture to leave their fortifications in pursuit.

By this time the male Dahoman army corps had crossed the ford, and, advancing across the plain, extended to the right of the Amazons, so as partly to encircle the town, and, if possible, embarrass the defence. The whole force then advanced within musket-shot, and a furious discharge took place on both sides. That portion of the plain which was occupied by the right of the Dahoman attack was still covered with dried and yellow grass reaching to the waist; the left being bare, through the grass having been burned some days before. An American missionary, who chanced to be in Abbeokuta, observing this, directed those Egbas near him to fire the grass; and, a strong wind blowing at the time towards the advancing Dahomans, in a few minutes a vast sheet of flame bore down upon them. To conceive the rapidity with which a fire will under favourable circumstances sweep across a plain of dried grass, it is necessary to have witnessed such a sight. The male Dahoman army corps, finding itself suddenly confronted by a roaring, crackling pyramid of flame, fairly turned and fled. They had come out to fight, not to be roasted, and they bolted for their lives. The king, as soon as he saw the course affairs were taking, hastily recrossed the river with some 200 followers, leaving orders for the Amazons to cover the retreat and hold the ford till nightfall.

The victorious Egbas sallied out in thousands, and threw themselves upon the devoted band of Amazons, who were extended in three lines, with the flanks drawn back. In this order they kept at bay the whole Egba force, the first line firing, retiring through the second and third line, and then forming up again in rear to reload, and the whole thus retreating slowly upon the river. Arrived at the ford, they formed up in a compact mass; and, in spite of the repeated furious charges of the Egbas, held their ground until nightfall, when the enemy drew off and retired within their walls.

Early next morning the Amazons picked up such of their wounded as the Egbas had not murdered, and retired in excellent order across the river to the village of Johaga, about fifteen miles from Abbeokuta, the Egbas hovering round them during their retrograde movement, but taking care to keep at a safe distance. At Johaga a sharp skirmish took place, resulting in the repulse of the Egbas; and from that point the retreat of the Dahomans was not further molested.

The Dahoman force employed in this expedition consisted of some 3,000 Amazons and 5,000 male Dahomans. The Amazons lost very heavily, nearly 1,800 dead women-soldiers being counted by the missionaries of Abbeokuta at the ford and under the walls of the town. The men being little engaged did not suffer much. The Egbas engaged outside the town, both before and after the assault, were estimated at over 20,000 and quite 40,000 persons bore arms during the defence of the fortifications. Very few Dahoman prisoners were taken: the Amazons even when disarmed refused to surrender, fighting on, and biting their foes, and were consequently hacked to pieces.

ELLIS: *The Land of Fetish*. 1883.

In regions beyond the reach of the tsetse fly the horse played its part in warfare. All the Hausa kings had detachments of cavalry.

The number of fighting men brought before the town could not, I think, be less than fifty or sixty thousand, horse and foot, of which the foot amounted to more than nine-tenths. For the depth of two hundred yards, all round the walls was a dense circle of men and horses. The horse kept out of bow-shot, while the foot went up as they felt courage or inclination, and kept up a straggling fire with about thirty muskets, and the shooting of arrows. In front of the sultan, the Zegzeg troops had one French fusil: the Kano forces had forty-one muskets. These fellows, whenever they fired their pieces, ran out of bow-shot to load; all of them were slaves; not a single Fellata had a musket. The enemy kept up a sure and slow fight, seldom throwing away their arrows until they saw an opportunity of letting fly with effect. Now and then a single horse would gallop up to the ditch, and brandish his spear, the rider taking care to cover himself with his large leathern shield, and return as fast as he went, generally calling out lustily, when he got among his own party, "Shields to the wall!" "You people of the Gadado, or Atego," etc., "why don't you hasten to the wall?" To which some voices would call out, "Oh! you have a good large shield to cover you!" The cry of "Shields to the wall" was constantly heard from the several chiefs to their troops; but they disregarded the call, and neither chiefs nor vassals moved from the spot. At length the men in quilted armour went up "per order". They certainly cut not a bad figure at a distance, as their helmets were ornamented with black and white ostrich feathers and the sides of the helmets with pieces of tin, which glittered in the sun, their long quilted cloaks of gaudy colours reaching over part of the horse's tails, and hanging over the flanks. On the neck, even the horses's armour was notched, or vandyked, to look like a mane; on his forehead and over his nose was a brass or tin plate, as also a semicircular piece on each side. The rider was armed with a large spear; and he had to be assisted to mount his horse, as his quilted cloak was too heavy; it required two men to lift him on; and there were six of them belonging to each governor, and six to the sultan. I at first thought the foot would take advantage of going under cover of these unweildy machines; but no, they went alone, as fast as the poor horses could bear them, which was but a slow pace. They had one musket in Coonia, and it did wonderful execution, for it brought down the van of the quilted men, who fell from his horse like a sack of corn thrown from a horse's back at a miller's door; but both horse and man were brought off by two or three footmen. He had got two balls through his breast; one went through his body and both sides of the tobe; the other went through and lodged in the quilted armour opposite the shoulders.

CLAPPERTON: *Journal of a Second Expedition.* 1829.

9. SLAVES

The following views on the subject of slaves are attributed by Dupuis to the King of Ashanti:

If I fight a king, and kill him when he is insolent, then certainly I must have his gold, and his slaves, and the people are mine too. Do not the white kings act like this? Because I hear the old men say, that before I conquered Fantee and killed the Braffoes and the kings, that white men came in great ships, and fought and killed many people; and then they took the gold and slaves to the white country: and sometimes they fought together. That is all the same as these black countries. The great God and the fetische made war for strong men every where, because then they can pay plenty of gold and proper sacrifice. When I fought Gaman, I did not make war for slaves, but because Dinkera (the king) sent me an arrogant message and killed my people, and refused to pay me gold as his father did. Then my fetische made me strong like my ancestors, and I killed Dinkera, and took his gold, and brought more than 20,000 slaves to Coomassy. Some of these people being bad men, I washed my stool in their blood for the fetische. But then some were good people, and these I sold or gave to my captains; many, moreover, died, because this country does not grow too much corn like Sarem, and what can I do? Unless I kill or sell them, they will grow strong and kill my people. Now you must tell my master that these slaves can work for him, and if he wants 10,000 he can have them. And if he wants fine handsome girls and women to give his captains, I can send him great numbers."

DUPUIS: *Journal of a Residence in Ashantee.* 1824.

*

Under the mats and in the enclosures are to be seen male and female slaves, from the age of five up to thirty. Some of these children of misfortune, more intelligent than others, are to be seen sitting pensive and melancholy, apparently in deep thought, while their poor legs are swelled from confinement in irons, or being closely stowed at the bottom of a canoe; some are eating yams and Indian-corn bread, while their owners are making a bargain or bartering them away for elephants' teeth or cowries. It is painful to contemplate the number of slaves annually sold at this market, most of whom are forwarded to the sea-side: allowing there to be fifty canoes—which there are, and nearly double—and each canoe generally take eight or ten slaves— calculating thus, fifty canoes, with ten slaves each, make five hundred. The market is held every ten days, but twice a month every eight days, and the number of markets is $300 \times 38 = 11,400$.

LAIRD and OLDFIELD: *An Expedition into the Interior of Africa.* 1837.

*

During the course of our march from Loko to Egga, via Kano, a distance of about eight hundred miles, we had frequent opportunities of observing the general insecurity of life and property which the existence of the slave trade produces. Soon after leaving Loko we entered the town of Nassarawa, where we were compelled to wait till the return of its king from a slave raid, on which he was then absent. Reaching Jimbambororo, a village a few miles further on, we were told that its king was not "feeling sweet", owing to the fact that twenty of his subjects had that very morning been seized as slaves by the people of an adjacent town. On leaving this village we passed a spot where two days before fifteen native merchants had been carried off as slaves; and again, shortly before reaching Katchia, we were shown another point on our path where, within the previous two days, a similar fate had befallen five other travellers. On arriving at the large town of Zaria, in the market place of which we saw about two hundred slaves ex- posed for sale, we were once again informed that the king was absent on a slave-raiding expedition. During our stay in Kano about a thousand slaves were brought into the town on a single occasion as the result of such an expedition. In the course of our march from Kano to Bida we passed towns and villages, literally without number, which had been recently destroyed and their inhabitants sold as slaves; and this, as has been already explained, not by any foreign invader, but by the king in whose territory the places themselves were situated.

ROBINSON: *Hausaland.* 1896.

For fifty years after the abolition of the slave trade in 1807 the Navy main- tained anti-slavery patrols along the Coast. Many slavers were caught; more probably escaped. The patrols were handicapped by the niceties of inter- national agreements. Slaves had actually to be found on board before a ship could be seized as a slaver, and this usually meant that, on sighting a patrol vessel, the slaver dumped his unhappy cargo into the sea. The following is extracted from a lively account by Sir Henry Huntley of a long chase of two Spanish slavers, the Rapido *and the* Regulo. *The slavers turned into one of the Niger's mouths and were followed by the two ships of the patrol, the* Rosamond *and the* Black Joke.

The wind now fell light; on a sudden the slavers were observed to haul out of the river and run up a large branch of it, stretching to the eastward; this was a most striking part of the chase, which had lasted from nine in the morning till the present hour, about half past four. A low sandy spit of more than a mile in length, covered with jungle and high grass, now only separated the hostile vessels, and as the slavers ran up inside, the *Rosamond* sailed down the other. This spit of land was not more than a quarter of a mile broad, and therefore they would, when abreast, be within range of the guns of each other—there were however other things to attend to as well as firing guns; one of which was the pilotage, which if not successfully accomplished, would render every effort futile; and the other was the necessity of obtaining the clearest evidence of the vessels having slaves on board; for these reasons, until this point had been rounded the firing was suspended, and Robin-son and two intelligent men were sent aloft to observe over the jungle the actions of the Spaniards.

"Canoes are going to the slavers," reported Robinson; "they are taking the slaves from the brigs! The headmost brig is also throwing her slaves overboard!" was also in succession reported by him; but now the *Rosamond* had taken in her steering sails, and was round the sandy spit, within point blank range of the *Regulo*; instantly the fire was opened upon her—the canoes struggled to get from her sides—those inside only pushed against the others, and they only presented, for a time, a black mass upon the waters—while the screaming, shout-ing, and firing, contrasted strangely with the otherwise tranquil aspect of the scenery.

The *Regulo* was now deserted by the canoes, by which more than two hundred slaves were kept on board, at the same time she struck her flag, and ran aground upon the muddy bank of the river in which they all were. The *Rosamond* passed under her stern, but could not afford to send men to take possession of her, seeing that the *Rapido*, at anchor about a mile and a half farther up the river, had evinced every determination to make a resolute defence, and at this time the *Black Joke*, from not being in this tributary branch of the river, could afford no very ready assistance; the *Regulo* was therefore hailed, and informed that if a canoe came alongside, or a man left the vessel by any means, she would be instantly fired upon.

The *Rapido*, to which vessel fewer canoes went, was still relanding her slaves, and when there were no canoes alongside, they were pushed overboard, shackled together by the legs, and drowned. By the help of the glass, it was seen that her guns were trained towards the *Rosamond*, and over her low bulwarks the pikes and bayonets of the armed crew bristled, apparently in meditated resistance, and her flag was still flying.

The breeze was very light, the water smooth as glass, excepting where it was ruffled by the death struggles of slaves recently plunged into it, and the *Rosamond* came steadily and silently on—she was nearly within point blank range, when observing some disturbed water close to her side, a small boat was pushed off to save if possible what seemed to be the drowning negroes; the man in the bow put his boat-hook down, and providentially it passed between the two slaves, hooking in the iron which shackled them together by the right and left leg of each other; they were brought on board and put below in safety.

Of the pugnacious intentions of the *Rapido*, there could be no reasonable doubt, and as the *Rosamond* was now within point blank shot, the commander thought considering the weakness of his force, it would be as well to try the effect of a shot amongst the men who lined the Spaniard's deck fore and aft, and then run him on board; the pivot gun was well laid, the vessel sheered off a point or two, to allow of its bearing upon the *Rapido*, and it was fired; the shot struck just before the foremost shroud, passed obliquely across the deck, and went out at the opposite quarter. The *Rapido's* men wavered, for the *Rosamond* was close enough now to see everything—the commander, instantly observing it, called out, "fire upon them, marines, keep panic up,"—and the marines (only four in number by the bye)—men who are sure never to be failing in the time of need—promptly discharged their pieces—there was but time for a second volley—the object was effected—and as the bowsprit of the *Rosamond* was ran into the fore-rigging of the *Rapido*, the commander exclaimed "out cutlasses," and followed by Robinson, the marines, and two fine fellows, Morris, and Oliver, simultaneously jumped on board, supported eagerly by the rest of the crew, the Spaniards making a precipitate retreat, when the *Rosamond's* intention to run alongside, was seen to be certain; the captain alone kept his station on the deck, armed with a sword, and brace of pistols; when deserted by his men, he calmly sat down to meet whatever fate should be awarded to him; Don Felippe, he named himself, a fine looking man, and would no doubt have been an intrepid guerrilla leader, should he have been destined to that life, as it was, he was a brave, but despicable slave dealer. . . .

Revisiting the scene of action afterwards, the course adopted to avert capture by the *Rapido* was awfully, and revoltingly illustrated—

ARRIVAL OF A CHIEF,
GOLD COAST

COURTESAN IN A ROBE OF AMBER BROCADE,
SOKOTO EMIRATE

that vessel had, when chased in, nearly five hundred slaves on board, at least one third of which number had been thrown overboard shackled together in pairs, and in this manner they were lying about on the muddy sides of the river, torn and half eaten by the sharks, and other voracious reptiles of the place.

HUNTLEY: *Service on the Slave Coast.* 1850.

10. BEASTS, BIRDS AND CREEPING THINGS

Shoals of dolphins and flying-fish appeared near us; grey doves flew round the ship, and lighted on the rigging; and several fly-catchers were taken, of the size and shape of larks. The breast and stomach were of a greenish yellow; the back of the neck, back, and tail were brown; two white bars were on the wings, and the half of the outer tail-feathers were white; the bill was small and black; and the nail of the fourth toe very long. At night, the sea was very phosphorescent from numerous animalculae.

ALEXANDER: *Narrative of a Voyage of Observation.* 1837.

*

On some West Coast boats excellent training is afforded by the supply of cockroaches on board, and there is nothing like getting used to cockroaches early when your life is going to be spent on the Coast—but I need not detail you with them now, merely remarking that they have none of the modest reticence of the European variety. They are very companionable, seeking rather than shunning human society, nestling in the bunk with you if the weather is the least chilly, and I fancy not averse to light; it is true they come out most at night, but then they distinctly like a bright light, and you can watch them in a tight packed circle round the lamp with their heads towards it, twirling their antennæ at it with evident satisfaction; in fact it's the lively nights those cockroaches have that keep them abed during the day. They are sometimes of great magnitude; I have been assured by observers of them in factories ashore and on moored hulks that they can stand on their hind legs and drink out of a quart jug, but the most common steamer kind is smaller, as far as my own observations go. But what I do object to in them is, that they fly and feed on your hair and nails and disturb your sleep by so doing; and you mayn't smash them—they make an awful mess if you do. As for insect powder, well, I'd like to see the insect powder that would disturb the digestion of a West African insect.

But it's against the insects ashore that you have to be specially warned. During my first few weeks of Africa I took a general natural historical interest in them with enthusiasm as of natural history; it soon became a mere sporting one, though equally enthusiastic at first. Afterwards a nearly complete indifference set in, unless some wretch aroused a vengeful spirit in me by stinging or biting. I should say, looking back calmly upon the matter, that seventy-five per cent. of West African insects sting, five per cent. bite, and the rest are either permanently or temporarily parasitic on the human race. And undoubtedly one of the many worst things you can do in West Africa is to take any notice of an insect. If you see a thing that looks like a cross between a flying lobster and the figure of Abraxas on a Gnostic gem, do not pay it the least attention, never mind where it is; just keep quiet and hope it will go away—for that's your best chance; you have none in a stand-up fight with a good thorough-going African insect. Well do I remember at Cabinda, the way insects used to come in round the hanging lamp at dinner time. Mosquitoes were pretty bad there, not so bad as in some other places, but sufficient, and after them hawking came a cloud of dragon-flies, swishing in front of every one's face, which was worrying till you got used to it. Ever and anon a big beetle, with a terrific boom on, would sweep in, go two or three times round the room and then flop into the soup plate, out of that, shake himself like a retriever and bang into some one's face, then flop on the floor. Orders were then calmly but firmly given to the steward boys to "catch 'em"; down on the floor went the boys, and an exciting hunt took place which sometimes ended in a capture of the offender, but always seemed to irritate a previously quiet insect population who forthwith declared war on the human species, and fastened on to the nearest leg. It is best, as I have said, to leave insects alone. Of course you cannot ignore driver ants, they won't go away, but the same principle reversed is best for them, namely, your going away yourself.

KINGSLEY: West African Studies. 1899.

★

But your tarantula is indeed a fearful wild fowl. Call him and class him amongst spiders, if you please, but he is most like a devil. I myself killed one in Cape Coast, quite a small demonkin, but too large to stand in a saucer. The full-grown monster stretches about the width of a breakfast plate. He has fur all over him, soft, and delicately mottled in brown and black and stone colour. Legs about as thick as a straw, furry and mottled like his body, ending in broad suckers, wherewith he takes a death grasp. On the under side huge red nippers, such as would doubtless tear out a piece of flesh. When this foul brute gets hold, it is necessary to cut his legs off with scissors, so firm is the grasp of his paws and jaw. The bite is very poisonous. Fantees have a dread beyond words for the tarantula. They believe he can spring a great

distance, and has the malignity to use his power with or without provocation. I do not know whether this is true, but the structure of his
paws leads one to doubt; suckers are not convenient for springing.
He certainly has no fear of man, putting up his great forelegs like a
mantis, when threatened with a stick; this I guarantee, for myself
have seen it.

BOYLE: *Through Fanteeland to Coomassie.* 1874.

*Locusts descended on Bathurst at the time Sir Henry Huntley was
Lieutenant-Governor.*

At length the whole body reached the town and settlement; in the
former, in less than twenty minutes, not a particle of green was to be
seen in any of the gardens; excepting when the plant bore within it
either an acid, or astringent juice, the ground nut and yam therefore
escaped, but all the farinaceous plants and those producing saccharine
matter were eaten to the roots; while of the leaves of trees, especially
those of the coco-nut, nothing remained but the mere fibre to which
the more vegetable part had been attached; besides this desolation, it
was almost impossible to move out of the house in consequence of the
severe blows inflicted on the face by the flight of the locusts, as it
whirled along in its devouring course. A horse could not be made to
face the flight, so incessant was the stream beating against his eyes. The
colour of the flag of a schooner sailing into the harbour not more than
a quarter of a mile distant could hardly be distinguished; lastly the
stench arising from the ground where they had fallen, and were dying
in layers, resembled, and equalled, the horrible effluvia exhaling from
the slave crowded deck of a slave ship; it was absolutely necessary to
keep men sweeping the exhausted locusts from the colonnades of the
government house, to remove the smell as far as might be possible
from the rooms; but it filled the atmosphere until the sun had completely dried up the dead bodies on the ground.

HUNTLEY: *Service on the Slave Coast.* 1850.

In the mangrove swamps are slimy things.

You often hear the utter lifelessness of mangrove-swamps commented on; why I do not know, for they are fairly heavily stocked
with fauna, though the species are comparatively few. There are the
crocodiles, more of them than any one wants; there are quantities of
flies, particularly the big silent mangrove-fly which lays an egg in
you under the skin; the egg becomes a maggot and stays there until

it feels fit to enter into external life. Then there are "slimy things that crawl with legs upon a slimy sea", and any quantity of hopping mud-fish, and crabs, and a certain mollusc, and in the water various kinds of cat-fish. Birdless they are save for the flocks of grey parrots that pass over them at evening, hoarsely squarking; and save for this squarking of the parrots the swamps are silent all the day, at least during the dry season; in the wet season there is no silence night or day in West Africa, but that roar of the descending deluge of rain that is more monotonous and more gloomy than any silence can be. In the morning you do not hear the long, low, mellow whistle of the plaintain-eaters calling up the dawn, nor in the evening the clock-bird, nor the Handel-Festival-sized choruses of frogs, or the crickets, that carry on their vesper controversy of "she did"—"she didn't" so fiercely on hard land.

But the mangrove-swamp follows the general rule for West Africa, and night in it is noisier than the day. After dark it is full of noises; grunts from I know not what, splashes from jumping fish, the peculiar whirr of rushing crabs, and quaint creaking and groaning sounds from the trees; and—above all in eeriness—the strange whine and sighing cough of crocodiles. I shall never forget one moonlight night I spent in a mangrove-swamp. I was not lost, but we had gone away into the swamp from the main river, so that the natives of a village with an evil reputation should not come across us when they were out fishing. We got well in, on to a long pool or lagoon, and dozed off and woke, and saw the same scene around us twenty times in the night, which thereby grew into an æon, until I dreamily felt that I had somehow got into a world that was all like this, and always had been, and was always going to be so. Now and again the strong musky smell came that meant a crocodile close by, and one had to rouse up and see if all the crews' legs were on board, for Africans are reckless, and regardless of their legs during sleep. On one examination I found the leg of one of my most precious men ostentatiously sticking out over the side of the canoe. I woke him with a paddle, and said a few words regarding the inadvisability of wearing his leg like this in our situation; and he agreed with me, saying he had lost a valued uncle, who had been taken out of a canoe in this same swamp by a crocodile. His uncle's ghost had become, he said, a sort of devil which had been a trial to the family ever since; and he thought it must have pulled his leg out in the way I complained of, in order to get him to join him by means of another crocodile. I thanked him for the information and said it quite ex-plained the affair, and I should do my best to prevent another member of the family from entering the state of devildom by aiming blows in the direction of any leg or arm I saw that uncle devil pulling out to place within reach of the crocodiles.

KINGSLEY: *Travels in West Africa.* 1897.

Jobson says this of the Gambian crocodile, "whom the people call by the name of Bumbo".

The people of the Country, stand in such dread of these, that they dare not wash their hands in the great River, much lesse, offer to swimme, or wade therein, reporting unto us many lamentable stories, how many of their friends, and acquaintance have beene devoured by them; neither do they at any time bring any of their Cattle, to passe the River, as within ebbing, and flowing, they have diverse occasions to doe, but with great dread, and ceremony: for at all Townes within that compasse, they have small boats, which we call Canoos, to ferry over withall, which cannot receive a live beefe, onely some five or sixe of the people: but when they passe a beefe over, he is led into the water, with a rope to his hornes, whereby one holds him close to the boate, and another taking up his tayle, holds in the like manner; the Priest, or Mary-bucke, stands over the middle of the beast, praying and spitting upon him, according to their ceremonies, charming the Crocodile, and another againe by him, with his bow and arrowes ready drawne, to expect when the Crocodile will ceaze, and in this manner, if there be twenty at a time, they passe them one another after, never thinking them safe, untill they be on the toppe of the River bancke: One thing more, to shew the feare they have of him, when I was going in my discovery up the River; having as I sayde, onely nine of our owne people with me, I did hire Blacke-men, as I had occasion to use them, to serve as Interpreters, likewise to send abroade, and to helpe to row, and get up the boate, so that when I came to pass the flowing, and to goe all against the currant, I did furnish my selfe, of foure able Black-men: the first place we found a stiffe gut to resist us, the water being not above foure foote deepe, for speedier and more easier passing, our men went into the water, and laying hands, some one the one side of the boate, and some likewise on the other, waded along, and led her through, which we found a good refreshing; the River being sweete and cleare, was comfortable in the heate, by no means I could not make any of my blacke people, go out of the boate, denying flatly to go into the water, saying that Bumbo would have them; after some two of these passages, there was another streight, where was a necessity of more hands, so that striping my selfe, I leapt into the water, the Blackes seeing me prepare, seeme much to diswade me, but when they

saw me in the water, they presently consulting together, stript themselves, and came likewise in, the businesse ended, and we all aboord
againe, I askt of them the cause made them come in, having so earnestly
denied it before, they made answere, they had considered amongst
themselves, the white man, shine more in the water, than they did,
and therefore if Bumbo come, hee would surely take us first.

JOBSON: *The Golden Trade.* 1623.

*An ingenious method of killing the "bumbo" was seen by Laird and Old-
field on the Niger. Having spotted one of the brutes basking on the river
bank two Africans cautiously approached.*

As soon as they were near the animal, one of the natives stood up
from his crouching position, holding a spear about six feet along, which
with one blow he struck through the animal's tail into the sand. A
most strenuous contest immediately ensued; the man with the spear
holding it in the sand as firmly as his strength allowed him, and clinging to it as it became necessary to shift his position with the agility of a
monkey; while his companion occasionally ran in as opportunity
offered, and with much dexterity gave the animal a thrust with his
long knife, retreating at the same moment from within reach of its
capacious jaws as it whirled round upon the extraordinary pivot
which his companion had so successfully placed in its tail. The battle
lasted about half an hour, terminating in the slaughter of the alligator,
and the triumph of his conquerors, who were not long in cutting him
into pieces and loading their canoes with his flesh, which they immediately carried to the shore and retailed to their countrymen.

LAIRD and OLDFIELD: *An Expedition into the Interior of Africa.* 1837.

*

On the plains of Accra are found hares and partridges, and small red
deer: the last of which are caught in traps, like hurdles supported by a
sloped stick, and baited with their favourite herbage. There are also
hyenas, held in such contempt by the natives, that they beat them off
with sticks from their folds; and beautifully-marked leopards, whose
activity is such, that they clear fourteen feet walls. One had lately
paid four visits to the fort, and killed a dozen sheep within it: sucking
the blood at the jagular vein so neatly, that it was necessary to remove
the wool to see the wound. Two wild elephants had also been seen a
short time since near Accra; but were pursued without effect. Among
the hills are large black baboons, and brown-backed and grey-sided

monkeys, remarkably handsome; also black poisonous snakes with red gills. While flights of Java sparrows with their crimson beaks, and bright-plumaged humming-birds, are rife among the foliage.

ALEXANDER: *Narrative of a Voyage of Observation.* 1837.

In earlier days elephants were often seen on the Accra plains.

We found him standing in the midst of the Garden; where, before our coming, he had broke down four or five Coco-Trees; which Number, either to divert himself, or shew us his Strength, he augmented with five or six more in our Presence. The Strength which he seemed to use in breaking down a Tree, may very fitly be compared to the Force which a Man exerts in order to knock down a Child of three or four Years old.

Whilst he stood here, above one hundred Shot were fired at him, which made him bleed to that degree, as if an Ox had been killed. During all which he did not stir, but only set up his Ears, and made the Men apprehend that he would follow them.

But this Sport was accompanied with a tragical Event; for a Negro fancying himself able to deal with him, went softly behind him, catched his Tail in his Hand, designing to cut a Piece of it off; but the Elephant being used to wear a Tail, would not permit it to be shortened in his Life-time: Wherefore, after giving the Negro a Stroke with his Snout, he drew him to him, and trod upon him two or three Times; and, as if that was not sufficient, he bored in his Body two Holes with his Teeth, large enough for a Man's double Fist to enter. Then he let him lye, without making any farther Attempt on him; and stood still also whilst two Negroes fetched away the dead Body, not offering to meddle with them in the least.

From both these Instances it is sufficiently clear, that, unprovoked, they do not often hurt any Body; but that they grow very fierce when shot at and missed, doth not so plainly appear, since this Elephant suffered above three hundred shot to be made at him, without any sign of being enraged, or Resistance: But as the same Actions have not always the same Success, I should be loth from hence to advise any Person rashly to fire at an Elephant, since this vast Number of Shot which were thundered at him were not sufficient to fetch him down; and those who pretend thoroughly to understand the Elephant-shooting, told us, that we ought to have shot Iron Bullets, since those of Lead are flatted, either by their Bones, or the Toughness of their Skin.

This seems probable; for after his Death, we found, of the vast

Quantity of Shot levelled at him, very few had passed the Bone into his Head. Some remained betwixt the Skin and the Bone; most of them, and more especially the small Shot, were thrown off by his Hide, as if they had been shot against a Wall. The Bullets were certainly too small, since what the English Factor told me, was confirmed by others, that as he was in the River Gamby in a Canoe, he killed an Elephant, which pursued him, with one Shot only. For to imagine that none of the Balls hit him in the proper Place, is not very reasonable, since in such a great Number, at least one must hit right, as appeared after his Death.

BOSMAN: Description of the Coast of Guinea. 1721.

"River horses" are to be seen in the Niger.

While engaged upon our dinner we came rather suddenly on a herd of ten or a dozen hippopotami, which were amusing themselves in shallow water, but did not appear much to mind our intrusion, merely expressing their disapprobation by loud snorting. Shortly afterwards, whilst passing between two islets, another popped its head above water, so close to our quarter that we could have almost touched it with an oar, but, alarmed by our unlooked-for proximity, it quickly disappeared. River-horses, as far as I have been able to observe them, seldom venture into deep water except when crossing from one spot to another, and, though gregarious, I have rarely seen them together in large numbers. During the day their favourite haunt is in still water over some shallow, or on sandbanks connected with an island. In such places they are to be seen tranquilly basking in the sun, frequently with the head only above the water. If at all alarmed they immediately disappear below, occasionally coming to the surface to breathe and to look around. They can remain under water for a long period, but I never had a good opportunity of ascertaining their extreme limits of endurance. When more sportively inclined they may be observed splashing clumsily about, opening their enormous jaws, displaying their tusks, and tossing their huge heads in anything but a graceful manner. When reposing on sandbanks they usually form one extended line, at which times nothing is visible but a profile view of a long row of faces, just above the water, the small eyes and the swollen muzzle then constituting the most remarkable features. It is from sunset to sunrise that they usually visit the shore for feeding, etc., and near marshy spots or grassy islets their peculiar noise, something between a grunt and a snort, may be heard throughout the night. Their flesh is greatly prized, for which they are much sought after by the natives, the hunters employing in the chase chiefly poisoned arrows: their tusks form excellent ivory, and bring a much higher price in the markets than that yielded by the elephant.

BAIKIE: Narrative of an Exploring Voyage.   1856.

Snakes are far less obtrusive than is commonly believed, but the naturalist has no difficulty in finding them.

Now and again on exposed parts of the hillside, one comes across great falls of timber which have been thrown down by tornadoes either flat on to the ground—in which case under and among them are snakes and scorpions, and getting over them is slippery work; or thrown sideways and hanging against their fellows, all covered with gorgeous drapery of climbing, flowering plants—in which case they present to the human atom a wall made up of strong tendrils and climbing grasses, through which the said atom has to cut its way with a matchette and push into the crack so made, getting the while covered with red driverants, and such like, and having sensational meetings with blue-green snakes, dirty green snakes with triangular horned heads, black cobras, and boa constrictors. I never came back to the station without having been frightened half out of my wits, and with one or two of my smaller terrifiers in cleft sticks to bottle. When you get into the way, catching a snake in a cleft stick is perfectly simple. Only mind you have the proper kind of stick, split far enough up, and keep your attention on the snake's head, that's his business end, and the tail which is whisking and winding round your wrist does not matter: there was one snake, by the way, of which it was impossible to tell, in the forest, which was his head. The natives swear he has one at each end; so you had better "Lef 'em," even though you know the British Museum would love to have him, for he is very venomous, and one of the few cases of death from snake-bite I have seen, was from this species.

KINGSLEY: Travels in West Africa.   1897.

★

When he was some four feet from my Houssa, he rose to his full height and leaned forward. The Houssa did not appear in the least disturbed; he finished rubbing the herbs in, and then extended the flat palm of his hand towards the cobra, so that it was only two or three inches from his head. The latter evidently thought that it was the most disgusting smell he had ever encountered, for he drew back considerably; the outstretched palm followed; the snake retreated further, and, finally, he threw himself full length on the floor and tried to crawl away. My Houssa then triumphantly picked him up, tied him round his neck, and walked out. I may add that this was witnessed by more than a dozen people.

ELLIS: *West African Sketches.* 1881.

As to fish, there are many oddities.

Amongst which fish, there was one, much like unto our English breame, but of a great thicknes, which one of the Saylers thinking for his turne, thought to take away, putting therefore his hands unto him, so soone as he toucht, the fellow presently cried out, he had lost the use both of his hands, and armes: another standing by sayd, what with touching this fish? and in speaking, put thereto his foote, he being bare-legged, who presently cried out in the like manner, the sence of his leg was gone: this gave others, of better rancke, occasion to come forth, and looke upon them, who perceiving the sence to come againe, called up for the Cooke, who was in his roome below, knowing nothing what had hapned, and being come willed him to take that fish, and dresse, which he being a plaine stayd fellow, orderly stooping to take up, as his hands were on him, suncke presently upon his hinder parts, and in the like manner, made grievous mone: he felt not his hands, which bred a wonderfull admiration amongst us: from the shore at the same time was comming a Canoe aboord us, in which was a Blacke man called Sandie, who in regard he had some small knowledge of the Portingall tongue, had great recourse amongst us, we brought him to the fish, and shewed it unto him, upon sight whereof, he fell into a laughter, and told us, it was a fish they much feared in the water, for what he toucht hee num'd, his nature being to stroke himselfe upon another fish, whom presently he likewise num'd, and then pray'd upon him."

JOBSON: *The Golden Trade.* 1623.

*

This River produces several Sorts of Fish, most of which are very good in their Kind, except the Oysters; of which there are vast Quantities growing to the Branches of Trees! I make no Doubt, but many will be apt at first to question the Truth of this Assertion; but the Fear of such like Objections shall, at no Time, hinder my giving a faithful Narrative of whatsoever I met with worth Notice throughout this whole Expedition. Therefore, I shall acquaint my Reader, that the Mangrove is a Tree which grows in shallow Water. The Leaf is exactly like that of an European Laurel, and the Branches have a natural Tendency downwards to the Water. These under Water are always stored with such Shell-fish as in hot Climates grow even to our Ships Bottoms, the chief of which are Oysters. And I have often cut off the Branch of a Mangrove so full of Oysters, Barnacles, etc., that I could scarce lift it into the boat.

SMITH: *A New Voyage to Guinea.*   1745.

BOOKS AND AUTHORS

RICHARD JOBSON: *The Golden Trade, or A Discovery of the River Gambia.* 1623.

Richard Jobson, Gentleman, was an enterprising captain in the service of the Company of Adventurers of London trading into Africa who in 1620–21 sailed farther up the River Gambia than had any European before him. In doing so he developed what current jargon is pleased to call "a thing" about trading opportunities in West Africa. In particular he established friendly relations with "a great blacke Merchant, called Bucker Sano", from whom he obtained reports of many wonders, including "houses covered with gold". So on his return he wrote *The Golden Trade* in order, as he says in the "Epistle Dedicatory", to induce others "to follow and proceede upon this hopeful enterprise".

WILLIAM BOSMAN: *A New and Accurate Description of the Coast of Guinea.* 1721.

By quoting from a Dutchman I confess to cheating, but Bosman's account is too important to be omitted, even when, to quote a contemporary English critic, he was "always sorry for speaking well of any Thing that belong'd to the English". He was chief agent on the Coast of the most important Dutch house trading there, and his "itch of scribbling" prompted a series of descriptive letters to his uncle in Amsterdam. The letters were written just before 1700, but were not "faithfully done" into English until this edition of 1721.

WILLIAM SMITH: *A New Voyage to Guinea.* 1745.

William Smith went to the Coast on behalf of the Royal African Company in order "to take exact Plans, Draughts and Prospects of all their Forts and Settlements: as also of all the principal Rivers, Harbours and other Places of Trade". He found it a congenial commission and cheerfully took soundings, wallowed in mangrove swamps, drew sketches and observed the habits and customs of Africans and Europeans.

T. EDWARD BOWDICH: *Mission from Cape Coast Castle to Ashanti.* 1819.

In 1817 the Committee of Merchants in the Gold Coast decided to "venture an embassy" to the King of Ashanti, and to "associate scientific with the political purposes of the mission". The embassy had four members, of whom Bowdich was to be responsible for carrying out the scientific purposes. In fact, the senior member proved so inept in negotiation that Bowdich took charge, with the support of the other two. He negotiated a treaty of "perpetual peace and harmony" with the King, and discharged his other duties by making copious notes on the habits and customs of the Ashantis.

JOSEPH DUPUIS: *Journal of a Residence in Ashanti.* 1824.

Four years after the Bowdich mission, Whitehall stepped in with a mission of its own. The King of Ashanti must have been puzzled by the purpose of this second mission, but he was prepared to be accommodating and signed another treaty. Dupuis, who led the mission on the strength of a "long residence in Barbary", alienates sympathy by his disparagement of Bowdich and vilification of the Committee of Merchants, but his book is nevertheless important.

MAJOR DIXON DENHAM and CAPTAIN HUGH CLAPPER-
    TON, R.N.: *Narrative of Travels and Discoveries in Northern and
    Central Africa.* 1826.

Denham is represented in the anthology by only one selection, and I have to deal rather with Clapperton, to whom goes the distinction of being the first white man to visit Kano and Sokoto. Clapperton came of a good Scottish family, his grandfather being a distinguished surgeon and classical scholar and his father also a surgeon. The fact that his father had twenty-eight children—seven, including Hugh, by his first wife, and twenty-one by his second—perhaps explains why Hugh received a wretchedly poor education and was packed off to sea when only thirteen. Four years later he was press-ganged into the Navy, with which he proceeded to serve with distinction in Mauritius and Canada until retired on half-pay after the Napoleonic Wars. He was then still only twenty-nine and not at all inclined to settle down. In 1820 in Edinburgh he met Dr. William Oudney, who was organising an official expedition into the interior of Africa, and to that meeting there could be only one result—Clapperton joined the expedition. The rest of Clapperton's story is told in "Perspective" at the beginning of this section.

COMMANDER HUGH CLAPPERTON, R.N.: *Journal of a
    Second Expedition, with a Journal* by RICHARD LANDER.
    1829.

This is the story of Clapperton's disastrous second expedition which ended in his death at Sokoto. Its only redeeming feature was the emergence of Richard Lander as a figure of first importance in African exploration. Lander was the son of a Cornish innkeeper, a cheerful, sturdy young man who sought adventure by offering his services as personal servant to wealthy travellers. In this way, by the time he was twenty-one, he had already travelled in the West Indies, parts of Europe, and South Africa. Now came the expedition to West Africa as Clapperton's personal servant. On Clapperton's death Lander found himself alone in the interior of Africa, but was more than equal to the occasion. Not only did he find his way back to the coast with Clapperton's papers, but also covered much new ground and kept a detailed journal of his own.

RICHARD and JOHN LANDER: *Journal of an Expedition to Explore the Course and Territories of the Niger*. 1832.

Lander's achievement saw him established at the age of twenty-five as an explorer in his own right. Lord Bathurst, then Secretary for the Colonies, was so impressed that he gave his blessing to a proposal that Lander should return and follow the "Great River" to its mouth. For these services Lander was to be provided with an outfit allowance and cash for expenses: in addition, his wife was to receive £100 in quarterly instalments and he himself a gratuity of £100 on his return (presuming he did return). In a final burst of generosity, Government gave permission for Richard's brother John to accompany him, though without salary "or even the promise of a reward". On this basis the two brothers solved the centuries-old mystery of the Niger by paddling from Bussa to the sea.

F. HARRISON RANKIN: *The White Man's Grave*. 1836.

In this instance the "White Man's Grave" is Sierra Leone as seen by a missionary fascinated by the "interesting and Malthusian characteristics" of "slavery, polygamy and cannibalism".

MACGREGOR LAIRD and R. A. K. OLDFIELD: *Narrative of an Expedition into the Interior of Africa*. 1837.

For more than thirty years after the Landers had traced the Niger to the sea, Laird was the driving force behind attempts to use the river as a commercial highway. He persisted in his plans despite disastrous setbacks due primarily to the unhealthiness of the Delta. First of these setbacks was the expedition of 1832, which proved the navigability of the Niger but cost the lives of thirty-nine of the forty-eight Europeans who set out.

J. E. ALEXANDER: *Narrative of a Voyage of Observation among the Colonies of Western Africa in the Flag-ship "Thalia".* 1837.

Sir James Alexander was a professional soldier who served with distinction in most parts of the world, and wrote travel books as a hobby. He is represented also in the West Indian section.

SIR HENRY HUNTLEY: *Seven Years' Service on the Slave Coast of Western Africa.* 1850.

The Coast first knew Sir Henry Huntley as commander of a British ship engaged in chasing "slavers". In 1840 he accepted appointment as lieutenant-governor of "His Majesty's Settlements upon the Gambia", despite the fact that the two previous holders of the post had died "within a twelve month of each other".

BRODIE CRUICKSHANK: *Eighteen Years on the Gold Coast of Africa.* 1853.

A Scotsman, a merchant, and a member of the Legislative Council at Cape Coast Castle, Brodie Cruickshank was as solid and worthy a citizen as the Gold Coast has known. His book has the same solid qualities, and gains in importance from the fact that he was a contemporary of Governor Maclean.

WILLIAM BALFOUR BAIKIE: *Narrative of an Exploring Voyage.* 1856.

This was the Niger expedition for which Laird had the *Pleiad* built, the first exploring vessel to be fitted with a screw propeller. "The peculiar features of this expedition," says Baikie, its leader, "were, first, the employment of as few white men as possible; secondly, entering and ascending the river with the rising waters, or during the rainy season, and lastly, it was anticipated that the use of quinine as a prophylactic or preventive would enable the Europeans to withstand the influence of the climate". The anticipation was justified, and the *Pleiad* spent 122 days in the river without loss of life.

SIR RICHARD BURTON: *Wanderings in West Africa.* 1863.

Burton was forty-two when he wrote this book, and had already achieved fame by his exploits in India, Arabia, Abyssinia and East Africa. It is not on the same plane as most of his other books and, as he says, records only "what a tolerably active voyager can see during the few hours allowed to him by halts of the mail packet".

WINWOOD READE: *The African Sketch-Book.* 1873.

It was during the travels he describes in the *Sketch-Book*, that Reade acquired much of the information he later embodied in his world-famous book *The Martyrdom of Man*. With the nice sense of humour which was not least of his attributes, Reade records that an African said of him: "You travel for sabby, come and see We country, put him for book and catch money for him."

FREDERICK BOYLE: *Through Fanteeland to Coomassie.* 1874.

Boyle was special correspondent of the *Daily Telegraph* during the Ashanti campaign of 1873.

CHARLES ALEXANDER GORDON: *Life in the Gold Coast.* 1881.

A soldier-doctor's recollections of two years' service in the Gold Coast compiled thirty years later from his private journal. Chief excitement on the Coast at that time was provided by the King of Appolonia, who went in for atrocities and sent a message to the Governor, "threatening to attack Cape Coast Castle, raze it to the ground, and dine off His Excellency's liver."

A. B. ELLIS: *West African Sketches*, 1881, and *The Land of Fetish*, 1883.

Except that Ellis was a soldier who knew his Coast well, had a ready pen and a lively sense of humour, I have no information about him.

CHARLES HENRY ROBINSON: *Hausaland.* 1896.

Canon Robinson, "a man of academic distinction, varied experience, and tried capacity in Oriental travel", spent some time in Kano and elsewhere studying the language and customs of the Hausas. He went at the invitation of the Hausa Association, which had been founded in memory of his brother, the Rev. John Alfred Robinson, a missionary, who died in Nigeria in 1891.

MARY H. KINGSLEY: *Travels in West Africa*, 1897, and *West African Studies*, 1899.

Any good reference book will tell you that Mary Kingsley was the daughter of George Kingsley and niece of Charles; that after her parents' death in 1893, when she was thirty, she travelled extensively in West Africa; and that she died in 1901 in South Africa from typhoid contracted while nursing Boer wounded. But no reference book can give any conception of the extraordinary charm and vitality of her personality and writings. In search of "fish and fetish", she went where no European had gone before, took the wildest adventures in

8

her stride, and made firm friends with the fiercest of African tribes. No one, said a friend, looked less like an explorer. In her dress she made no concessions to Africa. "Grand things, good old-fashioned skirts are for Africa," she declared, though she did admit that "petticoats, good as they are, do not prevent insects and catawumpuses of sorts walking up one's ankles". Some of the conclusions she reaches in her books do not go unchallenged, but for sheer readability she is without peer.

COMMANDER R. H. BACON, R.N.: *Benin, The City of Blood.*
    1897.
An account of the punitive expedition to Benin following the massacre of Vice-Consul Phillips and his party.

PART TWO

THE CARIBBEAN

The Colonies of British Guiana, in South America, British Honduras, in Central America, Barbados, Jamaica, Trinidad (with Tobago), the Bahama Islands, the Leeward Islands (including Antigua, Barbuda, Montserrat, Nevis, St. Kitts, and the British Virgin Islands), and the Windward Islands (including Dominica, Grenada, St. Lucia and St. Vincent).

Perspective

1. "A PLACE EXCEEDINGLY DELIGHTFUL"
2. "SIGHT, SCENT AND SOUND"
3. "THE SEVERITY OF GOD"
4. ANIMATE NATURE
5. ARAWAKS, CARIBS AND OTHERS
6. THE BUCCANEERS
7. SUGAR AND SLAVES
8. RACIAL MÉLANGE
9. THE "BUCKRA QUALITY"

Books and Authors: with biographical notes

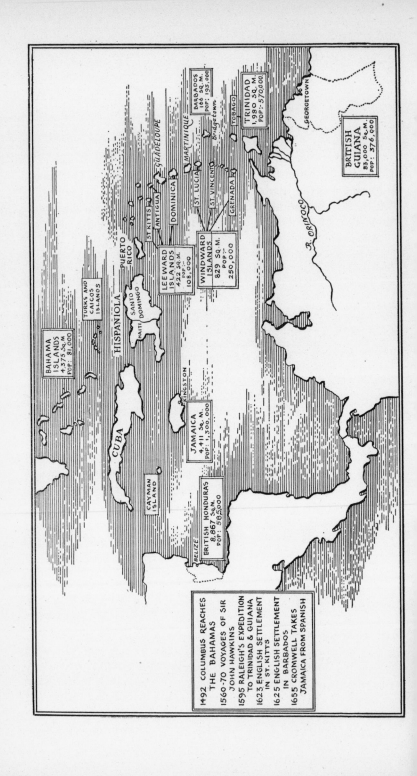

BAHAMA ISLANDS 4,375 Sq.M. POP: 81,000

TURKS AND CAICOS ISLANDS

CUBA

HISPANIOLA

HAITI | SANTO DOMINGO

PUERTO RICO

CAYMAN ISLAND

Kingston

JAMAICA 4,411 Sq.M. POP: 1,300,000

BELIZE

BRITISH HONDURAS 8,867 Sq.M. POP: 565,000

St KITTS
ANTIGUA
DOMINICA
GUADELOUPE
MARTINIQUE
St LUCIA
St VINCENT
Bridgetown
GRENADA
TOBAGO

LEEWARD ISLANDS 422 Sq.M. POP: 108,000

WINDWARD ISLANDS 829 Sq.M. POP: 250,000

BARBADOS 166 Sq.M. POP: 195,000

TRINIDAD 1,980 SQ.M. POP: 570,000

BRITISH GUIANA 85,000 Sq.M. POP: 376,000

GEORGETOWN

R. ORINOCO

1492 COLUMBUS REACHES THE BAHAMAS
1560-70 VOYAGES OF SIR JOHN HAWKINS
1595 RALEIGH'S EXPEDITION TO TRINIDAD & GUIANA
1623 ENGLISH SETTLEMENT IN ST. KITT'S
1625 ENGLISH SETTLEMENT IN BARBADOS
1655 CROMWELL TAKES JAMAICA FROM SPANISH

PERSPECTIVE

SIR JAMES ALEXANDER tells of the portly major who, when posted to a West Indian garrison, spent the days sitting in a tub of cold water, ejaculating from time to time: "Damn Columbus! Curse the fellow! Why did he discover these rascally islands!" As to the rascality of the islands there is precious little to support the major's view, but the responsibility of Columbus for their discovery is undisputed. In four voyages between 1492 and 1504 he visited and named most of the important islands, and went beyond them to the mainland of Central America. The fact that he had discovered a completely new continent was probably never known to him, since he had set out to find the East Indies by a westerly route and thought he had done so. The point he first touched was San Salvador in the Bahamas. The story has it that on October 8th, 1492, when his crews had become thoroughly mutinous because of the seemingly endless journey through an unknown sea to a problematical destination, he was compelled to enter into an agreement with them that if land was not sighted in three days they would return to Spain. On the night of 11th October, at precisely the moment the agreement was due to expire, a light was seen and the situation saved. So was America discovered. Most of the names Columbus gave to the islands have been retained, though his christening methods were somewhat empirical. Nevis he named, for example, because its cloud-topped summit reminded him of snow; Dominica because he sighted it on a Sunday; Trinidad in honour of the Trinity, because of the three peaks later known as the Three Sisters. One of the names which did not stick was St. Jago which he gave to Jamaica in honour of the patron saint of Spain, but which was afterwards discarded in favour of the original Indian name of Xaymaca, meaning "well wooded and watered".

For a century after these discoveries Spain did her best to keep the islands and the Main a private preserve while she mined gold and planted sugar. In this she was supported by a Papal decision, and on the whole she was successful. Yet neither the force of Spanish arms nor the authority of the Roman Catholic Church could entirely deter French and English traders and adventurers from intruding. The first Englishman on the scene was probably Sir Thomas Pert, vice-admiral of England, who in 1515 visited Hispaniola, where he was driven off by a salvo of artillery, and Porto Rico, where his treatment was less rough but yet sufficiently inhospitable to persuade him to return empty-handed. Later in the century, in the 1560's, the Spanish settlers needed African slaves and general merchandise so badly that they were prepared to do business with Sir John Hawkins despite censure from Madrid. Hawkins made two successful voyages, financed by a syndicate of London merchants, but on the third he met disaster. After selling his cargo at remote ports he was driven by a hurricane into the Spanish mainland stronghold of San Juan de Ulua. It was further his misfortune that on the following day a Spanish squadron arrived off the port, and though negotiations brought an agreement it was violated by the Spanish when once they were in the anchorage. In the fight Hawkins lost his own ship and two others and only two escaped, the *Minion*, to which Hawkins transferred, and the *Judith*, a still smaller vessel. Even then the *Minion* was so overcrowded with survivors that 100 men had to be put ashore to fend for themselves as best they could. Of the 100 who remained on board only fifteen survived the voyage to Plymouth. The *Judith* suffered less but only, it would seem, by virtue of the fact that she abandoned the *Minion* to her fate, an incident all the more remarkable because her captain was a gentleman named Francis Drake, Hawkins' cousin. Whatever the truth of the matter, it is at least clear that Drake arrived back in England impressed no less by the need to take an adequate revenge than by the great riches of the Main. So it was that Drake found congenial occupation during the next five years making piratical and profitable descents on Spanish shipping and towns in the Caribbean. Slowly but surely the Spanish monopoly was being broken, and with the defeat of the Spanish Armada in 1588 a new era began with the English, French and Dutch all making settlements in the islands and on the coast of Guiana.

Among the English Sir Walter Raleigh led the way in 1595 with an expedition up the Orinoco in search of the "Great and Golden City of Manoa (which the Spaniards call El Dorado)". In this he failed as he was bound to fail, since the place did not exist, but his account of the "Large, Rich and Bewtiful Empire of Guiana" focused new attention on the opportunities open to the adventurous and enterprising. During this voyage he called also at Trinidad where he destroyed the Spanish garrison and caulked his ships with pitch from the famous Pitch Lake. Others followed hard on his heels. In 1605 an English ship called the *Olive Blossom*, bound for Guiana, called at Barbados because of faulty navigation and the crew carved on a tree the words: "James, King of England and this island." This title a colonising mission made good twenty years later. The 1620's were, in fact, the decade in which England firmly staked claims in the islands.

A settlement in St. Kitts in 1623 was followed by the one in Barbados, and by others in St. Vincent (1627), Nevis (1628), Antigua and Montserrat (1632). None of these settlements was disputed by the Spanish, chiefly because they had never succeeded in taming the warlike Caribs who inhabited most of the islands of the Lesser Antilles. Yet the Spanish were by no means acquiescent. In 1650 they wiped out an English settlement at Santa Cruz, an island to the south-east of Porto Rico, killing more than 100 of the Colonists. It was a deed which paved the way for the downfall of Spanish power in the West Indies. To exact revenge Cromwell in 1655 despatched an armada, and though an assault on Hispaniola was repulsed, the Roundheads seized Jamaica instead and so gave England a base within the Spanish defences.

"The English being thus become masters of the island," said Sir Thomas Linch, "formed themselves into a Body or Colony. Then did they begin to settle themselves in Plantations, whilst others betook themselves to the Sea as Freebooters or Privateers, the better to secure themselves against the Spaniards".

This, indeed, is the pattern of developments during the seventeenth century. While some established plantations, usually sugar plantations, and manned them in part with indentured white servants but chiefly with slaves shipped from West Africa, the wilder spirits preferred to become buccaneers and sail under the skull and crossbones in attacks on Spanish towns and shipping from bases in Jamaica, Honduras and the Bahamas. With its many islands and dangerous reefs the coast of Honduras lent itself particularly well to use as a sally port, while the buccaneers who made it their headquarters found that they could spend their spare time very profitably fishing for turtle, catching wild cattle and cutting logwood and mahogany. So British Honduras had its beginnings. These beginnings are indicated in the name of the capital, Belize, which is thought to be a corruption of the name of the most famous of the Honduras buccaneers, a certain Captain Willis.

But pre-eminent among the buccaneers was Captain Henry Morgan, later knighted by Charles II, who operated from Jamaica. At one time he commanded a fleet of thirty-seven ships with 2,000 fighting men, "besides seamen and boys". His exploits are chronicled by John Esquemeling, himself a buccaneer, in *Bucaniers of America*. Morgan's personal story was similar to that of many other of the buccaneers. He was apparently the son of a Welsh farmer, and having an inclination to adventure he joined the crew of a ship sailing to Barbados from Bristol. When the ship arrived at Barbados the captain sold him to a planter for whom he had to work for three years. On getting his free-

dom he made his way to Jamaica and there joined the pirates. Esquemeling, who found himself in a like plight at Tortuga, explained his
predicament as follows: "Being now at liberty, though naked and
destitute of human necessaries, not knowing how to get my living, I
determined to enter into the wicked order of the Pirates."

Buccaneering reached its wildest and most impudent extremes in the
1660's, but in 1670 Britain concluded a formal treaty of peace and
commerce with Spain and thereafter the buccaneers lacked official
support. Many of them took advantage of an amnesty, and piracy
became but a tithe of what it had been. The buccaneers had played no
small part in undermining Spanish power in the New World, and by
the end of the century England and France were each as much concerned with the pretensions of the other as with those of Spain.

By now, indeed, the islands had been converted into sugar factories
of the greatest importance to the trade of the mother countries. In
consequence they figured largely in the disputes between the European
powers, and particularly the disputes between England and France,
which characterised the eighteenth century. Some of the islands
changed hands several times and it was not until the end of the Napoleonic Wars that the pattern of national ownership assumed its present
appearance. England emerged with her position in the islands strengthened by the acquisition of Trinidad, which had been captured from
Spain in 1797, and by confirmation of her claims to Grenada, St. Lucia
and Dominica which the French had heavily disputed. In all four islands
the influence of the earlier occupations is still discernible; for example
in the French patois of St. Lucia and in French architectural styles in
Grenada.

So far in West Indian history centuries and phases had coincided with
agreeable neatness. The sixteenth century was the phase of Spanish
monopoly; the seventeenth the phase of monopoly breaking; and the
eighteenth the phase of European dispute for possession of the islands.
With the nineteenth century came something quite novel—nothing
less than the emergence of a liberal and humane spirit which proclaimed the brotherhood of man. It was a spirit which could not
tolerate existence of the institution of slavery, however benevolently
that institution might be organised, and so the West Indies found itself
faced with a new kind of crisis.

In fairness to the planters let it be recognised that, with exceptions,
they treated their slaves well, if for no other reason than that a slave
represented an investment of hard cash. Nor does there seem much
doubt that most negroes found life as a slave in the West Indies more
congenial than life as a free man in West Africa. In particular, a slave

had his own "provision grounds", time to cultivate them and freedom to sell their products if he wished. In short, while his essential
requirements in food, shelter and clothes were provided by the estate,
he had the means to earn money, either to spend or to save for purchase of his freedom. Life as a slave could, in fact, be very tolerable.

Yet having said all that, the fact remained that slavery as an institution was indefensible and could not expect to survive in a world
which was developing a sense of human values. In 1807 Britain took the
first step by prohibiting the slave trade in all British possessions; in 1833
came the logical sequel of emancipation.

In the West Indies emancipation meant that the existing system of
economy was swept away. Everything had depended on cheap and
stable labour. Now labour was neither cheap nor stable. In lands
where life demanded a minimum of human effort there was no particular reason why the freed slave should exert himself. "But my friend
and brother over there," wrote Anthony Trollope in 1860, "my skin
polished, shining oil-fat negro, is a richer man than I. He lies under his
mango-tree, and eats the luscious fruit in the sun; he sends his black urchin up for a breadfruit, and behold the family table is spread. He
pierces a coconut, and lo! there is his beverage. He lies on the grass
surrounded by oranges, bananas and pine-apples. Oh, my hard taskmaster of the sugar-mill, is he not better off than thou? why should he
work at thy order?"

Had this been the only problem besetting the hard taskmaster of the
sugar-mill, the poor man would have been hard enough pressed. But
the Imperial Government had another blow to deliver. In 1854 it
removed the preference given to West Indian sugar in the home market, and so left the way clear for the cheaper slave-produced sugar of
Cuba and Brazil. Finally, just to make sure that the man was well and
truly down, Europe began to grow sugar beet.

Hard times had come to the West Indies, and a device such as the
importation of labour from India and China under an indenture system
could be only a palliative. The arrangement with China proved short-
lived, but from India the flow was to continue for seventy years with
the result that in Trinidad and British Guiana East Indians became an
important element in the population. Here was another facet to the
West Indian problem. Economies might shrink but populations grew,
not so much by the importation of new peoples as by natural increase of the predominant negro stock. No longer could a man who
felt so inclined lie back and "fatten in the genial heat."

As the twentieth century opened the twin problems of poverty and
over-population sat firmly in the saddle.

1. "A PLACE EXCEEDINGLY DELIGHTFUL"

Beauty is the first and obvious characteristic of the islands. Sir Hesketh Bell likens them to a necklace of gigantic jewels strung across the throat of the Caribbean.

Our first notice of the approach of land was the fragrant and aromatic smell of the continent of South America (or of the islands in its vicinity), which we sensibly perceived as a squall came from that quarter, and one of the boobies, flying round the ship, perched amongst the rigging, and suffered himself to be taken with apparent indifference. On the same day innumerable flights of small flying-fish rose on each side of the ship's bows from the water.

MCKINNEN: *A Tour through the British West Indies.* 1803.

One normally called first at Barbados. Its charm lies, not in spectacular scenery, but in what H. N. Coleridge called "its finished cultivation and the air of life and domestic comfort".

Barbados, that lies out to windward, guarding the other islands as it were! Barbados, that is and ever was entirely British! Barbados, that makes money, and is in all respects so respectable a little island! King George need not have feared at all; nor yet need Queen Victoria. If anything goes wrong in England—Napoleon coming there, not to kiss Her Majesty this time, but to make himself less agreeable—let Her Majesty come to Barbados, and she will be safe!

TROLLOPE: *The West Indies and the Spanish Main.* 1860.

★

It is about the size of the Isle of Wight, cultivated so far as eye could see with the completeness of a garden; no mountains in it, scarcely even high hills, but a surface pleasantly undulating, the prevailing colour a vivid green from the cane fields; houses in town and country white from the coral rock of which they are built, but the glare from them relieved by heavy clumps of trees. What the trees were I had yet to discover. You could see at a glance that the island was as thickly peopled as an anthill. Not an inch of soil seemed to be allowed to run to waste. Two hundred thousand is, I believe, the present number of Barbadians, of whom nine-tenths are blacks. They refuse to emigrate.

They cling to their home with innocent vanity as though it was the finest country in the world, and multiply at a rate so rapid that no one likes to think about it.

FROUDE: *The English in The West Indies*. 1888.

A little to the west of Barbados lie the Windward Islands which, with the Leewards to the north, make up what our great grandfathers preferred to call the "Caribbee Islands". "I had pictured them to myself a thousand times," says Charles Kingsley, "but I was altogether unprepared for their beauty and grandeur."

Under a cloudless sky, upon a sea, lively yet not unpleasantly rough, we thrashed and leaped along. Ahead of us, one after another, rose high on the southern horizon banks of grey cloud, from under each of which, as we neared it, descended the shoulder of a mighty mountain, dim and grey. Nearer still the grey changed to purple; lowlands rose out of the sea, sloping upwards with those grand and simple concave curves, which betoken, almost always, volcanic land. Nearer still, the purple changed to green. Tall palm-trees and engine-houses stood out against the sky; the surf gleamed white around the base of isolated rocks. A little nearer, and we were under the lee, or western side, of the island. The sea grew smooth as glass; we entered the shade of the island-cloud, and slid along in still unfathomable blue water, close under the shore of what should have been one of the Islands of the Blest.

KINGSLEY: *At Last: A Christmas in the West Indies*. 1871.

*

The islands, though green intensely, are not of one, but of every conceivable green, or rather of hues ranging from pale yellow through all greens into cobalt blue; and as the wind stirs the leaves, and sweeps the lights and shadows over hill and glen, all is ever-changing, iridescent, like a peacock's neck; till the whole island, from peak to shore, seems some glorious jewel—an emerald with tints of sapphire and topaz, hanging between blue sea and white surf below, and blue sky and white cloud above.

Ibid.

*

The next morning we were under the Pitons of Saint Lucia, two immense pryamidal rocks, which stand by themselves on the edge of the shores, like two giants, or Gog and Magog, who had walked down from the mountains to take a bath; and so tenacious are they of respect in passing them, that if you have not your haliards and sheets in hand, your vessel may be on her beam-ends, before you can call Jack Robinson to assist you, the sudden gusts, or invisible squalls, which are apt to come down upon you, affording you no time for preparation. Three English sailors—sailors love such exploits—because the steepest rock was deemed inaccessible, determined to gain the summit; two of them were never seen afterwards, but the third reached the apex, planted the British union on it, and "fell in mortal convulsions by its side;" so says the legend. Snakes, which are numerous and venomous in this island, are supposed to have caused their death.

The West India Sketch Book. 1834.

*

The appearance of Nevis is perhaps the most captivating of any island in the West Indies. From the south and west it seems to be nothing but a single cone rising with the most graceful curve out of the sea, and piercing a fleecy mass of clouds which sleeps for ever round its summit. It is green as heart can conceive, perfectly cultivated, and enlivened with many old planters' houses of a superior style and churches peeping out in the most picturesque situations imaginable. A complete forest of evergreen trees grows like a ruff or collar round the neck of the high land where cultivation ceases.

COLERIDGE: *Six Months in the West Indies, in* 1825.

Dominica claims a river for every day of the year, innumerable waterfalls, and the mighty Morne Diablotin, culminating peak of the Caribbean Andes. As its Administrator, Sir Hesketh Bell was possibly prejudiced in believing it the most beautiful of all the islands, but his descriptions are persuasive.

Everyone has gone to bed and the silence of the tranquil night is only broken by the indefinable hum of the countless insect creatures that haunt the great forest beyond the borders of the orange-grove. My trees are all in bloom and the scent of them is almost excessive. In the clear moonlight I can see the clusters of fragrant blossoms everywhere and the dark green foliage glistens under the luminous dew.

During the daytime the view, from my window, is almost indescribably beautiful. It dominates the whole of the interior of the island, with its vast basin of undulating valleys, all covered with dense virgin forest, and encircled by a coronet of lofty mountains. But now, under the mysterious gleams of a crescent moon, its loveliness is almost overwhelming.

Deep down, in the valley below, the moonbeams glisten on the little cascades in the restless course of the tumbling river that wends its tortuous way through the clearings in the forest. The foothills of the encircling mountains seem to glide gradually down into the rolling plains beneath and, in majestic undulations, spread softly away towards the towering mass of Morne Diablotin looming in the distance.

BELL: *Glimpses of a Governor's Life.*

Behind the beauty of the Caribbee Isles lies a menace. The islands are volcanic in origin; no more, in fact, than the tips of a range of volcanic peaks, not all of them extinct. The Souffrière of St. Vincent erupted as recently as 1902. Dominica has a famous Boiling Lake, 3,000 feet above sea level.

Finally we reached the crest of the mountain and were confronted by a magnificent and awe-inspiring sight. In lieu of the soft, enchanting beauty of the green and blossoming mountain-side, a picture of grey and gloomy desolation lay at our feet. We were facing a huge circular crater fully a mile in diameter. The sky had become overcast and everything was grey and doleful. A neutral-tinted mist filled the great cavity, and the steeply sloping sides of the huge basin were clothed only with slimy clay or blackened scoriæ. Jets of strangely coloured water issued from cracks and fissures, and small spurts of steam rose from many places. It was the Abomination of Desolation.

The floor of the crater was fully a thousand feet below, and in the centre of it we could just discern a small circular basin, which, the guide told us, was our objective. To our disappointment, it seemed to be only full of pale, grey sand, with no sign of any lake, boiling or otherwise. But our guide assured us that, if we stayed two or three hours, we should be amply repaid for our trouble.

The scramble down into the depths below was rather a painful affair. The lower we went the hotter and steamier conditions became, and if the sky had not been overclouded the temperature would have been almost unbearable. Finally we got to the bottom, and found that the famous "boiling lake" was merely a basin, about a hundred yards in diameter, covered with soft grey sand. A spring of warm water flowed into it from a crevice just above us, but the liquid sank almost immediately into a soft spot in the centre of the basin.

By this time we were very hungry and heartily consumed a picnic breakfast which we had brought with us. We had just finished our meal when the guide pointed out that the water was no longer disappearing into the centre of the space before us but was spreading rapidly over the sand. He said that we would very soon see what the Boiling Lake was like.

The depth of the water increased very quickly, and its volume was far greater than what the spring could supply. It was evident that large quantities of water were coming up from below, and we soon saw movements, like small geysers, appearing on the surface. It was also plain that the water was becoming very hot, as steam was rapidly rising from it. The volume of water increased so swiftly that we found it prudent to watch further developments from a spot higher up and farther from the eruption.

It was a wonderful and rather terrifying sight, and made one realize something of the extraordinary forces that were working just under our feet. In less than an hour the whole of the inner crater had become a seething cauldron of water boiling furiously. Five or six formidable geysers bubbled up in the centre to a considerable height and dense clouds of steam rolled off the broken surface.

Being anxious to get a good photograph of this remarkable phenomenon, I scrambled round a part of the circle in order to get a good viewpoint. Now and again, when the wind blew towards me, I was enveloped in a cloud of dense steam, and found that it was so impregnated by sulphurous fumes that I had to hold my sun-helmet in front of my face to avoid a sense of suffocation. I got some excellent shots which ultimately proved to be good clear pictures of the whole thing. As heavy rain seemed imminent, we decided to return home, especially as the force of the eruption seemed to be gradually diminishing. The guide told us that the water would soon go "off the boil" and would disappear entirely into the depths below, leaving the basin merely a surface of dull grey sand, just as we had found it. During our painful climb up to the top of the outer crater we saw, on looking back, that it was so, and by the time we reached the crest the Boiling Lake had entirely disappeared. We were told that it usually repeated its "turn" twice a day.

Ibid.

In the Greater Antilles, compared with Cuba and Hispaniola, Jamaica ranks in size as a junior partner, but it is none the less much the largest of all the British West Indian islands, and in beauty the equal of any.

The first appearance of Jamaica presents one of the most grand and lively scenes that the creating hand of Nature can possibly exhibit: mountains of an immense height seem to crush those that are below them; and these are adorned with a foliage as thick as vivid, and no less vivid than continual. The hills, from their summits to the very borders of the sea, are fringed with trees and shrubs of a beautiful shape, and undecaying verdure; and you perceive mills, works, and houses, peeping among their branches, or buried amidst their shades.

The sea is, in general, extremely smooth and brilliant; and, before the breeze begins to ripple its glassy surface, is so remarkably transparent, that you can perceive (as if there were no intervening medium) the rocks and sands at a considerable depth; the weeds and coral that adorn the first, and the stars and other testaceous fishes that repose upon the last.

Every passing cloud affords some pleasing variation; and the glowing vapours of the atmosphere, when the sun arises or declines, and when the picturesque and fantastic clouds are reflected in its polished bosom, give an enchanting hue, and such as is only particular to the warmer climates, and which much resemble those saffron skies which so strongly mark the Campania of Rome, and the environs of Naples.

BECKFORD: *A Descriptive Account of the Island of Jamaica.* 1740.

On his visit to Trinidad in 1595 *Raleigh caulked his ships with pitch from the famous lake. "It melteth not with the sunne as the pitch of Norway",* *he said.*

This iland of Trinedado hath the forme of a sheephook, and is but narrow; the north part is very mounteynous, the soile is very excellent and wil beare sugar, ginger, or any other commodity that the Indies yeeld. It hath store of deare, wyld porks, fruits, fish and fowle.

RALEIGH:
The Discoverie of the Large, Rich and Bewtiful Empire of Guiana. 1595.

*

We now perceived a strong sulphurous and pitchy smell, like that of burning coal, and soon after had a view of the lake, which at first sight seemed to be an expanse of still water, frequently interrupted by clumps of dwarf trees and islets of rushes and shrubs; but upon a nearer approach we found it to be in reality an extensive plain of mineral pitch, with frequent crevices and chasms filled with water. The singularity of the scene was altogether so great, that it was some time before I could recover from my surprise so as to investigate it minutely.

The surface of the lake is of the colour of ashes, and at this season was not polished or smooth so as to be slippery: the hardness or consistence was such as to bear any weight; and it was not adhesive, though it partially received the impression of the foot; it bore us without any tremulous motion whatever, and several head of cattle were browsing on it in perfect security. In the dry season, however, the surface is much more yielding, and must be in a state approaching to fluidity, as is shewn by pieces of recent wood and other substances being enveloped in it. Even large branches of trees, which were a foot above the level, had in some way become enveloped in the bituminous matter.

CARMICHAEL: *Five Years in Trinidad and St. Vincent.* 1834.

*

Trinidad has one wonder in it, a lake of bitumen some ninety acres in extent, which all travellers are expected to visit, and which few residents care to visit. A black lake is not so beautiful as an ordinary lake. I had no doubt that it existed, for the testimony was unimpeachable. Indeed I was shown an actual specimen of the crystallised pitch itself. I could believe without seeing and without undertaking a tedious journey.

FROUDE: *The English in The West Indies.* 1888.

Judged by the swampy environs of Belize, British Honduras has little in beauty to commend it, but Henry Fowler came back with enthusiastic descriptions of the hinterland.

For a few moments a magnificent scene burst on our view, on reaching the top. The sun shone out for a few minutes, but drifting clouds prevented the whole scene from being realized in one grand view. At our feet lay a broad valley some 1,500 feet below us running away to the right. In front was a range of mountains level with the ones we were on, with valleys winding up the side, and hills rising along the sweep of the slope opposite us, the foliage of the forest looked like an undulating green sward, bright where the sun shone, but sombre underneath the clouds. There was a break in the mountains opposite, a little to the left of us, through which a large stream wended its way to the coast; to the left in the distance was the head of the valley hemmed in by mountains, looking like a huge amphitheatre, with a large stream leaping over a precipice forming a magnificent water-fall of 300 or 500 feet; immediately to the north of us was another water-fall, which we could only hear, discharging the waters of the stream we had been following through a gorge into the valley below. We rested and admired the scene; which was perhaps all the more beautiful and wild from the varying shades of light thrown across the picture. Thick and fleecy clouds were driven alternately across the valley and mountains by a high wind. The roaring of the waters around us amidst the silence

FULANI GIRL WITH A BOWL OF MILK TO SELL,
NIGERIA

GRACE AND THIRST
BARBADOS

of the woods added another charm to the pleasing sensation we experienced.

FOWLER:
A Journey Across the Unexplored Portion of British Honduras.   1879.

At first sight British Guiana lacks charm. The principal recollections one has of British Guina, says Henry Kirke, are heat and dampness.

Guiana is an enormous extent of flat mud, the alluvial deposit of those mighty rivers which for so many years have been scraping together earth in those wild unknown upland countries, and bringing it down conveniently to the sea-board, so that the world might have sugar to its tea.

TROLLOPE: *The West Indies and the Spanish Main.*   1860.

In Victorian days Guiana had a reputation for unhealthiness which Anthony Trollope did his best to debunk.

I went over the hospital with the doctor there; for even in Demarara they require a hospital for the negroes. "And what is the prevailing disease of the colony?" I asked him. "Dropsy with the black men," he answered; "and brandy with the white."

Ibid.

★

When I settle out of England, and take to the colonies for good and all, British Guiana shall be the land of my adoption. If I call it Demerara perhaps I shall be better understood. At home there are prejudices against it I know. They say that it is a low, swampy, muddy strip of alluvial soil, infested with rattlesnakes, gallinippers, and musquitoes as big as turkey-cocks; that yellow fever rages there perennially; that the heat is unendurable; that society there is as stagnant as its waters; that men always die as soon as they reach it; and when they live are such wretched creatures that life is a misfortune. Calumny reports it to have been ruined by the abolition of slavery; milk of human kindness would forbid the further exportation of Europeans to this white man's grave; and philanthropy, for the good of mankind, would wish to have it drowned beneath its own rivers. There never was a land so ill spoken of—and never one that deserved it so little.

Ibid.

The "rich and bewtiful" Guiana of which Raleigh wrote lay to the north of what is now British Guiana, but his descriptions are applicable to the hinterland generally.

Both for health, good ayre, pleasure, and riches, I am resolued it cannot bee equalled by any region eyther in the east or west. Moreouer the countrey is so healthfull, as 100 persons and more which lay (without shift most sluttishly, and were every day almost melted with heat in rowing and marching, and suddenly wet againe with great showers, and did eate of all sorts of corrupt fruits, and made meales of fresh fish without seasoning, of Tortugas, of Lagartos, and of al sorts good and bad, without either order or measure, and besides lodged in the open ayre euery night) we lost not any one, nor had one ill disposed to my knowledge, nor found anie Callentura, or other of those pestilent diseases which dwell in all hote regions, and so nere the Equinoctiall line.

RALEIGH:

The Discoverie of the Large, Rich and Bewtiful Empire of Guiana.   1595.

Far in the interior lies Roraima, at 8,600 feet the highest peak in the British West Indies; and also the Kaietur waterfall which has a sheer drop of 740 feet. Raleigh was told of a great mountain and a great waterfall.

There falleth ouer it a mightie riuer which toucheth no parte of the side of the moutaine, but rusheth ouer the toppe of it, and falleth to the grounde with a terrible noyse and clamor, as if 1000 great belles were knockt one against another. I thinke there is not in the worlde so straunge an ouerfall, nor so wonderfull to beholde.

Ibid.

Kaietur was discovered in 1871, and Sir Everard im Thurn visited it seven years later in what was a very dry season.

Lying at full length on the ground, head over the edge of the cliff, I gazed down.

Then, and only then, the splendid and, in the most solemn sense of the word, awful beauty of the Kaietur burst upon me. Seven hundred and fifty feet below, encircled by black boulders, lay a great pool into which the column of white water, graceful as a ceaseless flight of innumerable rockets, thundered from by my side. Behind the fall, through the thinnest parts of the veil of foam and mist, the great black cavern made the white of the water look yet more white.

My first sensations were of a terrible and undefined fear. Those who visit the fall will understand this. When some of the men hurled down one of the big Bromeliads, the act seemed to cause me unbearable pain; I had as soon have hurled myself over as have allowed a repetition of the act just then. Gradually, however, these painful feelings gave way to others of intense wondering delight; and the whole scene, the gigantic weird fall, the dark and slippery places below, the grass-covered rocks at the gate of the amphitheatre, and beyond that the bright thickly wooded valley of the winding river, visible for many miles, were revealed, never to be forgotten.

IM THURN: *Among the Indians of Guiana.* 1883.

In 1879 Sir Everard visited the Fall a second time, on this occasion during a very wet season.

Crossing the savannah, and coming to the edge of the cliff over which the Potaro falls, we once more lay down, bodies along the top of the cliff, heads over its edge. It was a very different scene from the last time. Then it was beautiful and terrible; but now it was something which it is useless to try to describe. Then a narrow river, not a third of its present width, fell over the cliff in a column of white water, which was brought into startling prominence by the darkness of the great cave behind; and this column of water, before it reached the small, black pool below, had narrowed to a point. Now an indescribably, almost inconceivably, vast curtain of water—I can find no other phrase—some four hundred feet in width, rolled over the top of the cliff, retaining its full width until it crashed into the boiling water of the pool which filled the whole space below; and of the surface of this pool itself only the outer edge was visible, for the greater part was ceaselessly tossed and hurled up in a great and high mass of surf and foam and spray.

The fall, when the river was almost dry, had seemed as grand and beautiful a thing as it was possible to imagine; but now it was so infinitely more grand, so infinitely more beautiful, that it is painfully hopeless to try to express in words anything of its beauty and grandeur. Indeed the very words beauty and grandeur, and indeed all other words, seem absurdly weak when applied to such a scene as that. It is indeed possible to write down a few separate impressions that came to me as I looked at the fall, but it is impossible even to hint at the over-powering effect which the whole scene produced.

We made our camp at the old spot, at the actual edge of the fall. The river there had been choked by sedges (Cyperus) among which the water used to creep hidden to its fall; but this plant-growth was now quite covered by the rushing river.

About an hour before sunset on the first evening of our stay rain began to fall in light showers. Low down at our feet, across the river below the fall, the sun and rain built a coloured arch right across the ravine; and through this the river, narrowed by a seemingly endless series of projecting cliff buttresses, was seen winding through the forest-covered country till it passed the far-away sugar-loaf mountain at Amootoo, and then lost itself in the great wooded plain beyond.

An hour later heavy low-lying clouds had gathered, and almost shut us in our camp on the edge of the cliff. Then the mist and cloud and rain and wind made another wonderful scene. The great rocky ravine at our feet was filled by huge masses of rolling, driving cloud which hid everything, except when, now and then, a cold blast of wind, separating two clouds for a few seconds, showed in the gap some projecting cliff-ledge, or some tree-covered rock, apparently hanging suspended in a cloud world. And all the while the great river rushed swiftly at our side to the edge of the cliff, rolled over, and as it fell plunged through strange weird pillars of white mist, which continually rose from it and passed up into the low leaden-coloured sky overhead, down into the denser, unbroken mass of clouds below, and there hid itself. Night came on, and as it grew darker and darker, the few swifts (*Acanthyllis collaris*) which were about fell headlong down from the sky above; and they too were gone into the cloud. And the noise of the fall—the rustling sound of falling water and the deep boom rising from the unseen pool below—added to the effect. The whole world seemed unreal and grandly fantastic. In such a scene as that one forgets one's self, forgets real life, and seems carried into a new, hardly formed universe.

Ibid.

2. "SIGHT, SCENT AND SOUND"

"As regards flower displays," says Sir Harry Johnstone, "these lands of the West Indies and the Spanish Main are truly remarkable." In Montserrat, H. N. Coleridge walked along the road to the Souffrière.

It was like one of my native Devonshire lanes; no primroses or violets were there indeed, but the snowy amaryllis drooped her long and delicate petals like a love-sick girl; the thrice gorgeous hibiscus was unveiling his crown and feathers of scarlet, and the light limes and darker orange trees, which formed a verdant hedge on either side, were exhaling their perfumed incense to Him who made them so beautiful and so good. A thin grey cloud obscured the sun, whilst an Atlantic breeze blew gently and freshly upon my face and open neck. The air was as cool as on a May morning in England, but so inexpressibly soft, so rare and subtle to the senses that I think the ether which angels breathe cannot be purer stuff than this.

COLERIDGE: *Six Months in the West Indies, in* 1825.

Sir Everard im Thurn had an eye for beauty.

The next morning when I awoke I found that the tree, of a genus (Eugenia) new to me, to which one end of my hammock was tied, had burst into a marvellous sheet of pure white blossom. The branches touched the ground. Dense masses of its tiny feathery flowers, nestling along each branch and branchlet, made the whole look as if weighed down with snow. Its scent filled the air, and had attracted a host of humming-birds, butterflies, and bees, filling the air with their murmur. Sight, scent, and sound were equally grateful.

IM THURN: *Among the Indians of Guiana.* 1883.

★

It was in passing up this very creek, on a previous occasion, that I first understood the beauty of a tropical forest. On the main rivers the scenery is too large to be well understood; but these smaller streams give more definite impressions. Moraballi creek is about the width of the Cherwell at Oxford. The bright, dark red, wine-coloured water runs, arched over by gigantic trees and palms and ferns, through dense shade. The swampy banks are thickly set with ferns and large lily-leaved aroids. At the water's edge a carpet of half-transparent filmy ferns and mosses is kept continually moist. From the trees which meet overhead, roots and leafless stems of wiry creeping plants hang down to the water; and on some of these humming-birds fix their tiny nests. There is no colour; the light is very dim; the air is very cool and almost chilly. But in one place, where a tree had fallen and left a space in the forest roof, the glorious and intensely blue sky appeared, its colour thrown into extraordinary vividness by a wreath of scarlet-blossomed passion-flower which had thrown itself across the open space from tree to tree. On the fallen tree, now lying leafless and branchless across the stream, almost touching the water, perched a great grey-blue king-fisher, which, frightened by the approach of our boat, flew screaming down the dark, arched streamway which lay beyond us.

Ibid.

Nature in the tropics can be venomous as beautiful.

The tree called Mancanilla, or Dwarf apple-tree, groweth nigh unto the Sea Shoar; being naturally so low, that its branches, though never so short, do always touch the water. It beareth a fruit, something like, unto our sweet sented apples; which notwithstanding is of a very venemous quality. For these apples being eaten by any person, he instantly changeth colour, and such an huge thirst doth seize him as all the Water of the Thames cannot extinguish, he dying raving mad within a little while after. But what is more the Fish that eat as it often happeneth, of this fruit are also poysonous. This tree affordeth, also a liquor, both thick, and white; like unto the Fig-tree; which, if touched by the hand, raiseth blisters, upon the skin, and these are so red in colour, as if it had been deeply scalded, with hot water. One day, being hugely tormented with Mosquitos or gnats, and as yet, unacquainted with the nature of this tree, I cut a branch thereof, to serve me instead of a fan; but all my face swelled the next day, and filled with blisters, as if it were burnt to such a degree, that I was blind for three days.

ESQUEMELING: *Bucaniers of America.* 1684.

And merciful as venomous.

We could get no water except from the wild vines growing on the trees, from which, however, we obtained a sufficient supply for break-fast purposes. Three of the largest plants gave us a good gallon of water. The water vine is a wonderful provision of nature to furnish water to a traveller, and is common in the forest. A good vine is about the size of one's arm, and runs along the ground or hangs from tree to tree, you cut it in pieces of about two or four feet, and let one end drain into your mouth, or a cup. The water that you obtain from it is delicious and cool. A curious phenomenon in tropical vegetation is the fact that the flow of sap depends upon, or coincides with the changes of the moon, as in colder climates it corresponds with the seasons. A mahogany cutter will only fell trees at the fullest stages of the moon, and the reason he gives is that if felled at other times, the wood will be liable to split, in the same manner as trees cut elsewhere at a wrong season. India rubber is always collected at the new moon, when the sap flows freely. If a tree is tapped only at full moon, but little juice would ever be extracted. An Indian will only cut leaves to thatch his house in the same way. The sap certainly appears to correspond with the changes of the moon, but whether it is affected by the moon or not, I cannot venture an opinion, I merely state the above facts.

FOWLER:
A Journey Across the Unexplored Portion of British Honduras. 1879.

The "high woods" of Trinidad fascinated Charles Kingsley.

You can only wander on as far as you dare, letting each object impress itself on your mind as it may, and carrying away a confused recollection of innumerable perpendicular lines, all straining upwards, in fierce competition, towards the light-food far above; and next of a green cloud, or rather mist, which hovers round your head, and rises, thickening and thickening to an unknown height. The upward lines are of every possible thickness, and of almost every possible hue; what leaves they bear, being for most part on the tips of the twigs, give a scattered, mist-like appearance to the under-foliage. For the first moment, therefore, the forest seems more open than an English wood. But try to walk through it, and ten steps undeceive you. Around your knees are probably Mamures, with creeping stems and fan-shaped leaves, something like those of a young coco-nut palm. You try to brush through them, and are caught up instantly by a string or wire belonging to some other plant. You look up and round; and then you find that the air is full of wires—that you are hung up in a network of fine branches belonging to half-a-dozen different sorts of young trees, and intertwined with as many different species of slender creepers. You thought at your first glance among the tree-stems that you were looking through open air; you find that you are looking through a labyrinth of wire-rigging, and must use the cutlass right and left at every five steps. You push on into a bed of strong sedge-like Sclerias, with cutting edges to their leaves. It is well for you if they are only three, and not six feet high. In the midst of them you run against a horizontal stick, triangular, rounded, smooth, green. You take a glance along it right and left, and see no end to it either way, but gradually discover that it is the leaf-stalk of a young Cocorite palm. The leaf is five-and-twenty feet long, and springs from a huge ostrich plume, which is sprawling out of the ground and up above your head a few yards off. You cut the leaf-stalk through right and left, and walk on, to be stopped suddenly (for you get so confused by the multitude of objects that you never see anything till you run against it) by a grey lichen-covered bar, as thick as your ankle. You follow it up with your eye, and find it entwine itself with three or four other bars, and roll over with them in great knots and festoons and loops twenty feet high, and then go up with them into the green cloud over your head, and vanish, as if a giant had thrown a ship's cables into the tree-tops. One of them, so grand that its form strikes even the Negro and the Indian, is a Liantasse. You see that at once by the form of its cable— six or eight inches across in one direction, and three or four in another, furbelowed all down the middle into regular knots, and looking like a chain cable between two flexible iron bars. At another of the loops, about as thick as your arm, your companion, if you have a forester with you, will spring joyfully. With a few blows of his cutlass he will sever it as high up as he can reach, and again below, some three feet down; and, while you are wondering at this seemingly wanton destruction, he lifts the bar on high, throws his head back, and pours down his thirsty throat a pint or more of pure cold water. This hidden treasure is, strange as it may seem, the ascending sap, or rather the ascending pure rain-water which has been taken up by the roots, and is hurrying aloft, to be elaborated into sap, and leaf, and flower, and fruit, and fresh tissue for the very stem up which it originally climbed; and therefore it is that the woodman cuts the water-vine through first at the top of the piece which he wants, and not at the bottom; for so rapid is the ascent of the sap that if he cut the stem below, the water would have all fled upwards before he could cut it off above. Meanwhile, the old story of Jack and the Bean-stalk comes into your mind. In such a forest was the old dame's hut; and up such a bean-stalk Jack climbed, to find a giant and a castle high above. Why not? What may not be up there? You look up into the green cloud, and long for a moment to be a monkey. There may be monkeys up there over your head, burly red Howler, or tiny peevish Sapajou, peering down at you; but you cannot peer up at them. The monkeys, and the parrots, and the humming-birds, and the flowers, and all the beauty, are upstairs—

up above the green cloud. You are in "the empty nave of the cathedral", and "the service is being celebrated aloft in the blazing roof." . . . Round our feet are Arums, with snow-white spadixes and hoods, one instance among many here of brilliant colour developing itself in deep shade. But is the darkness of the forest actually as great as it seems? Or are our eyes, accustomed to the blaze outside, unable to expand rapidly enough, and so liable to mistake for darkness air really full of light reflected downward, again and again, at every angle, from the glossy surfaces of a million leaves? At least we may be excused; for a bat has made the same mistake, and flits past us at noonday. And there is another—— No; as it turns, a blaze of metallic azure off the upper side of the wings proves this one to be no bat, but a Morpho—a moth as big as a bat. And what was that second larger flash of golden green, which dashed at the moth, and back to yonder branch not ten feet off? A Jacamar—kingfisher, as they miscall her here, sitting fearless of man, with the moth in her long beak. Her throat is snowy white, her under-parts rich red brown. Her breast, and all her upper plumage and long tail, glitter with golden green. There is light enough in this darkness, it seems.

KINGSLEY: *At Last: A Christmas in the West Indies.* 1871.

3. "THE SEVERITY OF GOD"

Hurricanes are part of the pattern of life in the West Indies. From time to time there is one of exceptional violence and horror; as, for example, "the awful hurricane of 1831" in Barbados, of which the following is an account quoted in Sir Robert Schomburgk's history:

Fiery meteors were presently seen falling from the heavens; one in particular, of a globular form and a deep red hue, was observed to descend perpendicularly from a vast height. It evidently fell by its specific gravity, and was not shot or propelled by any extraneous force. On approaching the earth with accelerated motion it assumed a dazzling whiteness, and an elongated form, and dashing to the ground in Beckwith Square, it splashed around in the same manner as melted ore would have done and was instantly extinct. In shape and size it appeared much like a common barrel shape. Its brilliancy and the spattering of its particles on meeting the earth, gave it the resemblance of a body of quicksilver of equal bulk.

A few minutes after the appearance of this phaenomenon, the deafening noise of the wind sank to a solemn murmur, or more correctly speaking a distant roar; and the lightning, which from midnight had flashed and darted forkedly, with few and but momentary intermissions; now for a space of nearly half a minute played frightfully between the clouds and the earth, with novel and surprising action. The vast body of vapour appeared to touch the houses, and issued downward, flaming blazes which were nimbly returned from the earth upward. The coruscations, for the short space of time they continued, instantly succeeding each other, this strange quivering or darting of flashes down and up may be compared to the miniature blazing produced by the rapid and irregular discharges of opposing artillery closely engaged. Whilst this remarkable phaenomenon proceeded, the earth vibrated in a manner, and in time answering with the action of the lightning. Twice or more, when the coruscations were more brilliant and intense, but less rapid in succession, the earth received correspondent shocks. The moment after this singular alternation of lightning, the hurricane again burst from the western points with a violence beyond conception, hurling before it thousands of missiles, the fragments of every unsheltered structure of human art. The strongest houses were caused to vibrate to their foundations, and the surface of the very earth trembled as the destroyer raged over it. No thunder was at any time heard; had the cannon of a hundred contending armies been discharged, or the fulmination of the most tremendous thunder-claps rattled through the air, the sounds could not have been distinguished. The horrible roar and yelling of the wind, the noise of the tumultuous ocean, whose frightful waves threatened the town with destruction, if all the other elements might spare; the clattering of tiles, the falling of roofs and walls, and the combination of a thousand other sounds, formed the most hideous din, which appalled the heart.

SCHOMBURGK: *The History of Barbados.* 1848.

Earthquakes and eruptions occasionally bring great disasters. In an earth-quake in Jamaica in 1692 more than 2,000 people were killed and the capital city, Port Royal, destroyed. To replace Port Royal, Kingston was founded: it suffered a similar fate a little more than 200 years later, in 1907.

You would admire at the Goodness of God in the Preservation of the residue; some were very miraculously delivered from Death, swallowed down into the Bowels of the Earth alive and spewed up again, and saved by the violent Eruption of Water through those Gaps; some (as they say themselves, if they were alive at that time to know what was done to them) were swallowed up in one place, and by the rushing of Waters too and fro by reason of the agitation of the Earth at that time, were cast up again by another Chasm at places far distant. But the general Means of Preservation was by Peoples flying as fast as they could toward the back Seaside, or getting aboard the Ships in the Harbour by one means or another with all speed possible, which were presently crouded with Men, Women and Children. . . . The lofty blew Mountains lift up their Heads, but are now so rent and torn that they are fearful to behold, and are like to stand for lasting Marks of the Wrath of God.

The Truest and Largest Account of
the Late Earthquake in Jamaica, June the 7th, 1692.

The Souffrière in St. Vincent has made a habit of erupting at intervals of roughly 100 years. It did so in 1715, again in 1812 and, the last and worst occasion, in 1902. This is an observer's account of the 1812 eruption, quoted in The West India Sketch Book.

On Thursday the 30th, the reflection of the rising sun on this majestic body of curling vapour was sublime beyond imagination; it after-wards assumed a more sulphureous cast, and in the course of the day, a ferruginous and sanguine appearance, with much livelier action in the ascent, a more extensive dilatation, as if almost freed from every obstruction; in the afternoon the noise became incessant, and resembled the approach of thunder still nearer and nearer, with a vibration that affected the feelings and hearing. Terror and consternation now seized all beholders. The Caribs at Morne Ronde fled precipitately towards the town; the negroes became confused, forsook their work, looking to the mountain, and as it shook, trembled with dread of what they could neither understand nor describe: the birds fell to the ground over-powered with showers of farilla, unable to keep themselves on the wing: the cattle were starving from want of food, as not a blade of grass or a leaf was now to be found: the sea became discoloured, but in no wise uncommonly agitated, and throughout the whole of this violent disturbance of the earth, it continued passive, and did not at any time sympathize with the agitation of the land. Scarcely had the day closed, when the flames burst pyramidically from the crater through the mass of smoke: the rolling of the thunder became more awful and deafening; electric flashes quickly succeeded, attended with loud claps; and now indeed the hurly-burly began. Shortly after seven p.m. the mighty cauldron was seen to simmer, and the ebullition of lava to break out on the N.W. side: this, immediately after boiling over the orifice, and flowing a short way, was opposed by the acclivity of a higher point of land, over which it was impelled by the immense tide of liquefied fire that drove it on, forming the figure V in grand illumination. Sometimes, when the ebullition slackened, or was insufficient to urge it over the obstructing hill, it recoiled back like a refluence billow from the rock, and then again rushed forward, im-pelled by fresh supplies and scaling every obstacle; carrying rocks and woods together in its course down the slope of the mountain, until it precipitated itself down some vast ravine, concealed by the intervening ridges of Morne Ronde. Vast globular bodies of fire were at the same time seen projected from the fiery furnace, and bursting, fell back into it, or over it, on the surrounding trees and bushes, which were instantly set in flames. About four hours after the lava boiled over the crater, it reached the sea, as was observed by the reflection of the fire and the electric flashes attending it; and an hour after midnight, another stream of lava was seen descending in the opposite direction to the east-ward. The thundering noise of the mountain, and the vibration of sound, that had been so formidable hitherto, now mingled in the sullen monotonous roar of the rolling lava, and became so terrible, that dis-may was almost turned to despair. At this time the first earthquake was felt, as if producing the awful catastrophe which excited appre-hension had anticipated; and this was followed for two hours by showers of cinders, that fell with the hissing noise of millions of snakes writhing in agonies of protracted dissolution. A dreadful rain of stones and fire followed for the space of another hour, and was again succeeded by cinders from three o'clock till six o'clock in the morning. Earthquake followed earthquake almost momentarily, the whole of this part of the island being in a continual state of oscillation: not agitated by shocks, vertical or horizontal, but undulated like water shaken in a bowl. The break of day, if such it could be called, was truly awful. At eight o'clock, darkness was only visible, and the birth of the first of May, dawned like the day of judgment: a chaotic gloom enveloped the mountains, and an impenetrable haze hung over the sea with black sluggish clouds of a sulphurous cast. The whole island was covered with farilla, cinders, scoria, and broken masses of volcanic matter. It was not until the afternoon, that the muttering noise of the mountain sunk gradually into a solemn yet suspicious silence.

The West India Sketch Book. 1834.

4. "ANIMATE NATURE"

Birds strangely shaped and gorgeously coloured take first place among the fauna of the West Indies, but the insects are not to be despised and the mammals at any rate include some agreeable oddities.

Here are several Animals, and Insects, as Snakes a yard and a half long, Scorpions as big as Rats, but no ways hurtful to man or beast; Lizzards, which are exceeding harmless, much frequenting the houses, and loving the company of men; Musketoes, Cockroaches, and Merriwings, which are very troublesome in the night in stinging; also, here are land-Crabs in great abundance, which are found good to eat. And here is a small Fly which they call Cayouyou, whose Wings in the Night, as it flyeth, casts forth a great lustre, and the Indians do commonly catch them, and tye them to their hands or feet, and make use of them instead of a Candle, which is forbidden them.

LINCH: A Description of the Island of Jamaica. 1672.

Nearly every writer has something to say about the phenomenon of the glow-worm.

As I gazed, the air burst into atoms of green fire before my face, and in an instant they were gone; I turned round, and saw all the woods upon the mountains illuminated with ten thousands of flaming torches moving in every direction, now rising, now falling, vanishing here, re-appearing there, converging to a globe, and dispersing in spangles. No man can conceive from dry description alone the magical beauty of these glorious creatures; so far from their effects having been exaggerated by travellers, I can say that I never read an account in prose or verse which in the least prepared me for the reality.

There are two sorts, the small fly which flits in and out in the air, the body of which I have never examined; and a kind of beetle, which keeps more to the woods, and is somewhat more stationary, like our glow-worm. This last has two broad eyes on the back of its head which, when the phosphorescent energy is not exerted, are of a dull parchment hue, but, upon the animal's being touched, shoot forth two streams of green light as intense as the purest gas. But the chief source or splendor is a cleft in the belly, through which the whole interior of the beetle appears like a red hot furnace. I put one of these natural lamps under a wine glass in my bedroom in Trinidad, and, in order to verify some accounts, which I have heard doubted, I ascertained the hour on my watch by its light alone with the utmost facility.

COLERIDGE: *Six Months in the West Indies, in 1825.*

For stinging, the bottle fly of Honduras impressed Henry Fowler above all others.

I had often heard of the flies in this part of the world, and a portion being called the Mosquito Coast, I was prepared to meet considerable inconvenience from insects. In the Cascade range of the Rocky Mountains I have been driven off a glacier by mosquitos and horse flies, apparently improbable, but nevertheless a fact, but they will not compare with the effect the bottle flies produce here; or as the creoles call them—the bottlass. They are a small black fly, the shape of a bottle; their bite is most venomous, and leaves a black mark which is only obliterated when the poisoned skin peels off. During flood times they flourish most, and people living in their midst are obliged to shut themselves up in their houses, and stop every aperture to keep the flies out. The peculiarity about them is, they don't care for dark places, and after sun-down not one is to be seen. They punished us all very severely. This pest, with the other discomforts and exposure, caused every one to become more or less sick during the journey, and even the dog I had to pack on the horse the last day, whilst I walked, to save his life.

FOWLER:
A Journey Across the Unexplored Portion of British Honduras. 1879.

★

The most striking of all the butterflies are the huge Morphos, the large wings of which are entirely blue, and so gorgeous, brilliant, and shining, that the insect as it comes flaunting lazily down through the dark alleys between the tree-trunks, seems even from a considerable distance like a flash of blue light. They generally fly high, at the tops of the trees; but for a short time every morning, apparently when the sun is at a particular point in the horizon, they come down into the openings made in the forest by a fall of trees, and there flaunt—I use the word purposely—lazily in and out between the sunshine and the shade. They are so large that, as they passed high over such openings, I have tracked their movements, as I sat below, by the shadows they cast on the ground.

IM THURN: *Among the Indians of Guiana.* 1883.

★

One of the most curious sights I ever saw in the colony was a flight of butterflies which passed my house in Suddie. They were the common white and yellow kind, but a column of them, which darkened the sky in its flight, was passing my house for two days without intermission. The insects were flying swiftly, and were not more than two yards apart. The stream was more than a mile wide, for I walked for that distance across them, and how high they reached of course I could not tell. Whether they flew at night I cannot say. It would be impossible to calculate their numbers, and whence they came and whither they were going was equally unknown. The Indians say such flights are a sign of coming droughts.

KIRKE: *Twenty-five Years in British Guiana.* 1898.

★

We sawe birds of all colours, some carnation, some crimson, orenge tawny, purple, greene, watched, and of all other sorts both simple and mixt, as it was unto us a great good passing of the time to beholde them, besides the reliefe we found by killing some store of them with our fouling peeces, without which, having little or no bread and lesse drink, but onely the thick and troubled water of the riuer, we had been in a very hard case.

RALEIGH:
The Discoverie of the Large, Rich and Bewtiful Empire of Guiana. 1595.

★

An almost infinite variety of the Parrot kind can also be found. The greater part of the latter are quickly domesticated, and if taken young, are as suddenly taught to talk fluently. The kinds which are most esteemed for their aptness in this respect are the yellow, and the blue-headed. The former of which is extremely numerous in the country of the Mosquito Indians, and on the contiguous island of Ruatan. The confused, clamorous noise of these birds, may be heard from the last place some miles before the shore is gained. The smaller sorts, or Parakeets, are equally abundant, and many of them are extremely pretty.

HENDERSON: *An Account of the British Settlement of Honduras.* 1809.

★

The humming-bird, the most beautiful as well as the most small of the feathery tribe, is frequently heard to beat with a continual and drony murmur its little wings; is now observed to dart its slender bill into, and to extract with momentary taste, the blossoms of the orange

BARBADOS LANDSCAPE,
PARISH OF ST. JOSEPH

BATHSHEBA, BARBADOS

or the lime; or to hang suspended, and for a time stationary, in the air, to steal the odours from the logwood fences that happen to be in bloom; or is now seen to flit by like lightning, and to return again with drowsy hum, for a fresh supply of rifled sweets; while its various and splendid plumes, that glow with blue, with green, with purple, and with gold, afford a never-ceasing alternation of the most rich and vivid dies.

BECKFORD: *A Descriptive Account of the Island of Jamaica.* 1740.

*

Amuse my dear children, by shewing them a little Humming-bird's nest, the progress of which I have been watching for several days past. The little mother is scarcely larger than a bee, and her nest is like a very tiny tea cup. It is placed under the leaf of a tree, which shelters it like a roof, and keeps even the dew from her young. The nest has a small branch running through it, as a security, and contained two little eggs, which are now hatched. The young birds are really not larger than what we call in England horse-flies, and are indeed the most ridiculous things. We were much amused, in seeing the little mother taking such care of them; and it was with difficulty I could get George and Louisa to allow themselves to be carried into the house again, they were so delighted with the sight.

MARIA, LADY NUGENT:
A Journal of a Voyage to, and Residence in, the Island of Jamaica, from 1801 to 1805.

Daniel McKinnen delighted in the flamingoes of the Bahamas.

For several successive mornings I observed an extended flock of Flamingoes, from an eminence, feeding with their heads under water in the shoal part of a distant bay; but so great was their watchfulness and timidity, that it was impossible to approach them. Their colour at a remote view appears of a lively pink. The young birds, when taken, are found to be nearly white; and the feathers on the pinions and on the necks of the old ones are of a deep scarlet. The quill feathers of some of the birds I found tipt with black. As I saw them at a con-siderable distance, their glowing plumage, contrasted with the green surface of the water, was extremely beautiful.

MCKINNEN: *A Tour through the British West Indies.* 1803.

*

Very early one morning I had taken my gun and wandered into the forest, and having about dawn reached a clearing evidently made by fire, which seemed likely to be visited by birds, I sat down on a fallen tree near the centre to wait. For some fifty yards on every side of me there was a dreary waste of fallen and half-burned trees, some blackened, others whitened by exposure to the weather; the soil was covered with ash, and only a rank herb grew here and there. At the outskirts of the clearing some trees, burned and dead, yet stood erect; a little further off the trees were only scorched, and beyond that again was the dense, living forest. Not a sound was yet heard. As the sun rose the little weird field of white in which I sat literally glowed with light and heat. Presently, almost at my feet, something moved, and then a black vulture rose slowly from the ground, leaving two eggs exposed, and flew to one of the dead standing trees. While I watched this bird there was a slight sound behind me, and, turning, I saw another vulture standing on another burned tree on the other side of me. Once more, and again and again, this happened. Surprised at the presence of these living things where all had seemed to me strangely lifeless, I began to count the birds; and I had to count quicker and quicker, for every moment a new vulture woke and attracted my attention by stretching its wings to dry them in the morning sun, in which position it remained awhile motionless. The only sound was the slight rustle caused by this wing-stretching. At last I found myself the centre of a circle of thirty-seven vultures, each with outstretched wings, standing motionless on a gaunt, fire-blackened, sun-whitened tree, and all gazing curiously at me.

IM THURN: *Among the Indians of Guiana.* 1883.

At night in the Guiana forest one becomes acutely conscious of the sounds of birds and beasts.

By the time the camp was ready the daylight had faded, and our fires alone threw round a circle of flickering light, contrasting strangely with the darkness of the surrounding forest. Where the firelight was strongest the Indians lay, smoking and talking in their hammocks, close to each of which was a fire, which occasionally flared up and seemed to lick the naked skins of the Indians through the meshes of the hammock. Not content with this, the Indians sometimes made the boys take lighted palm-leaves and singe them as they lay in their hammocks, this strange proceeding being intended to destroy savage insects.

One by one the Indians fell asleep. Various kinds of frogs kept up an almost deafening concert of marvellously varied croaks, some musical, some most unmusical. One imitated the beat of paddles striking in regular time against the sides of a canoe after the Indian custom; and the likeness was the more deceitful because the sound alternately rose and fell gradually as though a canoe came up the river, passed the camp, and was then paddled up the stream out of ear-reach. Often and often I have lain long in doubt whether the sound heard was caused by paddles or by frogs. And while the frogs croaked, every now and then a night-jar flitted swiftly and most silently by, and then suddenly shrieked out its loud cry of "Work-work-work-to-hell." Or another and larger species began to moan out the four notes of its most hideous and depressing cry of "Who-who-who-who", each note sounded in rapid succession, the first shrill and high-pitched, each of the succeeding ones lower, and the last an almost inaudible moan. It is only comparable to the cry of a despairing and dying human being. At times was heard the noise—something between a snort and a bellow—of a cayman; and at other times mysterious sounds, resembling the crack of pistol-shots, which I afterwards found were caused by caymans raising their tails into the air and bringing them down sharply on the surface of the water.

Toward morning the loudest and most appalling noise of all broke out. Beginning suddenly in a deep roar, it became louder and louder, till the whole forest rang with the din. It is hardly possible on first hearing this to believe that the terrific roar is produced only by the somewhat small red howling monkey (*Mycetes seniculus*), called baboon in the colony.

Before daylight the Indians were out of their hammocks, making preparation for the coming day's journey. A plunge into the river was the first thing. In the early morning the temperature near the river is comparatively low; though the thermometer stands perhaps at 70°, the air feels as chilly as on an autumn day in England, and the water, having retained much of the warmth imparted by the sun of the previous day, seems by contrast like that of a warm bath.

And now the sound and sights of the day began. Some toucans, perched on the very highest boughs of a tall tree, were revelling in the morning sun, and greeting it with their usual yelping cries. Emphasis is given to each puppy-like yelp by an odd and comical antic; the head is jerked down, the tail lifted almost at right angles to the body. In the distance an Indian canoe appeared from behind a bend in the river. The naked skins of the Indians in it literally flashed red in the intense light. A scarlet ibis (*Ibis rubra*)—the only one, by the way, that I ever saw so high up on this river—flew by and settled upon a tree between us and the approaching canoe; but it hardly looked more red than did the Indians. Flights of parrots, crying shrilly, began to pass over the river to their feeding grounds, flying so high that their colours were not to be discerned. From the forest the "pi-pi-yo", or greenheart bird (*Lipangus cineraceus*), began incessantly to cry its own Indian name; this is, if not the commonest, yet certainly the most noticed bird in the forests of Guiana, for its shrill cry, heard nearly all day long, is the most characteristic sound of these forests.

IM THURN: *Among the Indians of Guiana.* 1883.

★

The queen of all the pets is a black and grey spider monkey from Guiana—consisting of a tail which has developed, at one end, a body about twice as big as a hare's; four arms (call them not legs), of which the front ones have no thumbs, nor rudiments of thumbs; and a head of black hair, brushed forward over the foolish, kindly, greedy, sad face, with its wide, suspicious, beseeching eyes, and mouth which, as in all these American monkeys, as far as we have seen, can have no expression, not even that of sensuality, because it has no lips. Others have described the spider monkey as four legs and a tail, tied in a knot in the middle; but the tail is, without doubt, the most important of the five limbs. Wherever the monkey goes, whatever she does, the tail is the standing-point, or rather hanging-point. It takes one turn at least round something or other, provisionally, and in case it should be wanted; often, as she swings, every other limb hangs in the most ridiculous repose, and the tail alone supports. Sometimes it carries, by way of ornament, a bunch of flowers or a live kitten. Sometimes it is curled round the neck, or carried over the head in the hands, out of harm's way; or when she comes silently up behind you, puts her cold hand in yours, and walks by your side like a child, she steadies herself by taking a half-turn of her tail round your wrist. . . . Her creed is, that yellow bananas are the summum bonum; and that she must not come into the dining-room, or even into the verandah; whither, nevertheless, she slips, in fear and trembling, every morning, to steal the little green parrot's breakfast out of his cage, or the baby's milk, or fruit off the side-board; in which case she makes her appearance suddenly and silently, sitting on the threshold like a distorted fiend; and begins scratching herself, looking at everything except the fruit, and pretending total absence of mind, till the proper moment comes for unwinding her lengthy ugliness, and making a snatch at the table. Poor weak-headed thing, full of foolish cunning; always doing wrong, and knowing that it is wrong, but quite unable to resist temptation; and then profuse in futile explanations, gesticulations, mouthings of an "Oh!—oh!—oh!" so pitiably human, that you can only punish her by laughing at her, which she does not at all like. . . . Her friends are, every human being who will take notice of her, and a beautiful little Guazupita, or native deer, a little larger than a roe, with great black melting eyes, and a heart as soft as its eyes, who comes to lick one's hand; believes in bananas as firmly as the monkey; and when she can get no hand to lick, licks the hairy monkey for merely love's sake, and lets it ride on her back, and kicks it off, and let's it get on again and take a half-turn of its tail round her neck, and throttle her with its arms, and pull her nose out of the way when a banana is coming; and all out of pure love; for the two have never been introduced to each other by man.

KINGSLEY: *At Last: A Christmas in the West Indies.* 1871.

The vampire, the iguana, and the tapir are among the Caribbean's curiosities.

Then we inspected a Coolie's great toe, which had been severely bitten by a vampire in the night. And here let me say, that the popular disbelief of vampire stories is only owing to English ignorance, and disinclination to believe any of the many quaint things which John Bull has not seen, because he does not care to see them. If he comes to these parts, he must be careful not to leave his feet or hands out of bed without mosquito curtains; if he has good horses, he ought not to leave them exposed at night without wire-gauze round the stable-shed—a plan which, to my surprise I never saw used in the West Indies. Otherwise, he will be but too likely to find in the morning a triangular bit cut out of his own flesh, or even worse, out of his horse's withers or throat, where twisting and lashing cannot shake the tormentor off; and must be content to have himself lamed, or his horses weakened to staggering and thrown out of collar-work for a week, as I have seen happen more than once or twice. The only method of keeping off the vampire yet employed in stables is light; and a lamp is usually kept burning there. But the Negro—not the most careful of men—is apt not to fill and trim it; and if it goes out in the small hours, the horses are pretty sure to be sucked, if there is a forest near. So numerous and troublesome, indeed, are the vampires, that there are pastures in Trinidad in which, at least till the adjoining woods are cleared, the cattle would not fatten, or even thrive; being found, morning after morning, weak and sick from the bleedings which they had endured at night.

KINGSLEY: At Last: A Christmas in the West Indies. 1871.

★

But of all the animals which may occasionally be discovered in this country, the most extraordinary is unquestionably the Tapir; or as it is here vulgarly, and certainly with no great accuracy, named, the Mountain Cow. This animal is an inhabitant of the thickest and most retired woods in the neighbourhood of rivers and creeks. It is described as being about the size of a small cow, and is gregarious. It swims, dives, and is considered to possess the property of walking beneath the water. It may frequently be traced on the sands by the large, flat, and nearly round impression of its feet. As this animal cautiously avoids the day, it is but rarely met with. Sometimes, however, as the traveller pursues his course up the distant rivers, and when but little noise is made, it is surprised on the banks and shot. The meat of the Tapir, contrary to what has been pronounced of it, is in this country considered exceedingly coarse and rank.

HENDERSON: An Account of the British Settlement of Honduras. 1809.

The iguana is repulsive but edible.

They make excellent pepper-pot, and their eggs are delicious. The negroes had caught them on the trees with a long stick and hair noose at the end of it. They whistle, fix their eye upon them, and approach them cautiously; the guana is fascinated, allows itself to be tickled with the end of the stick, the noose is slipped over the neck, and it is thus dexterously fished from the trees.

ALEXANDER: Transatlantic Sketches. 1833.

In and around the water are many weird and repulsive creatures.

The nervous bather remembers that from the moment when he throws off his clothes, every part of his body not covered by water is exposed to the attack of mosquitoes, sandflies, and many other sharply stinging insects; but, on the other hand, that every part of his body covered by water may at any moment be bitten by perai, may receive a violent shock from an electric eel, or may be horribly lacerated by the poisoned spine of a sting-ray, or a limb may be snapped off by a passing cayman or alligator, or his whole body may be crushed, and thus prepared for swallowing by a huge water serpent; or, even if none of these pains come upon him, he may remember that the egg of a certain worm, of which I shall presently have to speak, may be deposited unnoticed on his flesh, there to develop and become exceedingly painful. Now all these dangers are real enough, and any one of them may make itself felt at any moment. But on the other hand, of all the men who trust themselves in these waters day after day, and many times a day, for years together, not ten per cent. have ever felt even any of the smaller evils which had been described, except perhaps the bites of mosquitoes or sandflies; and not one in a thousand has suffered any serious or permanent harm. While therefore the nervous man feels all the pain of anticipation of evils, neither he nor the less timid man as a rule feel the actual evil.

IM THURN: *Among the Indians of Guiana.* 1883.

★

We waded stream after stream under the bamboo clumps, and in one of them we saw swimming a green rigoise, or whip-snake, which must have been nearly ten feet long. It swam with its head and the first two feet of its body curved aloft like a swan, while the rest of the body lay along the surface of the water in many curves—a most graceful object as it glided away into dark shadow along an oily pool.

KINGSLEY: *At Last: A Christmas in the West Indies.* 1871.

★

The Caymanes are ordinarily busied in hunting and catching of flies; which they eagerly devour. The occasion is, because close unto their skin, they have certain little scales, which smell with a sweet sent, something like unto Musk. This aromatick odour is coveted by the flies, and here they come to repose themselves and sting. Thus they both persecute each other continually, with an incredible hatred, and antipathy. Their manner of procreating, and hatching their young ones, is as follows. They approach the sandy banks of some River, that lies exposed to the rays of the South Sun. Among these Sands they lay their eggs, which afterwards, they cover with their feet: And here they find them hatcht, and with young generation, by the only heat of the Sun. These as soon as they are out of the shell, by natural instinct, run unto the water. Many times those eggs are destroyed by Birds, that find them out, as they scrape among the Sands. Hereupon, the Femals of the Caymanes, at such times, as they fear the coming of any flocks of Birds, do oftimes, by night, swallow these their eggs, and

keep them in their stomach,till the danger is over. And from time to
time, they bury them again in the Sand, as I have told you bringing
them forth again out of their belly, till the season is come, of being
excluded the Shell. At this time, if the Mother be nigh at hand, they
run unto her and play with her as little Whelps would do with their
Dams, sporting themselves according to their own custom. In this
sort of sport, they will oftentimes run in and out of their Mother's
belly, even as Rabbets into their holes. This I have seen them do many
times, as I have spyed them at play, with their Dam, over the water,
upon the contrary banks of some River. At which time, I have often
disturbed their sport by throwing a Stone that way, causing them on a
suddain to creep into the Mothers Bowels, for fear of some imminent
danger.

ESQUEMELING: *Bucaniers of America.* 1684.

*

   We directed our Course for a Place, called Boca del Dragon, there
to make Provisions of Flesh. Especially of a certain Animal, which the
Spaniards call Menentines, and the Dutch, Sea-Cows, because the
Head, Nose, and Teeth, of this Beast, are very like unto those of a
Cow. They are found commonly in such places, as under the depth of
the Waters, are very full of Grass, on which, it is thought, they do
pasture. These Animals have no Ears, and only in place of them are to
be seen two little Holes, scarce capable of receiving the little Finger of
a Man. Nigh unto the Neck, they have two Wings, under which are
seated two Udders, or Breasts, much like unto the Breasts of a Woman.
The Skin is very close, and united together, resembling the skin of a
Barbary, or Guiney-Dog. This Skin upon the back is of the thickness
of two Fingers, which being dryed, is as hard as any Whale-bone, and
may serve to make Walking-staffs withal. The Belly is in all things
like unto that of a Cow, as far as the Kidneys, or Reins. Their manner
of Engendring likewise, is the same with the usual manner of a Land-
Cow, the Male of this kind being in similitude, almost one and the
same thing with a Bull. Yet notwithstanding they conceive and breed
but once. But the space of time that they go with Calf, I could not as
yet learn. These Fishes have the sense of Hearing extreamly acute, in
so much as in taking them, the Fishermen ought not to make the least
noise, nor row, unless it be very slightly. For this reason they make use
of certain Instruments for Rowing, which the Indians call Pagayos,
and the Spaniards name Caneletas, with which although they row, yet
is it performed without any noise that can frig..t the Fish. Meanwhile
they are busied in this Fishery, they use not to speak to one another, but

all is transacted by Signs. He that darteth them with the Javelin, useth it after the same manner as when they kill Tortoises. Howbeit, the point of the said Javelin is somewhat different, as having two Hooks at the Extremity, and these longer than that of the other Fishery. Of these Fishes, some are found to be of the length of 20, unto 24 Foot. Their Flesh is very good to eat, being very like in Colour unto that of a Land-Cow, but in Taste, unto that of Pork. It containeth much Fat, or Grease, the which the Pirats use to melt, and keep in earthen Pots, to make use thereof instead of Oyl.

ESQUEMELING: *Bucaniers of America.* 1684.

Guiana is the home of giant anaconda.

A friend of mine, living in a somewhat remote place surrounded by forest, was somewhat particular about having his morning coffee brought to him just at dawn. His cook, when she went in the dark into the shed which served as a kitchen, was in the habit of striking the match to light the fire on a particular corner post; but one morning she was surprised to find that one match after another broke instead of catching fire. At last she struck a light in a new place, and having done so, she found to her great horror that a thirty feet long camoodi was coiled round the corner post, and on this she had been rubbing her matches.

IM THURN: *Among the Indians of Guiana.* 1883.

Turtles are common.

These Creatures have certain customary places, whither they repair every year, to lay their eggs. The chiefest of these places, are the three Islands called Caymanes, situated in the altitude of twenty degrees, and fifteen minutes, Northern latitude; being at the distance of five and forty leagues, from the Isle of Cuba, on the Northern side thereof. It is a thing much deserving consideration, how the Tortoises can find out these Islands. For the greatest part of them come from the Gulf of Honduras; distant from thence, the whole space of one hundred and fifty leagues. Certain it is, that many times the ships having lost their altitude, through the darkness of the weather, have steered their course only by the noise of the Tortoises, swimming that way, and have arrived unto those Isles. When their season of hatching is past, they retire towards the Island of Cuba; where be many good places that afford them food. But the mean while they are at the Islands of Caymanes, they eat very little or nothing. When they have been about the space of one month in the Seas of Cuba, and are grown fat, the

Spaniards go out to fish for them; they being then to be taken in such abundance, that they provide with them sufficiently, their Cities, Towns and Villages.

ESQUEMELING: *Bucaniers of America.*   1684.

The following "exquisitely picturesque" directions for slaughtering a turtle are quoted from a book by an early French traveller.

When you are to kill one of these fishes, the manner is to lay him on his back on a table, and when he sees you come with a knife in your hand to kill him, he vapours out the grievousest sighes that ever you heard any creature make, and sheds as large tears as a stag, that has a far greater body and larger eyes. He has a joynt or crevis about an inch within the utmost edge of his shell, which goes round about his body from his head to his tail, on his belly side; into which joynt or crevis, you put your knife, beginning at the head, and so rip up that side, and then do as much to the other; then lifting up his belly, which we call his callipee, we lay open all his bowels, and taking them out, come next to his heart, which has three distinct poynts, but all meet above where the fat is; and if you take it out, and lay it in a dish, it will stir and pant ten hours after the fish is dead. Sure, there is no creature on earth, nor in the seas, that enjoyes life with so much sweetness and delight as this poor fish the turtle; nor none more delicate in taste, and more nourishing than he.

The West India Sketch Book.   1834.

5. ARAWAKS, CARIBS AND OTHERS

The gentle and timid Arawaks inhabited most of the northern islands when Columbus first touched at the Bahamas.

On the first arrival of the Spaniards this unsuspecting but devoted people were never satisfied with looking at them: they knelt down, lifted up their hands and gave thanks to God, inviting one another to admire the heavenly men. Twenty years, however, had scarcely elapsed, before these heavenly men found it convenient to transport them, by force or artifice, to dig in the mines of Hispaniola; a measure to which the court of Spain was tempted to give its assent by the plausible suggestion that it would be the most effectual mode of civilizing and instructing them in the christian religion. Upon this pretence 40,000 souls (probably the whole population of the islands) were transported to Hispaniola.

MCKINNEN: *A Tour through the British West Indies.* 1803.

The Spaniards found the Caribs of the southern islands a very different proposition and waged a merciless war against them.

The Spaniards, finding themselves to be cruelly hated by those Indians, and no where secure from their treachery's, resolved to extirpate, and ruine them every one. Especially seeing they could neither tame them by the civilities of their customs, nor conquer them with the Sword. But the Indians, it being their ancient custom to make their Woods their chiefest places of defence, at present made these their refuge, whenever they fled from the Spaniards that pursued them. Hereupon, those first Conquerors of the new World, made use of dogs, to range and search the intricatest thickets of Woods and Forests for those their implacable, and unconquerable Enemies. By these means, they forced them, to leave their ancient refuge, and submit unto the Sword, seeing no milder usage would serve turn. Hereupon they killed some of them, and quartering their bodies, placed them in the highways; to the intent, that others might take warning from such a punishment, not to incur the like danger. But this severity proved to be of ill consequence. For instead of frighting them and reducing their mindes to a civil society, they conceived such horrour of the Spaniards, and their proceedings, that they resolved, to detest and fly their sight, for ever. And hence the greatest part dyed in Caves, and subterraneous places, of the Woods and Mountains. In which places, I myself have seen many times, great numbers of human bones.

ESQUEMELING: *Bucaniers of America.* . 1684.

The Caribs survived to give English and French settlers many unpleasant ordeals but by the end of last century only isolated communities remained. In St. Vincent nearly all the remaining Caribs were killed in the Soufrière eruption of 1902. *H. N. Coleridge visited a mission for Indians in Trinidad.*

A projection of the roof in front is supported by posts, and forms a shady gallery, under which the Indians will sit for hours together in motionless silence. They seem to be the identical race of peoples whose forefathers Columbus discovered, and the Spaniards worked to death in Hispaniola. They are short in stature (none that I saw exceeding five feet and six inches), yellow in complexion, their eyes dark, their hair long, lank and glossy as a raven's wing; they have a remarkable space between the nostrils and the upper lip, and a breadth and massiveness between the shoulders that would do credit to the Farnese Hercules. Their hands and feet however are small-boned and delicately shaped. Nothing seems to affect them like other men; nether joy or sorrow, anger, or curiosity, take any hold of them. Both mind and body are drenched in the deepest apathy; the children lie quietly on their mothers' bosoms; silence is in their dwellings and idlesse in all their ways.

COLERIDGE: *Six Months in the West Indies, in* 1825.

On the mainland, both in Honduras and Guiana, the Indians have survived as a significant element in the population. In the seventeenth century the Buccaneers found the Mosquito Indians of Honduras excellent allies, and it is recorded that few of the pirates' ships did not have a fewMosquito Indians on board. Even, it is said, the Indians accompanied the English into Australasian waters, where their skill as turtle fishers proved of great value. In 1809 *Captain Henderson wrote that among the Mosquito Indians, "A tradition has long prevailed that the grey-eyed people, meaning the English, have been particularly appointed to protect them from oppression and bondage".*

They are tall in stature, and very nimble in running, which they perform almost as fast as horses. At diving also in the Sea, they are very dexterous and hardy. From the bottom of the Sea I saw them take up an Anchor that weighed six hundred pound, by tying a Cable unto it with great dexterity, and pulling it from a Rock. They use no other Arms than such as are made of Wood, without any Iron, unless that some instead thereof do fix a Crocodiles tooth, which serveth for a point.

ESQUEMELING: Bucaniers of America. 1684.

★

Every one of those Barbarian had, and hath still, a God to himself, whom he serveth and worshippeth. It is a thing that deserveth all admiration, to consider how they use in this particular a Child that is newly born into the world. As soon as this is issued from the Womb of the Mother, they carry it unto the Temple. Here they make a circle or hole, which they fill with ashes, without mingling any thing else with them. Upon this heap of ashes they place the Child naked, leaving it there a whole night alone, not without great danger; no body daring to come neer it. In the mean while the Temple is open on all sides, to the intent all sorts of Beasts may freely come in and out. The next day the Father and Relations of the Infant return thither, to see if the tract or step of any Animal appeareth to be printed in the ashes. Not finding any, they leave the Child there, until that some Beast hath approached the Infant, and left behind him the mark of his feet. Unto this Animal, whatsoever it be, they consecrate the Creature newly born, as unto its God; which he is bound to worship and serve all his life, esteeming the said Beast as his Patron and Protector in all cases of danger or necessity. They offer unto their Gods Sacrifices of Fire, wherein they burn a certain Gum called by them Copal; whose smoak affordeth a very delicious smell. When the Infant is grown up, the Parents thereof tell him and shew him whom he ought to worship, serve, and honour, as his own proper God. This being known, he goeth unto the Temple, where he maketh Offerings unto the said Beast. Afterwards, if in the course of his life any one hath injured him, or any evil happeneth unto him, he complaineth thereof unto that Beast, and sacrificeth unto it for revenge. From whence many times cometh, that those who have done the injury of which he complaineth, are found to be bitten, killed, or otherwise hurt by such Animals.

Ibid.

In Guiana, as in Honduras, English and Indians were good friends from the earliest days, finding a common cause in enmity for the Spanish. Raleigh reported that he had never beheld "a more goodlie or better favoured people, or a more manlie". Not least was he impressed by the comeliness of the women; of one chief's wife he writes:

She was of good stature, with blacke eies, fat of body, of an excellent countenance, hir haire almost as long as hir selfe, tied up againe in pretie knots, and it seemed she stood not in that aw of hir husband, as the rest, for she spake and discourst, and dranke among the gentlemen and captaines, and was very pleasant, knowing hir owne comelines, and taking great pride therein. I haue seene a Lady in England so like hir, as but for the difference of colour I would haue sworne might haue beene the same.

RALEIGH:

The Discoverie of the Large, Rich and Bewtiful Empire of Guiana. 1595.

Raleigh treated the Indians well and was treated well in return.

I suffred not anie man to take from anie of the nations so much as a Pina, or a Potato roote, without giuing them contentment, nor any man so much as to offer to touche any of their wiues or daughters: which course, so contrarie to the Spaniards (who tyrannize ouer them in all things) drew them to admire hir Maiestie, whose commandement I told them it was, and also woonderfully to honour our nation. But I confesse it was a very impatient worke to keepe the meaner sort from spoile and stealing, when we came to their houses, which bicause in all I could not preuent, I caused my Indian interpreter at euery place when we departed, to know of the losse or wrong done, and if ought were stolen or taken by violence, either the same was restored, and the party punished in their sight, or els it was paid for to their uttermost demand.

Ibid.

Though their weapons were primitive, the Guiana Indians were not to be despised as enemies. When hit by a poisoned arrow a man usually died—and died unpleasantly.

There was nothing whereof I was more curious, than to finde out the true remedies of these poisoned arrowes, for besides the mortalitie of the wound they make, the partie shot indureth the most insufferable torment in the world, and abideth a most uglie and lamentable death, sometimes dying starke mad, sometimes their bowels breaking out of their bellies, and are presently discoloured, as blacke as pitch, and so unsauery, as no man can endure to cure, or to attend them: And it is more strange to know, that in all this time there was neuer Spaniard, either by gift or torment that could attaine to the true knowledge of the cure, although they haue martyred and put to inuented torture I know not how many of them. But euery one of these Indians know it not, no not one among thousands, but their southsaiers and priests, who do conceale it, and onely teach it but from the father to the sonne. . . .

Some of the Spaniards haue been cured in ordinary wounds, of the common poisoned arrowes with the iuice of garlike: but this is a generall rule for all men that shall heerafter trauell the Indies where poisoned arrowes are used, that they must abstaine from drinke, for if they take any licor into their body, as they shall be maruellously prouoked thereunto by drought, I say, if they drink before the wound be dressed, or soone upon it, there is no way with them but present death.

Ibid.

Nearly 300 years later, Sir James Alexander gave this description of an Indian settlement in British Guiana.

The logies were open all round, and thatched with the leaves of the trooly palm, some of them twenty-four feet long. Suspended from the bamboo timbers of the roof were grass hammocks: in these the men were lazily swinging; one or two of those who were awake were fashioning arrow heads out of the cockarito palm. The men and children were entirely naked, with the exception of the blue lap or cloth for the loins, the lap of the former ending in a fringed tail, and bands of beads were round the wrists and ankles of the latter. The young women in their blue petticoats, braided hair, hands stained with the seed of the arnotto, like the rosy-fingered and gazelle-eyed beauties of Persia, were scraping the roots of the bitter or poisonous sassava tree into a trough of bark; it was then put into a long press of matting, which expressed the poisonous juice; the dry farina was afterwards baked on an iron plate, and the juice converted by boiling into cassereep for the savoury pepperpot.

The old women were weaving the square coeoo, or lap of beads, which they wear sometimes without a petticoat, also armlets and ankle ornaments of beads, the wampum of the North-American Indians. Some were fabricating clay pots, and all the females seemed actively employed. Parrots and saccawinkee monkeys were on the rafters, and little sharp-nosed dogs and spotted fly-catchers were below. I was attracted by the arms scattered about the logies—the short and heavy war-clubs, a rifle or two, bows and arrows, with many barbs for shooting fish, and with blunted heads for stunning birds, and above all the blow-pipe made of a straight reed sixteen feet long, by means of which the miniature arrows dipped in Wourali poison, and ending in cotton balls, are projected with deadly aim to the distance of three hundred feet.

The Indians stared at us without speaking, and we sat down in empty hammocks and commenced swinging like the rest. I caught up a red boy, a chubby-faced firm little rogue of a year and a half old, and tickled him till he screamed with laughing; his mother, who was pounding maize in a wooden mortar, ceased from her labour, and courteously offered us casseree in a gourd—a crimson liquor made from the sweet potato; of this I partook, and found it to taste like cider: however, I politely declined the pywarree. This intoxicating beverage is like thick rice-water, and is prepared by the sweet mouths of the Indian fair, old and young: they chew the cassava flower, spit it into a wooden trough, or sometimes a small canoe, add water, the liquor ferments, and at the pywarree feasts the men sit round the vessel, and the entertainers and their guests roll in the sand, drunk for two or three days together: their tender helpmates look after them, and keep them from being suffocated with the sand getting into their mouths. But pywarree is a harmless liquor, that is to say, it does not produce the disease and baneful effects of spirits; for after a sleep the Indians rise fresh and well, and only occasionally indulge in a debauch of this kind.

ALEXANDER: *Transatlantic Sketches.*   1833.

Sir Everard im Thurn records this Carib legend.

The Caribs say that when they first arrived on earth from skyland, cassava, plantains, and all useful vegetables grew on one huge tree. This tree was first discovered by a tapir, who grew fat on the fruit which fell from its branches. The Caribs, who as yet had found the new land a poor place and without food, were eager to find where the tapir fed. So they set the woodpecker to watch him. But the woodpecker as he flew through the forest after the tapir could not resist the temptation to tap the trees for insects, and the tapir, hearing the noise, knew he was followed, and went another way. Then the Caribs sent a rat, who stealthily succeeded in tracing the tapir to his food-tree; but the rat, having agreed with the tapir quietly to share the food, persuaded the Caribs that he too had failed in the quest. But the Caribs, finding the rat asleep one day with corn still in his mouth, woke him and compelled him to show the tree. Then the Caribs took their stone axes, and after many months' hard work, succeeded in felling it. Each man took pieces of the tree and planted them in a field of his own; so from that day each Indian has had his own cassava-field.

The story does not end here. When the tree was felled a flood began to flow from the stump and could be checked only by placing an inverted basket over the spring.

For some time the water was confined under the basket. But at last the brown monkey, curious, and suspecting that something very good must be hidden under the carefully tended basket, cautiously raised it and peeped under. In an instant the flood rushed out, carrying away the monkey, and overflowing the whole land. Then the man, with all manner of animals, took refuge up in a tall kokerite palm. Most of the fugitives remained patiently during the flood, but the red howling-monkey, getting excited, began to roar, and roared so loudly that his throat swelled, and has remained distended ever since. That is the reason of the curious bony drum in the throat of this animal. Meanwhile the man at intervals let single palm-seeds fall into the water, to judge by the splash of its depth. At last the flood seemed to have subsided, and all prepared to descend. But the trumpet-bird flew down in such a hurry that he alighted in an ants' nest, and the hungry insects fastened on his legs, which had before been fairly thick, and gnawed them down to their present spindle-like size. The others having descended more cautiously and safely, the man began to rub two pieces of wood to make fire. Now the first spark generated in this way is very small. The bush-turkey, at a moment when the man was looking away, swallowed this spark, mistaking it for a fire-fly, and then flew quickly away. The spark burned the bush-turkey's throat, and that is the reason why to this day those birds have a red wattle on their throats. Meanwhile, the man missing his spark, saw the alligator, who was then a gentle brute, but ugly, standing near. Immediately the other animals, agreeing in their abhorrence of the ugliness of the alligator, raised a shout that it was he who had taken the spark. Whereupon the man, angry and impatient, tore out the tongue of the supposed culprit. And this is the reason why alligators have ever since had such very rudimentary tongues, and also why they wage perpetual war on other beasts.

IM THURN: *Among the Indians of Guiana.* 1883.

6. THE BUCCANEERS

Prince of the Buccaneers was Sir Henry Morgan who organised his ex-peditions with due form and ceremony—and later evaded such obligations as he could.

He called all his Captains, and other Officers togerher, and caused them to sign some Articles of common Agreement betwixt them, and in the Name of all. Herein it was stipulated, that he should have the hundredth part of all that was gotten, to himself alone: That every Captain should draw the Shares of 8 Men, for the Expences of his Ship, besides his own: That the Surgeon, beside his ordinary Pay, should have 200 pieces of Eight, for his Chest of Medicaments: And every Carpenter, above his common Salary, should draw 100 pieces of Eight. As to Recompences and Rewards, they were regulated in this Voyage much higher than was expressed in the first part of this Book. Thus, for the loss of both Legs, they assigned 1500 pieces of Eight, or 15 Slaves, the Choice being left to the election of the Party. For the loss of both hands, 1800 pieces of Eight, or 18 Slaves. For one Leg, whether the right or the left, 600 pieces of Eight, or 6 Slaves. For a Hand, as much as for a Leg. And for the loss of any Eye, 100 pieces of Eight, or one Slave. Lastly, Unto him that in any Battel should sig-nalize himself, either by entring the first any Castle, or taking down the Spanish Colours, and setting up the English, they constituted 50 pieces of Eight for a Reward. In the head of these Articles it was stipulated, that all these extraordinary Salaries, Recompences and Rewards, should be paid out of the first spoil or Purchase they should take, according as every one should then occur to be either rewarded or paid.

ESQUEMELING: Bucaniers of America. 1684.

Buccaneering descents on the Spanish Main had a fairly uniform design. First came the assault executed with a maximum of surprise. Then the city was looted. Next the inhabitants were tortured to reveal the hiding place of their private treasures. Finally, a ransom was demanded as the price of not razing the city. The account which follows is of a characteristic exploit. It tells of Sir Henry Morgan's capture of Puerto Velo in Costa Rica. "It is judged," says Esquemeling, "to be the strongest place that the King of Spain possesseth in all the West Indies, excepting two, that is to say Havana and Cartagena. Here are two castles, almost inexpugnable, that defendeth the

City, being situated at the entry of the Port; so that no Ship nor Boat can pass without permission." Morgan's solution was to land at a convenient spot 10 leagues away and then march overland.

They had in their company a certain Englishman, who had been formerly a Prisoner in those parts, and who now served them for a Guide. Unto him and three or four more, they gave commission to take the Centry, if possible, or kill him upon the place. But they laid hands on him and apprehended him with such cunning, as he had no time to give warning with his Musket, or make any other noise. Thus they brought him, with his hands bound, unto Captain Morgan, who asked him, How things went in the City, and what Forces they had: with many other circumstances, which he was desirous to know. After every question, they made him a thousand menaces to kill him, in case he declared not the truth. Thus they began to advance towards the City, carrying always the said Centry bound before them. Having marched about one quarter of a league, they came unto the Castle that is nigh unto the City; which presently they closely surrounded, so that no person could get either in or out of the said Fortress.

Being thus posted under the walls of the Castle, Captain Morgan commanded the Centry, whom they had taken Prisoner, to speak unto those that were within, charming them to surrender, and deliver themselves up to his discretion; otherwise they should be all cut in pieces, without giving quarter to any one. But they would hearken to none of these threats, beginning instantly to fire; which gave notice unto the City, and this was suddenly alarmed. Yet notwithstanding, although the Governour and Souldiers of the said Castle made as great resistance as could be performed, they were constrained to surrender unto the Pirats. These no sooner had taken the Castle, but they resolved to be as good as their words, in putting the Spaniards to the Sword, thereby to strike a terrour into the rest of the City. Hereupon, having shut up all the Souldiers and Officers, as Prisoners, into one Room, they instantly set fire unto the Powder (whereof they found great quantity) and blew up the whole Castle into the air, with all the Spaniards that were within. This being done, they pursued the course of their Victory, falling upon the City, which as yet was not in order to receive them. Many of the Inhabitants cast their precious Jewels and Moneys into Wells and Cisterns, or hid them in other places underground, to escuse, as much as were possible, their being totally robbed. One party of the Pirats being assigned to this purpose, ran immediately to the Cloisters, and took as many Religious men and women as they could find. The Governour of the City not being able to rally the Citizens, through the huge confusion of the Town, retired unto one of the Castles remaining, and from thence began to fire incessantly at the Pirats. But these were not in the least negligent either to assault him, or defend themselves with all the courage imaginable. Thus it was observable, that amidst the horrour of the Assault, they made very few shots in vain. For aiming with great dexterity at the mouths of the Guns, the Spaniards were certain to lose one or two men every time they charged each Gun anew.

The assault of this Castle where the Governour was, continued very furious on both sides, from break of day until noon. Yea, about this time of the day, the case was very dubious which party should conquer or be conquered. At last the Pirats perceiving they had lost many men, and as yet advanced but little towards the gaining either this or the other Castles remaining, thought to make use of Fire-balls, which they threw with their hands, designing, if possible, to burn the doors of the Castle. But going about to put this in execution, the Spaniards from the Walls let fall great quantity of stones, and earthen pots full of Powder, and other combustible matter, which forced them to desist from that attempt. Captain Morgan seeing this generous defence made by the Spaniards, began to despair of the whole success of the Enterprize. Hereupon many faint and calm meditations came in to his mind; neither could he determine which way to turn himself in that straitness of affairs. Being involved in these thoughts, he was suddenly animated to continue the Assault, by seeing the English Colours put forth at one of the lesser Castles, then entered by his men. Of whom he presently after spied a Troop that came to meet him, proclaiming Victory with loud shouts of joy. This instantly put him upon new resolutions of making new efforts to take the rest of the Castles that stood out against him: Especially seeing the chiefest Citizens were fled unto them, and had conveyed thither great part of their Riches, with all the Plate belonging to the Churches, and other things dedicated to Divine Service.

Unto this effect therefore he ordered ten or twelve Ladders to be made, in all possible haste, so broad, that three or four men at once might ascend by them. These being finished, he commanded all the Religious men and women whom he had taken Prisoners, to fix them against the walls of the Castle. Thus much he had beforehand threatened the Governour to perform, in case he delivered not the Castle. But his answer was, He would never surrender himself alive. Captain Morgan was much persuaded that the Governour would not employ his utmost Forces, seeing Religious women, and Ecclesiastical persons, exposed in the front of the Souldiers to the greatest dangers. Thus the Ladders, as I had said, were put into the hands of Religious persons of both Sexes; and these were forced, at the head of the Companies, to raise and apply them to the Walls. But Captain Morgan was fully deceived in his judgment of this designe. For the Governour, who acted like a brave and couragious Souldier, refused not, in performance of his duty, to use his utmost endeavours to destroy whosoever came near the Walls. The Religious men and women ceased not to cry unto him and beg of him by all the Saints of Heaven, he would deliver the Castle, and hereby spare both his and their own lives. But nothing could prevail with the obstinacy and fierceness that had possessed the Governour's mind. Thus many of the Religious men and Nuns were killed before they could fix the Ladders. Which at last being done, though with great loss of the said Religious people, the Pirats mounted them in great numbers, and with no less valour; having Fire-balls in their hands, and Earthen-pots full of Powder. All which things, being now at the top of the Walls, they kindled and cast in among the Spaniards.

This effort of the Pirats was very great: Insomuch as the Spaniards could no longer resist nor defend the Castle, which was now entred. Hereupon they all threw down their Arms, and craved quarter for their lives. Onely the Governour of the City would admit nor crave no mercy; but rather killed many of the Pirats with his own hands, and not a few of his own Souldiers, because they did not stand to their Arms. And although the Pirats asked him if he would have quarter, yet he constantly answered, By no means: I had rather die as a valiant Souldier, than be hanged as a Coward. They endeavoured, as much as they could, to take him Prisoner. But he defended himself so obstinately, as that they were forced to kill him; notwithstanding all the cries and tears of his own Wife and Daughter, who begged of him upon their knees he would demand quarter and save his life. When the Pirats had possessed themselves of the Castle, which was about night, they enclosed therein all the Prisoners they had taken, placing the women and men by themselves with some Guards upon them. All the wounded were put into a certain apartment by itself, to the intent their own complaints might be the cure of their diseases; for no other was afforded them.

This being done, they fell to eating and drinking, after their usual manner; that is to say, committing in both these things all manner of debauchery and excess. These two vices were immediately followed by many insolent actions of Rape and Adultery committed upon many very honest women, as well married as Virgins: Who being threatned with the Sword, were constrained to submit their bodies to the violence of those lewd and wicked men. After such manner they delivered themselves up unto all sort of debauchery of this kind, that if there had been found onely fifty courageous men, they might easily have retaken the city, and killed all the Pirats. The next day, having plundred all they could find, they began to examine some of the prisoners (who had been persuaded by their Companions to say, they were the richest of the Town) charging them severely, to discover where they had hidden their Riches and Goods. But not being able to extort any thing out of them, as who were not the right persons that possessed any wealth, they at last resolved to torture them. This they performed with such cruelty, that many of them died upon the Rack, or presently after. Soon after, the President of Panama had news brought him of the pillage and ruine of Puerto Velo. This intelligence caused him to employ all his care and industry to raise Forces, with designe to pursue and cast out the Pirats from thence. But these cared little for what extraordinary means the President used, as having their Ships nigh at hand, and being determined to set fire unto the City, and retreat. They had now been at Puerto Velo fifteen days, in which space of time they had lost many of their men, both by the unhealthiness of the Country, and the extravagant Debaucheries they had committed.

Hereupon they prepared for a departure, carrying on Board their Ships all the Pillage they had gotten. But before all, they provided the Fleet with sufficient Victuals for the Voyage. While these things were getting ready, Captain Morgan sent an Injunction unto the Prisoners, that they should pay him a Ransom for the City, or else he would by fire consume it to ashes, and blow up all the Castles into the air. Withal, he commanded them to send speedily two persons to seek and procure the sum he demanded, which amounted unto one hundred thousand Pieces of Eight. Unto this effect, two men were sent to the President of Panama, who gave him an account of all these Tragedies. The President having now a body of men in a readiness, set forth immediately towards Puerto Velo, to encounter the Pirats before their retreat. But these people hearing of his coming, instead of flying away, went out to meet him at a narrow passage through which of necessity he ought to pass. Here they placed an hundred men very well armed; the which, at the first Encounter, put to flight a good party of those of Panama. This Accident obliged the President to retire for that time, as not being yet in a posture of strength to proceed any farther. Presently after this Rencounter, he sent a Message unto Captain Morgan, to tell him, That in case he departed not suddenly with all his Forces from Puerto Velo, he ought to expect no quarter for himself nor his Companions, when he should take them, as he hoped soon to do. Captain Morgan, who feared not his threats, as knowing he had a secure retreat in his Ships which were nigh at hand, made him answer, He would not deliver the Castles, before he had received the Contribution-money he had demanded. Which in case it were not paid down, he would certainly burn the whole City, and then leave it; demolishing beforehand the Castles, and killing the Prisoners.

The Governour of Panama perceived by this Answer, no means would serve to mollifie the hearts of the Pirats, nor reduce them to reason. Hereupon he determined to leave them; as also those of the City, whom he came to relieve, involved in the difficulties of making the best agreement they could with their Enemies. Thus in few days more, the miserable Citizens gathered the Contribution wherein they were fined, and brought the entire sum of one hundred thousand Pieces of Eight unto the Pirats, for a Ransom of the cruel Captivity they were fallen into. But the President of Panama, by these transactions, was brought into an extream admiration, considering that four hundred men had been able to take such a great City, with so many strong Castles: especially seeing they had no pieces of Cannon, nor other great Guns, wherewith to raise Batteries against them. And what was more, knowing that the Citizens of Puerto Velo had always great repute of being good Souldiers themselves, and who had never wanted courage in their own defence. This astonishment was so great, that it occasioned him, for to be satisfied herein, to send a Messenger unto Captain Morgan, desiring him to send him some small pattern of those Arms wherewith he had taken with such violence so great a City. Captain Morgan received this Messenger very kindly, and treated him with great civility. Which being done, he gave him a Pistol and a few small Bullets of lead, to carry back unto the President his Master, telling him withal, He desired him to accept that slender pattern of the Arms wherewith he had taken Puerto Velo, and keep them for a twelvemonth; after which time, he promised to come to Panama and fetch them away. The Governour of Panama returned the Present very soon unto Captain Morgan, giving him thanks for the favour of lending him such Weapons as he needed not, and withal sent him a Ring of Gold, with this Message, That he desired him not to give himself the labour of coming to Panama, as he had done to Puerto Velo; for he did certifie unto him, he should not speed so well here as he had done there.

After these transactions, Captain Morgan (having provided his Fleet with all necessaries, and taken with him the best Guns of the Castles, nailing the rest which he could not carry away) set sail from Puerto Velo with all his Ships. With these he arrived in few days unto the Island of Cuba, where he sought out a place wherein with all quiet and repose he might make the Dividend of the Spoil they had gotten.

They found in ready money two hundred and fifty thousand Pieces of Eight; besides all other Merchandizes, as Cloth, Linnen, Silks, and other Goods. With this rich Purchase they sailed again from thence unto their common place of Rendezvouz, Jamaica. Being arrived, they passed here some time in all sorts of Vices and Debauchery, according to their common manner of doing, spending with huge prodigality what others had gained with no small labour and toil.

Ibid.

7. SUGAR AND SLAVES

During the seventeenth and eighteenth centuries European settlers carved the islands into estates and organised the estates as sugar factories worked by African slaves.

A large windmill on each estate; the planter's dwelling-house and sugar-works, with the negro huts, in their beautiful groves of oranges, plantains, and cocoanut trees, completed a landscape that continually recurred in passing over the island.

MCKINNEN: A Tour through the British West Indies. 1803.

In addition to the slaves, most estates employed in the early days a number of indentured white servants, engaged for a period of years as artisans and supervisors.

The Masters, for the most part, live at the height of Pleasure.

The Servants, at the expiration of 5 years, become Freemen of the Island, and employ their times according to their abilities, and capacities; either to get a small Plantation, or to work at day-labour in other Plantations, or else to exercise their Trades, if so capacitated.

The Negro-Slaves are never out of their Bondage, and the Children they get, are likewise perpetual Slaves. They have but mean allowance of dyet, cloaths, and lodging; and although held to such hard Labour, and so ill treated, yet are they well contented with their Conditions; and if their Master is but any thing kind, they think nothing too much to be done for them; and therefore 'tis great pity to wrong such poor Creatures.

The chiefest Stock of a Planter, consists in his Servants and Slaves, but especially the Slaves, who are more numerous. And these they Buy on Shipboard, as men Buy Horses in a Fayr, and according as they are handsome, lusty, well-shapen, and young, either the men or women, they give more or less; the general Rates for the Christian-servants being about 10£ but if one that hath a good Trade, as a Carpenter, Joyner, Smith, or the like, then far more: Likewise, a Female that is young and handsome, is higher valued. The general Rate for the better sort of Negro-men, is 20£ or 25£ sterling; and for Women, about 15£ for the encrease of stock of Negroes, they generally take as many Men as Women.

The Maintenance of the Servants, and Negro-Slaves, as to their Dyet, Apparrel, and Lodging, is very inconsiderable.

For their Food, they are contented from weeks-end, to weeks-end, with Potatoes, Loblolly, made of beaten Maize mixt with water, Cassader-bread common in all the Indies, Bonavist, and such like food that the Plantation affordeth; as for Meat, they are seldome troubled with it, except at Christmas, Easter, and Whitsontide, and then they have Hoggs-flesh, according to the custome of the Island; but of late, the servants are allowed weekly, a small quantity of Swines-Flesh, or salted Flesh, or Fish; and when any of the Cattle dye of any distemper, or by accident, it is given to the Negroes, who feed like Princes on it.

Their Drinks are Mobbie, made of Potatoes soaked in water; Perino, made of Casavie-Root and water; Crippo, Kill-Devil, Punch, made of water and Sugar; Plantin-drink, made of Plantins and water; Beveridge, made of Spring-water, Sugar, and the juyce of Orenges; and wine of Pines, which is only made of the juyce of the Fruit, which is exceeding good and delicious; but this sort, as also the Beveridge, and Punch, the servants are not much troubled with.

But as for the Master-Planters, Merchants, Factors, and Strangers, their Faire is far otherwise, having their curious-made Dishes, as Custards, Cheese-cakes, Tansies; also, Sturgeon, Anchoves, Caviare, Botardo, Neates-Tongues, besides Poultrey, Fish, Fowl, Mutton, Beef, Kid, Porke, Beans, Pease, several Roots, and other good Dishes. And, besides the several sorts of Liquors already named, Wines, Strong waters, Brandy, and English-Beer; so that they find no want, and do not consider the condition of those poor wretches, their Servants and Slaves, who are constrained to so hard a labour.

The Apparrel they allow their Servants yearly, for the men, are 6 pair of Drawers, 12 pair of Shoes, 3 Monmouth-Caps, 6 Shirts; and for the women, 4 Smocks, 3 Petticoats, 4 Coifes, and 12 paire of Shoos, besides a Rug-Gown to each, to keep them warm, in the night, and to put on them when they come sweating from their labour. To the Negro-men, they allow but 3 pair of Canvas-Drawers, and to the Women, but three Petticoats.

But for themselves (especially the better sort) they are exceeding profuse and costly.

The Lodging of these poor wretches is worst of all, for having laboured all the day in so hot a Countrey, without any nourishing Dyet, at night they must be contented to lye hard, on nothing but a board, without any Coverled, in their Hutts, or rather Hogflies; but Christian Servants are something better Treated, being allowed Hamocks.

Every Sunday, (which is the only day of Rest, and should be set apart for the service of God) they employ either in the getting of the Bark of Trees, and making of Ropes with it, which they Truck away for Shirts, Drawers, and the like; or else spend the day in Recreation, as Dancing, and Wrestling, which they much delight in, though they are no great Proficients in either; for in their Dancing, they use antick actions, their hands having more of motion than their feet; and their head, than either; nor do the men and women Dance together, but apart; the Musique to which they Dance, being a sort of Kettle-drums, one bigger than another, which makes a strange and various noise, but whither Harmonious, I leave to the judgment of the Reader.

LINCH: *A Description of the Island of Jamaica.* 1672.

Most of the harshness had disappeared from plantation life when Mrs. Carmichael went to the islands, and the planter had become something of a paterfamilias of whom a full share in the hard work was expected.

The duties of a planter's wife are most arduous: distant from markets, and all the few comforts that a small West India town even does afford, she must continue to live upon the stock raised on the property, or absolutely go without. The stock, therefore, becomes her immediate care; and besides being forced to superintend pigs, poultry, etc. with sundry other occupations of the same nature, she must attend also to the garden, and that most minutely; otherwise, she would reap little from it. Then she has to listen to all the stories of the people on the estate—young, old, and middle-aged: all their little jealousies and quarrels she must enter into, and be in short a kind of mother to them all. The negro children must be daily watched; she must see them swallow their physic when necessary; reward the good, and admonish the bad; visit the sick—encourage them—and take, or appear to take, an interest in all that concerns them. It is more than probable, too, that she not only cuts out, but sews a great proportion of the clothes for her house servants. Then, again, the mode of washing in the West Indies greatly adds to the domestic labours of the planter's wife: the linen is dipped in the river, and soap rubbed upon it while it is laid over a stone, after which it is beat with a flat heavy piece of wood, made for the purpose; and, lastly, the article itself is dashed upwards and downwards upon the stone, with which the operation concludes.

It is utterly impossible for those who have not gone through such scenes, to comprehend the unnecessary accumulation of work thus thrown upon the mistress of a family, who must begin to button and string the whole wardrobe every time it returns from the wash, as it is a rare occurrence if any of those appendages return; the patching and mending of a West India family is, consequently, "never ending—still beginning:" all this a planter's wife must see done, and also give her own active assistance to the completion of it. The nature of the climate too, renders it necessary that all pantries and store-rooms be out of doors—at least with very few exceptions. A great increase of trouble and consumption of time is thus occasioned; and all is thrown upon the planter's wife, for none of her servants think of what is required, and indeed prefer making their mistress return again and again to the store-room during the day; as by this, more frequent opportunities of pilfering are offered to them.

All these avocations require more time, activity, and temper than many people may be aware of, and nothing short of a trial of such a life can give any one a perfect idea of the various annoyances attendant upon it: nor is this all; for very many, besides these labours, bake the pastry, and make the puddings, and custards. Let those who talk of the luxuries of a West India life, judge whether they would exchange their home in Britain, however poor it may be, to undergo all this. I can safely state, from personal experience, that so little reliance is to be put in any servant—even on him who may call himself head servant— that the every-day work of laying the table for dinner must be looked at in order to ascertain that nothing is wanting on the table. I need scarcely say that those ladies who have young children, have still more to do; and in their personal attention towards their offspring during infancy, they are the most anxious and affectionate of parents, always suckling their children, and generally to a longer period than is usual in England; and never, for any party of pleasure, trusting their infant to the hands of others. Their conduct in this respect is most exemplary, and very different from our fashionable mothers in Britain, who either stint their infant of its natural support, or abandon it to a mercenary nurse.

CARMICHAEL: *Five Years in Trinidad and St. Vincent.* 1834.

Mahogany, not sugar, ruled in Honduras, but again the slave from Africa was indispensable.

There are two seasons in the year for the cutting of mahogany: the first commencing shortly after Christmas, or at the conclusion of what is termed the wet season, the other about the middle of the year. At such periods all is activity, and the falling of trees, or the trucking out those that have been fallen, form the chief employments. Some of the wood is rough-squared on the spot, but this part of the labour is generally suspended until the logs are rafted to the different rivers' mouths. These rafts often consist of more than two hundred logs, and are floated as many hundred miles. When the floods are unusually rapid, it very frequently happens, that the labour of a season, or perhaps of many, is at once destroyed by the breaking asunder of a raft, and the whole of the mahogany being hurried precipitately to the sea.

The gangs of negroes employed in this work consist of from ten to fifty each; few exceed the latter number. The large bodies are commonly divided into several small ones, a plan which it is supposed greatly facilitates labour.

Each gang of slaves has one belonging to it, who is styled the huntsman. He is generally selected from the most intelligent of his fellows, and his chief occupation is to search the woods, or as in this country it is termed, the bush, to find labour for the whole. A negro of this description is often valued at more than five hundred pounds.

About the beginning of August, the huntsman is dispatched on his errand, and if his owner be working on his own ground, this is seldom an employment of much delay or difficulty. He cuts his way through the thickest of the woods to the highest spots, and climbs the tallest tree he finds, from which he minutely surveys the surrounding country. At this season, the leaves of the mahogany tree are invariably of a yellow reddish hue, and an eye accustomed to this kind of exercise can discover, at a great distance, the places where the wood is most abundant. He now descends, and to these his steps are directed; and without compass or other guide than what observation has imprinted on his recollection, he never fails to reach the exact point to which he aims. . . .

On some occasions no ordinary stratagem is necessary to be resorted to by the huntsman to prevent others from availing themselves of the advantage of his discoveries; for if his steps be traced by those engaged in the same pursuit, which is a very common thing, all his ingenuity must be exerted to beguile them from the true scent. In this, however, he is not always successful, being followed by those who are entirely aware of all the arts he may use, and whose eyes are so quick, that the lightest turn of a leaf, or the faintest impression of his foot, is unerringly perceived: even the dried leaves which may be strewed on the ground often help to conduct to the secret spot. Patents for discovery having never been contemplated by the Honduras wood-cutters, any invasion of the right appertaining to it has therefore seldom been very scrupulously regarded by them. And it consequently happens, that persons so engaged must frequently undergo the disappointment of finding an advantage, they had promised to themselves, seized on by others. . . .

The annual cost of the negro alone is estimated by each proprietor at Honduras, at something more than 35 pounds Jamaica currency: an expence which, in the history of slavery, is probably without parallel.

HENDERSON: *An Account of the British Settlement of Honduras,* 1809.

8. RACIAL MÉLANGE

By the second half of last century people of African descent formed by far the greater part of the population of the islands, but in Trinidad, following Emancipation, there had been an influx of Indians and Chinese under the indenture system. In the streets of Port of Spain were colourful scenes.

Here passes an old Coolie Hindoo, with nothing on but his lungee round his loins, and a scarf over his head; a white-bearded, delicate-featured old gentleman, with probably some caste-mark of red paint on his forehead; his thin limbs, and small hands and feet, contrasting strangely with the brawny Negros round. There comes a bright-eyed young lady, probably his daughter-in-law, hung all over with bangles, in a white muslin petticoat, crimson cotton-velvet jacket, and green gauze veil, with her naked brown baby astride on her hip; a clever, smiling, delicate little woman, who is quite aware of the brightness of her own eyes. And who are these three boys in dark blue coatees and trousers, one of whom carries, hanging at one end of a long bamboo, a couple of sweet potatoes; at the other, possibly, a pebble to balance them? As they approach, their doleful visage betrays them. Chinese they are, without a doubt: but whether old or young, men or women, you cannot tell, till the initiated point out that the women have chignons and no hats, the men hats with their pig-tails coiled up under them. . . .

There again is a group of coloured men of all ranks, talking eagerly business, or even politics; some of them as well dressed as if they were fresh from Europe; some of them, too, six feet high, and broad in proportion; as fine a race, physically, as one would wish to look upon; and with no want of shrewdness either, or determination, in their faces; a race who ought, if they will be wise and virtuous, to have before them a great future. Here come home from the convent school two coloured young ladies, probably pretty, possibly lovely, certainly gentle, modest, and well-dressed according to the fashions of Paris or New York; and here comes the unmistakeable Englishman, tall, fair, close shaven, arm-in-arm with another man, whose more delicate features, more sallow complexion, and little moustache, mark him as some Frenchman or Spaniard of old family. Both are dressed as if they were going to walk up Pall Mall or the Rue de Rivoli; for "go-to-meeting clothes" are somewhat too much *de rigueur* here; a shooting-jacket and wide-awake betrays the newly-landed Englishman. Both take off their hats with a grand air to a lady in a carriage; for they are very fine gentlemen indeed, and intend to remain such: and well that is for the civilization of the island; for it is from such men as these, and from their families, that the good manners for which West Indians are, or ought to be, famous, have permeated down, slowly but surely, through all classes of society save the very lowest.

KINGSLEY: *At Last: A Christmas in the West Indies.* 1871.

But numerically the Negro dominated the West Indian scene.

On the door-steps sit Negresses in gaundy print dresses, with stiff turbans (which are, according to this year's fashion, of chocolate and yellow silk plaid, painted with thick yellow paint, and cost in all some four dollars), all aiding in the general work of doing nothing: save where here and there a hugely fat Negress, possibly with her "head tied across" in a white turban (sign of mourning), sells, or tries to sell, abominable sweetmeats, strange fruits, and junks of sugar-cane, to be gnawed by the dawdlers in mid-street, while they carry on their heads everything and anything, from half a barrow-load of yams to a saucer or a beer-bottle.

Ibid.

*

On the quay, on the mole, on boats, on posts, on house tops, through doors and windows, wherever a human foot could stand, was one appalling mass of black faces. As the barge passed slowly along, the emotions of the multitude were absolutely tremendous; they threw up their arms and waved their handkerchiefs, they danced, and jumped, and rolled on the ground, they sung and screamed and shouted and roared, till the whole surface of the place seemed to be one huge grin of delight.

COLERIDGE: *Six Months in the West Indies, in* 1825.

*

I lounged awhile in the rocking-chair, watching two Negros astride on the roof of a shed, on which they were nailing shingles. Their heads were bare; the sun was intense; the roof on which they sat must have been of the temperature of an average frying-pan on an English fire; but the good fellows worked on, steadily and carefully, though not fast, chattering and singing, evidently enjoying the very act of living, and fattening in the genial heat.

KINGSLEY: *At Last: A Christmas in the West Indies.* 1871.

*

RIVER ROAD, GRENADA

BASSETERRE, ST. KITTS

Their costume on fete days and Sundays are perfectly marvellous. They are by no means contented with coloured calicoes; but shine in muslin and light silks at heaven only knows how much a yard. They wear their dresses of an enormous fulness. One may see of a Sunday evening three ladies occupying a whole street by the breadth of their garments, who on the preceding day were scrubbing pots and carrying weights about the town on their heads. And they will walk in full-dress too as though they had been used to go in such attire from their youth up. They rejoice most in white—in white muslin with coloured sashes; in light-brown boots, pink gloves, parasols, and broad-brimmed straw hats with deep veils and glittering bugles. The hat and the veil, however, are mistakes. If the negro woman thoroughly understood effect, she would wear no head-dress but the coloured handkerchief, which is hers by right of national custom.

Some of their efforts after dignity of costume are ineffably ludicrous. One Sunday evening, far away in the country, as I was riding with a gentleman, the proprietor of the estate around us, I saw a young girl walking home from church. She was arrayed from head to foot in virgin white. Her gloves were on, and her parasol was up. Her hat also was white, and so was the lace, and so were the bugles which adorned it. She walked with a stately dignity that was worthy of such a costume, and worthy also of higher grandeur; for behind her walked an attendant nymph, carrying the beauty's prayer-book—on her head. A negro woman carries every burden on her head, from a tub of water weighing a hundredweight down to a bottle of physic.

When we came up to her, she turned towards us and curtsied. She curtsied, for she recognized her "massa"; but she curtsied with great dignity, for she recognized also her own finery. The girl behind with the prayer-book made the ordinary obeisance, crooking her leg up at the knee, and then standing upright quicker than thought.

"Who on earth is that princess?" said I. "They are two sisters who both work at my mill," said my friend. "Next Sunday they will change places. Polly will have the parasol and the hat, and Jenny will carry the prayer-book on her head behind her."

TROLLOPE: *The West Indies and the Spanish Main.* 1860.

Something of the spirit of the swamp and jungle of Africa found its way across the Atlantic in the slave ships to persist in the form of "obeah".

Much has been told and written about that strange belief of the negro race called "obeah". It is similar to the ancient belief in witch-craft, and the obeah man is only another form of the witch or wizard of the past. Everything that is mysterious and incomprehensible to the negro is obeah. In practising my judicial functions I have often been made the subject of an obeah. On one occasion, on stepping on to the dais in court, I found it covered with small red things, which, on examination, proved to be hundreds of bits of red paper cut into the shape of hearts. Another time, on one arm of my chair was hung a sort of rag doll, which, on being opened, was found to contain a human tooth, some foul-smelling black powder, and some withered herb. This was great obeah, and it was with the greatest difficulty that I could compel any of the black policemen to touch the unclean thing. I have found similar articles suspended over my hammock when I was asleep, and the curious thing is one can never discover how the different articles are placed in the position in which they are found. Even if any one knows, they are too frightened to speak, for fear of the obeah working evil to themselves.

KIRKE: *Twenty-five Years in British Guiana.*   1898.

9. THE "BUCKRA QUALITY"

Society life in the West Indies was characterised above all things by hospitality.

The general character of the West Indians is extremely pleasing to strangers. They are frank, lively, and generous. Hospitality is carried to an extreme which is unknown in Europe; and there are few persons, I believe, who have ever visited these islands who have not separated from many of the inhabitants with regret.

MCKINNEN:
A Tour through the British West Indies, in the years 1802 *and* 1803.

★

I like the Grenadans much; they have a picture of an island, they give turtle, porter and champagne in abundance and perfection, they lend horses, and send pines and pomegranates on board your ship, in short they are right pleasant Christians.

COLERIDGE: *Six Months in the West Indies, in* 1825.

★

Country life in Jamaica certainly has its attractions. The day is generally begun at six o'clock, when a cup of coffee is brought in by a sable minister. I believe it is customary to take this in bed, or rather on the bed; for in Jamaica one's connection with one's bed does not amount to getting into it. One gets within the musquito net, and then plunges about with a loose sheet, which is sometimes on and sometimes off. With the cup of coffee comes a small modicum of dry toast.

After that the toilet progresses, not at a rapid pace. A tub of cold water and dilettante dressing will do something more than kill an hour, so that it is half-past seven or eight before one leaves one's room. . . . At this hour—eight o'clock, that is—the men ride, and sometimes also the ladies. And when the latter ceremony does take place, there is no pleasanter hour in all the four-and-twenty.

At ten or half-past ten the nation sits down to breakfast; not to a meal, my dear Mrs. Jones, consisting of tea and bread and butter, with two eggs for the master of the family and one for the mistress; but a stout, solid banquet, consisting of fish, beefsteaks—a breakfast is not a breakfast in the West Indies without beefsteaks and onions, nor is a dinner so to be called without bread and cheese and beer—potatoes, yams, plaintains, eggs, and half a dozen "tinned" productions, namely, meats sent from England in tin cases. Though they have every delicacy which the world can give them of native production, all these are as nothing, unless they also have something from England. Then there are tea and chocolate upon the table, and on the sideboard beer and wine, rum and brandy. 'Tis so that they breakfast at rural quarters in Jamaica.

Then comes the day. Ladies may not subject their fair skin to the outrages of a tropical sun, and therefore, unless on very special occasions, they do not go out between breakfast and dinner. That they occupy themselves well during the while, charity feels convinced. Sarcasm, however, says that they do not sin from over energy. For my own part, I do not care a doit for sarcasm. When their lords reappear, they are always found smiling, well-dressed, and pretty; and then after dinner they have but one sin—there is but one draw-back—they will go to bed at 9 o'clock.

But by the men during the day it did not seem to me that the sun was much regarded, or that it need be much regarded. One cannot and certainly should not walk much; and no one does walk. A horse is there as a matter of course, and one walks upon that; not a great beast sixteen hands high, requiring all manner of levers between its jaws, capricoling and prancing about, and giving a man a deal of work merely to keep his seat and look stately; but a canny little quiet brute, fed chiefly on grass, patient of the sun, and not inclined to be troublesome. With such legs under him, and at a distance of some twenty miles from the coast, a man may get about in Jamaica pretty nearly as well as he can in England. . . . The inspection of a pen or two, perhaps occasionally of the sugar works when they are about, soon wears through the hours, and at five preparations commence for the six o'clock dinner. The dressing again is a dilettante process, even for the least dandified of mankind. It is astonishing how much men think, and must think, of their clothes when within the tropics. Dressing is necessarily done slowly, or else one gets heated quicker than one has cooled down. And then one's clothes always want airing, and the supply of clean linen is necessarily copious, or, at any rate, should be so. Let no man think that he can dress for dinner in ten minutes because he is accustomed to do so in England. He cannot brush his hair, or pull on his boots, or fasten his buttons at the same pace he does at home. He dries his face very leisurely, and sits down gravely to rest before he draws on his black pantaloons.

Dressing for dinner, however, is *de rigueur* in the West Indies. If a black coat, etc., could be laid aside anywhere as barbaric, and light loose clothing adopted, this should be done here. The soldiers, at

least the privates, are already dressed as Zouaves; and children and
negroes are hardly dressed at all. But the visitor, victim of tropical
fashionable society, must appear in black clothing, because black
clothing is the thing in England. . . . After dinner no wine is taken—
none, at least, beyond one glass with the ladies, and, if you choose it,
one after they are gone. Before dinner, as I should have mentioned
before, a glass of bitters is as much *de rigueur* as the black coat. I know
how this will disgust many a kindly friend in dear old thickly-preju-
diced native England. Yes, ma'am, bitters! No, not gin and bitters,
such as the cabmen take at the gin-palaces; not gin and bitters at all,
unless you specially request it; but sherry and bitters; and a very pretty
habit it is for a warm country. If you don't drink your wine after
dinner, why not take it before? I have no doubt that it is the more
wholesome habit of the two. . . . And then men and women saunter
out on the verandah, or perhaps, if it be starlight or moonlight, into
the garden. Oh, what stars they are, those in that western tropical
world! How beautiful a woman looks by their light, how sweet the
air smells, how gloriously legible are the constellations of the heavens!
And then one sips a cup of coffee, and there is a little chat, the lightest
of the light, and a little music, light enough also, and at nine one
retires to one's light slumbers. . . . Such are the ordinary evenings of
society; but there are occasions when no complaint can be made of
lack of energy. The soul of a Jamaica lady revels in a dance. Dancing is
popular in England—is popular almost everywhere, but in Jamaica it is
the elixir of life; the Medea's cauldron, which makes old people young;
the cup of Circe, which neither man nor woman can withstand. Look
at that lady who has been content to sit still and look beautiful for the
last two hours; let but the sound of a polka meet her and she will awake
to life as lively, to motion as energetic, as that of a Scotch sportsman
on the 12th of August. It is singular how the most listless girl who seems
to trail through her long days almost without moving her limbs, will
continue to waltz and polka and rush up and down a galopade from ten
till five; and then think the hours all too short!

TROLLOPE: *The West Indies and the Spanish Main.* 1860.

*The matter-of-fact Mrs. Carmichael did not find West Indian social
occasions all they were cracked up to be.*

I will pass over the inconvenience of walking or riding, under a
tropical sun, even the few hundred yards that separated my house from
that of my entertainer—and the crowd of visitors arriving and arrived
outside the door—and suppose myself ushered in, having smoothed

down my dress, and arranged my curls, and in some degree recovered from the inconveniences of heat, a strong breeze, and abundance of dust. We were invited to dine at five in the afternoon, and as I had something short of a quarter of a mile to walk, I had the full benefit of the concentrated rays of the tropical sun.

Dinner being announced about six, we were ushered into a room by no means large or lofty: two long tables were soon filled, and we sat down, in number between thirty and forty—the gentlemen greatly predominating; there was very little general conversation during dinner, and, so far as I could see, not much even between those who sat next each other. Every thing looked brilliant, however, from the numerous lights (for it was already dusk), and the handsome shades, which are a great ornament to the candlesticks. The windows and doors all thrown open, displayed one of the most picturesque scenes imaginable; it was fine moonlight, and the beauty of a moonlight view in these latitudes, can be conceived by those only who have seen it. The dinner was like all West India dinners—a load of substantials, so apparently ponderous, that I instinctively drew my feet from under the table, in case it should be borne to the ground.

Turtle and vegetable soups, with fish, roast mutton (for in three weeks' residence I had not seen or heard of beef, lamb, or veal), and turtle dressed in the shell, with boiled turkey, boiled fowls, a ham, mutton and pigeon pies, and stewed ducks, concluded the first course. Ducks and guinea birds, with a few ill-made puddings and tarts, etc. formed the second course. The heat of the climate formed an excuse for the indifferent pastry; and experience soon taught me that it was impossible to make light flaky pastry, such as we see every day in England. However, it must be admitted that West Indies cooks do not excel in the art of making sweet dishes, if I except a dish yclept "floating island", which they always succeed in admirably.

I had heard so much at home of the luxury of the West Indies, and how clever black servants were, that I looked for something, not only good, but neat and even tasteful; but I was astonished to see the dishes put down without the least apparent reference to regularity, and I felt a constant inclination to put those even that were placed awry. Many of the guests brought their servants with them, and there was therefore an immense concourse of them, of all descriptions: some with livery, and some without; some with shoes, but generally without; some wore white jackets, others were of coloured striped jean; some were young, some old; some were coloured, and others negro men, there was no arrangement, co-operation, or agreement among the servants, save only in one thing, and that was in stealing; for a bottle of wine was hardly opened, until some clever hand whipped it away, and without any apparent fear of detection or sense of shame, openly handed it out of the window to those in waiting to receive it. In short, the servants' mouths were stuffed full the whole time; and so occupied were they all in making the most of a good opportunity, that the ladies' plates would never have been changed, had it not been for the repeated and loud reproof of the gentlemen. . . .

The ladies did not remain long at table, but soon retired to the drawing-room; but there, nothing like conversation took place—indeed the constant domestic drudgery of a female's life in the West Indies, married or unmarried (for the latter, although not occupied with the ménage, are engaged in dress-making and mending—negro servants being wretched needle women), leaves them no time for improving the mind—and in society, the ladies are too generally found distinguished for that listlessness, and meagreness of conversation, which arise from an uninformed mind.

As soon as the gentlemen came in, coffee and cake were handed round, and an almost immediate bustle followed; for a heavy though short shower of rain had fallen, and the ladies began to ponder upon the probable results of walking or riding down Mackay's Hill, through a miry, slippery road, in a cloudy night, between nine and ten o'clock. We had resolved to walk; and, wrapped in warm cloaks, bonnets, and thick shoes, we took our leave.

CARMICHAEL: Five Years in Trinidad and St. Vincent. 1834.

But it was during the Navy's visits that the islands knew their peaks of social enjoyment.

There, when the squadron comes in, officers in uniform dance at desperate sailors' pace with delicate Creoles; some of them, coloured as well as white, so beautiful in face and figure that one could almost pardon the jolly tars if they enacted a second Mutiny of the Bounty, and refused one and all to leave the island and the fair dames thereof. And all the while the warm night wind rushes in through the high open windows; and the fireflies flicker up and down, in and out, and you slip away on to the balcony to enjoy—for after all it is very hot—the purple star-spangled night; and see aloft the saw of the mountain ridges against the black-blue sky and below—what a contrast!—the crowd of white eyeballs and white teeth—Negros, Coolies, Chinese— all grinning and peeping upward against the railing, in the hope of seeing—through the walls—the "buccra quality" enjoy themselves.

KINGSLEY: At Last: A Christmas in the West Indies. 1871.

SIR WALTER RALEIGH: *The Discoverie of the Large, Rich and Bewtiful Empire of Guiana.* 1596.

"For gold, for praise, for glory" Raleigh sought new worlds: in particular he sought the "Great and Golden" city of El Dorado. At Trinidad he used the Spanish garrison treacherously and cruelly, kidnapped the Governor to serve him as a guide, caulked his ships at the Pitch Lake, and then, having safeguarded his lines of communication, he left the "Lion's Whelp" while he rowed up the Orinoco. The tale is told in *The Discoverie*, which, for all its bombast, is a very readable book, notable for vivid descriptions which time has, on the whole, proved accurate, though his contemporaries took them with a pinch of salt.

SIR THOMAS LINCH: *A Description of the Island of Jamaica.* 1672.

When in 1670 Spain agreed to recognise the English occupation of Jamaica and certain other islands, England in turn agreed not to countenance any longer the activities of the buccaneers. Sir Thomas Linch was accordingly appointed Governor of Jamaica to replace Sir Thomas Modyford who had worked hand-in-glove with the buccaneers. This *Description* of Jamaica, "with the other Isles and Territories in America to which the English are related", was published by Richard Blome, and described as "taken from the Notes of Sir Thomas Linch, Knight, Governor of Jamaica, and other Experienced Persons in the said Places."

JOHN ESQUEMELING: *Bucaniers of America.* 1684.

The sub-titling of *Bucaniers of America* says it is "A True Account of the Most Remarkable Assaults committed of late years upon the Coasts of the West Indies"; and further that it was written originally in Dutch "by John Esquemeling, one of the Bucaniers, who was present at Those Tragedies", then translated into Spanish and finally "faithfully rendred into English". Esquemeling went to the West Indies as an indentured servant of a French company owning plantations in Tortuga. He was sold to the Governor, "the most cruel Tyrant and perfidious man that ever was born of Woman", and having become ill from harsh treatment, he was sold again, this time "unto a Chirurgeon for the price of seventy pieces of eight". The doctor used him kindly and after a year granted him his liberty on the condition "that I should pay him one hundred pieces of eight when I was in a Capacity of Wealth so to do." Having no other recourse, Esquemeling then "determined to enter into the Wicked Order of the Pirates". His account of his subsequent adventures as a buccaneer in the service of Sir Henry Morgan and others bears the stamp of authenticity, and suggests that he was a man of unusual intelligence, perception and good sense.

The Truest and Largest Account of the Late Earthquake in Jamaica, June the 7th, 1692.

More than 2,000 people were killed in the earthquake, and Port Royal was razed to the ground. This account of the "amazing severity of God towards Jamaica" was written by "a Reverend Divine there to his friend in London", received "some Improvement by another Hand", and was printed in Worcester.

WILLIAM BECKFORD: *A Descriptive Account of the Island of Jamaica.* 1740.

A deep gloom emanates from Beckford's book, sufficiently explained by the fact that it was written in the Fleet, where he was presumably imprisoned as a debtor. Its second most apparent characteristic is prolixity. Yet, given patience, one can find in it both useful information and effective descriptive passages.

MARIA, LADY NUGENT: *A Journal of a Voyage to, and Residence in, the Island of Jamaica, from 1801 to 1805.*

Lady Nugent saw Jamaica from Government House as the wife of the Lieut.-Governor of the day.

DANIEL McKINNEN: *A Tour through the British West Indies, in the years 1802 and 1803.*

CAPTAIN HENDERSON: *An Account of the British Settlement of Honduras.* 1809.

Captain Henderson was serving with the 5th West Indian Regiment at the time of his visit to Honduras. The settlement then comprised only 200 white people, 500 people of colour or free blacks, and 3,000 negro slaves.

H. N. COLERIDGE: *Six Months in the West Indies in 1825.*

The poet Coleridge had only a moderate opinion of this book by his nephew Henry, praising it as generally amusing, but condemning it for lapses in both taste and style. Henry went to the West Indies as secretary to yet another Coleridge, William Hart Coleridge, who had just been appointed Bishop of Barbados. Though a young man of 28, he was suffering from a rheumatic complaint, and his chief motive in making the trip seems to have been to see if a change of climate would help.

J. E. ALEXANDER: *Transatlantic Sketches.* 1833.
  Sir James Alexander (1803–88) served as a soldier in many parts of the Empire, made detailed observations on the places he visited, and embodied his notes in agreeably written books. He is quoted also in the West African section.

The West India Sketch Book. 1834.
  The author is anonymous.

MRS. CARMICHAEL: *Five Years in Trinidad and St. Vincent.* 1834.
  As a good Scotswoman, Mrs. Carmichael brought a shrewd commonsense to the chronicling of her experiences as a planter's wife in St. Vincent and Trinidad. She went to the West Indies prepared to be horrified by conditions on the plantations, but eventually came to the conclusion that the slaves' lot was materially much better than that of the ordinary working man at home.

SIR ROBERT H. SCHOMBURGK: *The History of Barbados.* 1848.
  My only excuse for quoting from a history is that it is a very good history, containing quotations from sources otherwise difficult to tap, and that it was written by a man who did as much as anyone to consolidate Britain's position in the West Indies.

ANTHONY TROLLOPE: *The West Indies and the Spanish Main.*
    1860.
  Positively *the* Anthony Trollope. In 1859 his duties with the Post Office took him to the West Indies and a book was the inevitable result.

CHARLES KINGSLEY: *At Last: A Christmas in the West Indies.*
    1871.
  Charles Kingsley, the poet and novelist, visiting the West Indies "at last" at the age of fifty, six years before his death.

HENRY FOWLER: *A Narrative of a Journey Across the Unexplored Portion of British Honduras.* 1879.

As late as 1878 much of British Honduras was unknown to its administrators. As a conscientious Colonial Secretary, Henry Fowler did his own exploring.

SIR EVERARD F. IM THURN: *Among the Indians of Guiana.* 1883.

At twenty-five Sir Everard Im Thurn became Curator of the British Guiana Museum, and during the five years he held the post, undertook the studies which resulted in *Among the Indians.* In all, he spent twenty-two years in British Guiana and was subsequently Colonial Secretary in Ceylon and Governor of Fiji. The latter appointment he held for six years until his retirement in 1910. He died in 1932 at the age of eighty.

J. A. FROUDE: *The English in the West Indies* or *The Bow of Ulysses.* 1888.

"I visited the West India Islands in order to increase my acquaintance with the condition of the British Colonies," says Froude. "I have related what I saw and what I heard, with the general impressions which I was led to form." Those impressions were typically forthright and uncompromising, and caused resentment in many quarters. Briefly, he recorded neglect and called for a firm hand. Froude undertook his journey late in life, in his seventieth year, when he was already famous as a historian and, in particular, for his biography of Carlyle.

HENRY KIRKE: *Twenty-five Years in British Guiana.* 1898.

Late in life Henry Kirke sat down to write the story of his experiences as a law officer in British Guiana. He was aware, he said gruffly, that books of Reminiscences and Recollections were thought by some to be written only to "gratify the vanity of garrulous old men": all the same such books often did contain facts and anecdotes of value to future historians or sociologists, and so, be damned to the critics, he was going to have his say.

SIR HESKETH BELL: *Glimpses of a Governor's Life.*

Few men had a more distinguished record in the Colonial Service than Sir Hesketh Bell, who became Administrator of Dominica in 1899, at the age of thirty-four, and spent the rest of his career as a Governor—in Uganda, Northern Nigeria, the Leeward Islands and Mauritius.

PART THREE

EAST AFRICA

KENYA, TANGANYIKA, UGANDA AND ZANZIBAR

Perspective

1. HINTS TO TRAVELLERS
2. THE MASAI
3. THE RIFT VALLEY AND OTHER NATURAL WONDERS
4. "THE WHOLE ZOOLOGICAL GARDENS"
5. "UGANDA IS A FAIRY TALE"

Books and Authors: with biographical notes

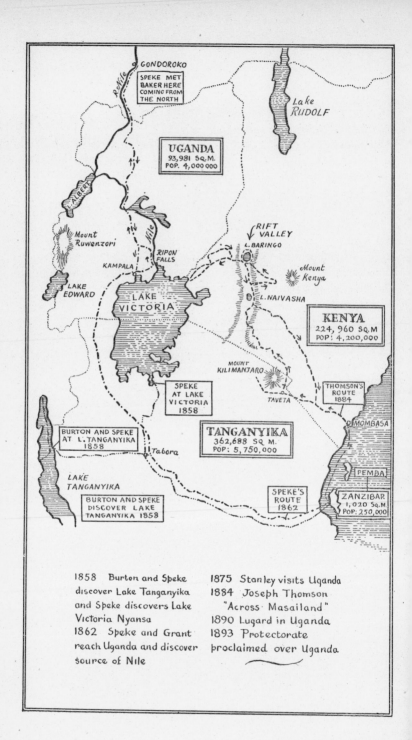

1858 Burton and Speke
discover Lake Tanganyika
and Speke discovers Lake
Victoria Nyansa
1862 Speke and Grant
reach Uganda and discover
source of Nile

1875 Stanley visits Uganda
1884 Joseph Thomson
    "Across Masailand"
1890 Lugard in Uganda
1893 Protectorate
    proclaimed over Uganda

PERSPECTIVE

THE modern East Africa has a pleasantly neat look about it on the map, and, what with this and the way Kenya pushes itself into the news, one cannot easily cast back to the days at the end of last century when East Africa was unknown territory and Kenya no more than the name of a snow-capped mountain.

In those days what excited Europe as travellers began to push into the interior were the reports they brought back of the existence far inland of a flourishing African kingdom called Buganda. This kingdom, said the reports, possessed a degree of civilisation far beyond anything yet seen in equatorial Africa. It possessed also many striking natural features. It lay on the northern shores of a huge lake: in that lake the Nile had its birth: and on its western boundary stretched a range of snow-capped mountains believed to be none other than the fabled Mountains of the Moon.

"In the Uganda Protectorate," Sir Harry Johnston was to say a little later, "one finds nearly all the wonders, most of the extremes, the most signal beauties, and some of the horrors of the Dark Continent."

So it was that nearly all the curiosity and effort of these energetic Victorians was directed towards making contacts with Uganda; and the intervening area, the area which now comprises the territories of Kenya and Tanganyika, was regarded primarily as a tiresome barrier, much of it barren and inhospitable, some of it of outstanding scenic beauty, and a substantial part of it held in thrall by a terrible warrior people called the Masai.

The reputed ferocity of the Masai was, indeed, one of the reasons why Europeans were so late in seeking out the wonders of the interior; that and the extreme unhealthiness of the coastal belt. Probably both were exaggerated by the Arabs who for many centuries had held settlements along the coast and did not relish the prospect of European competition in their trade with the interior. Their instincts were sound for when the Europeans did come, in the persons of the British, it was with the declared intention of destroying entirely the mainspring of Arab economy. As this was the trade in slaves the Arabs could perhaps not legitimately complain, but resist they could and did, and Her Majesty's Government had to resign itself to spending a great deal of British money, and expending a good many British lives, in maintaining naval patrols along the coast. The efforts of the sailors were reinforced by those of the diplomatists whose part it was to win the co-operation of the Sultan of Zanzibar. This was, indeed, essential to any real success since the Sultan, from his island capital, ruled in varying degree or effectiveness several hundred miles of the coastal fringe of the mainland. By degrees his co-operation was obtained, and with it the period covered by this section of the anthology begins.

Given the key of the gate, and Zanzibar was the key, it was only a matter of time before Europeans were pushing into the interior. A German missionary named Rebmann, from his station at Mombasa, ventured far enough inland to get a glimpse of snow-capped Kiliminjaro in 1848, and from then on the learned societies of Europe were jostling one another to sponsor expeditions.

First of the journeys deep into the hinterland was that in which Burton and Speke, striking south-west from Zanzibar, discovered Lake Tanganyika. On the return journey Speke made a detour from the main route of the expedition to check Arab reports that a still greater lake lay to the north. The reports were correct and so Speke became the first white man to see Victoria Nyanza. Without any obvious justification except his intuition Speke asserted that Victoria Nyanza was the source of the Nile, and in doing so started an angry feud with the irascible Burton which was to last many years and to end in tragedy.

In order to justify his contention Speke embarked on a second expedition, this time with himself as leader and Grant as second-in-command. He struck inland to the point where he had first sighted Victoria Nyanza, and then turned northwards along the lake's western shore. In this way he came eventually to the "singular, barbaric civilisation" of the Kingdom of Uganda, where he was most hospitably received by the king, Mutesa. With Mutesa's help Speke achieved his primary objective, discovery of proof positive that the Nile began its journey to the Mediterranean from Victoria Nyanza. Not only did he visit the point at which the river left the lake, but also traced part of its course northwards. Leaving the river at the point where it turned westwards towards Albert Nyanza he continued to trek northwards and eventually found it again in the vicinity of Gondoroko in the Sudan.

It was here that he met Baker who had got as far as Gondoroko in his effort to trace the Nile to its source by working down through Egypt and the Sudan. The unlucky Baker had thus been forestalled, but Speke was able to give him enough information to encourage him to continue his journey, and so to achieve the distinction of discovering Albert Nyanza and the Murchison Falls.

Next on the scene was H.M. Stanley, fresh from his historic meeting

KAIETUR WATERFALL,
BRITISH GUIANA

BLACK AND SILVER
THE SYMBOL OF ARAB INFLUENCE ON THE EAST COAST OF AFRICA

with Livingstone far away to the south, in Nyasaland. With substantial financial backing from the *Daily Telegraph* and the *New York Herald Tribune*, Stanley organised his expeditions ambitiously. On this occasion he took with him, in sections, a boat called the *Lady Alice*, in which he circumnavigated, first Victoria Nyanza, and then Lake Tanganyika. From Tanganyika he took the boat overland to the River Congo, which he followed along the whole of its enormous length to the South Atlantic and so crossed the continent from east to west, a truly remarkable achievement. During his journey on Victoria Nyanza Stanley called on Mutesa who gave him a welcome no less warm than that accorded to Speke. Stanley describes in particular how he witnessed a great naval battle on the lake and, in fact, took a decisive part in it by inventing a secret weapon. Stanley made considerable efforts to convert Mutesa to Christianity, and had sufficient success to inspire him to write the famous letter, which the *Daily Telegraph* published in 1875, calling for missionaries to visit Uganda. This letter had an adventurous journey to England. A second white man, a Belgian named Linant de Bellefonds, arrived at Mutesa's court while Stanley was there He came on a mission from Gordon in the Sudan, and to him Stanley entrusted the letter, thinking it would reach England more quickly if sent northwards to Gordon. In fact, de Bellefonds' party was massacred on its way back to Khartoum, and the letter lay in the dead Belgian's boot until it was recovered by the punitive expedition sent by Gordon. With this dramatic history behind it, the letter had immediate results on publication. One party of missionaries left for Uganda via Egypt, and a second via Zanzibar, and both arrived, though several of the Zanzibar party died on the way, and the rest were in very bad shape when they reached Uganda.

Until then, the late 1870's, no attempt had been made to brave the Masai by crossing their country in a direct line from the coast to Uganda. The Royal Geographical Society accordingly commissioned an engaging young man named Joseph Thomson to perform this feat, and gave him £3,000 with which to do it. His precise terms of reference said that he was to undertake "the ascertaining of a practicable direct route for European travellers through the Masai country from any one of the East African ports to Victoria Nyanza, and to examine Mount Kenia: to gather data for constructing as complete a map as possible in a preliminary survey: and to make all practicable observations regarding the meteorology, geology, natural history and ethnology of the regions traversed". All this he did very fully and recorded the results in *Through Masai Land*. Among other things, he brought back graphic descriptions of the Rift Valley—he called it the "meridional trough"—which is such a remarkable feature of East African topography. But he could not claim to be the first white man to penetrate into Masai country. A year earlier a German, Dr. Fischer, travelled as far as Lake Naivasha before the Masai turned him back. Thomson got far beyond Naivasha, however, and came back across the Kenya highlands into the bargain.

Fischer's journey was a symptom of the ideas which Bismarck's Germany had begun to entertain about colonial expansion, ideas which precipitated the "scramble for Africa" in the 'eighties. German merchants appeared on the coast, and their Society of German Colonisation received a charter of protection from Berlin. Britain countered by granting a royal charter to the Imperial British East Africa Company, in which the moving spirit was Sir William Mackinnon. This clash was marked by two years of uneasy sparring for advantage, and had then to be resolved in the Anglo-German treaty of 1890. The treaty drew a line between the coast and Victoria Nyanza, and it was agreed that north of the line (Uganda and what is now Kenya) should be recognised as a sphere of British influence, and south of the line (what is now Tanganyika) as a sphere of German influence.

Having performed all that it considered its duty, Her Majesty's Government heaved a sigh of relief and prepared to sit back and forget all about East Africa, content to leave management of affairs to the Company. The latter set about the task with more courage and energy than resources. Notable among the men it engaged were Lugard and Jackson, the former destined to become the outstanding British administrator in Africa, and the latter Governor of the East African Protectorate and of Uganda in turn.

Lugard at that time was a young Army captain placed on extended sick leave as the result of service in Burma. His idea of recuperative leave was to work his way to Zanzibar with the general idea that he "might embark in some useful undertaking in Africa, if possible in connection with the suppression of the slave trade". He proved his mettle in a prolonged battle with the slave traders established on the northern shores of Lake Nyasa, and was then recruited by the East Africa Company to lead an expedition to Uganda to make a treaty with King Mwanga, who had succeeded to the throne on the death of the famous Mutesa.

Mwanga, unhappily, had inherited his father's more capricious qualities but none of his breadth of vision. Seeing the threat to his despotic rule which lay in the spread of Christianity, for the missionaries had made remarkable progress, he initiated a persecution of the Christian converts. R. P. Ashe wrote of this period: "Frequently

furnaces were smoking, in which the agonised bodies of persons, innocent of any crime, were writhing in slow torture, till death, more
merciful than their tormentors, ended their anguish and despair." One
incident he records is the killing of three of the Mission Readers. These
three, it was reported by others who escaped, "had been tortured by having their arms cut off and were then bound alive to a scaffolding under
which a fire was made, and they were slowly burnt to death. Mufta
and his men mocked them, and bade them pray now to see if Isa
Masiya (Jesus Christ) would rescue them from his hands. The dear
lads clung to their faith and died rather than deny their Lord and
Master". The missionaries themselves were humiliated and threatened,
and in 1885, on Mwanga's orders, Bishop Hannington was speared to
death on his arrival at the eastern frontier of Uganda.

It was on this scene of persecution and civil war that Lugard arrived.
Within six months, largely by force of his own personality, he had
imposed order and obtained Mwanga's signature to a treaty. But it
was an uneasy order, and the Company lacked the resources, either to
maintain it indefinitely, or to build the railway which it was thought
would provide the key to the situation by connecting Uganda to the
coast, and so opening up the interior to profitable trade. The Company
accordingly sought to transfer its responsibilities to the Government,
and was powerfully supported by the missionary societies which had
been thoroughly roused by the incidents in Uganda.

The Government, however, showed a remarkable coyness. It could
see little to justify expenditure of the British taxpayers' money. As a
result one had the strange spectacle—strange, at any rate, in these days
when ideas of the white man's burden are not in vogue—of Lugard
trying to think up hard-boiled reasons for official intervention. "If
our advent in Africa," he wrote, "introduces civilisation, peace and
good government, abolishes the slave trade and effects other advantages for Africans, it must not therefore be supposed that this was our
sole and only aim in going there. However greatly such objects may
weigh with a large and powerful section of the nation, I do not believe
that in these days our national policy is based on motives of philanthropy only. Though these may be our duties, it is quite possible that
here (as frequently if not generally is the case) advantage may run
parallel with duty". In the end pressure of public opinion proved so
strong that the Government decided to send a Special Commissioner,
Sir Gerald Portal, to Uganda to "advise on the best means of dealing
with the country". What, in fact, he did recommend was the establishment of an official administration and the building of a railway. So
the Government at last agreed, a treaty was signed with Mwanga, and

in 1894 a British Protectorate over Uganda was proclaimed. The following year the Company sold their remaining rights to the Government for £250,000, and the East African Protectorate (re-christened Kenya in 1919) came into official being.

Eighteen-ninety-five saw also the beginning of the Uganda railway, which took six years to complete. "One of the most romantic and wonderful railways in the world," was how Winston Churchill described it. "The two iron streaks of rail that wind their way among the hills and foliage of Mombasa Island do not break their smooth monotony until, after piercing Equatorial forests, stretching across immense prairies, and climbing almost to the level of the European snow-line, they pause—and that only for a time—upon the edges of the Great Lake."

With the railway began the modern history of East Africa, a history which has developed rather differently from expectations at the turn of the century. All interest then was directed towards Uganda. "East Africa," wrote Sir Harry Johnston, "is mainly valuable as being the region furnishing the best seaports for the outlet of the products of Uganda." It is only fair to add that he also said of the railway that, "as it passes through the disappointing territories of British East Africa, it will cause those territories to cease their disappointment, just as French railways in Tunis and Algeria are making the desert habitable and profitable".

1. HINTS TO TRAVELLERS

A traveller proposing to venture into the interior of East Africa customarily assembled his caravan at Zanzibar. To penetrate inland he had to cross the belt of unhealthy swamp which fringed the sea. He did it usually before he was fully acclimatised, and while he was still "soft" from the ways of civilisation. Before the 'nineties, moreover, the mosquito was still unsuspected as the carrier of fever so that the precautions he took did not include those that really mattered. The upshot was that he reached the interior full of fever and in no condition to endure the hardships of trekking and living on the country. Joseph Thomson gives this description of the coastal swamps:

Whichever way the traveller chooses, he finds foul swamps and marshes, swarming with horrid creeping, slimy things, and through these he must wade by the hour together. He leaves the swamp, to slip and flounder over black fetid mud from which rise unpleasant exhalations. Rain falls frequently in torrents, and numerous almost unfordable streams obstruct his way. Rotting vegetation fills the air with poisonous gases, and the water he drinks is charged with the germs of disease. It would be well if he had to encounter only such physical difficulties, but, alas! such is not the case. The spirits of disease, like hell-hounds let loose, seize hold of him. They present no shape to the material eye, but from every swamp, marsh, and mud-stretch they rise invisible. They are drawn in by every breath, or drunk in each drop of water. Ague shakes him with its mighty hand till his teeth rattle together, dysentery strikes agonizing darts into his most vital parts, or fever clings to him like the shirt of Nessus, burning into his very heart. You may think that this picture is overdrawn, but such is not the case. I speak from dire experience, and I need but refer the reader to the works of almost every traveller to find my description substantiated.

THOMSON: *Through Masai Land.* 1885.

Expeditions started at Zanzibar chiefly because it was there that over the centuries the Arabs had created a class of professional porters—slaves, descendants of slaves, and even free men, drawn by the excitements of what Burton called the "mart and capital" of East Africa. These men, the Zanzibari, figure prominently in all East African travellers' tales before the coming of the railway. Some travellers damned them with a will: others sang their praises. The truth probably lies in the skill with which they were handled. "*In Africa*," *says Gregory,* "*everything turns on a personality*," *and so it was in handling Zanzibari. Ashe paints this picture of Zanzibar:*

Fair-faced languid-looking Indian women sit and display their wares, waiting patiently for customers, as also men of the same nation, who, to judge by their appearance, have evidently grown fat upon their gains; their commodities include cotton-stuffs, spices, gold and silver thread, lamps, attar of roses, onions, and other miscellaneous articles of frequent barter. Fruit-shops too abound, kept by vivacious negroes; there are also not a few almost European establishments owned by Goanese, where anything in reason may be purchased, from a dress-suit to a packet of pins. Arabs are stalking along with an air of superb contempt—the Arab has certainly mastered the art of looking as if the place belongs to him. Here comes one of them riding a gaily-caparisoned donkey, his slaves running in front calling out, "simila, simila", "by your leave". Now we meet a big black man carrying two enormous bunches of bananas slung over his shoulder at each end of a stick, he also cries out "simila". At another place a bevy of women and girls, every one of them slaves, are at work carrying mortar and stones for the masons who are building a neighbouring house, all the while chanting some monotonous but not unmusical African melody.

ASHE: *Two Kings of Uganda.* 1889.

These are the terms on which Stanley took the Zanzibari into his service:

I was compelled to bind myself to them, on the word of an "honourable white man", to observe the following conditions as to conduct towards them:

1st. That I should treat them kindly, and be patient with them.

2nd. That in case of sickness, I should dose them with proper medicine, and see them nourished with the best the country afforded. That if patients were unable to proceed, they should not be abandoned to the mercy of heathen, but were to be conveyed to such places as should be considered safe for their persons and their freedom, and convenient for their return, on convalescence, to their friends. That with all patients thus left behind, I should leave sufficient cloth or beads to pay the native practitioner for his professional attendance, and for the support of the patient.

3rd. That in cases of disagreement between man and man, I should judge justly, honestly, and impartially. That I should do my utmost to prevent the ill-treatment of the weak by the strong, and never permit the oppression of those unable to resist.

4th. That I should act like a "father and mother" to them, and to the best of my ability resist all violence offered to them by "savage natives, and roving and lawless banditti".

They also promised, upon the above conditions being fulfilled, that they would do their duty like men, would honour and respect my instructions, giving me their united support and endeavouring to the best of their ability to be faithful servants, and would never desert me in the hour of need. In short, that they would behave like good and loyal children, and "may the blessing of God", said they, "be upon us".

STANLEY: *Through the Dark Continent.* 1878.

Gregory, too, was faithfully served. The reason is clear in this account he gives of an incident which occurred above the snow-line of Mount Kenya. A porter, Wadi, was reported missing.

I rushed back at once; but as the snow had hidden our trail, I missed it, and had to search for an hour before I found him. He was lying on his load about 300 feet below the level of the camp; he was covered with snow and nearly frozen to death. A little brandy revived him, but he was too weak to stand. As it was still snowing it would have been useless to have returned for help, for the porters were so cowed that they would have refused to move. I recollected that Wadi weighed less than the burdens some of my men had to bear all day long, so I resolved to carry him. He was able to cling to my back, and slowly, and with many halts, I struggled with him up the slope. If the porter had left his load when he first became too weak to carry it, he could no doubt have walked on with the others. I thought his action in staying out in the snow with it simply Quixotic, and, annoyed at the trouble it had given me, I rather brutally told him next morning that he was a fool. It is a point of honour among Zanzibari never to leave their loads, and I shall not forget the man's reproachful look as he asked, "How could I leave my load without my master's orders to do so?"

GREGORY: *The Great Rift Valley.* 1896.

Goods to barter for food formed an essential part of the traveller's equipment.

We were provided with Epsom salts by the stone, but found ourselves short of common table salt. Our large supply of castor oil was but a poor compensation for the entire absence of such a necessary as butter, and for my part I would gladly have exchanged our elaborate distilling apparatus for another common tea-kettle. The ordinary equipment of an African traveller consists of tents, camp-beds, chairs, stools, buckets, pots, pans, cups and saucers, plates, blankets, guns, pistols, boxes of clothes and books, scientific instruments, provisions and medicines. He carries with him also goods for barter, consisting of bales of cloth made up into loads of from sixty to seventy pounds; beads of various kinds, copper, brass and iron wire, gunpowder, and soap, which is a very important article of commerce in the interior.

ASHE: *Two Kings of Uganda.* 1889.

*

The question of currency on this journey had been most perplexing. Altogether in my trek northwards I passed through seven distinct peoples or tribes, and the food, etc., that I bought or bargained for had to be purchased with a bewildering variety of articles. Fortunately, taught by past experience, I had not come unprepared. In Uganda and Bunyoro, shells, pice and rupees were generally acceptable. The Chope, Acholi, and Madi preferred beads, and the beads had to be of the particular shape, size and colour of the prevailing fashion. White small beads might do for one district, but large blue beads were *de rigueur* in another, and this with people whose only dress apart from ornaments consisted of "sunshine and a smile". Cloth, in the shape of the strong unbleached calico known as amerikani, could be used almost anywhere, the unit being a "hand", or the length of the forearm from the elbow to the tip of the middle finger. If a considerable length of cloth had to be measured out, the method of effecting measurement made quite a difference, the vendor bringing his shortest-armed friend to measure the cloth, the buyer selecting the longest-armed. As time was of no moment to the natives, and their bargaining instincts were brisk, I always turned the matter over to my headman with resulting satisfaction on both sides. As scarcity of food became more pronounced the further north we got, even beads lost their potency. I then found that a large bale of salt I had brought came in very handy, for salt was a very coveted luxury in those parts. Finally this failed and I then tried the last arrow in my quiver, a large bale of native tobacco. This instantly did the trick, and I bought the needed food.

COOK: *Uganda Memories.*

The passage of the "mlango" (door or gate) of a district was, in Thomson's words, "always the most ticklish matter". If all went well, the traveller and the chief went through a ceremony of blood brotherhood.

A goat was brought, and, taking it by one ear, I was required to state where I was going, to declare that I meant no evil, and did not work in uchawi (black magic), and finally, to promise that I would do no harm to the country. The other ear was then taken by the sultan's ambassador, and he made promise on his part that no harm would be done to us, that food would be given, and all articles stolen returned. The goat was then killed, and a strip of skin cut off the forehead, in which two slits were made. The M-swahili, taking hold of this, pushed it on my finger by the lower slit five times, finally pushing it over the joint. I had next to take the strip, still keeping it on my own finger, and do the same for the M-swahili, through the upper slit. This operation finished, the strips had to be cut in two, leaving the respective portions on our fingers, and the sultan of Shira and I were sworn brothers.

THOMSON: *Through Masai Land*. 1885.

Even then it was unwise to take too much for granted.

The goat was killed, the stomach cut out, and filled with blood, which was mixed with the contents of the stomach. Nathan Nyuki and the elders stood on the bridge and sang a kind of chant. The chief then said that he was ready to lead us, while the warriors formed up in two lines, one on each side of the path, on the opposite bank. I explained that I also had a religion, and to this religion I was devotedly attached. The first article in its creed was never to put your head into a lion's mouth; the second was always to get out of the way when an elephant was coming to walk over you; the third was never to place a line of your own men between two lines of spearsmen. I pointed out that according to their arrangements this last article would be infringed, and that my religion must be respected as well as theirs. So the warriors were all sent ahead.

GREGORY: *The Great Rift Valley*. 1896.

According to Lugard, finding one's way though unknown country requires only a compass and common-sense.

There is always a path. In country absolutely uninhabited there are the paths followed by game. When you have lived in Africa some time you will be able to distinguish to some extent *whose* path it is. We all know a *man's* path. An elephant's is different. It is some eighteen inches broad (a man's is generally not more than eleven or twelve); it has no central depression, but its distinctive difference is that the edges are clean cut; there is no *partly* trampled vegetation at the side, and the higher grasses lean over from the sharply defined margin. It is a peculiarity of game that it thus follows paths. Though an elephant should pass across a piece of open veldt, with grass but a foot high, which would be absolutely unfelt by him in walking, he will invariably follow a beaten track. If scared, he may rush across country, and then the densest jungle and most impenetrable scrub give way before him like dry flax before fire; but, however panic-struck, he will follow the first track he crosses. These tracks intersect each other in an elephant country in all directions, and it is difficult to decide with what object they first became well-used paths. A hippo path is different. This animal does not put one foot into the footprint of the last, like an elephant, but his near and off feet each make paths for themselves, so to speak, so that generally there is a narrow ridge of grass or soil in the centre. Rhinoceros again are different, and they use their paths to connect their dunging-places. On the bare plains, where the grass is no higher than the turf on a lawn, you may see the game tracks, worn still more bare by the hoofs of countless animals. In high grass, in forest, through tangled scrub and brushwood, of course the rule applies with still more force. Even the very field-mice and vermin keep to their runs, though the ground be flat and without a blade of grass.

If the caravan is proceeding along game tracks (as now on our journey up the Sabakhi) I select such as bear in the direction I wish to go by my pocket compass. Each path that branches away is "closed" by the men who follow me. This is done either by throwing upon it a few green twigs, leaves, or grass, or by drawing a line across it—if no leaves are handy—with a stick or spear. By this means, should you wish to follow up the track of the caravan, you can do so with ease among a network of paths; and thus, should a gap occur in the caravan, those behind have no difficulty in selecting the path we have followed.

LUGARD: *The Rise of our East African Empire.* 1893.

A white man's caravan had enormous entertainment value.

Our party was a source of continual wonder to these unsophisticated people. I recollect one day, when separated from my companions, being found by a group of Wagogo. I was evidently a new sort of man, and the first specimen of the kind which they had ever seen. Their astonishment knew no bounds. One old man ventured to approach while I stood still for inspection; he cautiously advanced one finger till it touched my beard, and then timidly withdrew it. The next thing which attracted his attention was my ear; he again put out his hand and very gently took hold of it, feeling it to see what it was made of, but I had no time to spare them for more minute examination.

ASHE: *Two Kings of Uganda.* 1889.

Who but a white man would do such ridiculous things?

She was another of those wonders of obesity, unable to stand excepting on all fours. I was desirous to obtain a good view of her, and actually to measure her, and induced her to give me facilities for doing so, by offering in return to show her a bit of my naked legs and arms. The bait took as I wished it, and after getting her to sidle and wriggle into the middle of the hut, I did as I promised, and then took her dimensions —round arm, 1 ft. 11 ins.; chest, 4 ft. 4 ins.; thigh, 2 ft. 7 ins.; calf, 1 ft. 8 ins.; height, 5 ft. 8 ins. All of these are exact except the height, and I believe I could have obtained this more accurately if I could have had her laid on the floor. Not knowing what difficulties I should have to contend with in such a piece of engineering, I tried to get her height by raising her up. This, after infinite exertions on the part of us both, was accomplished, when she sank down again, fainting, for her blood had rushed into her head. Meanwhile, the daughter, a lass of sixteen, sat stark-naked before us, sucking at a milk-pot, on which the father kept her at work by holding a rod in his hand, for as fattening is the first duty of fashionable female life, it must be duly enforced by the rod if necessary.

SPEKE: *Discovery of the Source of the Nile.* 1863.

The life of a caravan lacked neither colour nor incident.

From sunset till about nine o'clock was generally the noisiest time in camp. Men were sitting about the fires, many cooking, others smoking, and all talking. Sometimes a song with a chorus was indulged in. Then probably the head-man, Simba, would give directions for the next day's march. At any rate, this was the time chosen for an harangue to the men. They would sit round in a circle and he would commence with a short sentence. Then a man on the other side of the crowd would give a word of assent and so on until the speech was ended. Then every one listened for the sound of Stokes's drum. If it gave what is known as the "safari" beat, or the beat for the march, it was known that the caravan would leave as usual in the morning, and there would be a responsive roar from 2,000 throats, prolonged for two or three minutes. Then gradually men composed themselves for sleep and silence crept over the camp—a silence broken only by the ecstatic cry of some wretched bhang smoker, of whom there were many in the caravan—or the howl of some wild beast seeking its prey.

It was a weird sight, the great camp at night—with its almost countless fires, and bright gleams of light and black shadows in telling contrast, the stacks of loads, the white tents, the moving forms of wild-

looking men in every imaginable combination—then almost imperceptibly movement ceasing, first one and then another lying down to
rest until at length the huge encampment was almost as still and silent
and as weird as a city of the dead.

TUCKER: Eighteen Years in Uganda and East Africa.   1908.

★

On Saturday, September 20, we reached the Ututuru Wells. These
wells are narrow and the shafts deep—some seventy feet. According to
our custom we arrived first at the camping-ground, and were able,
with the assistance of our tent-ropes, to get sufficient water for our use
before the arrival of the huge caravan itself. The scene on its arrival is
one that will never fade from my memory. There were three wells to
supply 2,500 men.

The struggle for the water was terrible, not that the men fought—
they did not do that. But the crowding the well tops and the eager
pressing into vacant places almost amounted to a fierce struggle,
terrible to witness. In the course of the day three lives were lost by
men losing their foothold, and falling headlong down the well. All
night long the crowding continued, and when morning dawned there
were yet men with their thirst unquenched.

Ibid.

★

We were awakened in the middle of the night by a tremendous
noise, and on getting out of my tent I found about half the caravan in a
state of nudity, apparently executing a dance round the fires, but not
singing the cheery song that generally accompanies this performance.
In fact, their exclamations were the reverse of cheerful. It transpired
that one-half of the camp had been invaded by an army of large red
ants. These ants march in regular columns, with advanced guard,
scouts and flankers, and constitute a formidable and well-drilled army.
They had at once attacked the sleeping men, and, needless to say, in a
very brief space of time had cleared the camp. Those whose quarters
had escaped were busy barring the further progress of the ants by lines
of fires and red-hot embers, while the sufferers were engaged in picking
the ants off each other. This operation is not by any means easy, as the
ant will part with its body rather than release the hold it has obtained
with its powerful jaws. As a consequence, the first proceeding is to
tear off the body, and then pick off the head and jaws which remain
fixed in the flesh. In three-quarters of an hour or so the legions of ants
had marched on, and the camp resumed its normal condition. The

progress of these insects through grass causes a curious hissing sound not unlike that of a snake. On one occasion, while sitting by the road-side with Mr. Jackson, we were startled by this ominous hiss, and sprang to our feet, imagining we were attacked by a snake, but were relieved to find it was only the noise made by the advance guard of a column of these red ants.

MACDONALD: *Soldiering and Surveying in British East Africa.* 1897.

Physical toughness, the inevitable sense of humour, and a capacity for philo-sophical endurance were essential to the traveller.

Shortly after this, in chasing a rhinoceros, I met with an accident attended with the most unfortunate consequences; I fell and dislocated one toe and severely strained another. So far, however, that was a mere matter of detail. Next day, as ill luck would have it, I slipped when going over some rocks and hurt my foot again, and this led to synovitis. That also was detail, though next morning I could not walk. In defiance of the Zanzibari proverb, "Never mount a donkey that has no saddle", a sack was tied on to the remaining donkey, and I rode. During the day the beast shied, the improvised saddle slipped, and I was thrown and dragged a few paces along the ground. During this the accident happened. In a collision with a basalt boulder my watch sustained a blow which smashed the glass and stopped the works. I did all I knew to start it again; I oiled it, and patted it, and sang hymns to it. But it would not go, and for the rest of the expedition I had to guess the time as best I could.

GREGORY: *The Great Rift Valley.* 1896.

*

The chill brought on neuralgia, which after two days became localized to one of my wisdom teeth. In the absence of a dentist it became dismally evident that I must extract the wretched tooth myself. I had only taken one pair of dental forceps with me, but fortunately they fitted the tooth. From 2 to 3 a.m. I lay under my mosquito netting, revolving the situation, and then got up with the resolve to get through with the job. I tried to inject a little cocaine, not very easy to do at the back of one's own mouth, and then kneeling down before a little camp mirror fixed the forceps on to the offender. It hurt so abominably, that I couldn't take it off again, but twisted and wrenched till it came out.

COOK: *Uganda Memories.*

*

I had a fine big Unyamwezi donkey, of which, when I reached the neighbourhood of the Masai, those ignoble savages robbed me and left me to proceed on foot. However, I had the help of the donkey for the first five hundred miles of the march, which was an important consideration. I was by this time quite an old traveller, and I had in the boy Mwana awulira, whom I have before mentioned, an excellent interpreter, for he knew four African languages. He was also armour-bearer, as he carried my rifle, and combined this function with that of cook and general servant. Affectionate and as honest as the day, he was seldom tired and never out of temper. Add to this that he was my nurse when I was ill, and when I became blind my leader, it will be seen that if ransoming a slave be an act of charity, in this case I received an ample reward. I was far from well on the march, and was laid up six days at one village with bad fever. However, I struggled on to Ugogo, where I was attacked with ophthalmia. The prostration caused by frequent fevers had made me liable to this terrible complaint and to violent and prolonged toothache. The light caused me so much agony that I had to completely blindfold myself, and so in utter darkness for seven days I made the journey through Ugogo. Mwana awulira, the obedient child, did everything for me, and indeed all my followers were as kind as could be. . . . And so, in spite of the fact that I was blind and had toothache, I had a pleasant journey.

ASHE: *Two Kings of Uganda.* 1889.

2. THE MASAI

The two great curses of Africa, said Lugard, were the slave trader and the "awfu and intolerable tyranny of the dominant tribe". In East Africa, between the Lake and the coast, the rôle of dominant tribe was filled by the Masai. "One can talk to none of the peaceful agricultural tribes without hearing sad stories of Masai raids," recorded Gregory. "The people tell you of the impossibility of cultivating exposed districts—generally the most fertile ones—and they complain bitterly of the uselessness of keeping cattle, which serve only as incentive to Masai attack." For the Masai fighting was an end in itself. Only that and cattle keeping were occupations considered worthy of their attention. They wandered over East Africa with their herds and were a terror and scourge wherever they went. Their whole tribal organisation was directed towards the maintenance of a powerful warrior group. Between the ages of thirteen and seventeen a youth passed through stern initiation ceremonies and became a warrior. His membership of the warrior group lasted for between ten and fifteen years, and during the whole of this time he was subjected to the severest discipline, living apart from the rest of the tribe, barred from smoking and drinking, and limited to a diet of meat, milk and blood. Living with the warriors were the young, immature girls of the tribe, the theory apparently being that if the girls lived apart from the warriors they would allow themselves to be courted by the enemy. At twenty-seven or thirty the warrior became an elder, married and settled down.

Passing through the forest, we soon set our eyes upon the dreaded warriors that had been so long the subject of my waking dreams, and I could not but involuntarily exclaim, "What splendid fellows!" as I surveyed a band of the most peculiar race of men to be found in all Africa.

After a most ceremonious greeting performed with much gravity and aristocratic dignity, their great shovel-headed spears were stuck in the ground, their bullock's-hide shields rested against them on their sides, and then the oil-and-clay-bedaubed warriors assumed a sitting posture, with their knees drawn up to their chins, and their small neat kid-skin mantles enveloping them. We on our part took position opposite them, holding our guns in our hands. I, of course, as became my dignity, occupied a camp-stool.

After a few words among themselves in a low tone, a spokesman arose, leisurely took a spear in his left hand to lean upon, and then with his knobkerry as an orator's baton, he proceeded to deliver his message

with all the ease of a professional speaker. With profound astonishment I watched this son of the desert, as he stood before me, speaking
with a natural fluency and grace, a certain sense of the gravity and
importance of his position, and a dignity of attitude beyond all praise.

THOMSON: *Through Masai Land*. 1885.

*

As we emerged from the mountain pass by which we gained access
to the valley in which lies Lake Naivasha, we saw in a moment that
our entrance into Masai land would not pass unchallenged. About
mid-way between ourselves and the lake we saw a knot of figures,
which we knew at once to be Masai, but whether they were El-Moran
(warriors) we were ignorant. However, in a little while our doubts
were resolved. As they came near us we saw by the sunlight glinting
on their spears that they were warriors. Their shields and other warlike
trappings were soon revealed. On they came without the slightest
hesitation until they were within a dozen yards of us.

Then they stuck their spears in the ground and commenced to question us. They were magnificent specimens of humanity. Some of them
were certainly 6 ft. 3 in. and more in height. Their limbs shining with
grease, looked like burnished bronze. They were savages—but noble-
looking savages—as they stood there questioning us in all the assurance
of physical power. "Where had we come from? Whither were we
going? Were we traders? Had we wire? Would we give them some?"
and so on—until the main body of our caravan came in sight. Seeing
its length, and no doubt estimating its powers, they concluded their
catechism and courteously signed to us that we were free to proceed
on our way.

TUCKER: *Eighteen Years in Uganda and East Africa*. 1908.

*The traveller quickly learnt that among the Masai to be spat upon was a
courtesy much to be sought.*

Spitting, it may be remarked, has a very different signification with
the Masai from that which prevails with us or with most other tribes.
With them it expresses the greatest good-will and the best of wishes.
It takes the place of the compliments of the season, and you had better
spit upon a damsel than kiss her. You spit when you meet, and you do
the same on leaving. You seal your bargain in a similar manner. As I
was a lybon of the first water, the Masai flocked to me as pious catholics
would do to springs of healing virtue, and with the aid of occasional
draughts of water I was equal to the demand. The more copiously I

AN ARAB SHOPKEEPER FROM PEMBA
IN HIS TURBAN OF YELLOW, ACID PINK AND PURPLE

LOCAL WATER TRANSPORT, PEMBA, NORTH-EAST OF ZANZIBAR

spat upon them, the greater was their delight; and with pride they
would retail to their friends how the white medicine-man honoured
them, and would point with the greatest satisfaction to the ocular proof
of the agreeable fact. It was certainly rather drying work for me when
I had a large number to operate upon, and I required the aid of bullets
and stones in my mouth to stimulate the production of the precious
fluid.

THOMSON: *Through Masai Land*. 1885.

Gregory's experiences with the Masai were a good average sample.

Our route lay over rich turf, on which roamed many antelope and
enormous herds of cattle guarded by Masai. I had been told that the
terrible havoc wrought by cattle disease had annihilated the vast herds
once possessed by this tribe; I was therefore surprised to see so many.
I was also rather sorry, for the abundance of cattle showed that there
would be a large force of Masai near the lake. But my men assured me
that they would be quite friendly, and not interfere with my plans. I
was very anxious to examine the structure of the Mau scarp to the
west of Naivasha, in order to discover if its structure corresponded with
that of the eastern wall of the Rift Valley; and also to make a collection
to illustrate the flora and fauna of the lake. I had brought with me
presents for the Masai chiefs; for I intended to make friends with
them, to leave most of the porters on the lake shore, while with fifteen others I made a branch excursion to the west.

Great, therefore, was my disappointment when, on our arrival at
the camping-ground, a band of insolent young warriors came crowding round us and forbade my men erecting the tents. We had un-
wisely divided into two parties; Omari, the Askari, and eight porters
were with the donkeys, while I had hastened on with the other men
to get the camp into order before dark; so for a while I was bound to
temporise. The attitude of the El-Moran was insolent in the extreme;
they bullied the porters, who were in a cringing state of terror, but
fortunately they were rather in awe of me. One of them stepped up
to the door of my tent and wanted to enter it. I asked in a polite tone
"El Moru?" (Are you an elder?) and when he cheekily replied "El
Moran" (Warrior), I kicked him away from the tent, and told him at
once to leave the camp, an order which the other Masai made him obey.
At last, to our intense relief, Omari and the men with the donkeys came
in, and a temporising policy was no longer necessary. I ordered two
El-Moran to go and fetch some of the elders, as I wanted a "shauri".
Two elders came at the head of a powerful body of El-Moran, and the
shauri began. I could see that the idea of stopping at Naivasha for a

14

week was absolutely impracticable. I therefore simply stated that I wanted to go through the country on my way to Baringo. I asked for permission to rest there for that night, to buy some firewood and water from the women, and next morning to continue my march to the north. The reply was short and emphatic. I was not to go through their country; I had no right to pitch my camp in it without permission; and I was to pack up at once and return by the way I had come. Omari and the interpreter Ramathan both looked as distressed as I was disappointed at this reply. They begged for a peaceful answer, but I had been advised on the coast that the right way to manage Masai was by "bluff"; so I replied that we were not going back, that we intended to stay where we were for that night, and next morning march on to Baringo; and that we should leave it to them to decide whether we were to be friends or foes. They then altered their tone, and said I might go on if I paid them "hongo"—a kind of toll for passage through their country. Hongo seems to me a very fair tax, at least when a caravan uses the paths and wells made by the natives; I had therefore no *a priori* objection to paying it. But the amount demanded exceeded my whole stock of goods; I therefore pointed to the stack of loads and then to the men, who with rifles ready were standing round the camp, and told the Masai that whatever hongo they wanted, they had better come and take. They did not seem to like the tone of the invitation, and left with threats as to what would happen next day.

As soon as the Masai had withdrawn we devoted all our energies to strengthening the camp, cutting down any thorn bushes that would have afforded shelter to the enemy, and adding them to our thorn zeriba. Omari then came into my tent to discuss matters. He said the Masai were certainly present in great force, and for some reason or other were determined not to allow us to proceed. The interpreter Ramathan said he had passed Naivasha several times before, and had never seen so many kraals, such great herds of cattle, nor experienced such a hostile reception. With his usual cowardice he begged me to return. Omari was also very ill at ease, but with his usual pluck said that whatever I decided on should be done. Everybody on the coast had told me that if we met Masai parties on the war-path, we should have to fight them; but that, except on Laikipia, the people of the villages would be friendly. The porters only the day before had said that we should find the Masai here most amiable; they would come up to camp, we should shake hands and spit on one another; they would sell us food and trinkets, and we should go in and out of their kraals like brothers. We were therefore all of us much disconcerted by our reception. The Masai never offered to shake hands, much less did they spit on us; and until these two expressions of peace and good will had been made, we knew we could not trust the people. We could not quite understand it, so we made every preparation to repel attack, and stood to arms all night. It poured with rain, and this added to the discomfort of our situation. We kept the fires burning, and piles of wet grass beside them, so as to smother them in case of an attack.

Rain was still falling heavily at dawn, and it was useless to think of continuing our march until it left off. To encourage the men, we served out an extra ration of food and let them prepare breakfast. Some Masai children were sent out to watch us, but we saw no one else till about eight o'clock. The elders and the El-Moran then visited us, and once again the game of brag and bluster was resumed. They repeated their taunts as to the weakness of our numbers, and boasted that they had massacred caravans of twenty times our strength. They said they had done this with much smaller forces than they could now bring into the field, for they claimed to have 9,000 warriors on the shores of Naivasha. Any hesitation or offer of hongo would have been mistaken for weakness, and probably have completely ruined the whole expedition. There was nothing for it but to put on a bold front and answer defiance with defiance. So, as soon as they repeated their refusal of permission to proceed, and again ordered us to return to the coast, I told them that we were going on, even though we had to fight our way through the lot of them. I warned them that if any harm befell us it would be the worse for them, for a great caravan of brave soldiers was even then approaching their country from Uganda. I said that the men in this caravan were more in number than there were papyrus stems around Lake Naivasha, that they would sweep upon their country, kill all the El-Moran, eat up all the cattle, and drive the elders and women and children out into the deserts, where not even their slaves, the Wanderobbo, could manage to live. This little speech had been translated by Ramathan during the night, and I had learnt it by heart. The Masai replied by driving their women and cattle back to the kraals, and it looked most uncomfortably like a fight. At about a quarter to ten the rain stopped, and a few minutes later we started north across the plain. When the elders saw that we were determined to go, they became more friendly As the first man moved out of camp the chief came up and for the first time held out a "knobkerry", cut from a rhinoceros horn, for me to shake. I of course shook it, glad of this expression of friendliness, though quite aware that if it stopped at this it meant nothing. But as I walked down the slope from the camp after the men, he came up again, and this time not only held out his knobkerry, but as I shook one end, he shook the other. After walking a few yards he repeated this more vigorously. Then at last he held out his hand; we shook hands, at first coldly, and then more cordially. Finally, after we had walked a couple of hundred yards, we repeated the process and the chief spat upon me, a salutation which I returned with perhaps unnecessary vigour. I had been warned that whenever Masai retire from a conference without spitting the spit of peace, squalls may be expected. I was therefore much relieved when this friendly rite had been performed.

We marched northwards over the plain beside the lake. We were followed by a crowd of El-Moran, who seemed at first disposed to be fairly friendly. But as soon as they had passed out of sight of the first kraal, their love of mischief became too much for them. They drove up some donkeys towards us; these brayed to ours, which tried to dash off to join the others. One broke through our line, threw its load, and succeeded in reaching the herd. The El-Moran tried to pillage the load, but Omari and I reached it as soon as they did, and by striking the butt end of our rifles on their naked feet, sent a few of them limping away. As it was obvious that there was nothing like bluff for impressing the Masai, I ordered the El-Moran to go and catch the donkey. I said they were trying to steal it, and that if they did not bring it back I would seize three other donkeys and burn the kraal. They soon brought back our pack animal, and after this behaved much better. They made, however, another attempt to seize a load while we were crossing a stream. As we had to march in square, and were much annoyed by the Masai, we only made four miles that day. We had to pitch our tents amid some rocks about a mile from the north-eastern corner of the lake. There was no thorn scrub with which to make a zeriba, so we arranged the tents in a small circle and filled up the interspaces with boulders and baggage.

Late in the afternoon a powerful force of Masai in full war costume marched up to camp and said they had been sent to dance to us. I put some marks on the ground at a little distance from the camp, and said they were not to come nearer to us than these. I insisted on a Masai elder taking a seat on a box before me, and saw that all the men were at their posts with their rifles ready and the reserve ammunition boxes in a convenient place. Then I gave permission for the dance to begin. It was certainly extremely picturesque; the men were all armed with great shovel-headed spears, with heads varying from 30 inches to 3 feet in length, and spikes a little longer; they carried thick oval shields 4 feet in height, which were coloured in various patterns. They had rattles on their ankles and their arms; their fingers were protected by bright iron knuckle-dusters; their heads were adorned with aureoles of feathers. At first they simply leapt into the air, throwing their heads violently backwards and forwards, and making a series of guttural grunts. Then they marked time with their feet while they hurled their spears upward, giving them a twist which made them flash in the sunlight. Meanwhile they shouted a kind of song without words, to the accompaniment of the music of their rattles. Next they marched and ran in Indian file, twining in and out in a series of complex evolutions, and finally arranging themselves so that the designs on their leather shields were symmetrically disposed. Then they executed the last dance performed before starting on a war raid; they followed this by a series of sham rushes at the camp. As they came on roaring and shouting, their bodies covered by their shields, and their long spears raised over their heads, they presented a weird spectacle. We watched them with breathless anxiety, expecting every moment that a sham rush would become a real one. My revolver covered the head of the Masai elder, while the men prepared to close the breeches of their rifles, which were kept not quite closed, so that if trigger were pulled accidentally no harm would be done. After this, the Masai gave us the dance with which they celebrate victory; I told them I wanted to see that, but that they need not trouble to perform their dance after a defeat, as, if they did not behave better than they had done the day before, they would soon dance it in earnest. At the close of this "Wild East Show" I distributed among the dancers a couple of shillings' worth of beads, with which they went away apparently contented.

The Masai elder offered to stay with us in camp, as a sign of friendship and to protect us from interference by any of the El-Moran. I said I should be most happy to entertain him for a night, but that our guns were our protectors, and to them alone did we trust. I had a long chat with our guest in the evening, and found out from him what I imagined to be the explanation of the hostile attitude of the usually friendly Masai of Naivasha. He said they were preparing for a great war raid, but would not tell us against whom. They appeared to think that the garrison of Fort Smith had heard of this, and that I was being sent on to hasten the caravan returning from Uganda, in order to stop the raid. Major Smith, however, who knows the Naivasha Masai very well, afterwards told me that they are sometimes very bumptious and troublesome: that they planned an attack on the Railway Survey, and tried at night to surprise the camp of Mr. Newman, the famous rifle shot, when on his way back from Uganda. It is therefore probable that it was the small size of my caravan that tempted them to display their innate love of bullying and thieving.

Although after my conversation with the elder I felt more at ease, I still did not deem it safe to go to sleep. I sat wrapped up in a blanket, with my revolver, shot-gun, and rifle ready loaded on a table beside me. Every half-hour I went round the camp to see that the sentries were awake, and that the fires were burning. We had fortunately lighted fires at a little distance from the camp, and these illuminated a considerable space around us. Shortly after midnight, just after returning to my seat beside the fire, I saw the cook spring to his feet in such haste that I guessed there was something wrong; I threw off my rug, seized my rifle from the table, and looked round. By the light of the outer circle of fire, we could see a party of about twenty Masai creeping up to camp. They were carrying their spears, but not their shields, apparently lest these should make noise that might betray them. The cook and I shouted "Masai", and this, with my order of "Bunduki tiari" (Guns ready), roused the camp.

The men took their places quietly and quickly, and looked as though they meant fight. Even my tent-boy Philip, whose cowardice was the joke of the camp, went to his station inside my tent and stood ready to serve out ammunition. Several of the men under the Kiringozi, Wadi Hamis, had been told off to climb the small cliff above the camp, to guard that approach, and to be able to fire down at a foe upon the plain. I forgave that surly old grumbler many of his sins, for the pluck with which he led his men to that important post. He found another party of Masai approaching from that side, and at once opened fire, while I discharged four shots over the heads of the men on the plain. As the Masai now saw that there was no chance of a surprise, they turned and fled. I sprang at once to the shelter tent where the Masai elder was supposed to be. But the savage had escaped unnoticed, leaving his goods behind him. He certainly left before the attempted attack, as I had set two men to guard him at the first alarm. His behaviour thus lends some support to the idea that the attack had been planned, and that it was not a mere attempt by a batch of thieves to rush through the camp and seize any objects that they could lay their hands on in the confusion. We stood on guard, expecting at any moment an attack in force by the main body. But as this was not delivered, and I knew there would be no lack of sentries for the rest of that night, I turned into the tent and enjoyed my first three hours of continuous sleep since I had left the protection of Fort Smith.

At four in the morning I had breakfast, and the men packed up the loads. We waited anxiously for dawn, for we dared not start in the dark, lest we should walk into an ambush. The moment the light was strong enough to enable us to guard against surprise, we marched northward across the plain. Unnoticed by the Masai we waded the swamps beside the streams that enter the north-eastern corner of the lake; but as soon as we lost the shelter of the papyrus in the swamps and the scrub on its borders, we were discovered by some shepherds. They took the news to the nearest kraal, and a party of El-Moran came out to watch us. On the open grassland they dared not attack, so they followed at a respectful distance. A few miles farther on we were stopped by the river Malewa or Murendat. To avoid passing near some kraals we had bent our course far to the west, and thus, instead of striking the river at the ford, we reached it where it flowed through a deep sinuous canon. We marched along this to find a place where we could descend to the river, so as to be able to get water even if we could not cross. We found a track which led down to a ford, but the river was impassable. The flood, however, was subsiding rapidly, for the bank was still wet for more than a foot above the level of the water. We placed some notched sticks in the river to mark its rate of decline and camped. For twenty long hours we sat beside the ford, watching successively the river, the Masai, and the clouds on the hills to the east, and feeling probably much like the Israelites, when they had the Red Sea in front of them and Pharaoh's hosts behind.

In the evening, as the river had fallen several inches, I tried again to cross; I reached a shoal in the middle, but the last channel was too much for me. A school of hippopotami was playing in the pool below the ford; as I had been carried down into it in the morning, I did not think it worth the risk of adding to their sport, and swam back to the southern shore. Twice during the night we had false alarms of the Masai; our rest was also disturbed by the attempt of a pair of hyenas to get at our donkeys. Fortunately the night was rainless, and by the morning the river had fallen sufficiently to permit us to cross. We did so, though with difficulty. Omari and two or three of the stronger porters carried over the loads, while the feebler members of the party pulled themselves across, hand over hand, along a rope. Some Masai watched us, but made no attempt to interfere. A short march farther brought us to the Gilgil river, the waters of which were unusually low. There were no Masai in the district, and nothing to lessen the luxury of a feeling of safety and peace. The porters were delighted to get into an uninhabited country, and I was glad to turn again to the subjects of geology and botany, after my experience of the over-exciting occupation often presented by African anthropology.

GREGORY: *The Great Rift Valley.* 1896.

For all their arrogance to the white man, the Masai rarely pushed things to the point of killing him. Here is Jackson's account of the killing of a missionary. The Masai considered themselves provoked because of an attempt to prevent a cattle raid.

When they arrived, early one morning, Houghton was on the roof of a church he was building, and when the alarm was given by an old woman who came running into the stockade, Mrs. Houghton ran out of her house, and tried to close the heavy gate, but a moran managed to get there first, push both her and the gate back, and promptly speared her. Houghton, in the meantime, scrambled down from the church, and ran to her assistance, but seeing he had come too late, tried to get back to the roof, but was speared as he was climbing a ladder. In all, eleven natives were killed inside the stockade, the cook and Makau only saving themselves by jumping into the river and swimming across. Only one moran was killed, and in rather a curious way, too. A local native, unarmed, and taken by surprise like every one else, had sought safety by hiding, but on the moran's near approach and fearing detection, he got up and ran. But the moran ran faster, and just when within range of his spear, the pursued man suddenly turned round and grappled with him, held him tight and shouted until a friend, also unarmed, came running up, wrenched the spear from the moran and killed him; and that spear, presented to me by the cook, is now in my possession.

JACKSON: *Early Days in East Africa.*

Masai womenfolk have an astonishing method of augmenting their charms.

Round the legs from the ankles to the knees telegraph wire is coiled closely in spiral fashion. So awkward is this ornament that the wearer cannot walk properly, she cannot sit down or rise up like any other human being, and she cannot run. Round the arms she has wire similarly coiled both above and below the elbow. Round the neck more iron wire is coiled—in this case, however, horizontally—till the head seems to sit on an inverted iron salver. When these ornaments are once on they must remain till finally taken off, as it requires many days of painful work to fit them into their places. They chafe the ankles excessively, and evidently give much pain. As they are put on when very young, the calf is not allowed to develop, and the consequence is, that, when grown up the legs remain at a uniform thickness from ankle to knee—mere animated stilts, in fact. The weight of this armour varies according to the wealth of the parties, up to thirty pounds. Besides the iron wire great quantities of beads and iron chains are disposed in various ways round the neck.

THOMSON: *Through Masai Land.* 1885.

★

Their conception of the Deity seems to be marvellously vague. I was Ngai. My lamp was Ngai. Ngai was in the steaming holes. His house was in the eternal snows of Kilimanjaro. In fact, whatever struck them as strange or incomprehensible, that they at once assumed had some connection with Ngai. Their prayers to him were incessant. Nothing could be done without hours of howling, whether it was to seek direction where to slaughter their enemies, or to ward off a disease. The most sacred thing among them is the grass. Held in the hand, or tied in a sprig to the dress, it is a sign of welcome and peace. Thrown at any one, or into some mysterious place, it is an invocation for a blessing on the person, or a propitiatory offering. Next to the grass comes the milk. No liberties may be taken with it. The milk must be drawn into calabashes specially reserved for its reception, into which water is not allowed to enter—cleanliness being ensured by wood-ashes. To boil it is a heinous offence, and would be accounted a sufficient reason for massacring a caravan. It is believed that the cattle would cease to give milk. The cows, it may be remarked, are never milked except in the dark.

Ibid.

3. THE RIFT VALLEY AND
OTHER NATURAL WONDERS

Gregory effectively described the topography of East Africa when he said one should imagine an inverted saucer with a deep cleft down the middle: the cleft being the Rift Valley. On each side of the Valley, he went on to say, the country falls into three distinct and parallel belts. On the east side, from the Valley to the sea, these are respectively high volcanic plateau, jungle, and swamp: and on the west side, from the Valley outwards, high volcanic plateau, the basin of Victoria Nyanza, and the valley of the Nile. To complete the picture it is then only necessary to mention that there are two snow-capped peaks—Kenya and Kilimanjaro—on the plateau to the east, and others—in the Ruwenzori range—marking the extreme western edge of the region; and that a chain of narrow lakes runs the length of the Rift Valley from Baringo in the north to Tanganyika in the south. It is a picture of quite remarkable variety and picturesqueness—but let the anthology speak for itself.

After leaving the coast and crossing the swamps, one climbs gradually through the forest belt towards the highlands. But before getting there a barren zone has to be crossed.

As far as the eye can reach extends the forest of cactus and thorn bush. It is a study in thorns. Each bush rivals its neighbour. The acacia takes the lead, with a straight thorn three or four inches in length, and for fear this should be broken off, Nature has supplied another variety with a bulb at its base as big as a marble; they are as hard and as sharp as though of cast steel. Other bushes grow a combination of both the straight and the hooked (or wait-a-bit) thorn, as though to inflict a wound, however approached. The decayed cactus rots and dies, but its thorns (like the ivory of an elephant) seem impervious to decay, and litter the ground in masses. From below—to meet the thorn-bushes from above—springs the spiked *Nkonge aloe*, with a blade like a triangular bayonet, tipped with a hardened spike, which will penetrate even the strongest shoe leather.

It is a marvel how game, less thick-skinned than a rhino, can live in this inhospitable jungle. The delicate little *pah* gazelle, no bigger than a rabbit, its skin no thicker than a kid glove, bounds off like lightning among the aloes and the cacti. One looks to see it impaled like a butterfly on a pin; but Nature has taught her creatures to live with safety among their surroundings, though it is hard to gauge the reason for this prodigal wealth of vegetable armament, or to understand against what enemy its terrors are directed.

LUGARD: *The Rise of our East African Empire.* 1893.

More than 20,000 Europeans have settled in the Kenya Highlands.

A more charming region is probably not to be found in all Africa, probably not even in Abyssinia. Though lying at a general elevation of 6,000 feet, it is not mountainous, but extends out in billowy, swelling reaches, and is characterized by everything that makes a pleasing land-scape. Here are dense patches of flowering shrubs; there noble forests. Now you traverse a park-like country enlivened by groups of game; anon, great herds of cattle, or flocks of sheep and goats are seen wandering knee-deep in the splendid pasture. There is little in the aspect of the country to suggest the popular idea of the Tropics. The eye rests upon coniferous trees, forming pine-like woods, and you can gather sprigs of heath, sweet-scented clover, anemone, and other familiar forms. In vain you look for the graceful palm—ever present in the mental pictures of the untravelled traveller. The country is a very network of babbling brooks and streams.

THOMSON: *Through Masai Land.* 1885

In striking contrast to the charm of the highlands is the oppressiveness of the tropical forest which takes hold of the land as it falls away to Victoria Nyanza.

I had travelled through tropical forests in Cuba and India, and had often before admired their enchanting, yet sinister, luxuriance. But the forests of Uganda, for magnificence, for variety of form and colour, for profusion of brilliant life—plant, bird, insect, reptile, beast—for the vast scale and awful fecundity of the natural processes that are beheld at work, eclipsed, and indeed effaced, all previous impressions. One becomes, not without a secret sense of aversion, the spectator of an intense convulsion of life and death. Reproduction and decay are locked struggling in infinite embraces. In this glittering Equatorial slum huge trees jostle one another for room to live; slender growths stretch upwards—as it seems in agony—towards sunlight and life. The soil bursts with irrepressible vegetations. Every victor, trampling on the rotting mould of exterminated antagonists, soars aloft only to encounter another host of aerial rivals, to be burdened with masses of parasitic foliage, smothered in the glorious blossoms of creepers, laced and bound and interwoven with interminable tangles of vines and trailers. Birds are as bright as butterflies; butterflies are as big as birds.

The air hums with flying creatures; the earth crawls beneath your foot. The telegraph-wire runs northwards to Gondokoro through this vegetable labyrinth. Even its poles had broken into bud!

CHURCHILL: *My African Journey*. 1908.

After the forest comes the gently undulating landscape of the lake shore.

The road wound upward to the summits of green hills which commanded exquisite prospects, and down again into the sheltered bosoms of woody nooks, and vales, and tree-embowered ravines. Streams of clear water murmured through these depressions as they flowed towards Murchison Bay. The verdure was of a brilliant green, freshened by the unfailing rains of the Equator; the sky was of the bluest, and the heat, though great, was tempered by the hill breezes, and frequently by the dense foliage overhead.

STANLEY: *Through the Dark Continent*. 1878.

In this pleasant land the Nile begins its 3,000-mile journey to the Mediterranean. Speke was first white man on the scene. Mutesa had told him that at the point where the river left the lake it descended through some "stones". So it proved, and Speke named them the Ripon Falls in honour of the then President of the Royal Geographical Society.

Though beautiful, the scene was not exactly what I expected; for the broad surface of the lake was shut out from view by a spur of hill, and the falls, about 12 feet deep, and 400 to 500 feet broad, were broken by rocks. Still it was a sight that attracted one to it for hours—the roar of the waters, the thousands of passenger-fish, leaping at the falls with all their might, the Wasoga and Waganda fishermen coming out in boats and taking post on all the rocks with rod and hook, hippopotami and crocodiles lying sleepily on the water, the ferry at work above the falls, and cattle driven down to drink at the margin of the lake—made, in all, with the pretty nature of the country—small hills, grassy-topped, with trees in the folds, and gardens on the lower slopes—as interesting a picture as one could wish to see.

The expedition had now performed its functions. I saw that old father Nile without any doubt rises in the Victoria Nyanza, and, as I had foretold, that lake is the great source of the holy river which cradled the first expounder of our religious belief.

SPEKE: *Journal of the Discovery of the Source of the Nile*.   1863.

Winston Churchill's reaction to the Falls was characteristic. So much power running to waste!

The Ripon Falls are, for their own sake, well worth a visit. The Nile springs out of Victoria Nyanza, a vast body of water nearly as wide as the Thames at Westminster Bridge, and this imposing river rushes down a stairway of rock from fifteen to twenty feet deep, in smooth, swirling slopes of green water. It would be perfectly easy to harness the whole river and let the Nile begin its long and beneficent journey to the sea by leaping through a turbine.

CHURCHILL: *My African Journey.* 1908.

More spectacular than the Ripon Falls are those which Baker discovered and named after Murchison, another President of the Royal Geographical Society. He was making his way along the Nile by canoe from Lake Albert to Lake Victoria.

As we proceeded the river gradually narrowed to about 180 yards, and when the paddles ceased working we could distinctly hear the roar of water. I had heard this on waking in the morning, but at the time I had imagined it to proceed from distant thunder. By ten o'clock the current had so increased as we proceeded, that it was distinctly perceptible, although weak. The roar of the waterfall was extremely loud, and after sharp pulling for a couple of hours, during which time the stream increased, we arrived at a few deserted fishing-huts, at a point where the river made a slight turn. I never saw such an extraordinary show of crocodiles as were exposed on every sandbank on the sides of the river; they lay like logs of timber close together, and upon one bank we counted twenty-seven, of large size; every basking place was crowded in a similar manner. From the time we had fairly entered the river, it had been confined by heights somewhat precipitous on either side, rising to about 180 feet. At this point the cliffs were still higher, and exceedingly abrupt. From the roar of the water, I was sure that the fall would be in sight if we turned the corner at the bend of the river; accordingly I ordered the boatmen to row as far as they could; to this they at first objected, as they wished to stop at the deserted fishing village, which they explained was to be the limit of the journey, farther progress being impossible.

However, I explained that I merely wished to see the fall, and they rowed immediately up the stream, which was now strong against us. Upon rounding the corner, a magnificent sight burst suddenly upon us. On either side the river were beautifully wooded cliffs rising abruptly to a height of about 300 feet; rocks were jutting out from the intensely green foliage; and rushing through a gap that cleft the rock exactly before us, the river, contracted from a grand stream, was pent up in a narrow gorge of scarcely fifty yards in width; roaring furiously through the rock-bound pass, it plunged in one leap of about 120 feet perpendicular into a dark abyss below.

The fall of water was snow-white, which had a superb effect as it contrasted with the dark cliffs that walled the river, while the graceful palms of the tropics and wild plantains perfected the beauty of the view. This was the greatest waterfall of the Nile, and, in honour of the distinguished President of the Royal Geographical Society, I named it the Murchison Falls, as the most important object throughout the entire course of the river.

> BAKER: *The Albert N'Yanza, Great Basin of the Nile, and Explorations of the Nile Sources.*   1872.

The German missionary Krapf was the first white man to see Mount Kenya. In 1849, from far to the south, he caught sight of its snow-cap glittering in the sun. Joseph Thomson approached it from the north. After travelling up the Rift Valley as far as Lake Baringo, he climbed the eastern face of the Valley and turned southwards through the highlands. It was then that unexpectedly he sighted the mountain.

I was suddenly arrested by an object which fairly took my breath away. Before me, in the foreground, lay a splendid interchange of grove and glade, of forest and plain, stretching in billowy reaches down to the marshy expanse of Kopè-Kopè. Beyond rose abruptly and very precipitously the black, uninhabited mountains of the Aberdare range. These features, however, were not what had fascinated me. It was something more distant. Through a rugged and picturesque depression in the range rose a gleaming snow-white peak with sparkling facets, which scintillated with the superb beauty of a colossal diamond. It was, in fact, the very image of a great crystal or sugar-loaf. At the base of this beautiful peak were two small excrescences like supporters to a monument. From these, at a very slight angle, shaded away a long glittering white line, seen above the dark mass of the Aberdare range like the silver lining of a dark storm-cloud. This peak, and silvery line formed the central culminating point of Mount Kenia.

> THOMSON: *Through Masai Land.*   1886.

Winston Churchill says this of Mount Kenya.

There never was a mountain which made so little of its height. It rises by long gentle slopes more like a swelling of ground than a peak, from an immense upland plain, and so gradual is the acclivity that, but for the sudden outcrop of snow-clad rock which crowns the summit, no one would believe it over eighteen thousand feet high. It is its gradual rise that imparts so great a value to this noble mountain; for about its enormous base and upon its slopes, traversed by hundreds of streams of clear perennial water, there grows, or may grow, in successive, concentric belts, every kind of crop and forest known in the world, from the Equator to the Arctic Circle. The landscape is superb. In beauty, in fertility, in verdure, in the coolness of the air, in the abundance of running water, in its rich red soil, in the variety of its vegetation, the scenery about Kenya far surpasses anything I have ever seen in India or South Africa, and challenges comparison with the fairest countries of Europe.

CHURCHILL: *My African Journey.* 1908.

Of Kilimanjaro I have found few striking descriptive accounts. As well as any I like these two brief passages:

Just as we got off at daybreak, on turning our eyes south-east we saw a wonderful sight. Through a rift in the towering clouds which covered the sky in that quarter there suddenly appeared a great glittering mass—Kibo—one of the twin peaks of the mountain, reflecting the beams of the rising sun and flashing them back in truly regal splendour. All that we saw, some four or five thousand feet, was above the snow line, which on the equator is in the neighbourhood of 15,000 feet, and for the first time we realized what a mass of snow and ice crowned the summit. Cut off below and above by clouds, it seemed to float in mid-air, exquisitely sharp cut and defined.

COOK: *Uganda Memories.*

*

The snow-cap shows here to great advantage, forming a close-fitted, glittering helmet artistically laid on the massive head of Kibo, and at times looking not unlike the aureole, as represented in many old pictures of saints, as it scintillates with dazzling effect under the tropical sun. The resemblance to an aureole is made all the more complete by the manner in which long tongues or lines of snow extend down the mountain side, filling up a series of seams or flutings, formed, doubtless, by the erosive action of the melting snow, which, going on incessantly, counterbalances the continuous fall. Here still more than on the south side is Kilimanjaro lacking in the picturesque. You are not startled or bewildered by a multiplicity of detail. The magnificent mass only suggests a divine repose and grandeur.

THOMSON: *Through Masai Land.* 1885.

Ruwenzori, too, has inspired surprisingly few purple passages. Sir Albert Cook saw the range for the first time in 1898 while on trek with Bishop Tucker.

That evening we caught our first glimpse of the snows of Ruwenzori. At 5.30 the clouds which had obstinately veiled its summits during the weeks we had spent in marching round it, began to roll up. Crag after crag stood out, peak after peak appeared, until one of the topmost spires of that marvellous mass was clearly visible with its snowfields and glaciers. Not for long however was this vision vouchsafed us, for while we looked and looked again, and took our fill through field glasses, the fleecy clouds softly gathered and tenderly wrapped round the craggy heights.

COOK: *Uganda Memories.*

Much has been written about the Rift Valley.

This curious fault in the earth's surface, which geologists trace across the four thousand miles of land and sea which separate us from Palestine, and onward still to the southern end of Lake Tanganyika, is traversed by the Uganda Railway at one of its most remarkable stages. For sixty miles the Highland plateau has been rising steadily by a succession of wooded undulations to a level of over six thousand feet. Now it falls abruptly, almost precipitously, more than two thousand feet. This frowning wall of rock and forest, which extends straight as a ruler farther than eye can see, is the Kikuyu Escarpment. As the train claws its way downwards by slant and zigzag along its face, a majestic panorama breaks upon the view. Far below, bathed in sunshine, stretching away to misty purple horizons, lie the broad expanses of the Rift Valley. Its level surface is broken by strangely moulded volcanic hills and shattered craters. The opposite mountain wall looms up in the far distance, brown and blue. We gaze down upon the plain as from a balloon, mistaking forests for patches of green grass, and mighty trees for thorn-scrub.

CHURCHILL: *My African Journey.* 1908.

★

On the third march we surmounted the last step of the escarpment, and then a magnificent view burst upon us. We were looking across a

UGANDA LANDSCAPE

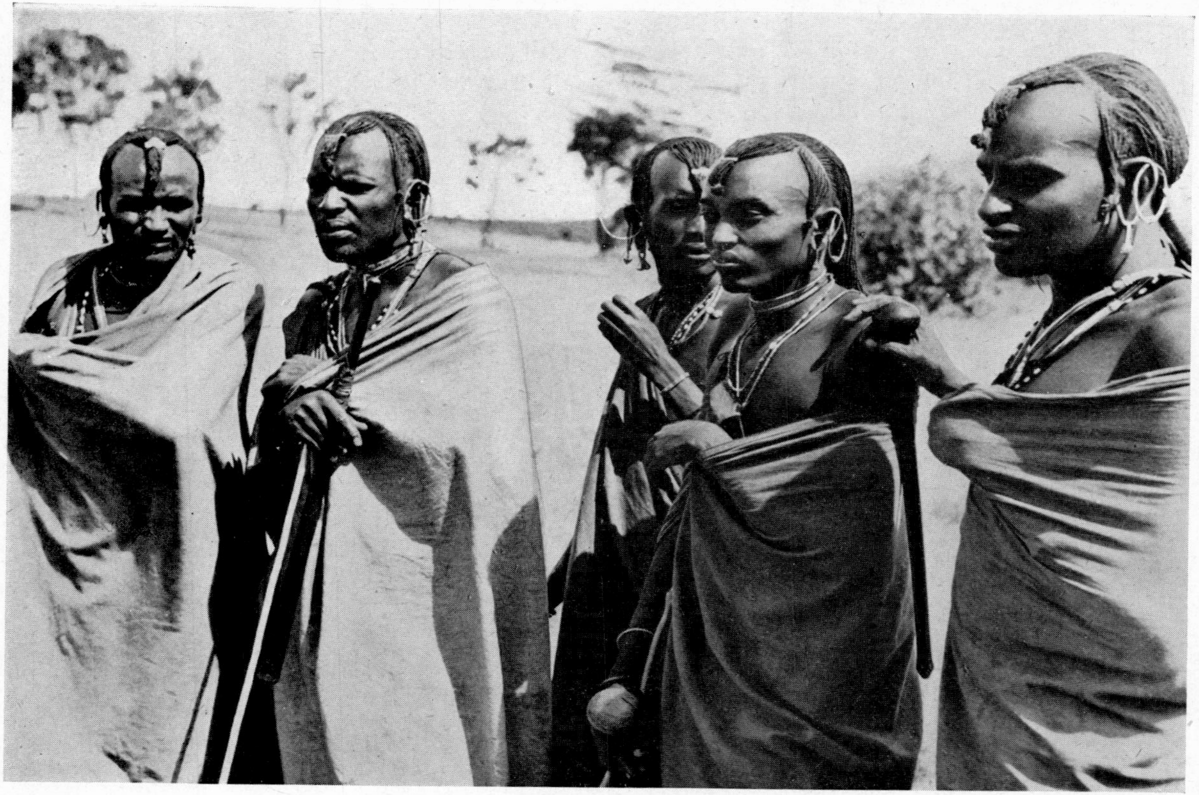

THE REDOUBTABLE MASAI

great plain, slightly undulating and perfectly treeless, bounded on the east by the magnificent mass of the Aberdare Range, with Donyo Kinangop rising picturesquely from the mass. Through a slight gap the snowy peak of Kenia glittered in crystal purity. To the south-east lay the wooded highlands of Kikuyu, with forests of bamboo in the foreground. To the south-west we saw the yawning pit of Donyo Longonot, and the romantic expanse of Naivasha. To the south the desolate plain of Dogilani and to the east the massive escarpment of Mau. I got myself held up to view this grand landscape—probably unsurpassed anywhere—and weak and weary as I was I surveyed the glorious panorama with infinite delight, though also with a spice of awe.

THOMSON: *Through Masai Land.* 1885.

Of the Rift Valley lakes Baringo is usually said to be the most beautiful.

I have now looked upon many striking and wonderful lake scenes in Africa. I have viewed Nyassa from the mountains to the north, Tanganyika from the south, the east, and the west, Lake Leopold from the Fipa Mountains. But not one of these spectacles approaches in beauty, grandeur, and variety the landscape that now spread out before me on the edge of the Lykipia plateau. Imagine, if you can, a trough or depression 3,300 feet above the sea level, and twenty miles broad, the mountains rising with very great abruptness on both sides to a height of 9,000 feet. In the centre of this depression lies a dazzling expanse of water, glittering like a mirror in the fierce rays of a tropical sun. Almost in its centre rises a picturesque island, surrounded by four smaller islets—a group of nature's emeralds in a dazzling setting of burnished silver. Round the irregular-shaped Lake appears a strip of pale green, which indicates a marshy border, and in an outer circle extending up to the mountains, spreads a very dark green area which you know to be table-topped acacia-trees.

Ibid.

From the floor of the Rift Valley rises the cone of an extinct volcano, known to the Masai as Donyo Longonot—"Mountain of the Big Pit". It was climbed by Joseph Thomson.

At last we reached the bottom of the cone proper, and with astonishment I viewed its extraordinary steepness. It beat anything of the kind I had ever seen. I made a determined sprint, literally on hands and knees, to ascend this point. The slightest slip would have landed me half-way down the mountain. At last I reached the top and the scene that lay before me fairly overwhelmed me with wonder. I found myself on the sharp rim of an enormous pit, as far as I could judge, from 1,500 to 2,000 feet in depth. It was not, however, an inverted cone, as volcanic craters frequently are, but a great circular cavity, with perfectly perpendicular walls, and about three miles in circumference, without a break in any part, though on the south-western side rose a peak, several hundred feet above the general line of the rim. So perpendicular were the enclosing walls, that immediately in front of me I could not trace the descent, owing to a slight angle near the top. So sharp, also, was the edge of this marvellous crater, that I literally sat astride it, with one leg dangling over the abyss internally, and the other down the side of the mountain. The bottom of the pit seemed to be quite eerie, covered with acacia trees, the tops of which, at that great depth, had much the general aspect of a grass plain. There were no bushes or creepers to cover over the stern and forbidding walls, which were composed of beds of lava and agglomerate.

The scene was of such an astounding character that I was completely fascinated, and fell under an almost irresistible impulse madly to plunge into the fearful chasm. So overpowering was this feeling that I had to withdraw from the side of the pit.

THOMSON: Through Masai Land. 1885.

4. "THE WHOLE ZOOLOGICAL GARDENS"

The world has no region richer in animal and bird life than East Africa. And no one has recorded its beauty and variety better—both in word and water-colour—than Sir Harry Johnston.

But giraffes are not the only large game on these glorious downs. Elephants may be seen in great herds close by, but they affect rather more the scattered forest than the open plains. Where you see the giraffes you see also numerous rhinos in couples, male and female, or a female alone with her snub-nosed calf. The rhino looks a purple-black or a whitish grey as he moves through the long grass, according as the light strikes him. It is a glorious sight, say an hour after the sun has risen, and the shadows are beginning to shorten, to traverse this grass country and see this zoological gardens turned loose. Herds of zebras and Jackson's hartebeest mingle together, and in face of the sunlight become a changing procession of silver and gold, the sleek coats of the zebras in the level sunlight mingling their black stripes and snowy intervals into a uniform silver-grey, whilst the coats of the hartebeests are simply red-gold. Dotted about on the outskirts of this throng are jet-black cock ostriches with white wings, a white bob-tail, and long pink necks. Red and silver jackals slink and snap; grotesque wart-hogs of a dirty grey, with whitish bristles and erect tails terminating in a drooping tassel, scurry before the traveller till they can bolt into some burrow of the ant bear. Males of the noble waterbuck, strangely like the English red deer, appear at a distance, browsing with their horn-less, doe-like females, or gazing at the approaching traveller with head erect and the maned neck and splendid carriage of Landseer's stags. Grey-yellow reedbuck bend their lissom bodies into such a bounding gallop that the spine seems to become concave as the animal's rear is flung high into the air. The dainty Damaliscus, or sable antelope, with a coat of red, mauve, black, and yellow satin bordered with cream colour, stands at gaze, his coat like watered silk as the sunlight follows the wavy growth of the glistening hair.

JOHNSTON: *The Uganda Protectorate.* 1902

★

From the windows of the carriage the whole zoological gardens can be seen disporting itself. Herds of antelope and gazelle, troops of zebras—sometimes four or five hundred together—watch the train pass with placid assurance, or scamper a hundred yards farther away, and turn again. Many are quite close to the line. With field-glasses one can see that it is the same everywhere, and can distinguish long files of black wildebeeste and herds of red kongoni—the hartebeeste of South Africa—and wild ostriches walking sedately in twos and threes, and every kind of small deer and gazelle. The zebras come close enough for their stripes to be admired with the naked eye.

CHURCHILL: *My African Journey.* 1908.

THE RHINO

Acacia, euphorbia, and all the thorn-trees, which thrive where nothing else can grow, flourished here, and among them wandered the rhino, who, like them, seems to thrive without water and sustenance, and to delight in barren rocks and a fierce sun. He is a beast with no fine feelings, he has no eye for scenery, no manners if you meet him unexpectedly. His palate lacks discrimination, unless it be in the comparative merits of thorns as appetisers. He is a pachyderm inside and out with whom I have no sympathy, and, like some people one has met, enforces his repartee with the point of his horn, and relies for his emphasis on the ponderous bulk of his own mass of insusceptibilities.

LUGARD: *The Rise of our East African Empire.* 1893.

★

When we were within 200 yards, it got a whiff of us, which made it spin round as if it had been struck, and trot off. The wind immediately veering, it lost our scent and turned round to look for us. Of course we simultaneously sank flat in the grass, and lay perdu. Once more it scented us and trotted away, while we sprang up, and with bent forms rushed after it, to fall flat when once more it turned round, perplexed by the uncertain character of our wind. We thus got nearer and nearer. The rhino, becoming furious, now varied its movements by charging aimlessly in the direction of the hidden foe, only to turn tail on getting another whiff. At last we got pretty close by carefully attending to our tactics, and were quite enjoying the excitement of the curious hunt, when with unexpected suddenness our game spun round, and before we were hidden in the grass we were sighted. Furiously it charged right towards us. Shouting to Brahim to have my second rifle at hand, I sprang to my feet and stood ready. The rhino's courage, however, proved to be all show, for within twenty yards it

turned. At the same moment a bullet struck its side with a dull thud.
A second was lodged in the creature as it ran off, but neither seemed to
have struck well, for we never got it.

THOMSON: *Through Masai Land.* 1885.

★

I fired. The thud of a bullet which strikes with an impact of a ton
and a quarter, tearing through hide and muscle and bone with the
hideous energy of cordite, came back distinctly. The large rhinoceros
started, stumbled, turned directly towards the sound and the blow,
and then bore straight down upon us in a peculiar trot, nearly as fast
as a horses's gallop, with an activity surprising in so huge a beast, and
instinct with unmistakable purpose.

Great is the moral effect of a foe who advances. Everybody fired.
Still the ponderous brute came on, as if he were invulnerable; as if he
were an engine, or some great steam barge impervious to bullets, insensible to pain or fear. Thirty seconds more, and he will close. An
impalpable curtain seems to roll itself up in the mind, revealing a
mental picture, strangely lighted, yet very still, where objects have new
values, and where a patch of white grass in the foreground, four or five
yards away, seems to possess astonishing significance. It is there that
the last two shots that yet remain before the resources of civilization are
exhausted must be fired. There is time to reflect with some detach-
ment that, after all, we were the aggressors; we it is who have forced
the conflict by an unprovoked assault with murderous intent upon a
peaceful herbivore; that if there is such a thing as right and wrong
between man and beast—and who shall say there is not?—right is
plainly on his side; there is time for this before I perceive that, stunned
and dazed by the frightful concussions of modern firearms, he has
swerved sharp to the right, and is now moving across our front,
broadside on, at the same swift trot. More firing, and as I reload some
one says he is down.

CHURCHILL: *My African Journey.* 1908.

THE LION

The lion in his habits, as in his character, is very different from the
tiger. He courts no concealment, and shirks no encounter. The tiger,
unless tracked up, or driven out of the fastnesses of the jungle, is
rarely or never seen. If come upon unawares, he will in ninety-nine
cases out of a hundred plunge into the jungle and escape from view.

If suddenly confronted at very close quarters he may charge in self-defence, as I have known him do, and on such occasions he will invariably roar terrifically to frighten his enemy: in fact it is, perhaps, the only occasion on which he *does* roar his best. A man-eater may assume the aggressive, and a tiger, should he hear sounds in front, and have cause to suspect that he is surrounded or entrapped, will fearlessly charge, but his natural instinct is to escape.

A lion, on the other hand, stalks majestically over the plain in the open. If he sights man he will generally go from him, but he scorns to run, and if pressed close or interfered with, will charge viciously. It would, indeed, appear as though the lion considered it *infra dig*, to bolt, even from man. I have fired shots at a lion and lioness, and though the bullets went so close that they must almost have singed the hair, they walked proudly along till they crested a rising ground and disappeared. Crossing a small ravine, I ran after them as fast as possible, hoping for a shot at the point where they had disappeared, but when I reached it, I saw them galloping fast on the far horizon. As long as they were in view they scorned to run, but when once out of sight they had made the best of their time! I have again and again remarked this, and often as I have seen lions I can never recall an instance where they may be said to have fled from me.

LUGARD: *The Rise of our East African Empire.* 1893.

Ashe tells this story of Bishop Hannington, whose impetuousness and fearlessness later contributed to his death on the frontiers of Buganda.

It was during this time that Hannington met with one of the most extraordinary lion adventures on record. He had gone out with his gun, followed by his servant boy Bakiti, when he saw a small animal at some distance moving in the long grass. He had no suspicion what it was; he raised his gun and fired, and the little creature rolled over dead. Instantly, with a terrific roar, there sprang out two great full-grown lions and came bounding towards him. His gun was empty, there was no time even to reload, so he turned and ran. The lions were almost upon him, and as his pace grew slower and more uncertain, he heard the agonized cry of his faithful Bakiti, "Hapana, hapana, kimbia!" "No, no, run!" urging him to swifter flight. He, however, translated it: "Don't, don't run," and immediately faced round. The lions then stood still, waving their tails and glaring at their strange opponent. It was an awful moment. At last the divinity which hedges the courageous conquered the lions, and they crept away abashed. Now it was Hannington's turn to be the pursuer, so waving his arms and shouting, he drove them away, and actually carried off the dead carcase of the fallen whelp.

ASHE: Two Kings of Uganda.   1889.

*

I cannot vouch for the accuracy of the most remarkable lion story that I know, and can only say that it was related very often by an excellent man who appeared to believe it himself and resented incredulity in others. It was to the effect that he was marching up country with a caravan of donkeys, which generally went very slowly. One day they went at the most unusual speed, all except one which lagged behind. It was as much as the rest of the caravan could do to keep up with them. When they arrived in camp a very simple and natural explanation of this haste was discovered. A lion had got in among the donkeys the previous night, and had devoured one entirely, ears, hoofs, and all, with the result that he over-ate himself to such an extent that he could hardly move. In the grey, uncertain light of dawn he had been taken for the missing donkey and saddled with the rest. In his gorged and torpid condition he offered no resistance, and trudged along under his load, but the other donkeys, recognising his smell, were much alarmed and ran ahead as fast as they could.

ELIOT: The East Africa Protectorate.   1905.

THE BUFFALO

Heedless of Brahim's admonition, I obstinately went forward, intending to give it its quietus at close quarters. I had got within six-yards, and yet I remained unnoticed, the head of the buffalo being turned slightly from me, and I not making much noise. I was not destined to go much further. A step or two more and there was a rustling among some dead leaves. Simultaneously the buffalo's head turned in my direction. A ferocious, blood-curdling grunt instantly apprised me of the brute's resolution to be revenged. The next moment it was on its feet. Unprepared to fire, and completely taken by surprise, I had no time for thought. Instinctively I turned my back upon my infuriated enemy. As far as my recollections serve me, I had no feeling of fear while I was running away. I am almost confident that I was not putting my best foot foremost, and that I felt as if the whole affair was rather a well-played game. It was a game, however, that did not last long. I was aware of Brahim tearing away in front of me. There was a loud crashing behind me. Then something touched me on the thigh, and I was promptly propelled skyward.

My next recollection was finding myself lying dazed and bruised, with some hazy notion that I had better take care! With this indefinite sense of something unusual I slowly and painfully raised my head, and lo! there was the brutal avenger standing three yards off, watching his victim, but apparently disdaining to hoist an inert foe. I found I was lying with my head towards the buffalo. Strangely enough even then, though I was in what may be called the jaws of death, I had not the slightest sensation of dread; only the electric thought flashed through my brain, "If he comes for me again I am a dead man." It almost seemed as if my thought roused the buffalo to action. Seeing signs of life in my hitherto inanimate body, he blew a terrible blast through his nostrils, and prepared to finish me off. Stunned and bruised as I was, I could make no fight for life. I simply dropped my head down among the grass in the vague hope that it might escape being pounded into jelly. Just at that moment a rifle-shot rang through the forest, which caused me to raise my head once more. With glad surprise I found the buffalo's tail presented to my delighted contemplation. Instinctively seizing the unexpected moment of grace, I with a terrible effort pulled myself together and staggered away a few steps. As I did so, I happened to put my hand down to my thigh, and there I felt something warm and wet; exploring further, my fingers found their way into a big hole in my thigh; as I made this discovery there was quite a volley, and I saw my adversary drop dead.

THOMSON: *Through Masai Land.* 1885.

THE ELEPHANT

In native stories the elephant does not figure as a particularly clever animal, but he is generally credited with being a human, respectable sort of beast. There is a story at Taveta that a native woman once met a huge tusker, who appeared to be in a furious temper and was disposed to stop her. The poor woman was half dead with fear, but with feminine intuition she picked a bunch of grass and offered it to the elephant. The creature's demeanour at once changed; he accepted the present, picked another bunch himself, and, with a graceful wave of the trunk, handed it to the lady, for whom he now most courteously gave way.

ELIOT: *The East Africa Protectorate.* 1905.

*

The Wangwana and Wanyambu informed me with the utmost gravity that the elephant maltreats the rhinoceros frequently, because of a jealousy that the former entertains of his fiery cousin. It is said that if the elephant observes the excrement of the rhinoceros unscattered, he waxes furious, and proceeds instantly in search of the criminal, when woe befall him if he is sulky, and disposed to battle for the proud privilege of leaving his droppings as they fall! The elephant in that case breaks off a heavy branch of a tree, or uproots a stout sapling like a boat's mast, and belabours the unfortunate beast until he is glad to save himself by hurried flight. For this reason, the natives say, the rhinoceros always turns round and thoroughly scatters what he has dropped.

Should a rhinoceros meet an elephant, he must observe the rule of the road and walk away, for the latter brooks no rivalry; but the former is sometimes headstrong, and the elephant then despatches him with his tusks by forcing him against a tree and goring him, or by upsetting him, and leisurely crushing him.

STANLEY: *Through the Dark Continent.* 1878.

THE FLAMINGO

On Lake Hannington it is no exaggeration to say that there must be close upon a million flamingoes. These birds are mainly collected round the northern end of the lake and on the submerged banks which break up the deep blue-green of its still surface. The shores where they cluster, and these banks in the middle of the lake where they are above the water's edge, are dazzling white with the birds' guano. These flamingoes breed on a flat plain of mud about a mile broad at the north end of Lake Hannington, where their nests, in the form of little mounds of mud with feathers plastered on the hollowed top, appear like innumerable molehills. The birds, having hitherto been absolutely unmolested by man, are quite tame. They belong to a rosy species (*Phoeniconais minor*), which is slightly smaller than the Mediterranean flamingo, but exquisitely beautiful in plumage. The adult bird has a body and neck of rosy pink, the colour of sunset clouds. The beak is scarlet and purple; the legs are deep rose-pink inclining to scarlet. Underneath the black-pinioned wings the larger feathers are scarlet-crimson, while beautiful crimson crescents tip the tertiaries and wing-coverts on the upper surface of the wings. Apparently the mature plumage is not reached until the birds are about three years old. The younger flamingoes very soon attain the same size as the rosy adults, but their plumage when they are full grown is first grey-white and then the colour of a pale tea-rose before it attains its full sunset glory. On the north coast of the lake the belt of flamingoes must be nearly a mile broad from the edge of the lake outwards. Seen from above, this mass of birds on its shoreward side is grey-white, then becomes white in the middle, and has a lakeward ring of the most exquisite rose-pink, the reason being that the birds on the outer edge of the semi-circle are the young ones, while those farthest out into the lake are the oldest. It is not easy to make the birds take to flight. When they do so suddenly and the shallow water is stirred the stench which arises is sickening. The noise of these birds can be heard from nearly a mile distant. The kronk-kronk-kronk of the million, mingled with hissings and squitterings and splashings and the swish-swish-swish of those who are starting on flight, combine to make a tumult of sound in the presence of which one has to shout to one's companions in order to be heard. It is curious to watch the ungainly motions of these birds when they wish to rise in the air. Their flight has to be preceded by an absurd gallop through the mud before they can lift themselves on their wings.

JOHNSTON: The Uganda Protectorate. 1902.

Lake Albert Edward is another wonderful haunt of bird-life.

There are rows of Tantalus storks, with lemon-yellow beaks, white heads and breasts, black-green wings, and shoulder feathers of exquisite rose-pink; squadrons of pelicans, cohorts of crowned cranes (wading, dancing, and feeding on the shore-line), flocks of russet-white and metallic-green Egyptian geese, blue-grey herons, fawn-coloured herons, white egrets, black cormorants, black-green and white saddle-billed storks with crimson beaks, purple and white ibises, and huge marabou storks, with the mottled beaks and faces of drunkards, the scraggy necks and white plumes of dowagers, and huge wings of satin-like grey-green. At certain hours of the day this immense concourse of birds will meet (no doubt attracted by shoals of fish) to feed, fight, court, play, and display.

Ibid.

SNAKES

Lying amongst the dead leaves on the path may be the dreaded puff-adder, with its beautiful carpet-pattern of pinkish grey, black, lemon-yellow, and slaty blue, and with its awful head containing poison glands more rapidly fatal than those perhaps of any other viper. Numerous pythons, from fifteen to twenty feet in length (generally disinclined to attack human beings, however), are coiled on the branches of the trees, or hang by their tails like a pendent branch swaying to and fro in the wind. Their chequered patterns of brown and white are rendered very beautiful sometimes by the bloom of iridescence which imports rainbow colours into the scales when the skin is new. The pythons may be disregarded as a dangerous element to human beings, and the puff-adder, though his bite may kill you in an hour or less, is too sluggish to attack, unless by some blunder you tread on him and wait to see the consequences.

Ibid.

*

Mr. George Wilson, when collector in Unyoro, was assured by the Chiope hunters in the northern part of that district that expert hunters were accustomed to catch puff-adders in a noose. They then nailed the living snake by the tip of its tail in the middle of a buffalo track so that the enraged reptile might strike at the bodies of the buffalo as they passed by. In this manner it was asserted that as many as ten buffaloes have been killed in one day by one puff-adder. The body of the first buffalo killed would be discarded as being poisoned, but the bodies of the other victims of the snake would be considered wholesome for eating.

Ibid.

*

I note in my diary a quaint custom or superstition with regard to the cobra, which I noticed on this march: "A very big black snake crossed my path slowly, and getting a man's sword-bayonet I let him have it on the tail-end. He reared, and expanded a big hood, like the picture-book cobra. I did not know there was so well-hooded a cobra in Africa. He spat furiously, on which my men with great energy spat back! Nor could I get them to speak until he (and they) had finished. He did not attack further, though he looked like it at first, and went his way in the thick grass. From the manner of this performance it was evident that the men seemed to think their safety lay in spitting back at the reptile."

LUGARD: *The Rise of our East African Empire.* 1893.

LOCUSTS

It is a grim and repulsive spectacle to find oneself in the middle of a locust swarm. You may not be thinking anything of the kind, and be riding through a charming country, the trees in rich foliage, and perhaps lit up with bright flowers, the birds singing and the sun shining. Far away in the distance on the horizon are low, ragged clouds of a copper colour, which the heedless traveller takes to be either strangely coloured cloudlets or the smoke of bush fires. Gradually, however, these clouds grow and spread out into the sky until they are seen to be composed of millions of locusts. The obscurity of a yellow London fog begins to tinge the landscape, sucking up all its brightness. Looking into the sky, the eye sees nothing but myriads of locusts diminishing in perspective from a hideous object three inches long just above one's nose to copper-coloured pin-points, and then to a copper-coloured haze. It is sickening to have to ride through these whizzing millions. They settle on your hair, on your hands, on your back, and I personally feel an inclination to vomit as I look at their monstrous horse-heads with the oblong, unintelligent eyes, and when I feel in contact with my skin the scratchy hooks and spurs of the long limbs. A disagreeable smell also accompanies these jostled millions of gluttonous insects. After a while the copper atmosphere may thin until at last the blue sky and sunshine appear again. The flight of locusts will now have settled on all the trees and herbage in the vicinity. It would seem as though some god had peppered all this beautiful vegetation with a sad reddish grey substance. So closely do the locusts on bare branches resemble dry seed pods or withered leaf shoots that you often take them to be such until, at your approach, hundreds of them swoop from the tree, and bang into your face leaving the poor stripped branches bare of any leaf or flower.

JOHNSTON: *The Uganda Protectorate*. 1902.

5. "UGANDA IS A FAIRY TALE"

Every traveller visiting Buganda recorded astonishment at its complete difference from anything else to be seen in Africa. Winston Churchill said it like this:

The Kingdom of Uganda is a fairy tale. You climb up a railway instead of a beanstalk, and at the end there is a wonderful new world. The scenery is different, the vegetation is different, the climate is different, and, most of all, the people are different from anything elsewhere to be seen in the whole range of Africa. Instead of the breezy uplands we enter a tropical garden. In the place of naked, painted savages, clashing their spears and gibbering in chorus to their tribal chiefs, a complete and elaborate polity is presented. Under a dynastic King, with a Parliament, and a powerful feudal system, an amiable, clothed, polite, and intelligent race dwell together in an organized monarchy upon the rich domain between the Victoria and Albert Lakes. More than two hundred thousand natives are able to read and write. More than one hundred thousand have embraced the Christian faith. There is a Court, there are Regents and Ministers and nobles, there is a regular system of native law and tribunals; there is discipline, there is industry, there is culture, there is peace. In fact, I ask myself whether there is any other spot in the whole earth where the dreams and hopes of the negrophile, so often mocked by results and stubborn facts, have ever attained such a happy realization.

CHURCHILL: *My African Journey.* 1908.

That was after the Baganda had been in contact with Europeans for thirty years or more. Some fifteen years earlier Lugard said the same kind of thing.

As we crossed the boundary of Usoga the country suddenly changed most completely. The rough, coarse grass and treeless undulations gave place to endless banana groves. The Great Unclad were replaced by a race of more intellectual appearance, completely clothed in voluminous bark-cloth.

The shady banana groves are a great relief after the burning sun, and the good paths after the jungle we have passed through; but they exclude the view, and make mapping difficult. The groves are wonderfully well kept; all old trees are promptly cleared away; the leaves are

225

neatly strewn on the ground in regular lines—to keep down weeds and as manure, I suppose.

The people are very much addicted to the banana wine (pombe). Even on the march a man carries a kitoma with a tube in it, and sucks; when talking, he sucks at intervals. He sucks, apparently, "from early dawn till dewy eve," and when he is not sucking he is smoking a long pipe—of bhang, I think. The liquor, however, appears to be very harmless, and I have not seen any one visibly the worse for drink, or boisterous and quarrelsome, as from the effects of tembo at the coast. The pipe is curious, too; a prettily-made clay bowl, with a long tube in it, is the usual one. Dried hemp leaves are put in it, and a live charcoal on the top. Sometimes a separate perforated tray, or false top, contains the live coal, the bhang being underneath. The people are very fond of music, and you may hear the "penny-whistles", made from reeds, from morning till night.

LUGARD: *The Rise of our East African Empire.* 1893. Abridged.

One of the first things to astonish the traveller was the extreme politeness of the Baganda.

If you say "Good morning" to a stranger on an English road, it is as like as not that his surprise will throw him into a posture of self-defence; but when two Baganda meet they begin to salute each other as soon as they come within earshot. "How are you?" cries the one. "Who am I that you should care to know?" replies the other. "Humble though I be, yet I have dared," rejoins the first. "But say first how are *you,*" continues the second. "The better for the honour you have done me," is the answer. By this they have already passed each other, and there is only time for the Parthian affability, "The honour is mine, and I shall treasure it," and a quavering of delicately-modulated, long-drawn "A-a-a's" of contentment and good will which gradually die away in the distance, leaving neither of them the worse circumstanced, nor the better informed.

CHURCHILL: *My African Journey.* 1908.

With courtesy goes love of music.

Every little goatherd has his flute. Almost every other man who walks along the road is playing on a reed flageolet. If he is carrying a burden on his head it makes no difference; he tries to make his load lighter with music. Harps, beautifully made, are twanged on all the roads about Mengo.

TUCKER: *Eighteen Years in Uganda and East Africa.* 1908.

Mutesa welcomed his European visitors with the greatest ceremony.

Here I was desired to halt and sit in the glaring sun; so I donned my hat, mounted my umbrella, a phenomenon which set them all a-wondering and laughing, ordered the guard to close ranks, and sat gazing at the novel spectacle. A more theatrical sight I never saw. The king, a good-looking, well-figured, tall young man of twenty-five, was sitting on a red blanket spread upon a square platform of royal grass, encased in tiger-grass reeds, scrupulously well dressed in a new mbugu. The hair of his head was cut short, excepting on the top, where it was combed up into a high ridge, running from stem to stern like a cockscomb. On his neck was a very neat ornament—a large ring, of beautifully-worked small beads, forming elegant patterns by their various colours. On one arm was another bead ornament, prettily devised; and on the other a wooden charm, tied by a string covered with snake-skin. On every finger and every toe he had alternate brass and copper rings; and above the ankles, halfway up to the calf, a stocking of very pretty beads. Everything was light, neat, and elegant in its way; not a fault could be found with the taste of his "getting up". For a handkerchief he held a well-folded piece of bark, and a piece of gold-embroidered silk, which he constantly employed to hide his large mouth when laughing, or to wipe it after a drink of plantain-wine, of which he took constant and copious draughts from neat little gourd-cups, administered by his ladies-in-waiting, who were at once his sisters and wives. A white dog, spear, shield, and woman—the Ugandan cognisance—were by his side, as also a knot of staff officers. with whom he kept up a brisk conversation. . . .

I now longed to open conversation but knew not the language, and no one near me dared speak, or even lift his head from fear of being accused of eyeing the women; so the king and myself sat staring at one another for full an hour—I mute, but he pointing and remarking with those around him on the novelty of my guard and general appearance, and even requiring to see my hat lifted, the umbrella shut and opened, and the guards face about and show off their red cloaks —for such wonders had never been seen in Uganda.

SPEKE: *Journal of the Discovery of the Source of the Nile.* 1863.

Speke's presents to the King included a number of carbines. With one of them he brought down a bird on the wing.

The Waganda were for a minute all spell-bound with astonishment, when the king jumped frantically in the air, clapping his hands above

his head, and singing out, "Woh, woh, woh! what wonders! Oh,
Bana, Bana! what miracles he performs!"—and all the Wakungu
followed in chorus. "Now load, Bana—load, and let us see you do it,"
cried the excited king: but before I was half loaded, he said, "Come
along, come along, and let us see the bird." Then directing the officers
which way to go—for, by the etiquette of the court of Uganda, every
one must precede the king—he sent them through a court where his
women, afraid of the gun, had been concealed. Here the rush onward
was stopped by newly-made fences, but the king roared to the officers
to knock them down. This was no sooner said than done, by the
attendants in a body shoving on and tramping them under, as an elephant would crush small trees to keep his course. So pushing, floundering through plantain and shrub, pell-mell one upon the other, that the
king's pace might not be checked, or any one come in for a royal
kick or blow, they came upon the prostrate bird. "Woh, woh, woh!"
cried the king again, "there he is, sure enough; come here, women—
come and look what wonders!" And all the women, in the highest
excitement, "woh-wohed" as loud as any of the men.

SPEKE: *Journal of the Discovery of the Source of the Nile.* 1863.

*Speke quickly discovered that the King's more amiable qualities were allied
with a total disregard for human life and for human suffering.*

The king now loaded one of the carbines I had given him with his
own hands, and giving it full-cock to a page, told him to go out and
shoot a man in the outer court; which was no sooner accomplished
than the little urchin returned to announce his success, with a look of
glee such as one would see in the face of a boy who had robbed a bird's
nest, caught a trout, or done any other boyish trick. The king said to
him, "And did you do it well?" "Oh yes, capitally." He spoke the
truth, no doubt, for he dared not have trifled with the king; but the
affair created hardly any interest. I never heard, and there appeared no
curiosity to know, what individual human being the urchin had
deprived of life.

Ibid.

*

I have now been for some time within the court precincts, and have
consequently had an opportunity of witnessing court customs. Among
these, nearly every day since I have changed my residence, incredible
as it may appear to be, I have seen one, two, or three of the wretched
palace women led away to execution, tied by the hand, and dragged
along by one of the body-guard, crying out, as she went to premature

death, "Hai Minange!" (O, my lord!) "Kbakka!" (My king!) "Hai N'yawo!" (My mother!) at the top of her voice, in the utmost despair and lamentation; and yet there was not a soul who dared lift hand to save any of them, though many might be heard privately commenting on their beauty.

Ibid.

Yet life at Mutesa's court had its lighter moments.

Then twenty naked virgins, the daughters of Wakungu, all smeared and shining with grease, each holding a small square of mbugu for a fig-leaf, marched in a line before us, as a fresh addition to the harem, whilst the happy fathers floundered n'yanzigging on the ground, delighted to find their darlings appreciated by the king. Seeing this done in such a quiet mild way before all my men, who dared not lift their heads to see it, made me burst into a roar of laughter, and the king, catching the infection from me, laughed as well; but the laughing did not end there—for the pages, for once giving way to nature, kept bursting—my men chuckled in sudden gusts—while even the women, holding their mouths for fear of detection, responded—and we all laughed together. Then a sedate old dame rose from the squatting mass, ordered the virgins to right-about, and marched them off, showing their still more naked reverses.

Ibid.

Stanley arrived in Buganda at a time when Mutesa was setting out on a punitive campaign against a tributary people called the Wavuma. Since the Wavuma were ensconced on Ingira Island in the Lake, Mutesa had to rely largely on the efforts of his admirals. Stanley was astonished to find that the fleet could muster 230 units, capable of taking between 16,000 and 20,000 men into action.

The largest canoe seen by me in this fleet measured 72 feet in length, 7 feet 3 inches in breadth, and was 4 feet deep within, from keel to gunwale. The thwarts were 32 in number, to seat 64 paddlers besides the pilot. There were probably over 100 canoes between 50 and 70 feet in length, and about 50 between 30 and 50 feet long; the remaining 80 fighting-boats were of all sizes, from 18 to 30 feet long. The rest of the fleet consisted of small boats fit only to carry from three to six men.

The largest class—100 in number—would require on an average fifty men each to man them, which would be equal in the aggregate to 5,000. The second class would require on an average forty men each, or 2,000 to man the fifty canoes. The third class would average twenty

16

men each, and being eighty in number, would require 1,600 men to
man them, the sum total standing therefore at 8,600.

A very respectable figure for a naval force, most men would think.
But in a battle on the lake, or for such an occasion as the present, when
the resources of the empire were mustered for an important war, they
would be further required to carry a strong force to assault Ingira
Island. The canoes for the assault would therefore be crammed with
fighting men, the largest class carrying from 60 to 100 men exclusive
of their crews; so that the actual fact is that Mutesa can float a force of
from 16,000 to 20,000 on Lake Victoria for purposes of war.

STANLEY: *Through the Dark Continent.* 1878.

In his historic letter to the Daily Telegraph, *appealing for missionaries to
visit Buganda, Stanley emphasised that the kind of man needed was "the
practical Christian tutor". But even he probably did not realise just how
practical the missionaries would have to be.*

The morning after the death of Mutesa's mother, Mackay and Mr.
O'Flaherty had gone to pay their respects to the king. They found all
the chiefs with their hands clasped above their heads, roaring and
shedding tears with all their might. When they entered, the king
bade these chiefs be silent, which they were instantaneously. His
majesty then asked Mackay how royalty was buried in England.
Mackay endeavoured to describe three royal coffins with cloth coverings, and one of them of lead to preserve the remains. At once the
king asked him if he would be undertaker and make the coffins; and,
thinking that they would be of ordinary dimensions, Mackay agreed
to do so, at which Mutesa was much pleased. Mutesa, however, had
no lead, but plenty of copper, which Mackay told him would do well
enough.

The court was dismissed, and soon after there arrived at the mission
a host of fine bronze trays of Egyptian workmanship (probably
presents from General Gordon), and copper pots and water jars of
Zanzibar (Hindu) make, with copper drums made in Buganda by
coast artisans. These were to be manufactured into a coffin.

Next morning, he went off to Rusaka, the residence of the late
queen-mother, some five miles distant, to measure the body. Much
objection was made by the royal ladies there, at his going in to measure
the corpse, but his friend, the chief Kyimbugwe, was the master of the
ceremonies, and he explained that Mackay had been commissioned by
the king to do so. Mackay was, however, somewhat taken aback,
when he was told by some of the other chiefs that he ought not to

have measured the corpse, but the dimensions of the grave, and have made the coffins to fit the latter. He told them that there was not copper enough in the land to make a box larger than what was necessary for the body alone, but that, if there were, he would willingly make one as large as a mountain, but that, as it was, he would make the inner coffins to suit the body, and the outer one as large as a house if they liked.

The grave was a huge pit, some twenty feet by fifteen feet at the mouth, and about thirty feet deep. It was dug in the centre of the late Queen's chief house, an enormous hut some hundred and fifty feet in diameter, as usual all roof, with no walls, and a perfect forest of poles inside, the centre ones being large enough for frigate masts. Rusaka stands on a hill of dry sandstone, clay, and gravel. It was well that the stratum was so firm, otherwise serious accidents might have happened if the sides of the grave had fallen in.

Nearly all the excavated gravel had been carried away, while the monster pit was nearly lined all round with bark-cloth. Into this several new bark-cloths were thrown, and carefully spread at the bottom, filling up much of the hole. Then the segments of the huge box, which, with the other coffins, had taken more than a month to make, were lowered in with much trouble, and Mackay descended and nailed the corners together. After this, he was summoned to the ceremony of putting the corpse into the first coffin. Thousands of women were yelling with all their might, a few with tears in their eyes. Only the ladies of the royal family were near the body, which by this time had been reduced to a mummy, by constantly squeezing out the fluids with rags of bark-cloth. It was wrapped in a new "lubugu", bark-cloth, and laid on the ground. The chiefs half-filled the nicely padded coffin with "bufta", finest Manchester shirting, then several bunches of petty charms belonging to the Queen were laid in, and the body was placed in the coffin, which was immediately filled up with more calico. Kyimbugwe, Kawuta, and the other chiefs in charge, carried the coffin to the court where the grave-house was, when much more yelling took place. Mackay then screwed the lid down, but such was the attachment of some of the royal ladies to the deceased, that he had to have them peremptorily ordered away, with their crying and tears, and hugging of the coffin, before he could get near to perform his duties as undertaker. Then came the copper coffin, into which the other was lowered by means of a huge sheet, and the lid of which had to be riveted down, a process that was new to the chiefs standing by. "He cuts iron like thread," they said, as the pincers snapped the nails. "Mackay is a proper smith," they all shouted.

With no mechanical contrivances, it was astonishing how they got this copper coffin, with its ponderous contents, lowered into the deep grave, without letting it fall end foremost into the great box below. The task was effected, however, by means of the great multitude of men. Thousands of yards of unbleached calico shirtings were then filled in, round and over the copper coffin, until the big box was half full. The remainder was filled up with bark-cloths, as also the space round the outside of the box. The lid was lowered, and Mackay descended once more to nail it down. Several thousands more of "Embugu," bark-cloths, were then laid on, until within three feet of the surface, when earth was thrown in, to the level of the floor of the house where the grave was.

ASHE: *Two Kings of Uganda.* 1889.

The missionaries quickly found that skill in healing was one of the things expected of them: though it was not until 1897 that the C.M.S. found it possible to appoint a resident missionary doctor. This was Dr. Albert Cook, later to be knighted. On trek a typical week-end's work would be like this.

Amongst others there were over forty lepers, with fingers and toes dropping off, some blind, alas! and others just starting the fell disease, including one a child of only eight or nine. Many had huge ulcers, with a lump of cow-dung clapped on by way of medicine. There were babies with malarial spleens. Enormous hydroceles, which in many cases reached the size of a child's head, or even bigger, were common. On Saturday we operated on thirty-one of these, on Sunday afternoon on forty-seven. With two Baganda boys from our hospital I went round, after making the sufferers sit down; one boy prepared the place antiseptically, the other dressed and bandaged it after tapping. I think that I shall never forget that Sunday afternoon. The heat of the day gradually diminished as the sun at length sank and the moon rose, but the crowds hardly seemed to get less. One after another the dusky forms pressed forward into the circle of light cast by the lamp, now it was a leper waving mutilated stumps of hands, now an anxious mother carrying a sick child, or again a daughter leading her blind father; their language I did not know, but we found a native who knew Luganda and Teso and so the work went on until at length the last one was seen and silence fell.

COOK: *Uganda Memories.*

There was no lack of appreciation for the white doctor's skill.

The impact of modern medical and surgical knowledge on their old

methods of treatment produced effects which have been very interesting to watch. The native, speaking generally, has a stoical indifference
to pain, but he is quick to appreciate anything that lessens it. His
method of extracting an offending tooth was to seize it between finger
and thumb, and waggle it backwards and forwards till it became loose
enough to jerk out, a process that took time and trouble, for their teeth
are astonishingly firmly embedded. Occasionally they would get a
friend to come along with a spear, and the sufferer, opening his mouth
wide, would get him to knock out the tooth with the spear blade. If
he got the right tooth, the method though rough and ready might succeed; but if he failed. . . ? It will therefore be easily understood that
when on visiting the Islands in 1898, a man with a painful tooth presented himself, and it was quickly extracted by dental forceps, he
looked upon it as painless dent istry, and in the next three days I had
some eighty teeth to extract, natives even wading into the lake as the
canoe was pushed off, opening their jaws and asking for painful teeth
to be removed!

Anæsthetics were at first a great marvel; and on seeing no signs of
pain shown, while extensive wounds were inflicted and large tumours,
etc., removed, with the necessary loss of blood, some thought we had
killed the patient. On the effects of the anæsthetic passing off and the
sufferer exhibiting signs of life, such credited us with raising the patient
from the dead.

One of the most spectacular results is, as always in uncivilized lands,
the restoration of sight to the blind. One such case lives in my memory.
A native groped his way up to the hospital, and asked if we could help
his blindness. An examination of the eye showed that though the pupils
were useless, owing to opaque scars in the cornea in front of them, a
little operation involving the cutting of a small window in the iris,
might be successful. This was done, and a few days later the bandages
were removed. The patient threaded his way up the very narrow ward
we had in the hospital in those days, avoiding table and stools, and
as he returned there was a great light shining on his face, for he found
he could see. He fell on his knees and called me God. As I hastily dis-
claimed Divine honours, he said: "Then you must be God's servant,"
and that title I felt we could all accept.

Far more recently we had the same wondering gratitude from an old
Somali Arab who came all the way from Berber in Somaliland, a distance of some two thousand miles, blind with double cataract, because
he heard that at Mengo was someone who could restore sight. The
rather risky proceeding of operating on both eyes at the same time was
adopted. I do not think any of us who stood round the old Moslem's

bed, as the bandages were removed for the first time, and listened to his broken expressions of wonder and gratitude, will ever forget the scene. "That's the Hakim," he exclaimed as he covered my hand with kisses, "and that's a lady," pointing to the white-robed nurse.

COOK: *Uganda Memories.*

Winston Churchill described the government of Buganda as "a complete and elaborate polity". It proved quite equal to organising a postal system.

Among other measures adopted by the Lukiko for dealing with the exigencies of the critical situation of the time, was the establishment of a very complete postal system. Huts were built at intervals of a mile along all the principal roads at which men were stationed, and in which they were supposed to live, ready at all times, night or day, to be called out for duty. A letter despatched say 100 miles in the interior is placed in the hands of a native runner, who at once, having tied it to the end of a split reed, starts at full speed holding aloft the missive and shouting at the top of his voice, "A letter, a letter, it is burning my hand—a letter, a letter." As he draws near the first hut on the road he finds a messenger standing ready, who, with his loins girded, starts off at full speed shouting the same cry, "It's burning my hand." And so, like the fiery cross of Scottish life of old days, the letter is speeded on its way until in an incredibly short space of time it reaches its destination.

TUCKER: *Eighteen Years in Uganda and East Africa.* 1908.

The Flame Tree, one of Africa's loveliest flowering trees, inspires this folk story told by the Baganda.

Once upon a time there was a little girl who lived in the village of Si. Her parents had no other children, and as she grew older they saw with joy that she was more beautiful every day. People who passed through the village saw her and spoke of her beauty until every one in Kyagwe knew that the most lovely girl in the country lived in the village of Si— and every one in the province called her "the Maiden". The Maiden was a gentle, sweet child, and she loved all the animals and birds and butterflies and flowers, and played with them and knew their language. Her parents were very proud of her, and often talked of the time when she should be grown up and marry a great chief with many cows and gardens and people, and bring great wealth to her tribe. When the time came to arrange her marriage, all the Chiefs came and offered many gifts, as the custom of the Baganda is; but the Maiden said, "I will marry none of these rich Chiefs, I will marry Tutu the peasant boy, who has nothing, because I love him." Her parents were very grieved when they heard this, and would have tried to persuade her, but just then a messenger arrived from the Sekibobo to say that the King of Uganda was going to war with Mbubi, the chief of the Buvuma Islands, and all the chiefs went away to collect their people for the King's army. Then the Chief of Si, who is called Kibevu, called all his men together, and Tutu the peasant boy went with them. The army marched down to the Lake shore to fight the Islanders who came across the blue waters in a fleet of war canoes, painted and decorated with horns and feathers and cowry shells and beads. The Maiden was very sad when she said good-bye to Tutu. "Be very brave and win glory," she said, "then my father will let me marry you, for I will never marry any one else." But when the men had marched away and only the women and children were left in the village with the old people, the Maiden forgot her brave words and only thought how she could bring Tutu safely back.

She called to her friend the hawk. "Come and help me, Double-Eye; fly quickly to the Lake shore and see my peasant boy—tell him I think of him day and night. I cannot be happy till he returns." The hawk knew Tutu well, for often on the hillside he had played with the children. The Baganda called him "Double-Eye", for they say, that, with one eye he watches the Earth and with the other he sees where he is going.

The Baganda reached the Lake, and there was a great battle, and Tutu the peasant boy was killed by a stone from an Islander's sling; but the Baganda rallied, and drove the enemy back to their canoes, and Mbubi beat the retreat drum, and his men returned to Buvuma. The hawk flies very quickly, and while he was still a long way off he saw Tutu lying where he had fallen on the Lake shore. The soldiers were burying the dead, and the hawk watched to see where they would bury the peasant boy of Si, that he might show the Maiden his grave.

The Maiden waited on the hillside for the hawk's return and the moments seemed like hours. She called to a bumble bee who was her friend. "Go quickly to the Lake side and greet my peasant boy, tell him I wait here on the hillside for his return."

The bumble bee flew away quickly, and when he reached the Lake shore he asked the hawk for news. "The Islanders have fled in their canoes, but Tutu the peasant boy is dead, a stone from a sling killed him. I wait to see his grave that I may show it to the Maiden." The bumble bee was afraid to go back with the news, so he stayed near the hawk and watched. Meanwhile the Maiden waited in a fever of impatience, ever gazing at the distant Lake and pacing up and down. She saw a flight of white butterflies playing hide-and-seek round a mimosa bush and called to them.

"Oh, white butterflies, how can you play when my heart is breaking? Go to the Lake shore and see if my peasant boy is well."

So the white butterflies flew away over the green hills to the Lake and arrived on the battlefield just as the soldiers were digging Tutu's grave, and they settled sadly down on a tuft of grass, their wings drooping with sorrow, for they loved the Maiden who had often played with them in the sunshine. Far away on the Si hills the Maiden watched in vain for their return. Filled with fear she cried to the Sun, "Oh, Chief of the Cloud Land, help me! take me on one of your beams to the Lake shore that I may see my peasant boy and tell him of my love." The Sun looked down on her with great pity, for he had seen the battle and knew that Tutu the peasant boy was dead. He stretched out one of his long beams and she caught it in her hands, and he swung her gently round until she rested on the Lake shore. When she saw the soldiers lifting Tutu's body to lay it in the grave she cried to the sun:

"Oh, Chief of the Cloud Land, do not leave me, burn me with your fire, for how can I live, now that my Love is dead?" Then the Sun was filled with pity and struck her with a hot flame, and the soldiers were very sorry for her too, and they dug a grave for her next to Tutu's.

And when the people of Si visited the graves the next year they found a wonderful thing, for a beautiful tree had grown out of them, with large flame-coloured blossoms which ever turned upwards to the sun, and they took the seeds and planted them in their gardens. And now the country is full of these beautiful trees which are called Flame Trees, but the old people call them Kifabakazi, because the stem is as soft as a woman's heart and a woman can cut it down.

BASKERVILLE: *The Flame Tree.*

Sir Harry Johnston suggests that the elves and gnomes of European fairy tales may have had their inspiration in the African pygmies, some of whom live in the western parts of Uganda.

The little Pygmies of the Congo Forest do not themselves cultivate or till the soil, but live mainly on the flesh of beasts, birds, and reptiles, on white ants, bee-grubs, and larvæ of certain burrowing beetles. Nevertheless, they are fond of bananas, and to satisfy their hankering for this sweet fruit they will come at night and rob the plantations of their big black agricultural neighbours. If the robbery is taken in good part, or if gifts in the shape of ripe bananas are laid out in a likely spot for the Pygmy visitor who comes silently in the darkness or dawn, the little man will show himself grateful, and will leave behind him some night a return present of meat, or he will be found to have cleared the plantation of weeds, to have set traps, to have driven off apes, baboons, or elephants whilst his friends and hosts were sleeping. Children, however, might be lured away from time to time to follow the Dwarfs, and even mingle with their tribe, like the children or men and women carried off by the fairies. On the other hand, it is sometimes related that when the Negro mother awoke in the morning her bonny, big, black child had disappeared, and its place had been taken by a frail, yellow, wrinkled Pygmy infant, the changeling of our stories. Any one who has seen as much of the Central African Pygmies as I have, and has noted their merry, impish ways; their little songs; their little dances; their mischievous pranks; unseen, spiteful vengeance; quick gratitude; and prompt return for kindness, cannot but be struck by their singular resemblance in character to the elves and gnomes and sprites of our nursery stories.

JOHNSTON: *The Uganda Protectorate.* 1902.

JOHN HANNING SPEKE: *Journal of the Discovery of the Source of the Nile.* 1863.

As the first European to reach Victoria Nyanza, the Kingdom of Uganda, and the source of the Nile, Speke was a man to whom much honour was due. But his life was embittered by the enmity of Sir Richard Burton with whom he had quarrelled following incidents during their two expeditions together. Burton challenged Speke's estimates of the size and importance of Victoria Nyanza, and poured scorn on his claim to have discovered the source of the Nile. In 1864 Speke failed to appear at a public meeting at which he and Burton were to debate their differences, and it was announced to the audience that he had been killed that morning while shooting. At the inquest the verdict was "Accidental Death". Speke was then only thirty-seven years old. His *Journal* is an entertaining book, particularly in those chapters describing life at the court of Mutesa.

SIR SAMUEL W. BAKER: *The Albert N'Yanza, Great Basin of the Nile and Exploration of the Nile Sources.* 1872.

The experiences described in Baker's book were in the main outside the present East African territories, and I have quoted only his description of the Murchison Falls, on the Nile between Lakes Albert and Victoria. Baker and his German wife were following the course of the Nile from the sea, and had reached Gondoroko in the southern Sudan when Speke appeared from the south with news that the river had its origin in Victoria Nyanza. However, Baker went on his way, aided by information collected by Speke, and after many hardships and adventures, discovered Albert Nyanza and the Murchison Falls. Baker achieved much fame in his day as a big-game hunter and a wanderer in strange places.

SIR HENRY M. STANLEY: *Through the Dark Continent.* 1878.

It is perhaps a little hard on Stanley that he should be remembered chiefly by what was in part a newspaper "stunt"—the meeting with Livingstone. The journey described in *Through the Dark Continent* was an altogether greater achievement, one of the greatest in the annals of exploration. During the first part of this journey Stanley covered much of the ground explored by Speke. In Uganda he obtained additional information about the course of the Nile, and made firm friends with Mutesa. His letter in the *Daily Telegraph* appealing for missionaries to be sent to Uganda, caused a stir and had rapid results. What was wanted, he said, was "the practical Christian tutor, who can teach the people how to become Christians, cure their diseases, construct dwellings, understand and exemplify agriculture, and turn his hand to anything, like a sailor". Stanley had a remarkable life. He was born at Denbigh in 1841, and spent the first nine years of his life in the workhouse of St. Asaph under the name of John Rowland. He then went to sea as a cabin-boy, and at New Orleans was adopted and educated by a wealthy cotton broker from whom he took the name Henry Morton Stanley. He fought in the American Civil War, and afterwards became a special correspondent of the *New York Herald Tribune*. In all he led four African expeditions, and then settled down in England where he was knighted and became an M.P. He had exceptional gifts as a descriptive writer, and all his books are highly readable.

JOSEPH THOMSON: *Through Masai Land.* 1885.

At the age of eleven "Joe" Thomson was studying the history of African exploration; at thirteen he was persuaded with difficulty that a small boy would be more hindrance than help in the search for Livingstone; and at twenty he made his first trip to Africa. He went as geologist and naturalist to an expedition to Lakes Nyasa and Tanganyika. The leader, Keith Johnson, died when the party was only a short distance inland, but Thomson took charge and completed the objectives of the expedition in a manner which gained him the approbation of the Royal Geographical Society and the acclamation of the general public. In 1881, on behalf of the Sultan of Zanzibar, he investigated reports of coal deposits (he found none which made him unpopular with the Sultan), and then in 1883-84, when he was still only twenty-five, came the famous journey across Masai land. Subsequently he undertook a successful mission to the Sultan of Sokoto on behalf of the National African Company, had an exciting journey into the Atlas Mountains in Morocco, and visited unexplored territory in what is now Northern Rhodesia for the British South African Company. Unhappily, his health was progressively undermined, and he died in 1895 at the age of thirty-seven. Thomson was the youngest of the five sons of a master builder in Dumfriesshire. As a child he was said to be "of a singularly gentle and lovable disposition", and as a man he retained—to quote his friend J. M. Barrie—"the generous exuberance of boyhood".

R. P. ASHE: *Two Kings of Uganda*. 1889.

The four years Ashe spent as a missionary in Uganda, 1882–86, saw the inception of Mwanga's persecution of the Christians. He records the anguish of the missionaries as they saw their converts tortured and burnt to death. They themselves lived in hourly expectation of a similar fate, but Mwanga never quite screwed his courage to the decisive point, though he did instigate the killing of Bishop Hannington in 1885. In the end the missionaries were forced to the conclusion that their presence in the country was a danger rather than a help to the converts and in 1886 Ashe left. He had to leave behind his colleague Mackay, whom Mwanga retained, partly as a hostage, partly because Mwanga wished to make use of his skill.

CAPTAIN F. D. LUGARD (later Lord Lugard): *The Rise of our East African Empire*. 1893.

In 1887 Lugard was a young Army captain, lately returned from a campaign in Burma. He had been awarded the Distinguished Service Order, but was shattered in health and had been placed on temporary half-pay, while he recuperated. The doctors ordered rest, quiet, comfort. Lugard had his own prescription. He sailed for Africa. "My hope was that I might embark on some useful undertaking in Africa, if possible in connection with the suppression of the slave trade." At Zanzibar he quickly found the "useful undertaking". It was a ten-months' campaign against Arab slave raiders in Nyasaland, followed by an assignment from the British East Africa Company to sort out the tangled affairs of Uganda. Through no wish of his own Lugard emerged as leader of the public opposition which developed in Britain to the Government's declared policy of abandoning Uganda to its own devices. "He is a frank man, a brave man, an able man, and an upright man," said Gladstone with characteristic fairness. The result was a mission of inquiry, and in 1894 Uganda became a British Protectorate. The tale of those exciting, critical years Lugard tells in *Rise of our East African Empire*. Already he had become a national figure, but this was no more than the beginning. His achievements as a soldier and administrator in West Africa lay ahead, and his advocacy of the principles of the "dual mandate" and indirect rule.

J. W. GREGORY: *The Great Rift Valley*. 1896.

Four rich English sportsmen decided in the early 1890's to organise an expedition to explore the little-known country round Lake Rudolf. From the British Museum they sought the services of a naturalist and the assignment fell to Gregory. The expedition was badly managed, encountered troubles, and collapsed at an early stage. Gregory then had six months remaining of his period of secondment, plus limited funds. He obtained permission to organise a small expedition of his own to Mount Kenya and Lake Baringo, and in five months covered 1,650 miles, climbed above the snow-line of Mount Kenya, and had some exciting adventures with the Masai. He came back with a wealth of new and valuable information which provided material for *The Rift Valley*, and for a second and rather different book, *The Foundation of British East Africa*, published when he was Professor of Geology at the University of Melbourne. In 1919—he was then Professor of Geology at Glasgow—he again visited East Africa, and subsequently published *The Rift Valleys and Geology of East Africa*.

SIR JAMES MACDONALD: *Soldiering and Surveying in British East Africa*. 1897.

As an Army engineer with a distinguished record in India, Macdonald was given the task of conducting the preliminary survey for the Uganda Railway. While in East Africa he also undertook an official inquiry into the religious disturbances in Uganda.

SIR HARRY JOHNSTON: *The Uganda Protectorate*. 1902.

As a young man, Sir Harry Johnston had every intention of becoming an artist. He studied painting at the Royal Academy and then had the conventional studio in Chelsea. But his painting led to an interest in tropical flora and fauna—for some years he held a student's ticket at the Zoo—and also took him to North Africa. The turning point came in 1882, when he was twenty-four, and had already decided that he had no future as a great painter, but might do very well in the service of the Foreign Office. He joined a private expedition to Angola and the Congo, and acquitted himself so well that in the following year he was asked to lead an expedition to study the flora and fauna of Mount Kilimanjaro. His first official appointment came in 1885 in West Africa—as Vice-Consul for the Oil Rivers and the Cameroons. Next he went to Mozambique, again with a consular appointment; in 1891 he was sent to organise Nyasaland and North Zambesia into an administered protectorate; 1897 saw him in Tunis as Consul-General; and then two years later came his appointment as Special Commissioner in Uganda. His task was to reorganise the finances and armed forces, and to report on the possibility of creating a local revenue sufficient to meet the costs of administration. This experience, like most of his earlier ones, resulted in a book. *The Uganda Protectorate* is a notable contribution to works on Africa, not only because he was a shrewd and thorough observer, but also because of the quality of his writing. It is further distinguished by reproductions from his own paintings. He was a prolific writer, his books including titles as diverse as *Science and Religion* and *Phonetic Spelling*, in addition to five novels, a series on Empire pioneers, and his many books of travel.

SIR CHARLES ELIOT: *The East African Protectorate*. 1905.

From January, 1901, to June, 1904, Sir Charles Eliot was H.M. Commissioner for the East African Protectorate. "Those were perhaps the happiest and most interesting years of my life," he writes. He resigned after a dispute with the Foreign Office. His book is obviously important, though for purposes of quotation I have called on it only for two "tall" stories about animals.

ALFRED R. TUCKER, BISHOP OF UGANDA: *Eighteen Years in Uganda and East Africa*. 1908.

"Simply a story of Episcopal Missionary life and work in Equatorial Africa," says Bishop Tucker of his book. But it is an exciting story of adventure and achievement. The Bishop took a leading part in marshalling British public opinion against the Government's declared intention of abandoning Uganda.

WINSTON SPENCER CHURCHILL: *My African Journey*. 1908.

In his early thirties Mr. Churchill was Parliamentary Under-Secretary of State for the Colonies. Characteristically, he decided that the affairs of the East African protectorates needed investigating on the spot. An entertaining account of the visit is given in the diary of Sir Hesketh Bell, who was then Commissioner for Uganda. "He is now in Nairobi and seems to be stirring up things there," says Sir Hesketh, adding apprehensively, "I am wondering how I shall get on with him." In fact, they seem to have got on very well, though at one ceremony the visitor made himself "a perfect nuisance, dodging about with his camera all the time," while at another the office of Under-Secretary was interpreted to the people as being similar to that of a toto—"the small black urchin which a cook or other servant pays to help him in his job". Bell came to the conclusion that there was "an awful lot in and about Winston Churchill". One piece of dialogue went like this: "Suddenly turning towards me, he said, 'How old are you?' On my admitting that I am forty-three, he exclaimed, 'Do you know I am ten years younger than you? I wonder where I shall be when I am your age,' looking at me as if I was Methuselah! 'Where do you think you will be?' said I. 'P.M.,' he replied in a tone characteristic of acute determination." Needless to say, Mr. Churchill's own account of his trip is first-class reading, both for its shrewdness of comment and its felicity of phrase.

ROSETTA BASKERVILLE: *The Flame Tree.* 1925.
Mrs. Baskerville made a study of Baganda folk stories, and reproduced some of the best in *The Flame Tree.*

SIR FREDERICK JACKSON: *Early Days in East Africa.* 1930.
For ten years, from 1907 to 1917, Sir Frederick Jackson was a dominant figure in East African affairs, first as Lieutenant-Governor of the East African Protectorate and then as Governor of Uganda. But for thirty years before that he had held important posts of one kind and another, including service with the British East Africa Company.

SIR ALBERT R. COOK: *Uganda Memories.* 1945.
Uganda has had no servant more faithful than Sir Albert Cook, who arrived in February, 1897, as the first medical missionary, and has been there ever since, apart from infrequent spells of leave. Writing from Kampala to give permission to quote from *Uganda Memories*, he admitted that fifty-one years in Africa had left him rather the worse for wear. Indeed, he said, the Government Specialist told him frankly some years ago that three months would see his end: "however, through God's goodness, I am still very much alive if not exactly kicking". Three years after his arrival he married Miss Timpson, the first fully-qualified nurse to go to Uganda, and his chief-of-staff. *Uganda Memories* is largely the story of how, together, they built up the C.M.S. Medical Mission.

PART FOUR

THE MALAY ARCHIPELAGO

The Federation of Malaya, the Crown Colonies of Singapore, Sarawak and North Borneo, and the Protected State of Brunei.

Perspective

1. "NATURAL PRODUCTIONS"
2. SINGAPORE
3. "AND HE THE MALAY"
4. THE FOREST PEOPLES
5. HEAD HUNTERS OF BORNEO
6. "THE CHINESE ARE EVERYTHING"
7. KING TIGER, FRIEND ELEPHANT AND OTHERS

Books and Authors: with biographical notes

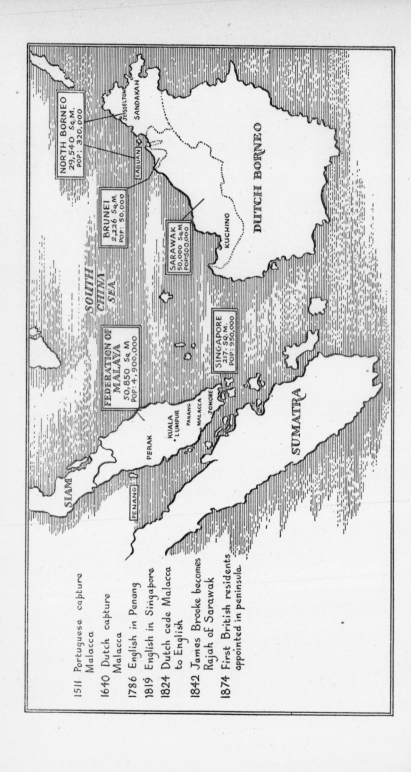

PERSPECTIVE

FOR as far back as reliable history can go, the Malay Peninsula and the northern islands of the Archipelago have been both a highway and a market place—a highway because of their situation on the trade route between India and China, and a market place because they themselves have products desired by the outside world. Tin was probably among the earliest of these products, and certainly benzoin, nutmegs, cloves and pepper. All were known in ancient times in the trading centres of western India and could have come only from the Archipelago. From India they found their way to the Middle East, and it has been argued that the tin used by the ancient Egyptians came in this way from the Malay Peninsula. If so, the Archipelago traded indirectly with the Eastern Mediterranean some 3,000 years before the "red-faced barbarians" from Western Europe appeared on the scene.

From the first the Malays seem to have been content to accept a passive rôle. Indians, Chinese, Arabs, and, later, Europeans all came seeking trade, and for the Malay it was sufficient that there should be some convenient centre where—when he felt like it—he could dispose of his products with a minimum of trouble. He himself lived a largely nomadic life. With his own family and probably a few others he would settle at a river's mouth, the settlement would grow, trouble of some kind would develop, or perhaps there would simply be a resurgence of his wanderlust, and away he would go again. He had the sun and the sea, Nature was bountiful, and there was space to move around in. Why then should he worry?

But others worried, and confronted by the easy-going Malay and his unwillingness to order affairs either energetically or efficiently, they did it for him. For a thousand years or more Indians dominated the trade and politics of the Archipelago, founding colonies and establishing dynasties. The stories and legends collected by Dr. Leyden in *Malay Annals* tell in the main of the heroic deeds of Hindu princes of Sumatra. Raja Suran, for example, "the mightiest prince of the land of Hind and Sind, and of all the rajas under the wind", who formed the design of subjugating China. So prodigious was his army that "the darkest night was illuminated by the light of their armour like the lustre of the full moon; and the noise of the thunder could not be heard for the loud noise of the champions and warriors, mixed with cries of horses and elephants". It should be added that Suran was nevertheless

247

outwitted by the Raja of China who heard of his coming and took refuge in a stratagem. A junk was filled with rusty needles, planted with trees and sent in charge of a crew of old toothless people to a port on Suran's route. The crew, cross-examined, told Suran that when they left China they were all young. "But now we have grown old and lost our teeth, and the seeds that we have planted have become trees. When we left the land of China, these bars of iron were thick as your arm, but now they have grown thus small by the corrosion of rust". Suran was suitably impressed, decided that the distance to China was too immense, and called off his campaign.

As far as the Malays themselves are concerned, the *Annals* say that a Hindu Prince of Sumatra came to the Peninsula to amuse himself hunting. From the Peninsula, he crossed to the island of Singapore, then known as Tamasak. "There they saw an animal extremely swift and beautiful, its body of a red colour, its head black and its breast white, extremely agile and of great strength." From descriptions given in ancient histories, the Prince concluded that the animal must be a lion or a singha. He liked the country so much that he sent to Sumatra for people, elephants and horses and formed a settlement, calling it Singha-pura. The settlement prospered and in course of time awakened the envy of the ruler of Java who succeeded at the second attempt in destroying it, the people taking refuge on the mainland. Their leader, Raja Secander Shah, eventually arrived at a riverside on the west coast of the Peninsula, and there established a new settlement which he called Malacca. So, if legend is to be believed, was founded the city which was to become for centuries the Archipelago's chief metropolis.

But though Hindus dominated the early history of the Archipelago, the more enduring influence was to be that of Mohammedans from Persia and Arabia, for it was they who introduced Islam, still the faith of the great majority of Malays. Arab merchants controlled much of the trade of Malacca at the time of the arrival of the Portuguese early in the sixteenth century, and the fanatical zeal with which the Portuguese conducted their campaign against Malacca had its inspiration not least in religious fervour.

First Europeans to visit the Archipelago were, not the Portuguese, but probably Greeks, who came at the beginning of the Christian era and were the channel through which the spices, tortoiseshell and perfumes of Malaysia found their way to Rome. Also preceding the Portuguese was Marco Polo, the Venetian traveller, who went over-land to China and subsequently accompanied a Chinese fleet on a voyage from China to the Persian Gulf in 1291: in his account of the voyage he gives some description of Sumatra, but otherwise has surprisingly little to say. It was some two hundred years later, in 1498, that Vasco da Gama crowned Portuguese exploration of the African coast by rounding the Cape and finding his way to India. His return with a rich cargo of Eastern products greatly stirred Europe, to a greater degree, indeed, than had the discovery of the West Indies a few years earlier by Columbus. The Portuguese acted energetically. From the Pope they obtained recognition of their exclusive right to possession of the Indian seas, and under the able and ruthless leadership of Albuquerque they quickly established a fortified base at Goa. It was then an easy step to destruction of the Arab trade between India and ports in the Persian Gulf and Red Sea, and to further exploration of the eastern seas.

The fame of Malacca inevitably drew the Portuguese there, and in 1509 the Malaccans saw white men for the first time. The *Annals* describe their astonishment at seeing "white Bengalis". "About every one of the Frangis the Malacca men were crowding by tens to view them, twisting their beards, and clapping their heads, and taking off their hats, and laying hold of their hands." The visit ended in hostility The people of Malacca, warned against the Portuguese by Mohammedan merchants in the city, attacked them, taking some prisoner, while the Portuguese commander retaliated by ordering that a man and woman who had come on board his ship should be sent to the king with an arrow passed through their skulls as a warning that he would return for revenge. Two years later, in 1511, Albuquerque himself appeared off Malacca in command of a fleet of nineteen ships, and the city was captured after a short but bloody battle, ending in a massacre. Thus, Europeans established themselves in the Archipelago and there they have been ever since.

Portuguese domination lasted for 130 years, a period of strife and bitterness, born in blood and maintained in oppression. "Their main object," says Crawfurd, "was the establishment of a commercial monopoly, and they made piratical war on all who opposed them in its prosecution". To the struggle was added the fanaticism of religious persecution, for the Portuguese sought to stamp out Mohammedanism, now the accepted faith of the Malays. Attempts to convert the people of Malacca proved so fruitless that before his final departure Saint Xavier publicly cursed the city. In the van of Malay resistance were the Achinese of Sumatra, who showed remarkable persistence. Massive sea-borne expeditions were undertaken against Malacca in 1582, 1615 and 1628, and all resulted in disaster, the expeditions of 1615 and 1628 each costing 20,000 men. But by the beginning of the seventeenth century, Dutch and English were infiltrating into the Archipelago, just as in the West Indies they were breaking the Spanish monopoly. In 1602 an English squadron of four merchant ships, commanded by Sir John Lancaster, visited Achin, bringing a letter and presents to the king from Queen Elizabeth, and the mission was greeted with much amiability. But it was as allies of the Dutch that the Achinese at last saw the downfall of the Portuguese at Malacca. Determined to capture the spice trade, and encouraged by the evident decline of Portuguese power, the Dutch first broke Portuguese sea control of the Straits and then, in 1641, took Malacca itself after a blockade, a siege and an assault. The victory no more than set the seal on Dutch success for already they had established themselves firmly in Java. Batavia had been founded in 1619, and the English driven out of the Spice Islands as a result of the Amboyna massacre in 1623. For 150 years from the capture of Malacca the Archipelago had the Dutch as its masters.

Unhappily, Dutch conceptions of trade proved no more liberal than those of the Portuguese. The Dutch Company's efforts to maintain a monopoly resulted in resentment and piracy among the Malays, and the piracy in turn involved the Company in expenditure that more than ate away the profits of monopoly. The English in the meantime retained the factory which Sir John Lancaster had set up at Bantam in 1603 following his visit to Achin. Bantam, a kingdom at the western end of Java, was then the centre of the trade in black pepper, and the English factory took its share for eighty years before the Dutch contrived to obtain monopoly rights by the expedient of backing the right side in a dispute for the throne of the country. Expelled from Bantam, the English Company established itself two years later, in 1685, at Bencoolen on the western coast of Sumatra. It was a sorry spot, swampy and unhealthy, but it was at least a foothold.

Not until the end of the eighteenth century did the English renew their interest in the Archipelago. By then the East India Company had become dominant in India, and was very willing to listen when Francis Light, "a navigating merchant" long engaged in trade with the more northerly of the Malay States, advocated the setting up of a British station in a position commanding the northern entrance to the Malacca Straits. Among the places suggested by Light was Penang, an uninhabited island belonging to Kedah, and this was the site the Company decided upon. In commissioning Light to conduct negotiations with the Sultan, the Company told him: "It is from the great reliance we have on your discretion, your experience in the navigation of the eastern seas, and knowledge of the views and dispositions and language of the Malay princes, that we have been encouraged to trust the success of the undertaking entirely to your superintendence." Light executed the commission successfully, but there seems little doubt that in obtaining cession of the island from the Sultan he promised more than he was in a position to perform. The Sultan understood from the agreement that the Company would protect him from attack by Siam, and would foot the bill for any campaign that took place, but the Company's undertaking was, in fact, no more than that it would maintain an armed vessel "to guard the island of Penang and the adjacent coast belonging to the king of Quedah". Subsequent squabbles about interpretation of the agreement did not reflect any great credit on the Company, and Light himself certainly had an uneasy conscience in the matter.

Having taken possession of the island in July, 1786, Light remained to administer it until his death in 1793. It prospered from the start, chiefly because the Company had the good sense to make it a free port, an object lesson which was later not lost on Stamford Raffles. The Dutch in Malacca felt the effects immediately, but far worse was about to befall them. In Europe, Napoleon invaded the Lowlands, and to forestall the French, Britain first seized Malacca in 1795, and then used the place as a jumping-off point for the expedition which captured Java in 1811. The assembling of the expedition is recorded by Abdullah in his autobiography. He was then only a boy and the great concourse of ships and men vividly impressed him. The anchorage, he says, looked like "a fence of masts", while "the length of the army was an hour's walking without break, and men were four and eight deep, all in scarlet". He even received a friendly pat on the head from the great Lord Minto, but what impressed him above all was the jumping of the officers' horses. "When they had done drilling and were returning, they did not take the horses through the gates, but leaped the fence, which was seven cubits high. This was the case daily. And the Malacca people in hundreds came every day to see the feat, and to witness the officers leaping the fence. Loud were they in their cries of astonishment at seeing the skill of the horses."

It was the Java episode which put Stamford Raffles into the forefront of Malay affairs. He had arrived in Penang as deputy-secretary to the Government in 1805 after nine years' service as a clerk at East India House in London. His father was master of a merchant ship in which Raffles was born off Jamaica. When he was still a boy his family fell on evil days, and he was only fourteen at the time he entered the service of the Company. His schooling was thus very incomplete, but he more than filled the gaps by the astonishing industry with which he studied in his spare time. There is some mystery about his promotion from an obscure clerkship in London to an important administrative post overseas, and contemporary rumour—which Raffles vigorously denounced—hinted that influence had been exerted by his wife's family. But whatever the cause, the event was destined to shape history. With his accustomed industry, Raffles not only applied himself to learning Malay, but seized every opportunity of travelling, of obtaining an understanding of the people, and of studying the flora and fauna. Abdullah describes how Raffles would work until midnight or one in the morning, and how he "kept four persons on wages" collecting natural history specimens. In the upshot he quickly became an authority on almost every aspect of Malayan affairs, so that his selection to administer Java after its capitulation in 1811 was but a logical development. This office he held for four years and then, after a period in England during which he published a *History of Java*, he returned to the East in 1817 as Lieutenant-Governor of Bencoolen.

For a man of his experience and ability it was a pitiful appointment, and obviously it could not contain his energies. In 1818, under the peace treaties concluded at the end of the Napoleonic Wars, Malacca and Java were returned to the Dutch, and Raffles, disgusted by the return to monopolistic trade practices which this implied, now conceived his plan for establishing a great free port at some key point within the Archipelago. He won acceptance of the idea from the Marquess of Hastings, Governor-General in India, and was given the task of acting on it. Singapore, then an almost uninhabited island, was one of the sites Raffles had in mind, and landing there in January, 1819, he quickly concluded agreements with the local chief and with one of the two disputants for the throne of Johore. The Dutch blustered, the Government at home hesitated, the Governor-General in India had some private misgivings but stood firm, and in the end the arrangement held. By 1823, when Raffles left Singapore, broken in health, the miserable fishing village he had found there four years earlier had already become a great port with an annual trade worth thirteen million dollars.

Singapore meant that Britain now shared with Holland dominant influence in the Archipelago and in 1824, by a treaty of friendship, the two Powers tied up loose ends. Holland gave up Malacca and promised to keep out of the Peninsula. Britain gave up Bencoolen and promised to keep out of Sumatra.

During the next fifty years the affairs of the Archipelago were notable chiefly for the continued and astonishing growth of Singapore, for attempts to suppress finally the piracy that menaced the whole internal trade of the Archipelago, and for the appearance on the scene of James Brooke.

Brooke's father was an official of the East India Company, and it was natural enough that the young James should enter the Company's service. He took part in the Burmese War of 1824–26 and received a wound from which he recovered only slowly. Fortunate in the possession of private means, he resigned his appointment in 1830 and went on a voyage from Calcutta to China in search of health. It was during this voyage that he saw Borneo for the first time and acquired as a result "an ardent desire to become better acquainted with a country combining the richest natural productions with an unrivalled degree of luxuriant beauty". To satisfy this "ardent desire" he returned to England, bought and fitted out the *Royalist*, a schooner of 142 tons, spent three years in finding and training a crew, and at last, in October 1838, sailed for Singapore.

Brooke was then thirty-five. His motives were mixed and possibly not entirely clear even to himself. Fame and fortune—but more especially fame—were admittedly among them, but they were linked from the start with a missionary zeal. Probably he saw himself as a second Stamford Raffles, spreading enlightenment and prosperity in benighted places. But whatever his motives, the outcome was that, in August, 1839, he sailed up the Sarawak river in Borneo to call on the Raja Muda Hassim, of whose character and disposition he had heard favourable reports.

Muda Hassim was the representative in Sarawak of the Sultan of Borneo, and had on his hands a particularly tiresome rebellion. He welcomed Brooke warmly, and, after a trade agreement had been concluded, he attempted to enlist his visitor's help in suppressing the rebellion. In return he offered, in Brooke's words, "to make over to me the government of Sarawak, with its revenues and trade". This offer Brooke refused. "I preferred interposing a delay," he says in his Journal, "because to accept such a boon when imposed by necessity, or from a feeling of gratitude for recent assistance, would have rendered it both suspicious and useless." However, he promised to reconsider the matter when he returned a year later with goods to exchange for antimony. When the year had elapsed, the rebellion was still in progress, Muda Hassim renewed the offer, and this time Brooke accepted. Putting an end to the rebellion he found an unexpectedly easy task, requiring no more than firm leadership and one determined charge by himself and a dozen of his crew. More difficult, indeed, was the task of persuading Muda Hassim to honour his side of the bargain, though it is only fair to say that Hassim was under pressure from a powerful opposition party, and also in some doubt about the approval of the Sultan. Brooke was patient but persistent and at length, in September

1841, he was formally declared Rajah of Sarawak, a title confirmed by the Sultan the following August. "I have a country," wrote Brooke in his Journal, "but, oh, how beset with difficulties, how ravaged by war, torn by dissentions, and ruined by duplicity, weakness, and intrigue."

In his first years as Rajah, Brooke applied himself to two principal policies—suppression of piracy and removal of Malay oppression of the Dyaks. In rooting out the pirates he had the assistance of the Singapore squadron of the Royal Navy, and three of the officers concerned—Keppel, Mundy and Marryat—recorded their experiences in books. Britain recognised Sarawak as an independent state in 1864, and in 1888 it was placed under British protection. In 1888 Britain also assumed a protectorate over the adjacent territory of North Borneo, which had come into existence some ten years earlier as a result of cessions of territory to a trading syndicate. Under this agreement responsibility for the internal administration of North Borneo remained in the hands of the British North Borneo Company.

Meanwhile, there had been a transformation in the affairs of the Peninsula. For fifty years after the agreement with the Dutch in 1824, the British Government resolutely turned its back on the Peninsula. The official attitude was summarised in a notice issued in reply to appeals from British subjects trading in the Malay States. Said the notice: "If persons, knowing the risks they run owing to the disturbed state of these countries, choose to hazard their lives and properties for the sake of large profits which accompany successful trading, they must not expect the British Government to be answerable if their speculation proves unsuccessful." But chaos and piracy in the Peninsula grew, with Chinese tin-miners contributing a nice line in internecine warfare, and in 1873 a new Governor of the Straits Settlements arrived with instructions to inquire into the state of affairs in the Peninsula, and to advise on the practicability of introducing a system of British Resident Advisers. In 1874 Perak, Selangor, and the Negri Sembilan all agreed to accept a Resident, and Pahang followed suit in 1888. These four in 1895 agreed to form a Federation providing for mutual assistance with men and money. With the remaining Malay States—Johore, Kedah, Perlis, Kelantan and Trengganu—agreements followed at intervals, and by 1914 the Peninsula had acquired for the first time a degree of genuine political coherency. With that coherency came peace and security and conditions under which the Peninsula could develop economically. Already its tin commanded a world market. Now the busy gentlemen of Europe and America invented the internal combustion engine and the pneumatic tyre, and rubber boomed. Rubber was not indigenous to Malaya, but in 1876 the

British authorities at Singapore had imported a few seedlings, and subsequent experiments there and on the mainland showed that both
climate and soil were ideal for its cultivation. With the boom the
rubber estates multiplied until, in little more than a decade, the Peninsula ranked as the world's leading producer. Rubber and tin—these
were the mainstays of the Peninsula's twentieth century prosperity,
these and the stable political conditions which made their development
possible.

1. "NATURAL PRODUCTIONS"

This region enjoys a climate more uniformly hot and moist than almost any other part of the globe, and teems with natural productions which are elsewhere unknown. The richest of fruits and most precious of spices are here indigenous. It produces the great green-winged Ornithoptera (princes among the butterfly tribes), the man-like Orang-Utan and the gorgeous Birds of Paradise. It is inhabited by a peculiar and interesting race of mankind—the Malay.

WALLACE: *The Malay Archipelago.* 1869.

Off the west coast of the Peninsula lies the island of Penang. Looking at the island with the critical eye of a "medical topographer", T. M. Ward came to the measured conclusion that it was "one of the fairest spots in the possession of the English in the East". In particular he delighted in Government Hill.

The lightness and purity of the atmosphere elevate the spirits and render the step free and buoyant, the splendid and varied scenery visible from its summit, the elegant tastefulness of the gardens, the inspiring breezes, and refreshing showers, render it literally a haven of health to the worn-out invalid. We wish not to encroach on the province of the poet; but cold must that heart be, and dead to the beauties of nature, which cannot be excited by the prospect from the summit of this mountain. The island itself with its numerous hills and dales; the town; the smooth roads in which vessels are riding in safety; the calm ocean around, studded with isles; the opposite coast of Quedah, with chains of mountains towering over chain, until they are lost in the distance, all inspire delight in the beholder. Nor are they undeserving of the attention of the medical topographer. Their influence is soothing to the mind of the invalid; and the convalescent from some dangerous malady, by looking on such scenes, must feel doubly grateful for the preservation of his existence.

WARD: *Medical Topography of Prince of Wales Island.* 1830.

The west coast of the Peninsula differs strikingly in appearance from the east.

On the western side of the Peninsula, more especially that part of it which forms one side of the Straits of Malacca, the shore-line is generally one long stretch of mud, covered with mangrove trees to the verge of high-water mark and rather further, for when the tide is up there are thousands of acres of mangrove whose roots and several inches of the stem are submerged. Beyond this forest the receding tide leaves great wastes of evil-smelling mire, soft and clinging, in which the searcher for shell-fish sinks almost to his waist.

Many rivers, small and great, find their way to the sea through this wide flat. At high water they look imposing enough, but when the tide is out a narrow and shallow channel is left winding about between low slimy banks, and right and left the eye wanders over a desolation of glistening mud with an almost imperceptible slope to the edge of the distant sea.

SWETTENHAM: *Malay Sketches.*   1895.

But on the east coast:

The waves dance, and glimmer, and shine in the sunlight, the long stretch of sand is yellow as a buttercup, and the fringes of graceful casuarina trees quiver like aspens in the breeze, and shimmer in the heat haze. The wash of the waves against the boat's side, and the ripple of the bow make music in your drowsy ears, and, as you glide through cluster after cluster of thickly-wooded islands, you lie in that delightful comatose state in which you have all the pleasure of existence with none of the labour of living. The monsoon threshes across these seas for four months in the year, and keeps them fresh, and free from the dingy mangrove clumps, and hideous banks of mud, which breed fever and mosquitoes in the Straits of Malacca.

CLIFFORD: *In Court and Campong.*   1897.

Down the centre of the Peninsula runs a chain of mountains. J. R. Logan climbed one of the foothills on the western side, behind Malacca.

A country, billowy like the sea, lay stretched before us, and above its farthest undulations rose the mountains, not now invested in the dim blue veil which they had hitherto worn, and which reduced them to mere geometrical figures, but raising their swelling forms in all the massiveness of close proximity. Ridges, descending from the highest summits and advancing slightly from the base, like vast buttresses, expanded in the warm shimmering sunlight, and broad and deep ravines reposed beneath their cool shadows, while one dense and continuous forest clothed the whole.

LOGAN: *Journal of the Indian Archipelago.*   1849.

The forests of Malaya, says Clifford, are "among the wonderful things of the earth".

Everything is damp, and moist, and heavy. The soil and the cool dead leaves under foot are dank with decay, and sodden to the touch. Enormous fungus growths flourish luxuriantly; and over all, during the long hot hours of the day, hangs a silence as of the grave. Though these jungles teem with life, no living thing is to be seen, save the busy ants, a few brilliantly-coloured butterflies and insects, and an occasional nest of bees high up in the tree tops. A little stream ripples its way over the pebbles of its bed, and makes a humming murmur in the distance; a faint breeze sweeping over the forest gently sways the upper branches of a few of the tallest trees; but, for the rest, all is melancholy, silent, and motionless. As the hour of sunset approaches, the tree beetles and cicada join in their strident chorus, which tells of the dying day; the thrushes join in the song with rich trills and grace-notes; the jungle fowls crow to one another; the monkeys whoop and bark like a pack of fox-hounds; the gaudy parrots scream and flash as they hunt for flies;

"And all the long-pent stream of life
Bursts downwards in a cataract."

Then, as you lie listening through the long watches of the night, sounds are borne to you which tell that the jungle is afoot. The argus pheasants yell to one another through the long night; the far away trumpet of an elephant breaks the stillness; and the frightened barking cry of a deer comes to you from across the river. The insects are awake all night, and the little workman bird sits on a tree close by you and drives coffin nails without number. With the dawn, the tree beetles again raise their chorus; the birds sing and trill more sweetly than in the evening; the monkeys bark afresh as they leap through the branches; and the leaves of the forests glisten in the undried dew. Then, as the sun mounts and the dew dries, the sounds of the jungle die down one by one, until the silence of the forest is once more unbroken for the long hot day.

CLIFFORD: *East Coast Etchings.* 1896.

Clifford adds that no man need ever lose himself in a Malay jungle, since running water can always be found and this will sooner or later lead to a village. This is no less true of Sarawak.

Two days we followed its course. Sometimes a solid wall of vegetation arose on either bank; sometimes, for miles on miles, extended the broad fringe of mangroves, whose light green foliage vainly strove to hide the foul slime from which they sprang. No song of bird or cry of beast broke the sultry silence. A heavy fruit fell from some giant branch into the water with resounding splash, or some laggard monkey rustled faintly among the leaves in escaping after his companions. The splendid blue kingfisher sat half asleep upon his bough, or suddenly swooped down on rainbow wing. The snow-white plumage of the solemn paddy-bird glimmered for a moment under the slimy bushes. Without a breath of wind our little craft swung slowly down the tide, and we lay under the awning in panting yet not unpleasant prostration. Hour after hour passed by without a sound reaching our ears, save the shrill voices of the sailors and the wash of the water. Is there a land in the temperate zone which can show, through all its length and breadth, the living beauty that exists in one acre of tropical jungle? Our seas, mountains, and skies are not so blue, our woods have not such a green, our trees are mere shrubs, our vegetation has no variety.

But when night comes in, and the silver moonlight spreads over the landscape, illumining the great masses of vegetation and rippling over the blackened water—when the bell of the wild deer comes in music from the glades, and a thousand vague but pleasant sounds arise from jungle and river—when the frogs boom in low thunder from the morass, and swarms of fire-flies flash among the trees in a sheet of living flame—then, indeed, the European must confess the poverty of his own scenery.

BOYLE: *Adventures among the Dyaks.* 1865.

No less characteristic of the Malay scene is the rice field.

If there is anyone who knows the Malay Peninsula and yet has never watched the sun set across the rice-fields, when the ripe grain hangs heavily in the ear, his knowledge of the beauties of Malay scenery is very incomplete.

A wide, flat plain covered by the golden harvest, the rice-stalks standing five or six feet above the ground from which they have sucked all the water which nourished them in the earlier stages of growth. One yellow sea of yellow ears, the green stalks only discernible in the near foreground.

This sea is broken by islands of palms and fruit-trees in which nestle the picturesque brown huts of cottagers, houses of wood, built on wooden piles with palm-thatched roofs and mat walls.

The setting sun strikes in great beams of saffron light across this wide expanse of grain bounded by distant ranges of soft blue hills. How greedily one drinks it all in! and, as the Eye of Day droops lower, there shoot from between its closing lids rays of fire which tinge the glistening palms with a rosy effulgence, followed all too soon by the pale opalescent shades which proclaim the approach of the fast-driving chariot of night.

A grey haze rises from the damp earth, spreads in thin wreaths across the darkening plain, thickens to a heavy dead-white vapour, and as the silver sickle rises over the distant hills it shines upon clustered plumes of dark fronds mysteriously poised above a motionless drift of snow-like cloud.   SWETTENHAM: *Malay Sketches.* 1895.

The bamboo is among the strange "natural productions" of which Wallace wrote. During an expedition into the country behind Malacca, J. R. Logan noticed "a succession of neat cottages".

On nearing one of these our ears were saluted by the most melodious sounds, some soft and liquid like flute notes, and others deep and full like the tones of an organ. These sounds were sometimes low, interrupted or even single, and presently they would swell into a grand burst of mingled melody. I can hardly express the feelings of astonishment with which I paused to listen and look for the source of music so wild and ravishing in such a spot. It seemed to proceed from a clump of trees at a little distance, but I could see neither musician nor instrument, and the sounds varied so much in their strength that their origin seemed now at one place and now at another, as if they sometimes came from mid-air and sometimes swelled up from the mass of dark foliage, or hovered, faint and fitful, around it. On drawing nearer to the clump my companions pointed out a slender bambu which rose above the branches, and whence they said the musical tones issued. I was more bewildered than before, but they proceeded to explain that the bambu was perforated, and that the breeze called forth all the sounds. Every one knows of the multiplied uses of the bambu, how, entire or split as the purpose requires, it forms posts, masts, yards, ladders, chairs, stools, screens, floors, roofs, bridges, etc., how, when smaller, it is an elastic material out of which a great variety of baskets and receptacles are formed for containing solids, and how its joints make neat and convenient bottles for holding and carrying liquids, or, when fine, are fashioned into flutes. But here was the crowning triumph of Malayan art, and the most wonderful of all the applications of the bambu, for what could be more bold and ingenious than the idea of converting an entire bambu, rough from the jungle and thirty or forty feet in length, into a musical instrument by simply cutting a few holes in it.

LOGAN: *Journal of the Indian Archipelago.* 1849.

*

JOHORE BAHRU, MALAYA

BEACH SCENE NEAR MALACCA

And the sound of the musical bamboos was extremely melodious; and the very birds lingered to hear their music; and the forest deer were all enchanted by their melody.

Malay Annals.

Nature has produced few fruits more extraordinary than the durian. Linschotten described it as growing on "a very great tree" and as being "of the bignes of a Mellon, covered with a harde husk, with many small and thicke sharpe prickles".

Such as will eat them, must first treade upon them softly with his foote, and breake the prickes that are about them: Such as never eate of it before, when they smell it at the first, thinke it senteth like a rotten Onyon, but having tasted it, they esteeme it above all other fruites, both for taste and savour. Here you must note a wonderful contrarietie, that is betweene this fruit Duriaoen, and the hearbe Bettele, which in truth is so great, that if there were a whole shippe, shoppe or house full of Duriaoens, wherein there lay certayne leaves of Bettele, all the Duriaoens would presently rotte and bee spoyled. And likewise by eating over many of those Duriaoens, they heat the Maw, and make it swell, and one leafe of Bettele, to the contrarie, being laide colde upon the hart, will presently cease the inflamation, rising or swelling of the Maw. And so if after you have eaten Duriaoens, you chance to eat a leafe or two of Bettele, you can receyue no hurt by the Duriaoens, although you have eaten never so many. Hereupon, and because they are of so pleasant a taste, the common saying is, that men can never be satisfied with them.

Journal of the Indian Archipelago (from Linschotten's *Voyages.*)

*

On a certain day, as Mr. Raffles was speaking to his writer regarding the answer to a letter from the Raja of Sambas, there suddenly came a Malay with six durians, with the hope that he would get them sold. So the smell of them reached the interior of the house as he stood at the door, and was sniffed by Mr. Raffles, on which he held his nose and made off upstairs. The people were astonished at this, not knowing his distaste to the smell of the fruit. On this he instantly called a sepoy, who was on the watch, asking, "Who brought these durians? Show me that Malay." So he was immediately ejected, with an injunction to the sepoy not to allow durians to be brought there again; and from that day no one dare bring a durian to his house.

Hikayat Abdullah.

*

The Durian, is however, sometimes dangerous. When the fruit begins to ripen it falls daily and almost hourly, and accidents not unfrequently happen to persons walking or working under the trees. When a Durian strikes a man in its fall, it produces a dreadful wound, the strong spines tearing open the flesh, while the blow itself is very heavy; but from this very circumstance death rarely ensues, the copious effusion of blood preventing the inflammation which might otherwise take place.

WALLACE: *The Malay Archipelago.* 1869.

I have been unable to find a descriptive passage about the orchids of Borneo which did not degenerate into a string of Latin names. But to the lotus justice has been done.

Not that there was anything wonderful about the lake beyond its picturesque setting. The wonder was that in it grew legions of lotus lilies, so that only occasional spaces of water—dazzling mirrors, reflecting the sapphire sky and the fleecy white clouds—lay, like everchanging pictures, amid their marvellous framing. But the frames! the lotus leaves! the lotus flowers! the lotus fruit! They were a sight to see. It was a very jungle of lotuses. Great circular leaves, spread flat on the surface of the mere, with fat globules of water, like gigantic dew-drops, sliding or resting on their green velvety faces. Forests of stalks, short and long, bearing the glorious wave-edged leaves, bending slightly over, and gleaming with the marvellous bloom which gives to their green softness an indescribable sheen of blue. Then there were thousands of flowers; beds and clusters and isolated stems, of buds and blossoms in every shade, from deepest to palest pink, only the fullblown flowers disclosing their yellow centres. Scattered about in every direction, amidst these leaves and blossoms, were hundreds of lotus fruit; the green pod, shaped like the rose of a watering-can, with a yellow seed peeping through every eyelet. As the fruit ripens, the stalk becomes black, the curious pod takes hues of heliotrope and brown, the eyelet holes open, and the seeds fall into the water, sink, take root, and shoot again.

Over the surface of the Mere flitted myriads of dragonflies, scarlet and orange and turquoise-blue; they dipped their transparent wings in the water, and, when tired of chasing each other, rested on the leaves and flowers of the lotus.

SWETTENHAM: *The Real Malay.* 1900.

2. SINGAPORE

The great city of Singapore has been the Archipelago's metropolis for well over a century, though to-day Kuala Lumpur is rising to world distinction as capital of the Federation of Malaya. Before Singapore Penang for a time held the centre of the stage, and before that, for several hundred years, Malacca.

Liberty in everything, commercial, civil, and religious, strictly and faithfully carried out, has attracted to this once uninhabited spot a greater amount of population and riches, than the Spaniards, Portuguese and Dutch have been able to bring together at Goa, Manilla and Java, with all their jealous laws, violent systems and intolerant religion.

YVAN: Six Months among the Malays. 1855.

★

On visiting this immense port for the first time, nothing astonishes you so much as the incredible number of vessels of various kinds which float on the breast of the calm waters—every species of craft and floating machine invented since the days of Noah, seem to have made this place a rendezvous—Chinese junks, looking like floating arches—heavy Cochin-China vessels, barbarous imitations of European ships—proahs from Holo, as thin and slender as a graceful fish—light Arab boats—tub-like machines from Siam—steam-boats belonging to the Company—the national colours of Holland, Spain, and Portugal, and last but not least, the French flag itself. The first sight of Singapore, from the port, is delightful—its white houses are overshadowed by nutmeg and clove-trees, and each looks as if the builder had consulted only his own taste and fancy.

Ibid.

★

The island of Singapore consists of a multitude of small hills, three or four hundred feet high, the summits of many of which are still covered with virgin forest.

WALLACE: The Malay Archipelago. 1869.

★

There are English, Chinese, Indian, and Malay streets; extraordinary activity and animation reign throughout; and in this city the useless and ineffectual quarrels of the West, are replaced by the general struggle

263

for commercial wealth and power. The phlegmatic Englishmen, in their immense shops, order everything with almost military precision, and overlook their numerous workmen as they heap up large quantities of pepper, clear away the refuse from the nutmeg, stow away the cloves into sacks, and fold up, or unpack the various stuffs and articles of wearing apparel. The Chinese, too, have a very different appearance from that which distinguishes them at Malacca—they are no longer to be seen indolently sitting on their coffins and smoking, contemplating the prospect of a future life, and yet enjoying to the very full all the comforts and luxuries of the present; but here, the sons of the Celestial Empire walk about the streets with a thoroughly business-like air, their sharp eyes on the watch, their necks bent forward—all alike in search of gain of some kind. That part of the city which is inhabited by them, is distinguished by its strong appearance, and the number of signs and marks they make use of; indeed, they may be called the very spiders of commerce, extending their nets in every direction, seizing upon every poor stupid fly that passes, and wringing from him all he possesses. Even the Hindoos themselves throw off a little of their habitual nonchalance, in the alleys with cloth awnings in which their shops are situated; their voices may be heard, crying their different kinds of merchandise, and vaunting forth their superiority in fine speeches.

YVAN: *Six Months among the Malays.* 1855.

*

There are always a few tigers roaming about Singapore and they kill on an average, a Chinaman every day.

WALLACE: *The Malay Archipelago.* 1869.

*

No public amusement whatever exists there, and the English inhabitants rarely meet except in their warehouses or on horseback. Each family gives one dinner party in six months and a ball once a year; the military band plays three times a week upon the Esplanade; races occur once in the twelve months. The environs of the town are dangerously infested with tigers, and a mountain five miles distant is alive with them. Under these circumstances the community is naturally addicted to gin and grumbling, but nevertheless a traveller is sure to be hospitably received among them.

BOYLE: *Adventures among the Dyaks.* 1865.

Here, in contrast, is a portrait of Malacca as it was when its fame was known from China to Europe.

At this time Malaca was in a very flourishing state, and the general resort of merchants; from Ayer Leleh (the trickling stream) to the entrance of the bay of Moar was one uninterrupted market place. From the Keling town, likewise, to the Bay of Penajar, the buildings extended along the shore in an uninterrupted line. If a person sailed from Malaca to Jagra, there was no occasion to carry fire with one, for wherever he stopped he would find people's houses. On the eastern side likewise, from Malaca as far as Batu Pahat (hewn-stone), there was the same uninterrupted succession of houses; and a great many people dwelt along the shore; and the city of Malaca, without including the exterior, contained nineteen lacsa of inhabitants (190,000).

Malay Annals.

3. "AND HE THE MALAY"

Home for the Malay is anywhere in the Archipelago, but preferably those parts of it which are currently enjoying a degree of peace and prosperity. One hundred years ago the Malay Peninsula was only thinly inhabited, but with the security which came with British influence the Malays began to settle in large numbers. So, too, did the Chinese and, to a lesser extent, the Tamils. Together these two now outnumber the Malays—the Chinese alone are almost as numerous—but of the three races only the Malays can truly say that this and none other is their homeland. In Sarawak and Borneo it is a claim they must share with the Dyak peoples.

The land is Malaya, and he is the Malay. Let the infidel Chinese and the evil-smelling Hindu from Southern India toil, but of their work let some share of profit come to him. They are strangers and unbelievers; and while he is quite willing to tolerate them, and to be amused, rather than angered, by their strange forms of idolatry, their vulgar speech in harsh tongues, and their repulsive customs, he thinks it only fitting that they should contribute to his comfort and be ready to answer to his behests. The Malay hates labour, and contributes very little to the revenues in the way of taxation. He cultivates his rice-fields, when he is made to do so by stern necessity, or the bidding of his headmen, and he is a skilful fisherman, because that is in the nature of sport. He plays at trade sometimes, but almost invariably fails to make a living out of it; because, having once invested his capital in a stock, he spends all the money he receives for sales, and then finds he has no means to continue his business. And yet, he is a delightful companion, a polite and often an interesting acquaintance, and an enemy who is not to be despised. He has aspirations. He loves power and place, and his soul hankers after titles of honour. In all these desires his women-folk are keenly interested. They apply the spur, and will readily consent to become the man's mouthpiece, when they think the good things of this world can be got by judicious flattery or tearful pleading.

SWETTENHAM: *The Real Malay.* 1900

★

Retaining much of that boldness which marks the Tartar stock, from whence they are supposed to have sprung, they have acquired a softness, not less remarkable in their manners than in their language. Few people attend more to the courtesies of society.

RAFFLES: Foreword to *Malay Annals.* 1821.

★

Malays are frank, courteous and honest; brave, generous and sen-
sititive to a fault; grave at times and anon overflowing with mirth in
youth, but invariably sedate when advanced in years; proud and re-
vengeful if ill-treated, but under generous treatment gentle, kind,
humane, grateful, docile and faithful. Capable of the warmest attach-
ments and yet impelled to madness and the commission of the most
revolting deeds by real or imaginary unkindness. They are kind
parents and dutiful children, they treat their aged kinsmen with the
greatest kindness and ever feel it a duty to relieve the wants of an in-
digent relative; old men and women are always regarded with respect.

VAUGHAN: *Notes on the Malays* (Logan's *Journal*). 1858.

*

I have frequently, on shooting excursions, been invited into their
houses, though a perfect stranger to the parties; a clean, white, sweet-
scented mat has been spread for me on the floor of lantei, a lad despatched to climb the tree bearing the best-flavoured and most juicy
cocoa-nut in the Campong; whilst the matron hands out from the
inner apartment a small cake of hard brown sugar, produce of the
sugar palm, neatly enveloped in its fan-like leaf. The young cocoa-nut
is opened with the ever ready parang, always in the presence of the
person to whom it is offered, to ensure its juice not having been
poisoned or charmed. The water forms a delicious cooling beverage,
and the tender kernel, sweetened by the addition of a little sugar, is a
repast by no means to be despised.

NEWBOLD: *Account of the British Settlements.* 1839.

*

Wheedlers are the men of Malacca.
Exaggerators are the men of Menangkabau.
Cheats are the men of Rembau.
Liars are the men of Trengganu.
Arrogant are the men of Pahang.

WILKINSON: *Malay Proverbs on Malay Character*
(from *Papers on Malay Subjects*). 1907.

*

The Pahang Malay, in his unregenerate state, thinks chiefly of deeds
of arms, illicit love intrigues, and the sports which his religion holds
to be sinful. He is a cock-fighter, a gambler, and a brawler; he has an
overweening opinion of himself, his country, and his race; he is at
once ignorant, irreligious, and unintellectual; and his arrogance has
passed into a proverb. He has many good qualities also, and is, above
all things, manly and reckless—as those who know him well and love

him can bear witness—but his faults are very much on the surface, and he is at no pains to hide them, being proud rather than ashamed of the reputation which they caused him to bear. He is more gracefully built than are other natives on the East Coast, he dresses within an inch of his life, and often carries the best part of his property on his back and about his person—for, like all gamblers, he is hopelessly improvident. He is a sportsman as soon as he can walk upon his feet without the aid of the supporting adan (a hand rail by means of which Malay children are taught to stand and walk); he is chronically in love, and will go to any length and run any risk in order to satisfy his desires; and, as he is exceedingly touchy and quick to take offence, he frequently seems to be in the condition which is known as "spoiling for a fight" . . . He is extraordinarily loyal to his Rajas and Chiefs, who have not always acted in a way to inspire devotion; he is capable of the most disinterested affection; he loves his wives and his little ones dearly; and, if once he trusts a man, will do anything in the wide world at that man's bidding. He is clean in his habits; nice about his food and his surroundings; is generally cheery; and is blest with a saving sense of humour, provided that the joke is at the expense of neither himself nor his relations.

CLIFFORD: *East Coast Etchings.* 1896.

The Kelantan Malay, Clifford goes on to say, had a reputation as a thief among thieves.

Their favourite weapon is an uncanny looking instrument called parang jengok—or the "peeping" knife—which is armed with a sharp peak at the tip, which stands out almost at right angles to the rest of the blade. Armed with this, on a dark night, the robber walks down a street, and just as he passes a man he strikes back over his left shoulder, so that the peak catches his victim in the back of the head, and knocks him endways. He can then be robbed with ease and comfort, and whether he recovers from the blow or dies from its effects is his own affair, and concerns the thief not at all. It is not very long ago that two men were found lying senseless in the streets of Kota Bharu, each having knocked the other silly with a parang jengok, striking at the same moment, in the same way, and with the same amiable intention. To save further trouble they each had their hands cut off, as soon as they came round, by the Sultan's order.

Ibid.

Clifford records this conversation with a Malay acquaintance:

"In Kinta, before Mr. Birch went to Perak, they had a game called Main China, each man betting on the number of the coins, which a passing Chinaman carried in his pouch, and whether they were odd or even. Thereafter, when the bets had been made, they would kill the Chinaman and count the coins."

"They might have done that without killing the Chinaman," I said.

"It is true," rejoined Raja Haji, "but it was a more certain way, and, moreover, it increased their pleasure."

Ibid.

The Malay was early noted for his disposition to "run amok", a peculiarity in his make-up which has prompted much speculation.

One day he went to divert himself at the town of Galang, and met an amok man. All the people with him fled here and there, but Radin Galang stood his ground, and drew his creese. The amok man made up to him, and they immediately began a-stabbing at each other, and pierced each other through the lungs, the one on the right and the other on the left, and both immediately expired. The people told the Prince, who came to take up his son's corpse, and having carried it to the palace, had it buried with befitting honour. He then put to death all those who had attended Radin Galang, for having deserted him, and the nobuts were not beat for forty days.

Malay Annals.

★

By far the greater number of Malay amoks results from a condition of mind which is described in the vernacular by the term *sakit hati*— sickness of liver—that organ, and not the heart, being regarded as the centre of sensibility. The states of feeling which are described by this phrase are numerous, complex, and differ widely in degree, but they all imply some measure of anger, excitement, and mental irritation. A Malay loses something he values; he has a bad night in the gambling houses; some of his property is wantonly damaged; he has a quarrel with one whom he loves; his father dies; or his mistress proves unfaithful; any one of these things causes him "sickness of liver". In the year 1888, I spent two nights awake by the side of Raja Haji Hamid, with difficulty restraining him from running amok in the streets of Pekan, because his father had died a natural death in Selangor. He had no quarrel with the people of Pahang, but his "liver was sick", and to run amok was, in his opinion, the natural remedy.

CLIFFORD: *In Court and Campong.* 1897.

★

These amoks result from an idiosyncrasy or peculiar temparament common amongst Malays, a temparament which all who have had much intercourse with them must have observed, although they cannot account for or thoroughly understand. It consists in a proneness to chronic disease of feeling, resulting from a want of moral elasticity, which leaves the mind a prey to the pain of grief, until it is filled with a malignant gloom and despair, and the whole horizon of existence is overcast with blackness.

LOGAN: *Journal of the Indian Archipelago.* 1849.

★

This is an isolated failing in the Malay which, by its awfulness and its peculiarity to the race, is apt to be too prominently set forth when estimating their general character.

THOMSON: *Description of the Eastern Coast of Johore.* Logan's Journal.

The element in Malay character leading to amoks sometimes made itself apparent in desperate deeds by pirates when they had been cornered.

One of the prahus was consequently taken possession of and brought alongside the *Ringdove*, the crew rowing it themselves, and having a guard over them of three marines and several seamen. On being made fast alongside the brig, without any previous warning, the pirates, for such it appears they were, though their arms had been skilfully concealed, suddenly rose, and simultaneously with their krises flew upon the seamen and marines, and, before they could defend themselves, one marine was killed, and two marines and a seaman severely wounded, they being all of the *Ringdove's* crew then on board the prahu. The prahu was at this time under the quarter, and touching the counter of the brig; so close, indeed, that one of the pirates actually took his spear, and lunging it through the port of the *Ringdove*, mortally wounded the master; and it was also reported, though I cannot ascertain exactly whether true or not, that the headman of the pirates, after killing the marine sentry dead with his krise, seized the musket as the man fell into the hold of the prahu, and fired it at the officers standing on the gangway. The pirates then cut the hawser adrift, and seizing their paddles made off for the shore. A desperate and well planned manœuvre, it must be admitted; and as it was at this time dark, there would have been a probability of escape, had not the boats of the brig been quickly manned and sent in chase. The prahu was overtaken and boarded in less than ten minutes, upon which the crew retreated below, and with their long spears, through the bamboo flooring, made a desperate defence, and finally refusing all quarter, they were slain to a man, and the prahu sunk by the gun of the pinnace.

MUNDY: *Operations of* H.M.S. Iris. 1848.

In organised land warfare Sir James Brooke found his Malay allies less resolute.

Though the shouts continued loud and furious from both sides, and a gun or two was discharged in the air to refresh their courage, the enemy did not attack, and a heavy shower damped the ardour of the approaching armies, and reduced all to inaction. Like the heroes of old, however, the adverse parties spoke to each other: "We are coming, we are coming," exclaimed the rebels; "lay aside your muskets, and fight us with swords." "Come on," was the reply; "we are building a stockade and want to fight you." And so the heroes ceased not to talk, but forgot to fight, except that the rebels opened a fire from Balidah from swivels, all of which went over the tops of the trees. Peace, or rather rest, being restored, our party succeeded in entrenching themselves, and thus gained a field which had been obstinately assaulted by big words and loud cries.

Journal of James Brooke.

In his dress the Malay has a style and distinction of his own.

The costume of the male sex is very simple but pretty, from its neatness of colour. It consists of a tight jacket of silk or cotton of a brilliant pattern, trousers usually white, a handkerchief for the head, and a "sarong" round the waist. This latter article is the distinctive feature of the Malay attire; it is made of silk or cotton, the pattern is always a tartan, and in shape it exactly resembles a wide sack with the bottom cut open. It is twisted around the body and looped up in graceful folds; the tying of his head handkerchief and the draping of his sarong are the great points of a Malay "swell".

BOYLE: *Adventures among the Dyaks.* 1865.

*

It is probably the simplest, most effective and least troublesome garment possessed by any nation. It is formed of a piece of cloth generally woven of the proper size, or about four yards long and two feet and a half broad. This is cut in two and the sides sewed together so as to form a cloth half as long and twice as broad as before. The ends are then sewed together and the sarong is formed. It may be said to be the gown in its simplest form, that is of the same width throughout and divested of all the additions from the waist upwards. From being nearly as long as the person, it forms in itself a complete envelope, as its name indicates, and is with the women, and often with the men, the only article of dress worn in the house and kampong on ordinary occasions. It forms also the sole sleeping dress of both sexes. In early morning the men may be seen standing in the serambi half torpid from the cold, with the arms folded in the sarong, which hangs down to the feet leaving nothing visible but the head and neck which are drawn down upon it. In the middle of the day, and generally when not in deshabille, it is worn fastened at the waist, the operation of a moment. In adjusting it, it is extended by the hand in front and to the left, till it embraces the person closely behind. It is then made to meet at the left haunch, so as to enfold the body tightly and the top of the remaining or loose half is gathered together into a knot in front, over which the border of the part next the person is drawn so as to confine it firmly. The lower end hangs to about the middle of the calf. The women fasten it in a different manner. When in deshabille, they generally wear it puckered and fastened immediately below the armpits, and reaching to the ankle. At night it is worn either loose or wrapped round the whole person including the head, according as the weather is close or chilly. Such are the modes in which the sarong is worn in and about the house.

LOGAN: *Journal of the Indian Archipelago.* 1849.

*

The Saputangan is worn in a hundred different styles and much taste is displayed in the way it is placed on the head. Certain localities are distinguished by the manner in which the inhabitants wear their Saputangans, and a man may be recognised as a native of this or that place by the manner in which he fixes his kerchief.

It is generally folded in a triangular shape and laid on the head with the apex of the triangle over the brow, the other ends are then brought forward, crossed over the forehead, taken back and tucked in under the folds according to the taste of the wearer, sometimes one end is concealed and the other left exposed, sometimes both ends are concealed or exposed.

The point left over the brow is raised and tucked in or left standing. To save trouble the Saputangan is frequently stiffened with starch and pinned into shape, and resembles the Persian head dress.

VAUGHAN: *Notes on the Malays* (Logan's *Journal*). 1858.

Malay houses are also distinctive.

Their habit of building on posts is so universal that they will do so even on high dry ground; the Chinese adopt an opposite course, they never raise their houses and if obliged to live on swampy ground they will raise the earth with much labour rather than build on posts.

Ibid.

*

The body of the house is about 40 feet square and, like all Malay cottages, rests on posts, so that the floor is some feet above the ground. It is divided by a partition into a large and a small room. A few steps lead down from the former into a broad verandah or gallery, which runs along the whole front of the house, and at one end extends about 24 feet beyond it. The sides and partition of the house are of pannelled wood work. The ends of the verandah are of similar wood work, with a curiously carved narrow window, or rather a row of slits, in each. In front and at the back of the projecting end, a wooden parapet about 2½ feet in height forms the only obstruction to the free ingress of the air and light. On the wall of the verandah are hung some deer's horns and skulls, the trophies of the house-holder's forest craft. Fine mats are spread on a portion of the floor, and others lie at one end in readiness for any unusual influx of visitors, for the verandah forms at once the visiting, eating, and sleeping place for guests. The large room into which we ascend from the verandah, is only used as a reception room on feasts and other great occasions, and ordinarily forms a convenient store-room for the less valuable household stuff, such as baskets of different kinds, mats, etc. Around a wooden post in the middle are hung an abundance of spears, swords, and other weapons of several sorts, for the Malayan armoury displays a motley and curious assortment of weapons. A number of baskets of paddy, which had been newly brought in from the field and were not yet cleaned for the granary, were placed on the floor. The smaller room was my host's bed chamber, the only place in the whole kampong sacred to privacy. At one end was a curtained bed, and on the other were stuck or suspended some fire-arms and a great variety of krises, swords and knives.

LOGAN: *Journal of the Indian Archipelago.* 1849.

The daily round begins at dawn.

In a Malay village all are astir very shortly after daybreak. As soon as it is light enough to see to walk the doors of the houses open one by one, and the people of the village come forth singly, huddled to the chin in their sarongs or bed coverlets. Each man makes his way down to the river to perform his morning ablutions, or stands on the bank of the stream, staring sleepily at nothing in particular, a black figure silhouetted against the broad ruddiness of a Malayan dawn. Presently the women of the village come out of the houses, in little knots of three or four, with the children pattering at their heels. They carry clusters of gourds in either hand, for it is their duty to fill them from the running stream with the water which will be needed during the day. It is not until the sun begins to rise, when morning ablutions have been carefully performed, and the first sleepiness of the waking hour has departed from heavy eyes, that the people of the village begin to set about the avocations of the day.

CLIFFORD: *In Court and Campong.* 1897.

When a Malay baby is born:

He is spat upon, morning and evening; his resting-places are smeared with sacrificial rice and with cosmetics that no ghost can approach; his cot is fumigated with the incense that the devil is known to abhor; his bath contains potent ingredients (such as manganese-dust and talismans of all sorts) that make the water purifying both to soul and body. On the seventh day the child begins to be taught the ways of the world. He is made to eat fruit—banana beaten into pulp and flavoured with salt. He is given a name, experimentally; but the name may be changed afterwards if it seems to bring ill luck. He is shown to the neighbours and receives his necessary quantum of feminine adulation. He has his head shaved. A sacrifice may be offered up on his behalf; feasts may be given in his honour. If his parents are unusually proud of him they offer up vows at some shrine, to be fulfilled in later years when the child has survived the perils of infancy. In short, the seventh day is the celebration-day of a baby's birth and everything possible is done to honour the child on that occasion.

WILKINSON: *The Incidents of Malay Life*
(from *Papers on Malay Subjects*). 1908.

Malay schools in Newbold's day were spartan in outlook and method.

The parents, at the time they deliver up a child to the master, offer a small present of plantains, sirih, tobacco, etc.; sometimes a few pice, and, when they can afford it, a rupee, or a dollar. They then say to the master, "This child we entirely surrender to you; he is not now ours, but yours; we only ask for his eyes and limbs, and that he may not be crippled, or severely wounded by chastisement. In every other respect he is solely at the disposal of the teacher." After these ceremonies, the child is regularly received by the master into the school, and entitled to all the advantages of the institution.

NEWBOLD: *Account of the British Settlements.* 1839.

★

In the school there were various modes of punishment for faults committed, and various instruments used; first there was the rattan, then the "Chinese crusher", that is, an instrument made with five pieces of rattans, which are tied close together at one end, and through the other end of each rattan a cord is passed; the punishment consists in placing a boy's fingers between the rattans and, pulling the cord, compressing or crushing the fingers, this punishment is inflicted for theft, and for beating each other. Then again there is the "Kayu palit", that is, a round stick about half a fathom long, bored with three holes, one at each end, and one in the middle, a cord is passed through, and knotted at each of the outer ends, and then passed through the centre hole. The punishment consists in placing a boy's feet beside the ends of the stick, and then tying them to the stick with the cord which passes through the centre hole, and, when thus fastened, beating the soles of the feet with a rattan—it is inflicted on boys who scheme from school, or who climb trees, or who make faces at their companions. Again, there is an iron chain, about a fathom or more in length, fastened to a block of wood, the other end of the chain is also fastened at the end of the block of wood; the punishment consists in fastening the chain round the boy's waist, and making him carry the block of wood on his shoulders round the school; sometimes the boy is not allowed to go home, but is confined with the block of wood at the Master's house, and his rice is sent to him there; it is inflicted on boys who run out every now and then from school, on boys who are always fighting, on boys who do not pay obedience to the instruction of their parents, and on boys who are slow in learning. Another is "singang" that is a punishment for boys who are of bad disposition and who are incorrigible, they are made to hold their ears with their hands, the right ear in the left hand and the left ear in the right hand, and thus made to sit down (on their haunches on the floor) and rise up, a great many times without stopping. There is another punishment for idlers, a dry cocoanut husk is set on fire, and made to smoke, and over this smoke the boy's head is held, sometimes dry Chinese chilli pepper is added, the smoke and pungency of the pepper entering the boy's nose and mouth and eyes cause him great pain. There is another punishment for boys who misbehave in school; a rope is tied round their waist, and then fastened to a post of the house; in this state they are made to learn their lessons, and are not let loose till the lesson is learned, their rice being sent there to the school by their parents. There is another punishment for very bad boys, and those who run away, and resist the authority of the teacher, and who steal, they are hung to a beam over head by cords round both wrists, and their feet are not allowed to touch the ground. There is another punishment also for very bad boys, they are laid down on their bellies on the ground, and flogged with a rattan. The punishment for boys who are great liars, and who abuse people, is to have chilli pepper rubbed in their mouths. All these punishments must be inflicted by the school-master in the school, there is no distinction made between the sons of the rich and the poor; the school-master can punish them even to the drawing of blood, and no complaint will be against him because he instructs well.

Hikayat Abdullah (Braddell's translation).

A village wedding begins with the bridegroom's procession to the home of the bride.

It cheers itself upon the way with the sound of much cracker-firing, with shouts, with shots, with the banging of drums, with the clanging of gongs and with as many other noises as the village is capable of producing. The bridegroom himself is borne in state by the best means of conveyance obtainable, be that conveyance a motor-car, a carriage and pair, a dog-cart, a horse, an elephant, a jinrikisha, or even the humble shoulders of a coolie. As he approaches his destination the noise becomes more and more deafening, and when he stops it is impossible to hear anyone speak. This is the signal for the bride's people to suddenly become awake to the fact that something is happening. "Who is this visitor? Whence comes he? Does he come in peace or in war?" A colloquy ensues. Sometimes the bridegroom's party apologize for his coming: "He comes by no wish of his own; he is drawn by some magnet of irresistible attraction, by the breath of the breeze, by the swirl of the tides." A duenna from inside the house shouts, "Let him be welcome then; but he must doff his weapons and pay tribute in the land where a queen holds sway." To which his supporters reply, "His wallet is torn, his money is lost, he can only give an earnest of the gifts that are to come." In this way he may be admitted on payment of "tribute" or little gifts to all and sundry of the old ladies of the house. Or, again, the bride's friends may affect complete ignorance of the bridegroom's personality; they may want him described so as to assure themselves that there is no mistake. All this, of course, gives unlimited opportunities for friendly chaff. Or again, they may pretend to resist him and hurl sweetmeats at the advancing host of the bridegroom's supporters. A mimic battle ensues and goes on until some well-meant act of treachery gives the bridegroom admission and prevents the jest from lasting too long. His followers crowd in after him.

It is usual at this stage for the young man to display a timid modesty that accords very ill with his truculent soldier-dress. He is Mars overcome by Venus; he is a poor fainting creature whose eyes have to be guarded with a fan lest a sudden glimpse of his betrothed should overpower him; he has to be held up by his friends lest his limbs should give way. Everyone hastens to reassure him and to lead him to the bridal

KUALA LIPIS, PAHANG

BUDDHIST IDOLS IN THE AYER ITAM TEMPLE IN PENANG

dais where his bride is waiting. There the pair have to be ceremonially seated together with their little fingers interlocked. The process is like an exercise in physical drill in which the performer is made to sink slowly down into a squatting posture and then to straighten his knees and stand erect. Bride and groom have to go on doing this together till they succeed in seating themselves slowly and exactly at the same moment—as custom requires. They also sometimes have to exchange vows that they will cherish each other and each other's good name. Once seated they are expected to remain motionless while the eyes of all the guests are fixed upon them. In Perak the guests are allowed to come up in strict order of precedence and lay offerings of silver on a platter before the newly-married pair. One by one they come up, doing obeisance, first to royalty (if present) and then to the bride and bridegroom, as king and queen of the evening. The married pair interchange mouthfuls of rice as evidence of their new relation to one another; the feast begins, and at last the guests are sent off in honour to their homes, the less distinguished being sometimes presented with packets of boiled rice and the more distinguished with the *telur joran* or coloured eggs stuck on branches. At the close of the "sitting in state" the bride is allowed to leave her husband and to return to her mother; and the hasty rush of the frightened girl, with the jingling and clanging of her ornaments, is a proverbial source of gratification to the bystanders, as a sign of her modesty after the uncomfortable splendour of her position.

WILKINSON: *The Incidents of Malay Life*
(from *Papers on Malay Subjects*). 1908.

Superstition plays its part in Malay life.

It is considered rather chic to have a *pelsit*. A Kedah lady the other day, eulogising the advantages of possessing a familiar spirit (she said that amongst other things it gave her absolute control over her husband and the power of annoying people who offended her), thus described the method of securing this useful ally:

"You go out," she said, "on the night before the full moon and stand with your back to the moon and your face to an ant-hill so that your shadow falls on the ant-hill. Then you recite certain *jampi* (incantations), and bending forward try to embrace your shadow. If you fail try again several times, repeating more incantations. If not successful go the next night and make a further effort, and the night after if necessary—three nights in all. If you cannot then catch your shadow, wait till the same day on the following month and renew the attempt. Sooner or later you will succeed, and, as you stand there in the brilliance of the moonlight, you will see that you have drawn your shadow into yourself, and your body will never again cast a shade. Go home and in the night, whether sleeping or waking, the form of a child will appear before you and put out its tongue; that seize and it will remain while the rest of the child disappears. In a little while the tongue will turn into something that breathes, a small animal, reptile or insect, and when you see the creature has life put it in a bottle and the *pelsit* is yours."

SWETTENHAM: *Malay Sketches*. 1895.

The art of composing Pantuns—defined by Crawfurd as a kind of rhyming enigma—was noted by the earliest observers as peculiar to the Malays.

The Pantun consists of two couplets, the lines of which rhyme alternately. The first couplet contains most frequently a simile drawn from some object of nature, more or less remotely alluding to the second couplet, the meaning of which is generally obvious, and conveys a moral apopthegm, a sentiment of love, defiance, anger, or a biting sarcasm, according to the subject of the Pantun. . . .

These Pantuns the Malays often recite in alternate contest for hours; the preceding Pantun always furnishing the catch word to that which follows, until one of the parties be silenced or vanquished. . . . The Malay youths, who pride themselves much on their skill in these compositions, are not unfrequently drawn by their desire to excel in them into serious disputes; and bloodshed sometimes terminates a poetical contest, which began probably in the same playful way as those of Virgil's shepherds.

NEWBOLD: *Account of the British Settlements*. 1839.

Newbold quotes the following as examples of the Pantun:

> How radiant is the sweet basil!
> Living wood is consumed by fire:
> If this be love, how intolerable are its pains.
> Than life, death is to be more desirable.

*   *   *

> Lofty, lofty grows the Limburi tree,
> Its branches sweep the clouds;
> It is over, my search is vain.
> I am like the wild dove bereft of its mate.

*   *   *

The deep waters have increased in depth,
The rains near the source of the stream have not abated:
The desire of my heart hath increased in strength,
Whilst its former language still remains unsatisfied.

*   *   *

The moon gives her light, the stars glitter,
The crows eat the young rice:
If my mistress believeth not my faith,
Lay open my bosom and view my heart.

Ibid.

The village story-teller has a rich stock-in-trade, particularly of jungle stories, in which the hero is the tiny Mouse-deer, first cousin of Reynard the Fox, Brer Rabbit and Ananse the Spider.

When the Great King of All the Tigers was sick, the Tiger-Crown-Prince made obeisance and said, "If my Lord will taste of the flesh of every beast of the field peradventure my Lord may recovery." So the Great King commanded the Crown-Prince to summon every kind of beast into his presence, and as they appeared the King ate of them. Only the Mouse-deer, who was likewise summoned, refused to appear.

Therefore the great King's wrath was kindled against the Mouse-deer and in the end he too was fain to appear. And when he appeared he was questioned by the King. "Why did you not attend at the first when we had summoned hither every kind of beast that lives in the field?" The Mouse-deer replied, "Your slave could not approach your Majesty because of a dream of certain medicine that would make your Majesty well." The King replied, "What medicine was this of which you dreamed?" "Your slave dreamed that the only remedy for your Majesty's sickness was for your Majesty to seize and devour *That which is Nearest your Majesty.*"

Immediately on hearing this the Great King of the Tigers seized the Prince of the Tigers and devoured him also. And straightway the King was cured, and the Mouse-deer himself became Crown-Prince in turn.

SKEAT: *Fables and Folk-Tales from an Eastern Forest.* 1901.

Here are other characteristic fables:

The Argus-pheasant and the Crow in the days of King Solomon were bosom friends, and could never do enough to show their mutual friendship. One day, however, the argus-pheasant, who was then dressed somewhat dowdily, suggested that his friend the crow should show his skill with the brush by decorating his (the argus-pheasant's) feathers. To this the crow agreed, on condition, however, that the arrangement should be mutual. The argus-pheasant agreed to this, and the crow forthwith set to work, and so surpassed himself that the argus-pheasant became, as it is now, one of the most beautiful birds in the world. When the crow's task was done, however, the argus-pheasant refused to fulfil his own part of the bargain, excusing himself on the plea that the day of judgment was too near at hand. Hence a fierce quarrel ensued, at the end of which the argus-pheasant upset the ink-bottle over the crow, and thus rendered him coal-black. Hence the crow and the argus-pheasant are enemies to this day.

SKEAT: *Malay Magic.* 1900.

*

Whenever it effects a capture the crocodile carries its victim at once below the surface, and either tries to smother him in the soft, thick mud of the mangrove swamp, or pushes him under a snag or projecting root, with the object of letting him drown, while it retires to watch him from a short distance. After what it considers a sufficient interval to effect its purpose, the crocodile seizes the body of the drowned man and rises to the surface, when it "calls upon the Sun, Moon, and Stars to bear witness" that it was not guilty of the homicide—

> "It was not I who killed you,
> It was water which killed you."

Ibid.

The Malay gift for sociability is nowhere more apparent than in the organisation of a party to meng-gelunchor.

Given a fine sunny morning (and that is what most mornings are in Perak) you will drive four or five miles to the appointed place of meeting, and there find a crowd of one or two hundred Malay men, women, and children, who have been duly bidden to *meng-gelunchor* and to take part in the picnic which forms a recognised accompaniment to the proceedings.

A walk of a couple of miles along a shady jungle path brings the party to the foot of a spur of hills, whence a clear mountain stream leaps down a succession of cascades to fertilise the plain. There is a stiff climb for several hundred feet until the party gains a great granite rock in the bed of the stream, large enough to accommodate a much more numerous gathering. In a "spate" this rock might be covered, but now the water flows round it and dashes itself wildly over the falls below. Upstream, however, there is a sheer smooth face of granite, about sixty feet long, inclined at an angle of say 45°, and, while the main body of water finds its way down one side of this rock and then across its foot, a certain quantity, only an inch or two deep, flows steadily down the face. The depth of water here can be increased at will by bamboo troughs, leading out of the great pool which lies at the head of the waterfall. At the base of the rock is an inviting lynn not more than four feet deep. On either side, the river is shut in by a wealth of jungle foliage through which the sun strikes at rare intervals, just sufficiently to give the sense of warmth and colour.

It is delightfully picturesque with all these people in their many-coloured garments, grouped in artistic confusion, on bank and rock. They only sit for a brief rest after the climb, to collect wood, make fires and get the work of cooking started, and you will not be left long in doubt as to the meaning of *meng-gelunchor*. It is to slide, and the game is to "toboggan" down this waterfall into the lynn at its base.

A crowd of little boys is already walking up the steep, slippery rock. They go to the very top, sit down in the shallow water with feet straight out in front of them and a hand on either side for guidance, and immediately begin to slide down the sixty feet of height, gaining, before they have gone halfway, so great a speed that the final descent into the pool is like the fall of a stone. They succeed each other in a constant stream, those behind coming on the top of those who have already reached the lynn.

But now the men, and lastly the women, are drawn to join the sliders and the fun becomes indeed both fast and furious. The women begin timidly, only half way up the slide, but soon grow bolder, and mixed parties of four, six, and eight in rows of two, three, or four each, start together and, with a good deal of laughter and ill-directed attempts at mutual assistance, dash wildly into the pool which is almost constantly full of a struggling, screaming crowd of young people of both sexes.

If you understand the game, the slide is a graceful progress, but, if you don't, if you fail to sit erect, if you do not keep your feet together, above all, if you lose your balance and do not remain absolutely straight on the slide, then your descent will be far from graceful, it may even be slightly painful, and the final plunge into the lynn will be distinctly undignified. It is well to leave your dignity at home, if you go to *meng-gelunchor* with a Malay party, for those who do not weary themselves with tobogganing become absolutely exhausted with laughing at the sliders. The fascination of the thing is extraordinary, and, to read this poor description, you would think it impossible that any sane person would spend hours in struggling up a steep and slippery rock to slide down it on two inches of water, and, having gained a startling velocity, leap into a shallow pool where half a dozen people will be on you before you can get out of the way. And yet I am persuaded that, if your joints are not stiff with age and you are not afraid of cold water, or ridicule, or personal damage (and you will admit none of those things) you would *meng-gelunchor* with the best of them, nor be the first to cry "hold, enough".

It is usual for the men, when sliding down the rock, to sit upon a piece of the thick fibre of the plantain called *upih*. It is perhaps advisable, but the women do not seem to want it. It is surprising that there are so few casualties and of such small importance—some slight abrasions, a little bumping of heads, at most the loss of a tooth, will be the extent of the total damage, and with a little care there need be none at all.

By 1 p.m. every one will probably be tired, dry garments are donned, and a very hungry company does ample justice to the meal. An hour will be spent in smoking and gossip, and, as the shadows begin to lengthen, a long procession slowly wends its way back, down the slippery descent, across the sunny fields, and through the forest, to the trysting-place where all met in the morning and whence they now return to their own homes.

SWETTENHAM: *Malay Sketches.* 1895.

Cock-fights and buffalo-fights are great occasions.

A cock-fight between two well-known birds is a serious affair in Pahang. The rival qualities of the combatants have furnished food for endless discussion for weeks or even months before, and every one of standing has visited and examined the cocks, and has made a book upon the event. On the day fixed for the fight a crowd collects before the palace, and some of the King's youths set up the cock-pit, which is a ring about three feet in diameter enclosed by canvas walls supported on stakes driven into the ground. Presently the Juara or cock-fighters appear, each carrying his bird under his left arm. They enter the cock-pit, squat down, and begin pulling at, and shampooing the legs and wings of their birds, in the manner which Malays believe loosen the muscles, and get the reefs out of the cocks' limbs. Then the word is given to start the fight, and the birds, released, fly straight at one another, striking with their spurs and sending feathers flying in all directions. This lasts for perhaps three minutes, when the cocks begin to lose their wind, and the fight is carried on as much with their beaks as with their spurs. Each bird tries to get its head under its opponent's wing, running forward to strike at the back of its antagonist's head as soon as its own emerges from under its temporary shelter. This is varied by an occasional blow with the spurs, and the Malays herald each stroke with loud cries of approval. Basah! Basah! Thou hast wetted him! Thou hast drawn blood! Ah itu dia! That is it! That is a good one! Ah sakit-lah itu! Ah, that was a nasty one! And the birds are exhorted to make fresh efforts amid occasional bursts of the shrill chorus of yells, called sorak, their backers cheering them on and crying to them by name.

CLIFFORD: *East Coast Etchings.* 1896.

★

The young Rajas stalk about, examine the bulls, and give loud and contradictory orders, as to the manner in which the fight is to be conducted. The keepers, fortunately, are so deafened by the row which everyone near them is making, that they are utterly incapable of following directions which they cannot hear. Malays love many people, and many things, and one of the latter is the sound of their own voices. When they are excited, and in the bull-ring they are always wild with excitement, they wax very noisy indeed, and, as they all talk, and no one listens to what anyone else is saying, the green sward, on which the combat is to take place, speedily becomes a pandemonium, compared with which the Tower of Babel was a quiet corner in Sleepy Hollow.

At last the word to begin is given, and the keepers of the buffaloes let out the lines made fast to the bull's noses, and lead their charges to the centre of the green. The lines are crossed and then gradually drawn taut, so that the bulls are soon facing one another. Then the knots are loosed and the cords slip from the nose rings. A dead silence falls upon the people, and for a moment the combatants eye one another. Then they rush together, forehead to forehead, with a mighty impact. A fresh roar rends the sky, the backers of each beast shrieking advice and encouragement to the bull which carries their money.

After the first rush, the bulls no longer charge, but stand with interlaced horns, straining shoulders and quivering quarters bringing tremendous pressure to bear one upon the other, while each strives to get a grip with the point of its horns upon the neck, or cheeks, or face of its opponent. A buffalo's horn is not sharp, but the weight of the animal is enormous, and you must remember the horns are driven with the whole of the brute's bulk for lever and sledge-hammer. Such force as is exerted would be almost sufficient to push a crowbar through a stone wall and, tough though they are, the hardest of old bull buffaloes is not proof against the terrible pressure brought to bear. The bulls show wonderful activity and skill in these fencing matches. Each beast gives way the instant that it is warned by the touch of the horn-tip that its opponent has found an opening, and woe betide the bull that puts its weight into a stab which the other has time to elude. In the flick of an eye—as the Malay phrase has it—advantage is taken of the blunder, and, before the bull has time to recover its lost balance, its opponent has found an opening, and has wedged its horn-point into the neck or cheek. When at last a firm grip has been won, and the horn has been driven into the yielding flesh, as far as the struggles of its opponent render possible, the stabber makes his great effort. Pulling his hind legs well under him, and straightening his fore-legs to the utmost extent, till the skin is drawn taut over the projecting bosses of bone at the shoulders, and the knots of muscle stand out like cordage on a crate, he lifts his opponent. His head is skewed on one side, so that the horn on which his adversary is hooked, is raised to the highest level possible, and his massive neck steams and quivers with the tremendous effort. If the stab is sufficiently low down, say in the neck, or under the cheek-bone, the wounded bull is often lifted clean off his fore-feet, and hangs there helpless and motionless "while a man might count a score". The exertion of lifting, however, is too great to admit of its being continued for any length of time, and as soon as the wounded buffalo regains its power of motion—that is to say, as soon as its fore-feet are again on the ground—it speedily releases itself from its adversary's horn. Then, since the latter is often spent, by the extraordinary effort which has been made, it frequently happens that it is stabbed, and lifted in its turn, before balance has been completely recovered.

Once, and only once, have I seen a bull succeed in throwing his opponent; after he had lifted it off its feet. The vanquished bull turned over on its back, before it succeeded in regaining its feet, but the victor was itself too used up, to more than make a ghost of a stab at the exposed stomach of its adversary. This throw is still spoken of in Pahang as the most marvellous example of skill and strength, which has ever been called forth, within living memory, by any of these contests.

As the stabs follow one another, to the sound of the clicking of the horns, and the mighty blowing and snorting of the breathless bulls, lift succeeds lift with amazing rapidity. The green turf is stamped into mud, by the great hoofs of the labouring brutes, and at length one bull owns himself to be beaten. Down goes his head—that sure sign of exhaustion—and in a moment he has turned round, and is off in a bee-line, hotly pursued by the victor. The chase is never a long one, as the conqueror always abandons it at the end of a few hundred yards, but while it lasts, it is fast and furious, and woe betide the man who finds himself in the way of either of the excited animals.

CLIFFORD: *East Coast Etchings*. 1896.

Though monarchy might be absolute, high standards of conduct were en-
forced on kings.

There are ten regulations for all Kings:
1st. Strength in their government.
2nd. Authority in their commands.
3rd. Mercy in their anger.
4th. Raise the weak.
5th. Lower the great.
6th. Honour the humble.
7th. Humble the splendid.
8th. Kill the living and bring to life the dead.
9th. Be affable to all.
10th. Be just and of good repute in all countries.

LOGAN: *Journal of the Indian Archipelago.* 1851.

The following were among the Laws of Johore in the middle of last century:

If a man borrow a slave for the purpose of climbing trees and say to
the master "peradventure he may be killed or maimed" and the master
shall have replied "if he be killed let him be killed and if he be maimed
let him be maimed", and this slave be killed, the borrower shall make
restitution to the extent of one-third of his value only, or in the event
of his being wounded or hurt, defray the expense of curing him and
restoration to his master.

*   *   *

If a number of neighbours unite to clear, cultivate and fence in a
portion of forest land, and one out of the number neglecting to build
his portion of the fence wild hogs or cattle shall destroy the corn, the
person so neglecting to construct his fence shall be compelled to make
good the corn which shall have been destroyed.

*   *   *

If a person go to hunt with toils, or nets or decoys, or to fish in
rivers or lakes, it shall not be lawful for the person in authority over
land to hinder him, for the animals he goes in quest of are wild animals.

*   *   *

If however a man take a rich bee-hive without the knowledge of the
owner of the ground, it shall be lawful for the latter to seize it and take
it from him, and he shall be further fined to the extent of half a tahil.
It is true the bees are wild animals, but the hives afforded the owner of
the ground a regular and certain revenue.

*   *   *

If either through the act of God or the invasion of an enemy, the country be afflicted with a famine and the poor shall say to the rich "give us food and let us become your slaves and sell us," and those who have food give it, and it afterwards comes to pass that the famine disappears, and those who supplied the food are desirous of selling as slaves the persons who are thus relieved, the Magistrates shall not permit it, and the persons relieved shall be considered indebted only to the amount of one-half of their estimated value.

*   *   *

If a gang of thieves commit a robbery and one of the party only enters the dwelling, that individual alone shall be punished by amputation of the hand, and the rest suffer correctional punishment, which correctional punishment is as follows:—The criminal shall be mounted on a white buffalo, have a posy of the shoe flower stuck behind his ear, shall be shaded by a dish cover of leaves in room of an umbrella, and shall have his face streaked with lime, with charcoal and with turmeric, and in this state shall be conducted through the town in mock procession, with the beat of the Crier's gong, and should the stolen property be found it shall be suspended round his neck.

*   *   *

If a slave give a free man a slap on the face his hand shall be cut off.

*   *   *

If a free man give a slave a slap on the face, without offence on the part of the latter, he shall be fined, if poor five mas, if rich ten mas. But if the slave should have been insolent, the free man shall not be considered in fault.

*   *   *

If one make an accusation and another deny it, and there be no evidence, the magistrate shall direct the parties according to the custom of the country to contend by ordeal; that is, by diving under water or submerging the hand in melted tin or burning oil. The person who fails in this trial, shall be deemed guilty and be put to death, fined, or otherwise dealt with, according to the custom of the country.

*   *   *

If a pilot forgets his reckoning or goes astray and the vessel strikes upon a rock or shoal and be lost the pilot shall suffer death.

*   *   *

If a man fish at the bow of a vessel while at anchor with a hook and line, and the line be carried down towards the stern and be taken hold of by any one, and the fisher mistake the resistance occasioned thereby for a fish and pull, and the person be hooked, such person shall become his property, even if the concubine of the commander.

LOGAN: *Journal of the Indian Archipelago.*   1851.

4. THE FOREST PEOPLES

In the forests of the Malay Peninsula, as of other parts of the Archipelago, tribes are still to be found who have shunned contact with the outside world and retained a primitive way of life. Most numerous are the Sakai. The Jakuns in the south are apparently of the same racial stock as the Malays.

He carried with him a bamboo which had holes in it, which he sounded, on which at once six Jakuns came out, with some old women and children. When I saw them, I was greatly astonished to see their condition. I praised God, who in His greatness had created various races of mankind, each with their peculiar gifts, nature, form, and such like. Their appearance, as I first saw them, was the same as human beings like ourselves, but with the dispositions of beasts; for beasts know also how to clean themselves, but they certainly did not. Their hair was like wickerwork clotted, and had no longer the colour of men's, being plastered with earth and gum, just like a buffalo's skin, and withal infested with lice and fleas to an extent which God alone could tell. They lived without clothes or coats, nor even an under-cloth to their body, but only a bit of bark as big as one's palm—this to hide their nakedness. Then as to the hair of the face, this was also as other people, their beards being entirely unshorn (or unplucked out, as the Malays do); and their skin had not the slightest appearance of being human, but just like earth in folds smeared with gum, while the eyes watered down the cheeks. I also perceived that each carried a creel or basket on their back, in which they put all kinds of food; two quivers below their armpits, with a sumpitan over their shoulders; also a fine piece of bamboo, like one's toe, filled with the ipoh poison, and which was thrust into the sash of their waist.

Hikayat Abdullah.

The Semangs, who are of Negrito stock, are noted huntsmen.

They handle the bow and the spear with wonderful dexterity and destroy the largest and most powerful animals by ingenious contrivances. 'Tis seldom they suffer by beasts of prey, as they are extremely sharp-sighted, and as agile in ascending the trees as the monkeys. Their mode of destroying elephants, in order to procure the ivory, or their flesh, is most extraordinary and ingenious. They lay in wait in small parties of two or three when they have perceived any elephants ascend a hill, and as they descend again, which they usually do at a slow pace, plucking the branches as they move along, while the hind legs are lifted up, the Semang cautiously approaching behind, drives a sharp pointed bamboo or piece of neebong which has been previously well hardened in the fire, and touched with poison, into the sole of the elephant's foot, with all his force, which effectually lames the animal and most commonly causes him to fall, when the whole party rushes upon him with spears and sharp pointed sticks and soon despatch him. The Rhinoceros they obtain with even less difficulty. This animal, which is of solitary habits, is found frequently in marshy places, with its whole body immersed in the mud, and part of the head only visible. The Malays call the animal *badak tapa* or the recluse rhinoceros. Towards the close of the rainy season, they are said to bury themselves in this manner in different places, and upon the dry weather setting in, and from the powerful effects of a vertical sun, the mud becomes hard and crusted, and the rhinoceros cannot effect its escape without considerable difficulty and exertion. The Semang prepare themselves with large quantities of combustible materials with which they quietly approach the animal, who is aroused from his reverie by an immense fire over him, which being kept well supplied by the Semangs with fresh fuel, soon completes his destruction and renders him in a fit state to make a meal of. The projecting horn on the snout is carefully preserved, being supposed to be possessed of medicinal properties and highly prized by the Malays, to whom they barter it for their tobacco, etc.

LOGAN: *Journal of the Indian Archipelago.* 1850.

Hugh Clifford quotes an aged patriarch of the Semangs as follows:

"The Malays were wont, when they could trace us, to surround our camps at nightfall, and attack when the dawn was about to break, but many and many a time, when we were so surrounded, we made shift by night to escape from the circle which hemmed us in. How did we win out? What then are the trees made for? Has the Tuan never heard of the bridges of the forest people that the Malays call *tali tenau*? When darkness was over the forest, the young men would ascend the trees, and stretch lines of rattan from bough to bough, over the places where the trees were too far apart for a woman to leap, and when all was ready, we would climb into the branches, carrying our cooking-pots and all that we possessed, the women bearing their babies at their breasts, and the little children following at their mother's heels. Thus, treading shrewdly on the lines of rattan, we would pass from tree to tree, and so escape from our enemies. What does the Tuan say? That it is difficult and hazarduous to walk by night on slender lines stretched among the tree-tops? No, the matter was easy. Where there is room to set a foot, why need a man fear to fall? And thus we baffled the Malays, and won our freedom."

CLIFFORD: *In Court and Campong.* 1897.

5. HEAD HUNTERS OF BORNEO

"Dyak, more correctly Dayak," says John Crawfurd in his Descriptive Dictionary of the Indian Islands, *"is a word used by the Malays as a generic term for all the wild races of Sumatra and Celebes, but more especially of Borneo, where they are most numerous." The head-hunting habits of the Dyaks gave them an early reputation for ferocity which their general disposition did not warrant. "The Dyaks preserve heads as we preserve banners, and for the same reason," says Crawfurd, "as trophies of victory and evidences of personal prowess." Most European accounts agree with that of A. R. Wallace who concluded that the moral character of the Dyaks was "undoubtedly high".*

They are middle-sized, averaging five feet five inches, but very strong-built and well-conditioned, and with limbs beautifully proportioned. In features they differ very much from the piratical inhabitants of these rivers. The head is finely formed, the hair, slightly shaven in front, is all thrown to the back of the head; their cheekbones are high, eyes small, black and piercing, nose not exactly flat—indeed in some cases I have seen it rather aquiline; the mouth is large, and lips rather thick, and there is a total absence of hair on the face and eyebrows.

MARRYAT: *Borneo and the Indian Archipelago.* 1848.

★

They were mostly fine young fellows, and I could not help admiring the simplicity and elegance of their costume. Their only dress is the long "chawat" or waist-cloth, which hangs down before and behind. It is generally of blue cotton, ending in three broad bands of red, blue, and white. Those who can afford it wear a handkerchief on the head, which is either red, with a narrow border of gold lace, or of three colours, like the "chawat". The large flat moon-shaped brass earrings, the heavy necklace of white or black beads, rows of brass rings on the arms and legs, and armlets of white shell, all serve to relieve and set off the pure reddish brown skin and jet-black hair. Add to this the little pouch containing materials for betel-chewing, and a long slender knife, both invariably worn at the side, and you have the every-day dress of the young Dyak gentleman.

WALLACE: *The Malay Archipelago.* 1869.

★

They are truthful and honest to a remarkable degree. From this cause it is very often impossible to get from them any definite information, or even an opinion. They say, "If I were to tell you what I don't know, I might tell a lie"; and whenever they voluntarily relate any matter of fact, you may be sure they are speaking the truth. In a Dyak village the fruit trees have each their owner, and it has often happened to me, on asking an inhabitant to gather me some fruit, to be answered, "I can't do that, for the owner of the tree is not here"; never seeming to contemplate the possibility of acting otherwise. Neither will they take the smallest thing belonging to an European. When living at Simunjon, they continually came to my house, and would pick up scraps of torn newspaper or crooked pins that I had thrown away, and ask as a great favour whether they might have them.

Ibid.

In warfare the Dyaks are resolute, with the sumpitan, or blow-pipe, as their principal weapon.

A body of four hundred men approached—no arms were used, not a spear was thrown or an arrow shot; but the Dyaks, covered with their shields, crouching along the ground, slowly marched under the house, and commenced cutting and burning the posts. The defenders, about fifty in number, with their wives and children cast down between the crevices of the bamboo floor, every implement they could collect, together with boiling water, but in vain. Their fate slowly, but surely approached. The fire and steel did their work. The besiegers retreated. The house fell with a dreadful crash, and ten men were killed, and fifteen women and children captured, the remnant escaping into the jungle.

Journal of James Brooke.

★

Several of our men were wounded by the sumpits; however, the arrows, on being drawn out, left a very small incision, which a kind messmate instantly sucked, and the poison (a black substance made from the upas tree) was extracted. These arrows are nine inches long, of tough wood, not thicker than moderate sized wire, very neatly made, and generally barbed with sharpened fish bones. At twenty yards' distance, the barb meeting the bare skin, would bury half the arrow in the flesh, but would not penetrate cloth at the distance of forty yards; the extreme range may be eighty or ninety yards. The length of the longest sumpitan I saw was between seven and eight feet, and much

resembled the cherry-stick pipes of Turkey. The beauty and straight-
ness of the bore is remarkable, and in order to give the greatest velocity
to the arrow, the head of it is made to fit exactly to the size of the tube,
and is formed of a sort of pith, or of very soft wood. The quiver for
these arrows is really curious, beautifully made from the large bamboo,
and besides the darts, usually contain a variety of amulets or charms in
the shape of pebbles, bones, and odd pieces of wood, with the skins of
monkeys.

MUNDY: *Operations of* H.M.S. *Iris.* 1848.

*Dyaks not infrequently took service with the Malay pirates, and in return
received the heads of victims. This incident took place during a naval raid on a
pirates' stronghold in Sarawak.*

Mr. Stewart, pulling in advance in a small canoe, with some of the
natives belonging to Kuchin, was suddenly pounced upon by three or
four of the enemy's prahus full of men. They ran down the canoe, and
thus were Mr. Stewart and his companions at their mercy. Mercy!—a
wrong term to use when speaking of those who never show any. They
were all krissed, to the number of seventeen, in sight of their companions in the other boats, who were too far behind to arrive in time
to render them any assistance, although it hardly need by said that
every effort was made. The last that was seen of poor Stewart was his
body being carried by one of the Dyaks into the jungle by the side of
the river, and the fellow was so anxious to obtain the much-valued
trophy of a white man's head, that, as he bore it along, he kept his
knife sawing at the head to sever it from the body. Indeed, so much do
these people value a white man's head, that they will build a separate
room on purpose to contain it.

MARRYAT: *Borneo and the Indian Archipelago.* 1848.

*James Brooke had the greatest difficulty in persuading his Dyak subjects that
head-hunting was not a respectable occupation, and in times of stress it reappeared (as it did, indeed, during the recent Japanese occupation). In* 1857
*there was a Chinese insurrection in Sarawak, and Bishop McDougall col-
lected the women and children of Kuching, placed them in charge of his wife,
and sent them to safety in a native boat.*

The only thing that troubled me was a nasty faint smell, for which
I could not account; but next morning we found a Chinaman's head
in a basket close by my corner, which was reason enough! We had
taken a fine young man on board to help pull the sweeps, a Dyak, and
this ghastly possession was his. He said he was at Kuching, looking

about for a head, and went into the court-house. Hearing someone in a little side room, he peeped in and saw a Chinaman gazing at himself in a bit of looking-glass, which was stuck against the wall. He drew his sword, and in one moment, stepping close behind him, cut off his head: and having obtained this prize, was naturally desirous of getting away from the place; so he came off as boatman in one of our flying boats, bringing the head in a basket, which he stowed in the side of the boat. It entirely spoilt my hand-bag, which lay near it.

HARRIETTE MCDOUGALL: *Sketches of Our Life at Sarawak.*

A Dyak village knew no greater occasion than the ceremonial bringing home of the heads after a battle.

On the following morning the heads were brought up to the village, attended by a number of young men all dressed in their best, and were carried to Parembam's house amid the beating of gongs and the firing of one or two guns. They were then disposed of in a conspicuous place in the public hall of Parembam. The music sounded and the men danced the greater part of the day; and towards evening carried them away in procession through all the campongs except three or four just about me. The women, in these processions, crowd round the heads as they proceed from house to house, and put sirih and betel-nut in the mouths of the ghastly dead, and welcome them! After this they are carried back in the same triumph, deposited in an airy place, and left to dry. During this process, for seven, eight, or ten days, they are watched by the boys of the age of six to ten years; and during this time they never stir from the public hall—they are not permitted to put their foot out of it whilst engaged in this sacred trust. Thus are the youths initiated.

For a long time after the heads are hung up, the men nightly meet and beat their gongs, and chant addresses to them, which were rendered thus to me: "Your head is in our dwelling, but your spirit wanders to your own country." "Your head and your spirit are now ours: persuade, therefore, your countrymen to be slain by us." "Speak to the spirits of your tribe: let them wander in the fields, that when we come again to their country we may get more heads, and that we may bring the heads of your brethren, and hang them by your head," etc. The tone of this chant is loud and monotonous; and I am not able to say how long it is sung, but certainly for a month after the arrival of the heads; as one party here had had a head for that time, and were still exhorting it.

Journal of James Brooke.

20

While H.M.S. Iris *was at Kuching, Brooke took a party of the officers to visit some of his Dyak subjects in the interior.*

It was towards noon before we saw the first mountain village, which we did not immediately enter, as we waited the arrival of the laggards: we stopped, therefore, at a spring of cold water, and enjoyed a refreshing wash. Here we fell in with some pretty Dyak girls, very scantily clothed, who were throwing water at each other in sport. We soon came in for a plentiful share, which we returned with interest; and in this amusing combat we passed half an hour, until all had joined the party. We then entered the village, which was situated in a grove of trees. The houses were built upon posts, as those down by the river side. They were immensely large, with a bamboo platform running the whole length of the building, and divided into many compartments, in each of which a Dyak family resides. We were escorted through a crowd of wondering Dyaks, to a house in the centre of the village, which was very different in construction from the others. It was perfectly round, and well ventilated by numerous port-holes in the roof, which was pointed. We ascended to the room above by means of a rough ladder, and when we entered we were rather taken aback at finding that we were in the Head House, as it is termed, and that the beams were lined with human heads, all hanging by a small line passed through the top of the skull. They were painted in the most fantastic and hideous manner; pieces of wood, painted to imitate the eyes, were inserted into the sockets, and added not a little to their ghastly grinning appearance. The strangest part of the story, and which added very much to the effect of the scene, was, that these skulls were perpetually moving to and fro, and knocking against each other. This, I presume, was occasioned by the different currents of air blowing in at the portholes cut in the roof; but what with their continual motion, their nodding their chins when they hit each other, and their grinning teeth, they really appeared to be endowed with new life, and were a very merry set of fellows. However, whatever might be the first impression occasioned by this very unusual sight, it very soon wore off, and we amused ourselves with those motions which were "not life", as Byron says; and, in the course of the day, succeeded in making a very excellent dinner in company with these gentlemen.

MARRYAT: Borneo and the Indian Archipelago.   1848.

Next to head-hunting, the Dyak custom most intriguing to European visitors was that of living communally.

The common habitation, as rude as it is enormous, measures 594 feet

in length, and the front room, or street, is the entire length of the building, and 21 feet broad. The back part is divided by mat-partitions into
the private apartments of the various families, and of these there are
forty-five separate doors leading from the public apartment. The
widowers and young unmarried men occupy the public room, as only
those with wives are entitled to the advantage of separate rooms. The
floor of this edifice is raised twelve feet from the ground, and the means
of ascent is by the trunk of a tree with notches cut in it—a most difficult
steep, and awkward ladder. In front is a terrace fifty feet broad, running partially along the front of the building, formed, like the floors,
of split bamboo. This platform, as well as the front room, besides the
regular inhabitants, is the resort of pigs, dogs, birds, monkeys, and
fowls, and presents a glorious scene of confusion and bustle. Here the
ordinary occupations of domestic labour are carried on—padi ground,
mats made, etc., etc. There were 200 men, women, and children
counted in the room and in front whilst we were there in the middle of
the day; and allowing for those abroad and those in their own rooms,
the whole community cannot be reckoned at less than 400 souls.
Overhead, about seven feet high, is a second crazy story, on which
they stow their stores of food and their implements of labour and war.
Along the large room are hung many cots, four feet long, formed of
the hollowed trunks of trees cut in half, which answer the purpose of
seats by day and beds by night. The Sibnowan Dyaks are a wild-look-
ing but apparently quiet and inoffensive race. The apartment of their
chief, by name Sejugah, is situated nearly in the centre of the building,
and is larger than any other. In front of it nice mats were spread on the
occasion of our visit, whilst over our heads dangled about thirty
ghastly skulls, according to the custom of these people.

Journal of James Brooke.

Bamboo is turned to ingenious uses.

Water is brought to the houses by little aqueducts formed of large
Bamboos split in half and supported on crossed sticks of various heights
so as to give it a regular fall. Thin long-jointed Bamboos form the
Dyaks' only water-vessels, and a dozen of them stand in the corner of
every house. They are clean, light, and easily carried, and are in many
ways superior to earthen vessels for the same purpose. They also
make excellent cooking utensils; vegetables and rice can be boiled in
them to perfection, and they are often used when travelling. Salted
fruit or fish, sugar, vinegar, and honey are preserved in them instead
of in jars or bottles. In a small Bamboo case, prettily carved and orna-

mented, the Dyak carries his sirih and lime for betel chewing, and his little long-bladed knife has a Bamboo sheath. His favourite pipe is a huge hubble-bubble, which he will construct in a few minutes by inserting a small piece of Bamboo for a bowl obliquely into a large cylinder about six inches from the bottom containing water, through which the smoke passes to a long slender Bamboo tube. There are many other small matters for which Bamboo is daily used, but enough has now been mentioned to show its value.

WALLACE: *The Malay Archipelago.* 1869.

*

A bridge of bamboos was thrown from one side to the other, and hung about sixty feet above the water. A single bamboo, eight or nine inches in diameter, affords quite sufficient support to a Dyak, whatever may be the depth of the abyss beneath. A slight hand-rail is placed on either side to assist the balance, but, in case of the traveller slipping, he carries bridge, hand-rail, and all together down on to the rocks beneath—a catastrophe which occasionally happens to the best of these structures. To suspend the bridge, a tree is selected on either bank whose branches conveniently overhang the water; long bamboos and ratans are attached to the boughs, sustaining the structure as well as is possible; but towards the middle it becomes very insecure. In this case the bridge was about eighty yards long, but the half of it was supported upon tressels on either bank. The part actually suspended may have been sixty or eighty feet long. Certainly, when we had crossed in safety, and could survey its arrangement from the opposite bank, it appeared a very strange and ingenious piece of architecture; but in passing over, the bamboos shook and swayed in a manner far too alarming for us to give any thought to the picturesque.

BOYLE: *Adventures among the Dyaks.* 1865.

Here is a Dyak folktale.

In the olden times, a certain Peninjauh Dyak was walking by the side of the Sarawak river, when he saw an alligator lying on a mud-bank, apparently in great distress, and evidently not shedding "crocodile tears". "What news? What is the matter with you?" asked the Dyak. "O my poor brother! Boo-oo-oo-oo." "What is the matter with your brother?"

"He is lying at the point of death, and no medicine that we alligators have is of any use to save him. Oh, my friend, do you know medicine?"

"A little," replied the Dyak.

"O do come and cure him."

"You alligators live in the water, and how am I brave enough to venture down to your house—I, who cannot swim a stroke?"

"Oh I will manage that."

"But then consider the trouble," it was objected.

"Only come and see the treasures of our house, gold and silver, gongs and jars, mats and weapons; and, if you doctor my brother successfully, you shall have your pick—we will make you the richest man in Peninjauh—only come."

Vanquished by these lavish promises, down went the Dyak, on the alligator's back, to the alligator's house, which was built in a hole of the rock on which Belidah Fort now stands. The house was decent and comfortable enough, there was no lack of necessaries, but there was, at the same time, no appearance of wealth. "The valuables are no doubt stowed away in the garret," thought the Dyak. The sick beast was stretched on his back in the midst of the floor—almost at his last gasp. The Dyak bade him open his mouth; he did so; down went the Dyak's hand into his gulf of a gullet, and up he brought a leg of a Malay, still covered with portions of a very dirty pair of trousers, half-strangling the sick alligator in his determined efforts to effect a clearance. The cure was complete; the thanks of the alligator-family were profuse, but no mention was made of a tangible reward to the expectant and impatient doctor; at length he ventured to mention that he would like to see the riches of which he had heard so promising an account, and was gruffly told that they did not exist, and that, instead of asking for anything, he ought to be thankful that he was not eaten for supper. He was then bidden mount the back of his deceiving guide, who set him ashore, angry, wet, frightened, and dirty, then laughed in his face, and finally dived off. From that time to this, however, alligators always run away when they see a Dyak, lest the debt then incurred should be demanded, and a very dirty action of their progenitors be thus unpleasantly forced upon their recollection.

ROTH: *The Natives of Sarawak and British North Borneo.* 1896.

6. "THE CHINESE ARE EVERYTHING"

A great deal has been written about the Chinese in Malaya, but since much of it is true of the Chinese anywhere, and since anthologies have been completed exclusively about the Chinese, I have not attempted here to do more than indicate their importance in the affairs of the Archipelago.

Wherever the Chinese are, the sound of the axe and the saw is to be heard in the woods as you approach, and all are industriously employed. They have their carpenters, sawyers, blacksmiths, and housebuilders whilst the mass work the antimony-ore, or are busy constructing the trench where they find and wash the gold. With such inhabitants a country must get on well, if they are allowed fair play.

Journal of James Brooke.

*

The character of the Chinese may be summed up in few words. They are active, industrious, persevering, intelligent, educated sufficiently to read, write, and to use the swampan or reckoning board. They are entirely free from prejudices of caste and superstition, which are grand stumbling blocks to the natives of India. On the other hand, they are selfish, sensual, ardent lovers of money, though not misers; inveterate gamblers, and often addicted to smoking opium.

NEWBOLD: *Account of the British Settlements.* 1839.

*

The fields of the Chinese are always first cleared, sown and reaped; it is surprising with what skill they will convey water to the most inaccessible spots and render them fertile. Water is usually conveyed by ditches from neighbouring streams to where it is needed, and where a selfish neighbour's land intervenes the water flows through troughs made by dividing the nibong tree into two parts lengthways and scooping the pith out, and these canals are led round the boundary of the field so as not to interfere with the owner.

VAUGHAN: *Chinese of the Straits Settlements.* 1879.

*

We mourn in black, they in white; we propel a boat with our backs

to the bow, they with their faces to the front; we make the north
point of the compass the chief point; they the south point; we take off
our hats and shoes as a token of respect, they keep them on for the
same purpose; we fan our faces to cool ourselves, they fan the anti-
podes to produce the same effect; in our names the surname is placed
last, in theirs they place the surname first; their place of honour at table
is on the left side, ours is on the right; they mount their horses on the
right side, we on the left; their books are written from right to left,
ours from left to right; in speaking of dates they mention the year
first, then the month and lastly the day of the month; we give the date
first then the month and lastly the year; their women wear no petticoats and men no shirts.

Ibid.

★

The Chinese merchant is generally a fat round-faced man with an
important business-like look. He wears the same style of clothing
(loose white smock and blue or black trousers) as the meanest coolie,
but of finer materials, and is always clean and neat; and his long tail,
tipped with red silk hangs down to his heels. He has a handsome ware-
house or shop in town and a good house in the country. He keeps a
fine horse and gig, and every evening may be seen taking a drive bare-
headed to enjoy the cool breeze. He is rich, he owns several retail
shops and trading schooners, he lends money at high interest and on
good security, he makes hard bargains and gets fatter and richer every
year.

WALLACE: *The Malay Archipelago.* 1869.

★

The streets of Singapore and the other towns in the Straits strongly
resemble those of Chinese towns. The houses are narrow, seldom exceeding twenty feet in width, and the sign boards are hung out on iron
rods and hooks into the thoroughfare, and are painted red or black with
gilt Chinese characters written thereon, setting forth the name of the
occupant and his trade. Over each doorway is placed a board with the
name of the shop, firm, or style of the master on it in colors strongly
contrasting with the colors of the boards. The fronts of the shops are
embellished by strips of red paper containing flowery passages from
the classics. The interior of the shops are most neatly arranged with
bottles, tin cannisters, boxes, almeirahs, cupboards, and other receptacles for goods; and samples of the latter are displayed in all parts of
the shop to attract attention. The owner and his servants are exceed-

ingly attentive to visitors and are as keen at driving a bargain as any
people in the world. A Chinese druggist's shop is quite a picture.
There are numerous drawers arranged round the walls filled with
drugs of every conceivable description; besides tin cannisters, bottles,
unique Chinese jars, pots, deers' horns, bones of different animals, and
other things.

People are constantly dropping in with prescriptions from Chinese
physicians, which are forthwith made up, and the medicines neatly
rolled up in paper parcels and handed to the messengers; whilst the
prescriptions are stamped with the druggist's seal or chop, and filed.
The Chinese doctors are considered very clever in curing fevers,
diseases of the bowels, or lungs and such like; but surgery they know
nothing of. They will not attempt the amputation of a limb unless it is
so crushed and broken, that it would be utterly useless to leave the injured part alone. It is simply cut off and thrown aside, and the bleeding
stump covered with something to staunch the hemorrhage. The writer
once pointed over to some bones and asked what they were good for;
the druggist replied, that they were tiger's bones, and if crushed and
boiled in water the decoction would make you brave. Several of the
drawers are always kept filled with black pills of various sizes; like
Morrison's and other quacks' pills, a vast number must be taken at a
time to prove effectual. The Chinese are famous for their liniments,
and balsams, which are considered infallible in attacks of rheumatism
and other inflammatory affections. Our doctors might discover most
important drugs, herbs, and wondrous medicines in the Chinese shops
if they would but carefully go over their contents and test them.

VAUGHAN: *Chinese of the Straits Settlements.* 1879.

*It was chiefly to mine tin that the Chinese went to the Peninsula during last
century.*

In the ore layer they showed me some ore which had been washed
for me and I was afterwards asked by a Captain China Ahin to be
present at the smelting. I consequently attended from the beginning
to the end of the sacrifices and feastings which were made previously to
the smelting. Several pigs were killed, the meat of which was dressed
with Chinese vegetables, which I enjoyed very much, especially as
I had had nothing but dry-fish and fowls to my rice for a long time. It
seemed as if the sacrifices would have no end, under an ear-deafening
firing of crackers and guns. The last ceremony consisted in lighting
several hundred small candles in the open air, making obeisance before
them and sprinkling them with samshu. The offering was concluded on

a certain signal, and now all tried to steal as many of the candles as they could, indeed some had not waited so long, but pilfered them before the ceremony was over. It was incomprehensible to me, how these people could believe that by the application of these means the smelting would turn out better, or that the ore would yield more tin than it actually contains.

The Tin Mines of Malacca (Logan's *Journal*). 1854.

Though far from home, the Chinese retained his habit of smoking opium and his disposition to join a secret society.

His second pipe being finished, he can now look round and has time to gaze on what is going on; but his soul is still wrapt in the bliss that is anticipated from what remains of his allowance, for not until a third or a fourth whiff do the feelings of positive pleasure arise. Then is felt a lightness of the head, a tingling in every limb, the eyes seem to be enlarged, and the ears sharpened to hearing, an elasticity, an inclination to mount on high is experienced, all pains have gone and pleasure now remains. All weariness is left and freshness takes its place. The loathing of food that was lately experienced is changed to a relish for what is piquant, and a great desire is frequently felt for some particular food. The tongue is now loosened and tells its tale, for whatever is secret becomes open, and what was intended for one becomes known to all. Still there is no excitement; but a calmness, soft, soothing and sedative. He dreams no dreams, nor thinks of the morrow; but, with a smile in his eye, he fills his pipe with the last of his allowance. Slowly inhaling it, he seems to brighten up, the smile that was sparkling in his eye extends to other features, and his appearance is one of complete yet placid enjoyment. Presently the pipe is slowly displaced or drops by his side, his head if raised, is now laid on the pillow, feature after feature gives up its smile, the eye becomes glazed. Now droops the upper eyelid and falls the chin with the lower lip, deeper and deeper inspirations follow, all perception is gone, objects may strike the eye but no sights are seen, sounds may fall on the ear, but no sensations are excited, and so he passes into sleep, disturbed and broken, from which the wretched being awakes to a full conception of his misery.

LITTLE: *The Habitual Use of Opium in Singapore* (Logan's *Journal*.) 1847.

During Singapore's first fifty years the influence of the secret societies seemed mostly evil, manifesting itself in large-scale fighting between rival societies and in organised thieving. Munshi Abdullah gives one of the few first-hand accounts of the proceedings of a secret society at this time. A Chinese friend agreed to smuggle him into a meeting outside Singapore.

Two days afterwards, on Saturday morning, at 5 o'clock, my friend came to call me, saying, "I have brought bread, and soft sugar, and plantains, so that you can eat on the road." I committed myself to God's safe-keeping, and then set out. I was dressed in an old pair of torn trowsers, an old cloth for covering my shoulders, with a torn handkerchief round my head. I had a rupee's worth of pice, a small knife, a pencil, and a sheet of paper. There were six of us, five Chinese and myself, we did not follow the usual road, but took short cuts over stumps of trees, across swamps and through water; I asked my friend why they did not improve the road, so that they might get with ease to the place. He laughed and said, "why, if the road was good we should have every one coming along—police, soldiers and Europeans; so that if there were any offenders they would very soon be caught." . . .

In the evening a drum was beaten, the sound of which was heard at a great distance, and soon after the people began to collect. In my opinion there were 500 or 600 people in the Bangsal at one time, and, of these, there were not 20 who were not opium smokers. When they were all assembled the noise in the Bangsal was such as if people were fighting a battle. At this time I was taken to the chamber at the side, which had a curtain, and belonged to the secretary. I remained here very quietly, my friend brought some rice in a plantain leaf, a roast potato, and two plantains. I ate in order to prevent me from being hungry during the night. In a short time my friend came, and said, "sit here quietly, there is a hole through which you can see, and be very careful, as the people will soon be all collected." I asked him to come and sit with me, but he said, "don't be afraid, I am an officer of the society, how can I be absent from the duty which brought me here? I will come every now and then to see you, but don't be alarmed as no one will dare to molest you." I said "very well."

About 7 o'clock they had all arrived and commenced to eat and drink spirits, which they did with a noise like battle. In about an hour this finished, when they commenced to play on drums, etc., the music of which was exceedingly loud. On this they all arranged themselves in order, sitting opposite the Datu (idol) but I observed that their faces were as red as the Bunga Rayah, from drunkenness. Among them all there was one chief, who sat on a lofty chair, with 2 men standing at his right, and 2 at his left. After them came 8 men, with drawn swords, who arranged themselves at the right and left; then came one man, who burned paper in front of the idol (sacrifice), after him came 8 men, with drawn swords, who guarded a man with dishevelled hair, and without any upper garments, in fact he had only a pair of trowsers. This man came in front of the chief, and bowed down, till his head touched the ground, the armed men on the right and left now advanced, shouting, and laid their swords on his neck, they remained silently in this position, for a short time, when a man advanced to the candidate's side; the chief then spoke as follows in the Chinese language, (this was translated afterwards at my request):—"Who are you, and from whence come you? Who are your father and mother? Are they still alive or are they dead?" These questions were explained to the candidate by the man who stood at his side, and were answered as follows: "I am such a one, of such a country, and my father and mother are both dead;" even if his father and mother were alive, he would be obliged to say they were dead, because no one whose father and mother are alive, can be admitted into the society, as the existence of all those is as if they were dead to the world and its ties. The chief then said, "will you swear that your father and mother are dead?" he answered, "I will," and performed the oath, by burning paper in front of the idol, saying at the same time, "my father and mother are dead." The chief then said, "what have you come here for?" answer "I wish to join the Tan Tae Hoey." This word means the sky, the earth and man.

The chief then said "you are deceiving, your thoughts are not as your speech," answer "I will swear that I am in good faith"—"then swear," the candidate then taking paper, burned it, while he repeated his assertion. The chief then said, "are you acquainted with the rules of the society?" answer "yes, I understand that I am required to take an oath by drinking blood." The chief then said something to which the following answer was made: "I promise not to divulge the secrets of this society to any one under penalty of death." The chief said, "truly"— answer "truly". A vessel was then brought, containing arrack and a little blood from each of the members of the society, and, with a knife, was placed in front of the idol. The candidate, then taking up the knife, made a slight cut in his finger, from which he allowed some blood to fall into the cup. The chief then said "drink in presence of Datu Peking." The candidate then drank a small cupfull, on which the chief, and all the confederates, drank a little, each in his turn. The chief then said "to-morrow go to our Secretary, and ask him for a book, in that book you will find all our rules and secret signs; you will pay one dollar for it." The chief then rose, and himself raised the candidate from his prostrate position and now being initiated, he can take his place among those who, before, would have considered him an enemy.

In this way four members were admitted, and during the ceremony,

I wrote down on paper every thing which I saw going on. My friend now came to see me, and after having asked if I was satisfied, went away. After these four had been admitted they brought a man with his hands tied with a cord, he was placed in front of the chief, and ordered to prostrate himself, but he remained erect. A man then came and gave him 10 or 20 blows with a bambu, he was then asked if he would join the society, he remained silent, the question was repeated 3 or 4 times, without getting any answer. The chief made a sign to those who were armed with the drawn swords, they advanced and made a motion as if they were about to cut off his head, indeed, I thought he was killed, but the chief ordered them to desist, and again asked if he would become a member of the society, still he refused. The chief then ordered him to be stretched on the ground, and 2 men came and beat him on the back with bambus. This beating frightened him greatly, but, on being questioned again, he still refused, when the chief said "to-morrow morning let him be put to death." They confined him for that night, and the next morning he was killed in consequence of his not wishing to join the society. In this way how many tens of people have been murdered. Unfortunate people were taken with violence, at night in town, and, to increase the number of members, were forced to join the society; and, if any of them dared to divulge the secrets, they would be put to death without mercy; they could not escape, as, wherever they went, they would meet members of the society.

Each member, when he enters, gets a book, in which are written the rules and regulations, and secret signs, and marks of knowing each other, in eating, and by the different ways of wearing clothes, so that when one arrives as a stranger in any country, he can easily make himself known to his brethren by these signs, but it is not necessary for me to enlarge on this subject at present.

By the time the occurrences which I have described above were finished, it was 2 o'clock in the morning; they then blew a horn, and the people separated, some went to smoke opium, some to sleep, and some went down to town to rob.

Hikayat Abdullah (Braddell's translation).

Green and harmless snakes hang like tender branches. Others of deeper and mingled colours, but less innocuous, lie coiled up, or, disturbed by the human intruder, assume an angry and dangerous look, but glide out of sight. Insects in their shapes and hues imitate leaves, twigs and flowers. Monkeys, of all sizes and colours, spring from branch to branch, or, in long trains, rapidly steal up the trunks. Deer, and amongst them the graceful palandoh, no bigger than a hare and celebrated in Malayan poetry, on our approach fly startled from the pools which they and the wild hog most frequent. Lively squirrels, of different species, are everywhere met with. Amongst a great variety of other remarkable animals which range the forest, we may, according to our locality, encounter herds of elephants, the rhinoceros, tigers of several sorts, the tapir, the babirusa, the orangutan, the sloth; and, of the winged tribes, the gorgeously beautiful birds of paradise, the loris, the peacock, and the argus pheasant. The mangrove rivers and creeks are haunted by huge alligators. An endless variety of fragile and richly coloured shells not only lie empty no the sandy beaches, but are tenanted by pagurian crabs which, in clusters, batten on every morsel of fat seaweed that has been left by the retiring waves. The coasts are fringed with living rocks of beautiful colours, and shaped like stars, flowers, bushes and other symmetrical forms. Of multitudes of peculiar fishes which inhabit the seas, the dugong or Malayan mermaid, most attracts our wonder.

LOGAN: *Journal of the Indian Archipelago.* 1847.

*

In entering the river mouth, we passed a large assembly of the youthful population of Muka, catching fish with great enthusiasm. They had bivouacked upon the sand, and around their tents and huts were piled up all sorts of extraordinary monsters ready for sale or salting. All possible colours of scale and skin were displayed among the captures. One of the most remarkable species had a slender body and a long nose, glowing with the tints of an illuminated carbuncle; another kind, which seemed to be used as bait, was flat and fleshy when first captured, but disappeared in a thick black liquid after a few moments. On examining the pool thus created, we discovered a shapeless mass about a quarter of the monster's original size, which appeared to be all that remained of him. Then there were skates, blue, crimson, and spotted, great eels, young sharks, flat bony fish like bream, and others all over spines and prickles. On that tongue of sand was a year's enjoyment for an ichthyologist.

BOYLE: *Adventures among the Dyaks.* 1865.

★

I had here an opportunity of seeing a turtle deposit its eggs, which it did in the following manner: when on the sand it wandered from place to place, and tried several by digging a little, apparently rejecting them as unfit: at length, having made its choice, it buried its nose, and began scooping the sand with its hinder feet in a most deliberate and easy manner, throwing the sand to a considerable distance. It often stopped in its work, and recommenced, and so dug till the body was pretty well buried, and the hole a depth of three or more feet. It then took its station over the hole, and began to lay its eggs, which it did at intervals, for a length of time, to the number of two hundred and thirty; and all the while was perfectly indifferent to the proximity of numerous spectators. Having desposited its eggs, it filled the hole with its hinder fins, and beat down the sand both on the spot and all around, and then retired, not directly (for the track would have been a guide to the nest), but in numerous tortuous courses, round and round, and finally took its departure for the sea at a point distant from its eggs. The Malays on watch have small sticks with flags on them, and as each turtle deposits its eggs, they mark the spot with one of these, and the following morning take the eggs, and store them ready for sale. With all their vigilance, however, numbers escape their observation, and some nests they purposely spare. When the young come forth, the sand (which is small) is said to be literally covered with them, and as they make directly for the sea, the sharks and other fish devour great numbers.

Journal of James Brooke.

★

We passed through extensive forests, along paths often up to our knees in mud, and were much annoyed by the leeches for which this district is famous. These little creatures infest the leaves and herbage by the side of the paths, and when a passenger comes along they stretch themselves out at full length, and if they touch any part of his dress or body, quit their leaf and adhere to it. They then creep on to his feet, legs, or other part of his body and suck their fill, the first puncture being rarely felt during the excitement of walking. On bathing in the evening we generally found half a dozen or a dozen on each of us, most frequently on our legs, but sometimes on our bodies, and I had one who sucked his fill from the side of my neck, but who luckily missed the jugular vein. There are many species of these forest leeches. All are small, but some are beautifully marked with stripes of bright yellow. They probably attach themselves to deer or other animals which frequent the forest paths, and have thus acquired the singular habit of stretching themselves out at the sound of a footstep or of rustling foliage.

WALLACE: *The Malay Archipelago.* 1869.

*

A Boa constrictor was sent for my inspection, which had that morning swallowed a pig belonging to some Chinese at Sungi Kranjie. It would appear that the snake had been seen lurking about the stye several days previous to his last meal which cost him so dear; he artfully however escaped the owner of the swine, who had ineffectually attempted his capture or destruction on these occasions; but on the morning in question, the Boa succeeded in getting entrance into the stye, and, having helped himself to a Porker, found himself in the dilemma of the Weasel in the Barn—he could not get out again. The owner came upon him in this state of helplessness, and, having called comrades to his assistance, secured the victim, torpid from his voracious exertions, and brought him in triumph into Town.

Now you will say there is nothing novel in all this, nevertheless the disparity of size between the carcase of the pig and the jaws and body of the snake struck me so forcibly, and appeared so extraordinary, that I forthwith proceeded to ascertain the exact relative proportions, and found them as follow. The snake was twelve feet, nine inches long, transerve diameter of jaw inside three and a half inches, neck round nine inches, greatest girth of body at thickest part, when pig was out, eleven and a half inches. The pig weighed thirty seven catties and a half, or rather more than fifty pounds, was a good three fourths grown young sow, and lay apparently without a mark of violence upon its body, not a hair ruffled, legs unbroken; indeed old Isaac Walton never dealt more tenderly with his frog than the Boa had seemingly done with young Piggy. Upon closer examination it was however discovered that the ribs were broken, but as the animal remained in its place of sepulture some hours, sufficient gases had been generated to rectify the effects of the crushing and restore Piggy to her pristine comeliness of shape; the contrast therefore was the more striking, but still it is quite inconceivable, how the animal was ever swallowed; how the head of the pig passed the jaws of the snake, would I think puzzle a conjuror to determine; and how the snake felt I leave to the consideration of some hopeless Dyspeptic. So distended were the walls of the abdomen by the unusual meal, that the whole pig could be seen plainly through them; they became diaphanous and thin as gold beater's skin. The vitality of the monster equalled his voracity, for, despite the numberless blows of clubs on its head, two hours after the pig had been cut out of the abdomen, I saw the tail firmly coil itself around a stake. Boa met with poetical justice, for, the same evening, he descended into the very little less ravenous maws of some Chinese, who looked upon the flesh as something exceedingly piquant and appetizing, and eagerly they strove amongst themselves who should possess the largest share of it.

Journal of the Indian Archipelago. 1847.

Borneo is the home of the Orang-Utan ("Man of the Woods").

It is a singular and very interesting sight to watch a Mias making his way leisurely through the forest. He walks deliberately along some of the larger branches, in the semi-erect attitude which the great length of his arms and the shortness of his legs cause him naturally to assume; and the disproportion between these limbs is increased by his walking on his knuckles, not on the palm of the hand, as we should do. He seems always to choose those branches which intermingle with an adjoining tree, on approaching which he stretches out his long arms, and, seizing the opposing boughs, grasps them together with both hands, seems to try their strength, and then deliberately swings himself across to the next branch, on which he walks along as before. He never jumps or springs, or even appears to hurry himself, and yet manages to get along almost as quickly as a person can run through the forest beneath.

WALLACE: *The Malay Archipelago.* 1869.

Wallace quotes a Dyak chief as follows:

"The Mias has no enemies; no animals dare attack it but the crocodile and the python. He always kills the crocodile by main strength, standing upon it, pulling open its jaws, and ripping up its throat. If a python attacks a Mias, he seizes it with his hands, and then bites it, and soon kills it. The Mias is very strong; there is no animal in the jungle as strong as he."

Ibid.

FISHING IN SUNLIT WATERS
EAST COAST OF MALAYA

A FIJIAN BEACH

Raffles was among those who kept a young Orang-Utan as a pet. Dr. Yvan also adopted one when he arrived in Singapore and it subsequently travelled to India and China with him.

The first time I introduced Tuan at my table, he made use of rather eccentric means for the purpose of pointing out the different objects which took his fancy, and stretching out his brown hand, endeavoured to put on his plate everything within his reach. I endeavoured to teach him better manners by giving him a sharp blow, upon which he had recourse to stratagem, and covering his face with one hand, played all sorts of tricks with the other; however, this ruse was unsuccessful, for I struck the offending hand with the handle of my knife, and ever after that time my intelligent pupil understood that he was to wait until he was helped. He very soon learned how to take his soup with a spoon; a plate of thin soup being put before him he got upon the table, in the position of a dog, and endeavoured to lap it up slowly; but this mode of proceeding being inconvenient, he again sat down, and seized the plate with both hands; but in carrying it to his lips spilled a portion of the contents over his chest, so I took up a spoon and shewed him what to do with it: he immediately imitated me, and from that time always made use of it.

YVAN: *Six Months among the Malays.* 1855.

*

A good many years ago I was travelling, with two other Europeans, towards the Perak River. We had nineteen elephants, only about a dozen of them carrying burdens. The others were not sufficiently trained for that purpose, or were too young, and one of them was quite a baby, about a year old, and not more than three feet high. We had already been travelling for several days, when one afternoon we crossed the pass dividing the Larut and Perak River valleys, and descended a steep incline into the latter. The small elephant had been a constant source of amusement to us; his gambols were so quaint; his naughtiness so varied and engaging, that he kept the party in continual laughter. If ever he found a log of wood lying parallel to the path, he invariably tried to walk on it, and though he repeatedly fell off, he would always get up again and persevere to the end. So enamoured was he of this amusement, that if he saw a log a little way off, he would not miss it, though it gave him great trouble to get at it. Then he took a fiendish delight in chasing stray Chinese woodcutters, charcoal-burners, and all the tribe of burden-bearers. Chinese are not used to elephants, don't like them, and avoid them as far as possible. But for any one carrying two heavy loads on a stick, it was impossible to avoid this irrepressible baby; and the invariable result was that, after a short chase and a use-less effort to distance his pursuer, the coolie would drop his burden and dash into the jungle, where the elephant, having accomplished his pur-pose, disdained to follow the yellow man.

These constant alarums and excursions retarded the baby's progress considerably. Though he was often left behind for a few minutes, and would come up to the party with a terrible rush, threading his way between the legs of the older and more sedate members of the trans-port train, his mother became anxious if there was any long absence, and his nurse would go back and look for him, driving the truant before her. The mother was a carrier, and therefore not at liberty to give the necessary attention to her erring offspring, but still, she de-clined to go on without him, if she thought he had got too far away. She had, however, delegated her duties to another quite grown-up elephant, which was not carrying any one or anything, so had plenty of time at her disposal. This was the nurse.

We were travelling over a jungle track, which necessitated walking in single file, and as we neared the foot of the slope leading into the Perak Valley, we came to a gigantic forest tree, which had fallen right across the path. Exactly in the path, a great slice of the tree had been sawn out and thrown on one side, so that coolies carrying loads might pass without having to get over the obstruction. All the elephants went a little way along the tree, to where the diameter was smaller, scrambled over, and then waited in a bunch on the other side. We asked the reason, and the drivers said they were waiting for the baby, which had last been seen, higher up the hill-side, chasing a Chinese coolie.

We tried to persuade the drivers to go on, but either they could not or would not. They said the elephants wanted to see the baby past the difficulty. Suddenly there was a noise of scattering leaves and rolling stones, and the baby ambled down the steep decline at a really hazard-ous pace, made straight for the cleft in the tree, dashed headlong into it, and there stuck fast! Then he squealed lustily, and his mother thumped her trunk on the ground, trumpeted in a very high-pitched voice, and moved about in such an uneasy way that she nearly threw her passen-gers off her back.

The baby was caught very fairly by his ribs. He seemed to fit the aperture exactly; his head out in front, his tail behind, and his body held as in a vice. We were very curious to see what would happen, and we had not long to wait.

The nurse went to the tree, and clambered over it, where she had passed before. Then she slowly walked to the path, looking at the imprisoned culprit out of the corner of her eye as she passed his tail. She took a couple of steps up the path, and then, lowering her head, ran at the baby, smote him in the hinder parts with her forehead, and sent him about ten feet down the path on the other side of his house of detention. The ungrateful little beast never even looked round, but, with the impetus given him, started off on a quest for new opportunities of mischief. The nurse rejoined the party with—or so it seemed to me—a curious twinkle in her eye, as though she had administered chastisement, while apparently only discharging her duties in the most orthodox fashion.

The next day I saw the eighteen elephants take the baby across the wide and (for him) deep Perak River, and though, during the crossing, only the end of his trunk was visible, waving about in the air in vague and anguished protest, they managed to push him safely across; some of them always getting on the down-stream side of him to prevent his being carried away by the current. He crawled up the opposite bank with some lack of energy, but in a few minutes he was scouring the plain for goats and Malay children, with all his accustomed eagerness and resolution.

SWETTENHAM: The Real Malay. 1900.

King of the Malay jungle is the tiger. The Pahang tiger about which this tale is told was reputed to have carried off nearly one hundred human beings.

Seven men and two women were passing the night in a house in that village, when they were startled by hearing the long-drawn howling, snarling moan of a hungry tiger, about half a mile up-river. The Malays call the roar of a tiger aum. The word, as pronounced by natives is vividly onomatopoeic, as those who have heard the sound in the jungle can bear witness. The howl came nearer and nearer, and, at length, sounded close to the house. Then came a roar, a rush, and a thud as the tiger charged the house, and fell back to the earth having failed to effect a landing on the roof. The women screamed, and six of the men seized their spears. They had no firearms. The seventh man climbed up into the para—or shelf-like upper apartment—where the little virgins of the household live during the short days of their celibacy, amid a miscellaneous collection of dusty grimy rubbish. Three times the tiger charged the house, and, at its third attempt, it landed on the roof, and tore the thatch apart with its great claws. The men held their spears to wait its descent, and for a space they stood gazing on the great square face, with its fierce eyes and teeth framed in the hole which it had made in the thatch. The timbers of the roof bent and cracked for a moment under the unwonted weight, and then, with a crash, the beast came through and landed inside the house. It was slightly wounded with the spears, but it never stopped to use its jaws, the soft pit-pat of its paws, as it sat up and struck out rapidly, speedily disposing of all its enemies. Six of the men and one of the women were killed outright, but the other girl was only wounded; and, for as long as it would take to cook rice, says the only survivor, he lay trembling with fear on the shelf while the tiger played with the wounded girl exactly as a cat plays with a mouse. At length it wearied of the sport, and put her out of her pain. Then, it sucked the blood from each of its victims in turn, tore down the door, as dawn was breaking, and betook itself to the jungle. When the neighbours came to see, next day, the house was a shambles, and the only survivor lay upon the shelf with his reason tottering in the balance.

CLIFFORD: *East Coast Etchings*. 1896.

When a man-eater is seen, the whole village takes up arms.

It takes little time to tell the story, and the men of the house, armed with spears and krises and an old rusty gun, quickly spread the news throughout the kampong, as each cluster of huts and orchards is called. Every one arms himself with such weapons as he possesses, the boys of sixteen or seventeen climb into trees, from which they hope to see and be able to report the movements of the beast. The men, marshalled by the ka-tua kampong, the village chief, make their plans for surrounding the spot where the tiger was seen, and word is sent by messenger to the nearest police-station and European officer.

Whilst all this is taking place, the tiger, probably conscious that too many people are about, leaves his lair and stealthily creeps along a path which will lead him far from habitations. But, as he does so, he passes under a tree where sits one of the young watchmen, and the boy, seizing his opportunity, drops a heavy spear on the tiger as he passes, and gives him a serious wound. The beast, with a roar of pain, leaps into the jungle, carrying the spear with him; and, after what he considers a safe interval, the boy climbs down, gets back to the circle of watchers, and reports what has occurred.

For a long time, there is silence, no one caring to go in and seek a wounded tiger—but this monotony is broken rudely and suddenly by a shot on the outskirts of the wide surrounding ring of beaters where a young Malay has been keeping guard over a jungle track. Instantly the nearest rush to the spot only to find the boy badly wounded, after firing a shot that struck the tiger but did not prevent him reaching and pulling down the youth who fired it.

Hardly has a party carried the wounded man to shelter, than news arrives that, in trying to break the ring at another point, the tiger has sprung upon the point of a spear held in rest by a kneeling Malay, and the spear, passing completely through the beast's body, the tiger has come down on the man's back and killed him. The old men say it is because, regardless of the wisdom of their ancestors, fools now face a tiger with spears unguarded, whereas in the olden time it was always the custom to tie a crosspiece of wood where blade joins shaft to prevent the tiger "running up the spear" and killing his opponent.

The game is getting serious now and the tiger has retired to growl and roar in a thick isolated copse of bushes and tangled undergrowth from which it seems impossible to draw him, and where it would be madness to seek him.

By this time, all the principal people in the neighbourhood have been collected. The copse is surrounded and two elephants are ridden at the cover, in the hope of driving the wounded tiger from his shelter. A vain hope, for, when the huge beasts get inconveniently near to him, the tiger, with a great roar, springs on to the shoulder of the nearest elephant and brings him to his knees. The terrified occupants of the howdah are thus deposited on the ground, but lose no time in picking themselves up and getting away. The elephant with a scream of terror whirls round, throwing off the tiger with a broken tooth, and accompanied by his fellow, rushes from the place and will not be stopped till several miles have been covered and the river is between them and their enemy.

Severe maladies want desperate and heroic remedies. After a short consultation, a young Malay chief and several of his friends, armed only with spears, express their determination to seek the tiger where he lies. They immediately put the plan into execution. Shoulder to shoulder and with spears in rest, they advance to the copse. They have not long to wait in doubt for the wounded and enraged beast, with open mouth and eyes blazing fell purpose, charges straight at them. There is the shock of flesh against steel, an awful snarling and straining of muscles and the already badly wounded tiger is pinned to the ground and dies under the thrusts of many spears.

SWETTENHAM: *Malay Sketches.* 1895.

BOOKS AND AUTHORS

MALAY ANNALS: *Translated by Dr. John Leyden.* 1821.

In an introduction, Sir Stamford Raffles describes the *Annals* as "a compilation of the most popular traditions existing among the Malays". Dr. Leyden, a Scotsman of humble birth, distinguished himself at Edinburgh University, where he was a friend of Sir Walter Scott. He joined the Indian Medical Service, and in 1811 accompanied the expedition which captured Java. While at Batavia he contracted fever and died. Though he was then only thirty-five, and had been in the East only eight years, he had already published a number of works dealing with the history and languages of the Malays and other Eastern peoples.

T. H. WARD: *Contributions to the Medical Topography of Prince of Wales Island, or Pulo Penang.* 1830.

Ward was Assistant Surgeon in charge, 35th Regt., Madras Native Infantry. This paper, published with a number of others, was designed "to remove the vague and erroneous reports that have gone abroad respecting the insalubrity, especially of Prince of Wales Island".

T. J. NEWBOLD: *Political and Statistical Account of the British Settlements in the Straits of Malacca.* 1839.

As an officer in the service of the East India Company, Newbold was stationed in the Straits for three years. He engaged Munshie Abdullah to help him in his study of Malay customs and traditions, and the latter says of him: "He was a gentleman of graceful manners to all, and of excellent sense, thus drawing the affection of all men."

CAPTAIN RODNEY MUNDY, R.N.: *Narrative of Events in Borneo and Celebes down to the Occupation of Labuan: from the Journals of James Brooke: Esq. Together with a Narrative of the operations of* H.M.S. Iris. 1848.

Mundy for some time commanded the Straits station, was closely associated with James Brooke in suppression of the pirates of Borneo, and published a book which included extracts from Brooke's *Journal.* In 1846 he conducted the negotiations with the Sultan of Brunei which led to cession to Britain of the island of Labuan, and subsequently he took formal possession of the island.

FRANK S. MARRYAT: *Borneo and the Indian Archipelago*. 1848.

Serving as a midshipman in H.M.S. *Samarang*, a surveying vessel, Marryat became familiar with Sarawak and other parts of the Archipelago. His book is agreeably written and exceptionally well illustrated. He should not be confused with Captain Frederick Marryat, the novelist, who also served in the East but did not visit Borneo.

J. R. LOGAN, FOUNDER AND EDITOR: *Journal of the Indian Archipelago and Eastern Asia*. 1848-57.

The *Journal*—usually known as "Logan's Journal"—was issued in monthly or occasional numbers over a period of twelve years, commencing in 1847. Eleven bound volumes were published. They contain many important papers, dealing with all aspects of life in the Archipelago. Logan was himself a frequent contributor. The *Journal* was a labour of love and had to be run at a financial loss. Logan, a Scotsman, came to Singapore in 1839 at the age of twenty, and was for some years in practice as a lawyer with his elder brother. In 1853 he went to Penang and died there in 1869.

DR. YVAN: *Six Months Among the Malays*. 1855.

Dr. Yvan, a Frenchman, visited the Archipelago and China as physician to a scientific mission. He comments amusingly, though in details not very accurately, on the British Settlements. He admired British achievement, and thought the Malays "had much reason to bless the manner in which they are now governed by the English, whose power is so gently wielded."

FREDERICK BOYLE: *Adventures Among the Dyaks of Borneo*. 1865.

Boyle and his brother visited Sarawak in 1863, though for what reason, apart from a general interest in its affairs, he does not state.

ALFRED RUSSEL WALLACE: *The Malay Archipelago: The Land of the Orang-Utan and the Bird of Paradise. A Narrative of Travel, with Studies of Man and Nature*. 1869.

It was while in the Moluccas during this expedition that Wallace formed his theory of evolution. He sent his draft notes to Darwin, but the latter had already come to similar conclusions and was about to publish *Origin of Species*. On Wallace's return the two men read a joint paper on the subject. The purpose of this expedition, as of an earlier one to the Amazon, was to collect natural history specimens. After eight years Wallace came back with "nearly 3,000 bird-skins, of about a thousand species; and at least 20,000 beetles and butterflies, of about seven thousand species; besides some quadrupeds and land-shells."

HARRIETTE McDOUGALL: *Sketches of Our Life at Sarawak.*

Reminiscences by the wife of Bishop McDougall, Sarawak's first Christian missionary. The McDougalls went out in 1848 at the invitation of Sir James Brooke, and spent most of the next twenty years in Sarawak.

J. T. THOMSON: *Translations from the Hikayat Abdullah.* 1874.

As a young man Munshi Abdullah was a Malay writer in the service of Sir Stamford Raffles. He saw the assembly at Malacca of the Java expedition and was with Raffles in Singapore immediately after the city had been founded. His reputation was such that at various times he was employed by most of the leading British personalities who came to Singapore and Malacca during his life-time. "His remarks on their familiar conversation in unrestrained moments and daily doings," says Thomson, "picture them more interestingly than can be found in grave history." Abdullah wrote his autobiography in the early 1840's and asked J. T. Thomson to translate it, but the latter was then too busy—he was Government Surveyor—and was unable to undertake the work until nearly thirty years later in New Zealand. Abdullah had then been dead for ten or fifteen years. Thomson was a frequent contributor to Logan's *Journal*, and in one paper tells in detail of the designing and building of the Horsburgh Lighthouse for which he was responsible.

J. D. VAUGHAN: *The Manners and Customs of the Chinese of the Straits Settlements.* 1879.

Starting life as a sailor, Vaughan saw much active service in Eastern waters, including the operations against the pirates of Borneo when he served under Captain Rodney Mundy. He then became successively Superintendent of Police at Penang and Magistrate of Police at Singapore. In 1869 he set up in private practice in Singapore as an Advocate and Solicitor. In his spare time he did much writing, and this book, his chief work, was based on a paper originally written for Logan's *Journal*. His object, he said, was to convince his readers "that the Chinese of the Colony are a superior race and worthy of all encouragement by our Government, so long as the indulgencies accorded to them do not infringe on the liberties or comfort of their fellow citizens."

SIR FRANK ATHELSTANE SWETTENHAM: *Malay Sketches,* 1895, and *The Real Malay,* 1900.

Swettenham is as famous a name as any in the history of Malaya since the 1870's. In the thirty critical years when British influence was penetrating into the Malay Peninsula he played a decisive rôle in Perak and Selangor. When these two States, with the Negri Sembilan and Pahang, became a Federation in 1895—an end for which he had worked —he became the first Resident-General. Later he was High Commissioner for the Federated Malay States and Governor of the Straits Settlements. He retired in 1904, and died in 1947 at the age of 97. He made important contributions to literature on Malaya, including the two books from which I have quoted. In 1942 he published an autobiography, *Footprints in Malaya.*

SIR HUGH CLIFFORD: *East Coast Etchings,* 1896, and *In Court and Campong,* 1897.

Clifford came on the Malay scene later than Swettenham, but in time to perform important services, particularly in Pahang, where for a time in the 1890's affairs were critical. He later served in the West Indies and went on to achieve the highest distinctions in the Colonial Service. From 1912 until his retirement in 1927 he held important governorships—in Gold Coast, Nigeria, Ceylon and, finally, the Straits Settlements, so that his official career ended, as it began, in Malaya. While Swettenham wrote in his early books chiefly of life on the western side of the Peninsula, Clifford wrote of Pahang and the east coast, so that their books are complementary. They collaborated in the compilation of a Malayan dictionary.

HENRY LING ROTH: *The Natives of Sarawak and British North Borneo.* 1896.

With its several hundred illustrations and handsome production, Roth's book is remarkably attractive. It is also an uncommonly useful work of reference.

W. W. SKEAT: *Malay Magic,* 1900, and *Fables and Folk Tales from an Eastern Forest,* 1901.

No greater claim is made for *Malay Magic* than that it is an "introduction to the study of Folklore, Popular Religion, and Magic as understood among the Malays of the Peninsula". It is nevertheless recognised as an outstanding work in its field. *Fables and Folk Tales* is a simpler and more "popular" work, pleasantly illustrated, and telling chiefly of the adventures of Friend Mouse-deer, favourite character in

Malayan folk-tales. Material for *Malay Magic*, Skeat obtained as a member of the Civil Service for the Federated Malay States, chiefly in Selangor, and for *Fables and Folk Tales* during a Cambridge University expedition to the Peninsula in 1899.

R. J. WILKINSON, GENERAL EDITOR: *Papers on Malay Subjects.* 1907 and 1908.

The *Papers* were published "by direction of the Government of the Federated Malay States", and were intended to "furnish an introduction to the study of Malay matters" for Cadets, and also to provide references for the "more advanced student". Wilkinson, a member of the F.M.S. Civil Service, was appointed General Editor, and himself contributed a number of the *Papers*. It is from two of these that I have quoted.

NOTE: I have not included in the list of authors a number of contributors to Logan's *Journal*. Among them is T. BRADDELL, who contributed several translations from the *Hikayat Abdullah*, and also a long and valuable article on *The Ancient Trade of the Indian Archipelago*. In addition to the *Journal*, I found JOHN CRAWFURD's *Descriptive Dictionary of the Indian Islands* exceptionally useful for reference (Crawfurd succeeded Raffles at Singapore.)

PART FIVE

THE WESTERN PACIFIC

The Colonies of Fiji and the Gilbert and Ellice Islands, the Solomon Islands Protectorate, and the Protected Kingdom of Tonga.

Perspective

1. CORAL SETTING
2. HORNBILL, MEGAPODE AND SLUG
3. THREE PEOPLES
4. CANNIBALS AND HEAD HUNTERS
5. HOMES AND OCCUPATIONS
6. PLEASURES AND PASTIMES
7. FABLES AND FOLK TALES

Books and Authors: with biographical notes

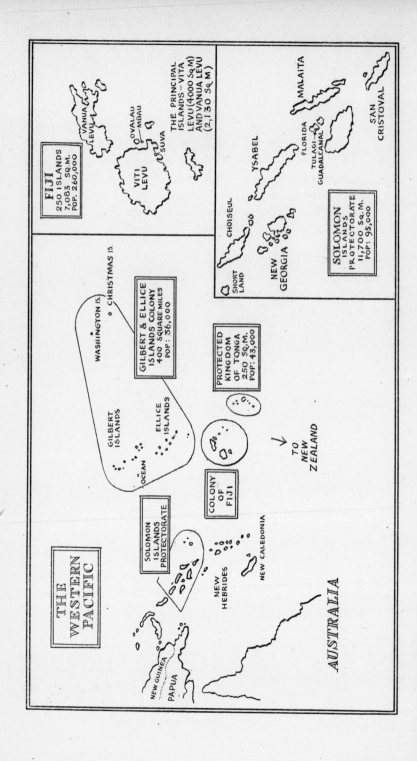

THE WESTERN PACIFIC

FIJI
250 ISLANDS
7,063 SQ.M.
POP. 260,000

VANUA LEVU

OVALAU
MBAU
VITI LEVU
SUVA

THE PRINCIPAL
ISLANDS — VITA
LEVU (4000 SqM)
AND VANUA LEVU
(2,130 SQ.M)

MALAITA
YSABEL
FLORIDA
TULAGI
GUADALCANAL
SAN
CRISTOVAL

CHOISEUL

SHORT
LAND

NEW
GEORGIA

SOLOMON
ISLANDS
PROTECTORATE
11,700 SQ.M.
POP: 95,000

WASHINGTON IS.
CHRISTMAS IS.

GILBERT & ELLICE
ISLANDS COLONY
400 SQUARE MILES
POP: 36,000

GILBERT
ISLANDS

ELLICE
ISLANDS

OCEAN

PROTECTED
KINGDOM
OF TONGA
250 Sq.M.
POP: 43,000

COLONY
OF FIJI

TO
NEW
ZEALAND

SOLOMON
ISLANDS
PROTECTORATE

NEW
HEBRIDES

NEW CALEDONIA

NEW GUINEA
PAPUA

AUSTRALIA

PERSPECTIVE

As soon count sparrows in London as islands in the South Pacific, but of those directly concerning Britain—by which I exclude condominiums —there are between five and six hundred in four main clusters: Fiji, Tonga, the Solomons, and the Gilbert and Ellice Colony. Fiji constitutes the geographical, administrative and commercial hub. The Solomons are still wild and undeveloped; the Gilbert and Ellice group lives unobtrusively apart; and Tonga, which differs from the others in being an independent kingdom under British protection, also stands apart (though in the past it decisively influenced the affairs of Fiji).

As usual the Portuguese and Spanish were the first Europeans on the scene, the Portuguese approaching from the west after establishing themselves in India, and the Spanish from the east from the Pacific seaboard of their South American empire. Discovery of the Solomons is credited to Alvaro de Mendana, a young Spanish nobleman who commanded an expedition despatched from Peru in 1569. To quote a contemporary account: "He discovered a parcel of islands, very pleasant and abounding in gold, amber-grease, and other valuable commodities, and gave them the name of the Islands of Solomon." Both in naming the islands, and in subsequently exaggerating their riches, he was prompted by the enthusiasm of an empire-builder, since he desired to see a Spanish settlement in the islands and had to combat the doubts of the hard-headed gentlemen in Peru and Madrid. To his credit he was prepared to sink his own fortunes in the venture, and after more than twenty-five years' lobbying, by which time he was in his early fifties, he was appointed to lead a colonising mission to the islands. It comprised four ships carrying 400 soldiers, sailors and emigrants. His goal was San Cristoval, but the navigators erred and he arrived instead at Santa Cruz. This was in 1595. The colony lasted just two months. Disease killed some: poisoned arrows others. A mutiny broke out and the ringleaders were hanged. Then Mendana himself died, and his wife, to whom he had delegated command of the expedition, led the survivors back to the Phillipines and Peru.

The Solomons saw no more Europeans for 170 years; not until the second half of the eighteenth century when the English and French began to probe their way into the South Seas. But in the meantime the Dutch had made discoveries. In 1616 two Dutch ships touched at one of the outlying Tongan islands, and in 1643 came Tasman's historic voyage. From Batavia he went to Mauritius and then sailed steadily to the south to discover "whatever God had ordained to be there". So far south did he go that when eventually he turned to the east he missed Australia entirely, discovering instead the island which now bears his name (he called it Van Diemen's Land). Continuing eastwards from Tasmania he discovered New Zealand. After that he headed in the direction of Batavia, calling at the Tongan Islands, where he was hospitably received by the people, and then nearly losing his ships on reefs in the Fiji group, where he named about a dozen islands, but did not land or make contact with the people. As with the Solomons there was no subsequent European contact with either Tonga or Fiji until the arrival of the English and French late in the eighteenth century.

In 1767 an English expedition of two ships—the *Swallow* and the *Dolphin*—was sent into the South Seas to discover unknown lands. The two ships became separated, and while the *Dolphin*, under Captain Wallis, visited Tahiti, Tonga and Pitcairn, the *Swallow*, a decrepit sloop commanded by Captain Philip Carteret, made a landfall at Santa Cruz, and later sighted several of the islands of the main Solomons group without identifying them as those discovered by Mendana. At about the same time various islands in the Gilbert and Ellice groups were discovered by English captains, from one of whom the Gilbert Islands received their name.

But to Captain James Cook fell the greatest fame. In 1769 the Admiralty appointed him to take the *Endeavour*, of 370 tons, to Tahiti in order that the Transit of Venus might be accurately observed. This done, Cook went in search of the Southern Continent which geographers of the day postulated as a necessary counterpoise to the land masses of the northern hemisphere. Coming to New Zealand, last visited some 130 years before by Tasman, Cook circumnavigated the islands, thoroughly examined their coastline, and formally took possession of them in the name of George III. From New Zealand he sailed westwards which brought him to the east coast of Australia (the Dutch had earlier discovered the west coast, but neither then nor for some time afterwards was it realised that these were the opposite sides of one and the same land mass). Cook charted the Great Barrier Reef as he sailed slowly northwards, and eventually reappeared in the known world at Batavia.

Shortly afterwards Cook was again in the South Seas. On this occasion he revisited New Zealand and, still seeking the hypothetical Southern Continent, went far to the south before icebergs turned him back. He then paid a return visit to Tahiti, visited Tonga, and sighted an outlying island in the Fiji group. On his third voyage, in 1777, Cook spent three months in the Tonga Islands, and compiled the first full and accurate account of the people. At Lifuka he found them so amiable that he called it Friendly Island, though it was learnt later that in fact they plotted his death and abandoned the plot only because of disagreement about the precise method. The Hawaians shortly afterwards had no such second thoughts and killed him most treacherously.

On this last voyage Cook had two ships under his command, the *Discovery* and the *Resolution*. Master of the *Resolution* was a certain William Bligh, and it is Bligh who succeeds Cook in the forefront of South Seas exploration. At the end of 1788 Bligh took the *Bounty* to Tahiti to collect breadfruit plants which it was desired to introduce into the West Indian islands. From Tahiti he sailed via Tonga where he stopped to take on wood and water. Off the island of Tofua Fletcher Christian's mutiny took place, and Bligh found himself with eighteen companions in a ship's launch, twenty-three feet long, badly provisioned and without firearms. The launch landed at Tofua, but the people drove them away, killing one man. Because the prevailing winds were against a return to Tahiti, Bligh elected to make for Timor, 3,600 miles away, and in getting there achieved one of the greatest feats of seamanship in history. His course took him through the Fiji group, where he roughly charted the position of some of the islands, though he landed at none and avoided contact with two large sailing canoes which tried to intercept him. Three years later Bligh was back at Tahiti and, having collected his breadfruit plants, he revisited Fiji. During the six days he spent in the group he charted the position of many more of the islands, including Vitu Levu which he described as "very high and extensive" with one mountain among others which he christened the Cockscomb "because of its likeness to one". He again made no landings and only at one point was contact established with the people. Two men from among four in a canoe came on board. "One of them, says Bligh, "had his hair plaited about four inches long on his neck—hanging in a number of tails loaded with black grease—the other wore it short and lime burnt. Some of them had lost both little fingers as far as the second joint and the others only of one hand. They had very few marks of tattooing; one of their ears was remarkably long and had a hole in it that would have taken a large knife for an ornament. The others were bored in the common way: their beards were rough and untrimmed and they were dirty in person."

Thanks to Cook and Bligh and the other British captains, and to information obtained by the French, there existed by the end of the eighteenth century, a fairly accurate idea of the position and extent of

the main groups of islands, and in the nineteenth century the story of
the islands is largely concerned with the efforts of traders and missionaries to achieve their respective ends. The first and obvious results
were the introduction of alcohol, firearms and European diseases, and
the aggravation of internecine warfare. The islanders already had some
ignoble habits of their own, notably cannibalism, which was particularly prevalent in Fiji and caused the group to become known as the
Cannibal Isles. Physically a paradise, the islands were turned into a
hell on earth for most of the first sixty years of the century.

It was to Fiji that the white men at first chiefly came. The fat profits
to be made from the trade in sandalwood and beche-de-mer proved
irresistible, despite the hazard of shipwreck on the islands' coral reefs.
One result of shipwrecks was the stranding of their crews, some of
whom were killed and eaten, while others ingratiated themselves with
local chiefs to whom they made themselves useful in warfare and as
craftsmen. Their number was swollen by escaped convicts from New
South Wales, who were only too glad to enter into service of this
kind. A particularly ruthless group collected at the tiny island of Bau,
one of the seven warring states of Fiji, and with their aid Bau made itself feared throughout Fiji. Their leader was a man named Charles
Savage whose evil exploits came to a fitting end in 1813 when he was
killed and eaten and his bones made into sail needles. But Bau continued to be a storm centre, and by the middle of the century, under an
astute and ambitious young chief named Thakombau, it had achieved
an uneasy supremacy.

Meanwhile the missionaries had been persistent in the face of seemingly hopeless odds. Among several missionary societies founded in the
1790's was the London Society, which decided that its first mission
should be to the South Seas. From several hundred volunteers it chose
thirty young men of many trades and professions (only four were
ordained), and despatched them to Tahiti and Tonga, the ten appointed
to Tonga arriving there in April, 1797. "The men from the sky" were
at first welcomed, but when their novelty value had worn off, and
their usefulness had been exploited, the situation deteriorated rapidly.
The ten were soon at loggerheads with three white men already resident,
and of doubtful antecedents, and one of these three spread rumours that
the missionaries had been sent by the King of England to bring a pes-
tilence upon the people. In the end several of the missionaries were
killed, and the rest left in 1800. For twenty-two years Tonga remained
beyond the pale, but a clergyman from New South Wales then took up
residence in the islands. He stayed for fourteen months and in 1826
his work was continued when the Wesleyan Missionary Committee

A SOUTH SEAS' HARBOUR

A TYPICAL FIJIAN

sent out the Rev. John Thomas, a young man of exceptional ability and good sense, whose efforts during the next quarter of a century were largely responsible for the transformation which took place. By the end of that period almost the whole population had embraced Christianity, and the missionaries had gained the all-important support of the dominant ruler, Taufa'chau Tubou, who on baptism took the name of George. This was Tonga's famous King George Tubou I, who died in 1893 at the age of ninety-six, after a reign which unified the kingdom and gave it a constitution on the British model.

The king also exercised a critical influence in the affairs of Fiji. There had long been intercourse between the two groups, and many islands in Fiji had resident Tongan colonies, whose skill as canoe-builders and as warriors the Fijians held in high esteem. Such a colony existed on the island of Lakeba, and it was through the good offices of the Tongans that the chief of Lakeba agreed to accept two European missionaries as residents. The two men, William Cross and David Cargill, arrived in 1835, and four years later the mission transferred its headquarters to Rewa, in the south-east corner of the principal island of Viti Levu. Here they were cheek by jowl with Thakombau, but it was to be fifteen years before his conversion marked the abandonment of cannibalism and the beginning of a new era in Fijian affairs. Here again it was the Tongan king who influenced Thakombau's decision, warning him after a visit to Sydney in 1854 that the newspapers were calling for action against him because he had made Bau the trouble centre of the islands and practised cannibalism.

In the 1840's Thakombau's attempts to establish his pre-eminence were meeting with no little resistance. In particular, he found himself opposed by the equally ambitious and wily personality of Ma'afu, a Tongan chief who had achieved a position of supremacy in the eastern islands and was now bidding fair to supplant Thakombau on his own ground. This, too, was the time when unruly white settlers had caused it to be said of Fiji that no ship needed a chart to get there since the way was marked by floating gin bottles. A new trouble beset Thakombau in 1849. The United States commercial agent in Fiji, John Brown Williams, was celebrating the Fourth of July by the firing of cannons when one burst and set fire to the house. In the confusion the Fijians seized what they could, and in due course John Brown Williams presented the bill to Thakombau. His claim was supported by the United States Government, which in 1855 sent a warship to investigate this and other complaints by American citizens, and a bewildered Thakombau signed an agreement to pay 43,000 dollars within two years. This, of course, he could not do, and in his predicament he turned to W. T.

Pritchard, who in 1857 had been appointed British consul in Fiji, with an offer to cede the sovereignty of Fiji to Britain and to transfer 200,000 acres of land to the British Crown in return for payment of the 43,000 dollars. Pritchard took the offer to London, but its validity was questioned, and at the end of 1859 Her Majesty's Government sent Colonel W. T. Smythe to Fiji to investigate the position. Influenced apparently by the Maori war in New Zealand, Symthe advised against acceptance of the offer of cession (later he changed his views), and the Government took his advice.

But meanwhile the possibility that British rule would be established had drawn several hundred settlers to Fiji, and the numbers increased following the formation of a Polynesian Company in Australia to take over Thakombau's debt in return for the transfer of 200,000 acres of land. By 1870 Fiji had a white population of some 2,500, and the demand for labour for their sugar plantations, added to a much larger demand from Queensland, introduced a new element into the situation. Ships ranged the South Pacific, and in particular the Solomon Islands, in search of recruits for the plantations, and if volunteers were not forthcoming the labour traders resorted to kidnapping. To the natural ferocity of the Solomon Islanders was added a just anger, and whenever the opportunity presented itself they attacked visiting white men. In this way Bishop Patteson met his end in September, 1871, an event which greatly excited public opinion in Britain, and feeling was exacerbated when details became available of a massacre on board a labour ship called the Carl.

A public clamour for adequate control of the labour traffic coincided in 1874 with a new offer of cession by Thakombau, prompted by failure of the Polynesian Company and collapse of attempts to set up a stable form of government in which the interests of both Fijians and Europeans could be met. As before, Her Majesty's Government sent a commission, but this time the Commissioners strongly advocated acceptance of Thakombau's offer, which was supported by other chiefs, including Ma'afu, and on the 10th October, 1874, Fiji was formally ceded to the British Crown. The cession was made without conditions. "If I give a chief a canoe," said Thakombau, "and he knows that I expect something from him, I do not say, 'I give you this canoe on condition of your only sailing it on certain days, of your not letting such and such a man on it, or of your only using a particular kind of rope with it;' but I give him the canoe right out, and trust to his generosity and good faith to make me the return he knows I expect. If I were to attach conditions, he would say, 'I do not care to be bothered with your canoe; keep it yourself.' Why should we have any anxiety about the future? What is the future? If matters remain as they are, Fiji will become like a piece of drift-wood on the sea, and be picked up by the first passer-by. The whites who have come to Fiji are a bad lot. They are mere stalkers on the beach. . . . Of one thing I am assured, that if we do not cede Fiji, the white stalkers on the beach, the cormorants, will open their maws and swallow us. By annexation the two races, white and black, will be bound together, and it will be impossible to sever them. The 'interlacing' has come; law will bind us together, and the stronger nation will lend stability to the weaker."

The extension of British authority to the other groups followed by degrees. In the Solomons and in the Gilbert and Ellice Islands chaotic conditions arose from the absence of any stable form of government, and protectorates were accordingly declared. In Tonga, where King George Tubou I had established constitutional government on the British model, such intervention was unnecessary, but in 1900 a treaty of protection was signed with Britain and this continues in force.

1. CORAL SETTING

Volcanic action and zoophytes make Pacific Islands the lovely things they are. The islands fall into two sharply contrasting types—the large, mountainous and densely vegetated, and the low, circular atoll, enclosing a lagoon and providing a foothold for little more than the palm. Fijian islands nearly all belong to the first type: as, for example, Ovalau, where until the 'eighties the group had its capital at Levuka.

Towns and villages perched upon apparently inaccessible cliffs overhanging picturesque and secluded valleys; the broken and fantastic peaks of the various mountains towering against an azure sky, and the surrounding calm, blue, boundless sea dotted with innumerable islands, each more interesting than another for its own peculiar beauty; and then the foamy reefs stretching far beyond, fading imperceptibly away, until lost in the hazy distance.

DE RICCI: *Fiji: Our New Province in the South Seas.* 1875.

Most of the islands boast a coral reef.

These reefs usually girdle the islands at a distance of from half a mile to two miles. Within the barrier the water is as smooth as a lake, but the trade winds, which blow for nine months in the year upon the shore, send the long rollers of the Pacific against the reef, which varies from 5 ft. to 30 ft. in width. Dashing upon this impregnable barrier, they rise in columns of rosy foam to a height of from 10 ft. to 20 ft., and, glittering in the rays of the tropical sun, fall like obelisks of diamonds.

BRITTON: *Fiji in* 1870.

At Levuka, for example:

The rich blue of the harbour is separated from the purplish indigo of the great ocean by a submarine rainbow of indescribable loveliness. This is caused by the coral-reef, which produces a gleaming ray as if from a hidden prism. The patches of coral, sea-weed, and sometimes white sand, lying at irregular depths, beneath a shallow covering of the most crystalline emerald-green water, produce every shade of aquamarine, mauve, sienna, and orange, all marvellously blended. The shades are continually varying with the ebb and flow of the tide, which at high water covers the reef to the depth of several feet, while at low tide patches here and there stand high and dry, or are covered by only a few inches of water; treacherous ground, however, on which to land, as the sharp coral spikes break under the feet, cutting the thickest leather, and perhaps landing you in a hole several feet in depth, with still sharper coral down below. The highest edge of the reef lies towards the ocean, and a line of dazzling white surf marks where the great green breakers wage their ceaseless warfare on the barrier; but the passage through the reef is plainly marked by a break in the white line, and a broad roadway of deep blue connecting the inner waters with the great deep; and this, again, passes in gradual gradations of colour, from the intense blue of the harbour to the glittering green of the shallow water on the inner side of the reef. Altogether it is most fascinating. The scene is loveliest at noon, when the sun is right overhead, and lights up the colours beneath the water on the coral caves.

CUMMING: *At Home in Fiji.* 1881.

Among attempts to describe the beauty of the reefs I like these.

The water is usually from seven to fifteen fathoms in depth. Its crystal clearness reveals at the bottom subaqueous gardens of exquisite beauty, composed of marine plants and coral trees of divers form, upon which sport the peculiar kinds of fish whose habitat is here. There is among these a canary-coloured fish; another striped with yellow, green, brown, and black; and notably one of a deep ultramarine, which is always seen lying at the bottom, and is at first taken for some inanimate object. On the surface of the waters all the colours of the solar prism are condensed, and the occasional shifting of shadows thrown from the clouds or neighbouring promontories, produces ever-changing hues, which rival the fleeting shades of the expiring dolphin.

BRITTON: *Fiji in* 1870.

*

The first essential is to go in a boat which draws very little water, and which has no new paint to be considered. Then when the tide is low, and the sea without a ripple, you float idly over the coral-beds, suffering your boat to lie at rest or drift with the current, as a stroke of the oars would disturb the clear surface of the water, beneath which lie such inexhaustible stores of loveliness. Every sort and kind of coral grow together there, from the outstretched branches, which look like garden shrubs, to the great tables of solid coral, on which lie strewn shells and sponges, and heaps of brain and mushroom corals.

These living shrubs assume every shade of colour: some are delicate pink or blue; others of a brilliant mauve; some pale primrose. But vain is the attempt to carry home these beautiful flowers of the sea; their colour is their life. It is, in fact, simply a gelatinous slime, which drips away, as the living creatures melt away and die, when exposed to the upper air. So the corals we know in England are merely skeletons, and very poor substitutes for the lovely objects we see and covet in their native condition.

Besides, like everything in that submarine garden, much of its charm is derived from the medium through which we behold it—the clear translucent water, which spreads a glamour of enchantment over objects already beautiful, glorifying the scarlet corallines and the waving branches of green and brown weed, wherein play exquisite fish of all vivid hues and sizes, from the tiniest gem-like atoms which flash in the light like sapphires and rubies, to the great big-headed parrot-fish, which has strong white teeth specially adapted for crunching the coral, and thence extracting the insects on which he feeds.

There are great red fish, and purple-green fish, and some of bright gold, with bars or spots of black; but loveliest of all are the shoals of minute fish, some of the most vivid green, others of a blue that is quite dazzling. Some have markings so brilliant that I can only compare them to peacocks' feathers.

CUMMING: *At Home in Fiji.* 1881.

Atolls do not always conform to preconceived ideas.

It was a grey morning, threatening rain again, when the *Maori's* engines ceased to vibrate, and we heard the skipper's cheery voice ring out, "There's your island, Professor!" We dragged our limp bodies into an approximately perpendicular attitude, and looked round hopefully. We saw what was apparently the open ocean with several islands near, and several more looking like grey clouds on the horizon. I thought one of these islands must be Funafuti, and that we should soon steer for a narrow opening leading into the still waters of a tiny lagoon round which would lie a green ring of palm trees. You know that poetical utterance about the "garland of green in an ocean of blue," don't you? Well, I did, and, although the ocean wasn't blue that morning, I was keen to see the garland of green, chiefly because I steadfastly believed that the water enclosed by it would be perfectly still. So I ventured to ask the skipper when we should get in. "Get in where?" said he. "Why," said I, "into the lagoon, of course. I'm just pining to reach that small enclosure of perfectly smooth water, where all the gorgeous coral gardens grow." He looked at me pityingly and then said, "You're in it now." In it now! This enormous piece of the ocean a lagoon! Those scattered misty grey islands so far away from us and each other, do they compose the garland of green? It was necessary to enlarge one's conception of a lagoon, evidently. This lagoon is about fourteen miles across in one direction and eleven in another, and it isn't circular at all; and the islets bounding it are of all shapes and sizes— some close together, others far apart, and connected only by a thin white line of breakers just distinguishable on the horizon. There are two passages into this lagoon, formed by breaks in the reef, both large enough to admit the largest ship, as well as a strong current and heavy sea from the ocean outside.

DAVID: *Funafuti, or Three Months on a Coral Island.*   1899.

The beauty of Tonga is less spectacular than that of Fiji and the Solomons. Of Tongatapu, Captain Cook says:

The island may, with the greatest propriety, be called a low one, as the trees, on the West part, where we now lay at anchor, only appeared; and the only eminent part, which can be seen from a ship, is the South East point; though many gently rising the declining grounds are observable by one who is ashore. The general appearance of the country does not afford that beautiful kind of landscape that is produced from a variety of hills and valleys, lawns, rivulets, and cascades; but, at the same time, it conveys to the spectator an idea of the most exuberant fertility.

COOK: *A Voyage to the Pacific Ocean.*   1776–80.

The two largest Fijian islands—Vitu Levu (4,000 square miles) and Vanua Levu (2,130)—are well watered.

There is something extremely melancholy, and yet interesting, about the Fijian rivers. They are so still. There is scarcely a sound to be heard except the solitary cry of a water-bird, or the sudden grating screech of a parrot in the adjoining woods. It is rare even to meet a canoe; but, floating gently past, you may see a cocoa-nut or a shaddock, which having dropped into the water from an over-hanging tree, is slowly making its way down to the open sea, perhaps to sow itself on some distant island. The chief interest is in watching each new turn of the river, and the ever-varying mass of luxuriant vegetation on either side, including palm-trees, tree-ferns, creeping plants, and flowering trees and shrubs.

SMYTHE: *Ten Months in The Fiji Islands.*   1864.

The largest of Fijian rivers is the Rewa on Viti Levu.

The stream, of course, narrowed rapidly as we ascended, and in doing so gained immensely in interest. Gradually we approached beautiful mountain-ranges, and whenever we landed and ascended even the smallest rising ground, we found ourselves encircled by a panorama of rare loveliness. But of course, so long as we were on the water-level our horizon was bounded by the river-banks, and after a while the mere loveliness of vegetation became almost monotonous, and we found ourselves gliding unheeding past forests of tree-ferns and grand old trees, festooned with a network of lianas, rich and rare, such as a few days previously would have driven us into ecstasies of delight. Here and there, where some quiet pool in a rocky stream offered a tempting bathing-place, we called a halt, and therein revelled, while the boatmen were boiling the kettle and preparing breakfast or lunch in some shady nook at a respectful distance. No words can describe to you how delicious are such impromptu bathes in clear sparkling streams, embowered in exquisite ferns, which meet overhead, throwing a cool shade on the water, and forming a lovely tracery, through which you get glimpses of the bluest sky. And the light that does reach you is mellowed, and the colour of the great fronds is like that tender green of beech-woods in early spring; and the water is so fresh and delightful that you would fain prolong your bathe all day.

CUMMING: *At Home in Fiji.*   1881.

The profusion of ferns in Fiji inspires this passage.

Innumerable species grow in richest profusion in every damp ravine, and great tufts of birds'-nest and other ferns cling to the mossy boughs of the grey old trees. Every here and there you come on a rocky stream or shady pool round which they cluster in such luxuriance and variety, that it makes you long to transport the whole fairy-like dell to some place where all fern lovers might revel in its beauty. And this is only the undergrowth; for the cool shade overhead is produced by the interwoven fronds of great tree-ferns—their exquisite crown of green supported by a slender stem from twenty to thirty feet high, up which twine delicate creepers of all sorts, which steal in and out among the great fronds, and so weave a canopy of exquisite beauty. Loveliest of all are the delicate climbing-ferns, the tender leaves of which—some richly fringed with seed—hang mid-air on long hair-like trails, or else, drooping in festoons, climb from tree to tree, forming a perfect network of loveliness. It is a most fairy-like foliage, and the people show their reverence for its beauty by calling it the *Wa Kolo*, or God's fern.

Ibid.

In the Solomons Nature resents the intrusion of Man.

After being provokingly entangled in a thicket for some minutes, the persevering traveller walks briskly along through a comparatively clear space, when a creeper suddenly trips up his feet and over he goes to the ground. Picking himself up, he no sooner starts again when he finds his face in the middle of a strong web which some huge-bodied spider has been laboriously constructing. However, clearing away the web from his features, he struggles along until, coming to the fallen trunk of some giant of the forest which obstructs his path, he with all confidence plants his foot firmly on it and sinks knee-deep into rotten wood. With resignation he lifts his foot out of the mess and proceeds on his way, when he feels an uncomfortable sensation inside his helmet, in which, on leisurely removing it from his head, he finds his old friend the spider, with body as big as a filbert, quite at its ease. Shaking it out in a hurry, he hastens along with his composure of mind somewhat ruffled. Going down a steep slope, he clasps a stout-looking areca palm to prevent himself falling, when down comes the rotten palm, and the long-suffering traveller finds himself once more on the ground. To these inconveniences must be added the peculiarly oppressive heat of a tropical forest, the continual perspiration in which the skin is bathed, and the frequent difficulty of getting water.

GUPPY: *The Solomon Islands and Their Natives.*   1887.

Two types of palm characterise the Pacific scene—the coconut and the pandanus, each a remarkable product of Nature.

The flowers of the cocoa-nut tree are small and white. The fruit does not, as a rule, come to perfection in less than twelve months after the blossoms have fallen. A branch will sometimes contain twenty or thirty nuts, or even more, and there are often six, seven, or eight branches to a tree. The tough fibrous husk is about two inches in thickness, and this torn away, and the eyes of the nut pierced, you get at the milk as it is called; and when the nut is not quite ripe, this will be found to measure a pint or a pint and a half. The milk is perfectly clear, and in taste combines acidity and sweetness equal to the finest lemonade. It is deliciously cold, but to drink much of it is bad for most Europeans. The mixture of a little good brandy or gin with it is a first-class corrective.

In a few weeks after the nut has reached its full size, a soft white pulp, remarkably delicate and sweet, resembling in appearance and consistence the white of a slightly-boiled egg, is formed around the inside of the shell. If allowed to hang two or three months longer on the tree, the outside skin becomes yellow and brown; the skin hardens, the kernel increases to an inch or an inch and a quarter in thickness, and the milk is reduced to about half a pint.

One of the most extraordinary facts in natural history is the reproduction of the cocoa-nut tree by itself; and although this may be an oft-told tale, an account of it should, I think, not be omitted from a work treating of the land of cocoa-nuts as well as coral. If the nut be kept long after it is fully ripe, a white, sweet, spongy substance is formed in the inside, originating at the inner end of the germ which is enclosed in the kernel immediately opposite one of the three apertures in the sharpest end of the shell, which is opposite to that where the stalk is united to the husk. This fibrous sponge ultimately absorbs the water and fills the concavity, dissolving the hard kernel, and combining it with its own substance, so that the shell, instead of containing a kernel and milk, encloses only a soft cellular substance. While this marvellous process is going on within the nut, a single bud or shoot of a white colour, but hard texture, forces its way through one of the holes or "eyes" of the shell, perforates the tough fibrous husk, and after rising some inches, begins to unfold its pale green leaves to the light and air; at this time also two thick white fibres, originating in the same point, push away the stoppers or coverings from the other two holes in the shell, pierce the husk in an opposite direction, and finally penetrate the ground. If allowed to remain, the shell, which no knife would cut, and which no saw would hardly divide, is burst by an expansive power generated within itself. The husk and shell gradually decay, and forming a light manure, facilitate the growth of the young plant, which gradually strikes its roots deeper, elevates its stalk and expands its leaves, until it becomes a lofty, fruitful, and graceful tree.

COOPER: *Coral Lands.* 1880.

★

The pandanus tree grows usually upon coral, gravel, and clean sand, where there is no particle of mould, or soil, so that it seems beyond measure surprising that its roots could there find either moisture or nourishment. Nevertheless it contains a super-abundance of oily sap which exudes freely wherever it is cut with an axe. Growing as it does on the seashore, it would be liable to be blown down easily by a strong wind, were it not for a most marvellous protection given it by a beneficent God. From the ground upwards round and round the stem in a spiral row following the twist of the tree (to the height of about twelve feet), are what at first appear to be excrescences, looking like warts; these continue to protrude in the form of horns growing downwards, straight, and about the thickness of a man's arm, until they touch the ground, where they take deep root and send out suckers in all directions, and so form a series of stays round the tree on every side, so that it safely defies the power of the most furious storms.

These stays, when macerated and freed from their oily pulp, yield a fibre similar in appearance to jute, exceedingly white and exceedingly strong. The trunk of the pandanus tree, at maturity, is as hollow as a stove-pipe; the wood, never more than a few inches thick, is as hard as bone, and takes a very fine polish.

The leaves of the pandanus tree are more than six feet in length, and from two to four inches wide, of a bright green, with a rib down the centre and edged on both sides with a row of sharp prickles. Roofs of houses, sails of canoes, flooring mats, and clothing of all sorts are manufactured from the leaf. Wonderful and beautiful fabrics are made from it, all plaited by hand and dyed various colours. Waist-clothes and sashes, as white as linen and as soft as silk, are also made from the leaves of this rich tree.

I do not know of anything that will approach the leaves of the pandanus tree as a paper-making material. The tree grows from one end to the other of Coral Lands. Its leaves can be had for the trouble of cutting, and all that is wanted is to steep them in salt water, pound them and bleach them in the sun, and they will become as soft and white as a linen rag.

Ibid.

2. HORNBILL, MEGAPODE AND SLUG

Pacific fauna is notable chiefly for birds and sea creatures.

You must hear about my pets. I have got two—a turtle and a kula, a kind of parroquet. They are both beauties of their kind, though not equally companionable. The kula is the tamest and handsomest little bird you can imagine: it is something larger than a robin; the throat and body a bright scarlet, the head purple, the back and wings a varied green. It seems to be absolutely fearless: it will perch on my finger, teacup, or pen, a pert friendship it has acquired after a three days' acquaintance. The kula lives by suction, being furnished at the end of its long tongue with a beautiful little apparatus like a small brush or the fine suckers of a sea-anemone, which it has the power of protruding or withdrawing at pleasure. These charming little birds are, however, extremely delicate, and I believe have never been taken alive even as far as Sydney. The turtle is as happy as the day is long. We have bored a small hole in the hindermost plate of his armour, put a ring of wire through it, and to that attached a rope. Thus tethered, he is dropped overboard whenever we anchor, and can swim, dive, or graze at the bottom as he pleases.

SMYTHE: *Ten Months in The Fiji Islands.* 1864.

★

The most exquisite of all are the Kulas, tiny miniature parrots, combining green, scarlet, and purple in their gem-like plumage, and capable of being so thoroughly tamed that we have had them walking about the table at breakfast, climbing over the flowers, or sitting on our fingers, caressing us with their little rough tongues, and eating brown sugar and water, which, I believe, is the only safe food to give them. They are plucky little birds, and walk about the verandah on guard, and drive away the great big ducks, who stand in much awe of them. They also fight with the beautiful wee kingfisher. The latter is useful in the way of killing cockroaches. The other day Abbey observed one of the laughing-jackasses half choking with the effort to swallow something, and going to the rescue found the dear little kingfisher half-way down its throat; neither seemed any the worse however. A few days afterwards he again heard a scuffle, and found both the jackasses trying to swallow the same rat; as neither would yield its prize, he carried out Solomon's judgment with good effect, and both were satisfied!

CUMMING: *At Home in Fiji.* 1881.

Hornbills abound in the Solomons.

I once counted no less than thirty-seven feeding in the same tree. They are conspicuous objects when on the wing, as, in addition to the singular noise made by their flight, the jet black colour of the wings and body contrasts strongly with the great fan-shaped white tail. In the male the head and neck is of a golden straw-colour, so that they can be readily distinguished from the female, in which the head and neck is black, like the body. But the most remarkable thing about the bird is its immense beak, like a veritable horn. In very old birds it becomes chipped and serrated like a saw from continual use. Although of great strength and apparently of greater weight than the bird can conveniently carry, it is in reality, from its beautiful interior cellular formation, much lighter than it appears.

WOODFORD: *A Naturalist among the Head-Hunters.* 1890.

The Solomons also claim an unusual bird called the megapode.

I look cautiously; a dark-coloured bird, in size and shape not unlike a moor-hen, is scratching for insects, flinging the earth and leaves away with vigorous backward strokes of its large feet. It sees us, and runs quickly away among the undergrowth. It is that very singular bird, the *Megapodius Brenchleyi*. The natives highly prize its eggs as an article of food. They are considerably larger than a duck's egg, and out of all proportion to the size of the bird. The birds lay in open sandy clearings, generally near the sea, which are kept clear of shrubs and undergrowth by the natives, and by the sand being constantly turned over by the birds. The eggs are buried sometimes as deeply as two feet from the surface, and are hatched by the natural heat of the hot sand. Many thousands of birds congregate at the same place, the laying-yards being often some acres in extent. At the island of Savo, where these birds especially abound, they become so tame that I have seen a native digging out eggs and birds digging fresh holes to lay in within a few yards of one another.

Ibid.

A butterfly so large that at first he mistook it for a pigeon was seen by Woodford. It proved to be a female of the rare Ornithoptera Victoriae, *with a wing expanse of almost nine inches.*

In the afternoon it was proposed to take all the boys on shore—we had at the time nearly a hundred—to bathe in the fresh water. Posting our sentries, the whole ship's company were soon engaged splashing and diving in the pool, myself among the rest. All at once I saw one of the same huge butterflies that I had seen at Uru a day or two before flying slowly along the beach over my head. I scrambled out of the water, seized my net, and, *puris naturalibus*, started in pursuit. I tread upon a sharp stone and fall head over heels, but picking myself up again, continue the chase along the beach, till at last, just as my quarry is rising among the trees, I come up with it, and by a well-directed stroke enclose it in the net. I leave it to any ardent entomologist to imagine my feelings.

WOODFORD: *A Naturalist among the Head-Hunters.*   1890.

The oppossum, records Guppy, makes a useful addition to diet in the Solomons, and in some islands is also kept as a pet. It sleeps during the day which makes it relatively easy to catch.

One man climbs the tree in which the animal is ensconced whilst three or four other men climb the trees immediately around. By dint of shouting and shaking the branches, the opossum is started from its retreat, and then the sport commences. This clumsy looking creature displays great agility in springing from branch to branch, and even from tree to tree. Suspended by its prehensile tail to the branch above, the Cuscus first tests the firmness of the branch next below, before it finally intrusts its weight to its support. It runs up and down the stouter limbs of the tree like a squirrel; but its activity and cunning are most displayed in passing from the branches of one tree to those of another. At length, scared by the shaking of the branches, and by the cries of the natives who have clambered out on the limbs as far as they can get with safety, the opossum runs out towards the extremity of the limb, proceeding cautiously to the very terminal branchlets, until the weight of its body bends down the slender extremities of the branch, and it hangs suspended by its tail in mid-air about ten feet below. The gentle swaying of the branches in the wind, aided probably by its own movements, swings the opossum to and fro, until it approaches within grasp of the foliage of the adjoining tree. Then the clever creature, having first ascertained the strength of its new support, uncoils its tail. Up goes the branch with a swish when relieved of its weight; and in a similar manner the opossum swings by its tail from the slender branches of the tree to which it has now transferred its weight. Finally the opossum reaches the ground, where its awkward movements render it an easy capture.

GUPPY: *The Solomon Islands and Their Natives.*   1887.

Crabs and sea-worms are common. Of the gigantic land-crab Cooper says:

He lives in burrows under ground, and feeds on the cocoa-nuts as they fall from the trees. He first tears off the husk, and then, with his strong pincers, breaks through the shell at the extremity that holds the eyes. The strength of his claws is sufficient to crush a lath in two, and he can suspend himself on the branch of a tree for an hour or more. It may be useful to know that if, when intruding on their privacy, a human hand is grasped by them in a manner more engaging than desirable, a gentle titillation of the under soft parts with any light material will directly cause the crab to loose his hold.

COOPER: *Coral Lands.* 1880.

It was partly because of Chinese partiality for the beche-de-mer, or sea slug, as an ingredient in soup, that traders first found it profitable to visit Fiji.

It is from two to nine inches in length, resembles a caterpillar in its motions, and feeds by suction. There are several different sorts, and they are of various colours, being red, white, gray, yellow, brown, or black. They live among the rocks and in the holes of the coral reefs, where the water is from one to two fathoms deep, and are caught by the natives, who either dive for them, or fish by moonlight or torch-light. Traders frequently visit the islands, and make arrangements with a prominent chief for the services of the natives in procuring the desired supply. After the animals are caught, they are placed in bins, where their entrails are ejected; the next process is to cut them open, and they are then boiled, and throughly dried in a building erected for the purpose by the person engaged in the fishery. When completely cured in this manner, they are fit for market, and find a ready sale in China, where they are esteemed as one of the richest ingredients of their soups.

JENKINS: *Expeditions to the South Seas and the Pacific.* 1853.

While at Levuka, Miss Cumming witnessed the "Balolo Festival" which she described as "an extraordinary fact in natural history".

The balolo is a small sea-worm, long and thin as ordinary vermicelli. Some are fully a yard long; others about an inch. It has a jointed body and many legs, and lives in the deep sea.

Only on two days in the whole year do these creatures come to the surface of the water. The first day is in October, which is hence called "Little Balolo", when only a few appear. The natives know exactly when they are due, and are all on the look-out for them. They make their calculations by the position of certain stars. After this no more are seen till the high tide of the full moon, which occurs between the 20th and 25th of November, which hence takes the name of "Great Balolo," when they rise to the surface in countless myriads, always before daybreak. In the Samoan Isles the day occurs about a fortnight earlier. At certain well-known points near the reefs, the whole sea, to the depth of several inches, is simply alive with these red, green, and brown creatures, which form one writhing mass, and are pursued by shoals of fish of all sizes, which come to share the feast with the human beings. The latter are in a state of the wildest excitement, for it is the merriest day of the year, and is looked forward to from one November to the next by all the young folk.

About midnight they go out in their canoes, and anxiously await the appearance of the first few worms, and great is the struggle to secure these, which herald the approach of untold myriads. For several hours, there is the merriest sport and laughter, every one bailing up the worms and trying who can most quickly fill his canoe, either by fair sport or by stealing from his neighbour. All is noise, scrambling, and excitement, the lads and lasses each carrying wicker-baskets with which they capture the worms without carrying too much salt water on board. As the day dawns, these mysterious creatures with one accord sink once more to their native depths, and by the moment of sunrise not one remains on the surface; nor will another be seen for a twelve-month, when, true to its festival, the balolo will certainly return. Never has it been known to fail, in the memory of the oldest inhabitant, white or brown. Nor is there any record of any one having seen one rise to the surface on any save the two appointed days, which are known as the "Little Balolo" and "Great Balolo".

Well do the natives know how needless it would be to look for one after sunrise, so all the canoes then return to land, wrap their balolo in bread-fruit leaves, cook them in ovens dug on the beach, and have a great feast—a regular whitebait dinner, in fact. So now you know the true meaning of the "Diet of Worms". So great is the quantity taken, that the supply generally lasts for several days, being warmed up when required; and basketfuls are sent to friends at a distance, just as we in Scotland sent a box of grouse. Such is our prejudice against all manner of worms, that few Europeans appreciate this dainty, which neverthe-less is really not nasty, especially when eaten like potted meat, with bread and butter. It is rather like spinage, with a flavour of the sea.

CUMMING: *At Home in Fiji.* 1881.

A BEAUTIFUL LAGOON

A FISHERMAN IN THE SOUTH SEAS

3. THREE PEOPLES

Melanesians, Polynesians and Micronesians make up the population of the Pacific islands. In Fiji and the Solomons the people are predominantly Melanesian, which relates them to the Negro. The Tongan is a Polynesian, a light coloured, straight-haired relative of the European.

The skin of the pure Fijian is dark, rough, harsh. His hair, naturally black and copious, is bushy, persistently frizzled, almost wiry; indeed, it seems something between hair and wool. His beard, of the same texture, is equally profuse and bushy, and is his greatest pride. His stature is large, but somewhat less than that of the Tongan or Samoan; his muscular development is more perfect, while his limbs are less rounded, and his figure generally slighter. His eye is restless, his manner suspicious, his movements light and active. The skin of the pure Tongan or Samoan is a dark reddish-brown, smooth and soft. His hair, though naturally black and copious, is coarse, seldom wavy, generally straight. He is almost beardless, and abhors a hairy chin. His stature is herculean, his limbs well rounded, his figure symmetrical. His manner is quiet and confiding, his action pre-eminently graceful. His eye is soft and subdued, and his movements, lacking energy and quickness, are deliberate and stately.

PRITCHARD:
Polynesian Reminiscences; or, Life in the South Pacific Islands. 1866.

All the early visitors to Fiji commented on the elaborate hair styles of the men.

It is usual among the Feejeans to wear moustaches, and to allow the beard to grow long. The hair of the boys is kept cropped short, in order to keep out all strange intruders, with the exception of a single lock which is allowed to grow, till they arrive at man's estate, when it is spread out in a mop-like form, and often frizzled with great care and skill by the native barbers. Instead of the curling-irons of the *friseur*, a long and slender hair-pin, made of tortoise-shell or bone, is used for this purpose. Some of the chiefs keep several barbers among their retainers, and spend a great deal of time in dressing their heads, and their beards, and moustaches. Cocoa-nut oil, scented with sandal-wood, is liberally applied to their hair. This singular mode of wearing that useful appendage gives the Feejeean dandies a most strange appearance; but they pride themselves much on the exquisite finish of their toilet, and like other fops, will spend hour after hour in surveying themselves in a mirror. The loss of the hair is esteemed a great misfortune, and its place is always supplied by wigs, in the manufacture of which the native barbers display considerable skill, and often imitate nature so closely, that it is impossible to distinguish the counterfeit except by careful observation.

JENKINS: *Expeditions to the South Seas and the Pacific.* 1853.

*

Whatever may be said about the appearance being unnatural, the best coiffures have a surprising and almost geometrical accuracy of outline, combined with a round softness of surface, and uniformity of dye, which display extraordinary care, and merit some praise. They seemed to be carved out of some solid substance, and are variously coloured. Jet black, blue black, ashy white, and several shades of red, prevail. Among young people bright red and flaxen are in favour. Sometimes two or more colours meet on the same head. Some heads are finished, both as to shape and colour, nearly like an English counsellor's wig.

WILLIAMS: *Fiji and the Fijians.* 1870.

Feminine charm in the Pacific is proverbial.

The Fijian maidens quite understand the art of making themselves attractive. Flora is their jeweller, and they delight to ornament their ears with the purple blossom of the Chinese rose. They also frequently decorate their heads with chaplets of flowers, and wear curiously carved shell armlets, and long pendant necklaces made of wild flowers and vari-coloured seaweed skilfully interwoven. As regards excellence of physical form, which their simple dress (when in their own towns a narrow girdle of native grasses or liku, as the women's petticoat is called) displays in all the simplicity of nature, many of these girls might be taken for a sculptor's model. Their teeth, like those of the men, are of marvellous regularity and whiteness, owing to the almost uninterrupted vegetable diet of these people, and when in their gala attire the effect produced by their natural gaiety and vivacity, which never seem to flag, is often of a kind not readily to be effaced.

BRITTON: *Fiji in* 1870.

Universal and sole garment of feminine wear before the acceptance of Christianity was a tiny petticoat of grass or fibre.

The ridi is its name: a cutty petticoat or fringe of the smoked fibre of cocoanut leaf, not unlike tarry string: the lower edge not reaching the mid-thigh, the upper adjusted so low upon the haunches that it seems to cling by accident. A sneeze, you think, and the lady must surely be left destitute. "The perilous, hairbreadth ridi" was our word for it; and in the conflict that rages over women's dress it has the misfortune to please neither side, the prudish condemning it as insufficient, the more frivolous finding it unlovely in itself. Yet if a pretty Gilbertine would look her best, that must be her costume. In that and naked otherwise, she moves with an incomparable liberty and grace and life, that marks the poetry of Micronesia. Bundle her in a gown, the charm is fled, and she wriggles like an Englishwoman.

STEVENSON: *In the South Seas.* 1900.

A custom common to most of the islands was the cutting off of finger joints as a sign of mourning.

You rarely meet a woman above middle age who has not lost one or both her little fingers. The operation is performed with a sharp shell, with which the mourner saws the first joint till she cuts it off. On the next occasion of mourning, she sacrifices the second joint. The little finger of the other hand supplies a third and fourth proof of sorrow. After this, the Fijian equivalent of wearing crape is to rub the poor mutilated stumps on rough stones till they bleed.

CUMMING: *At Home in Fiji.* 1881.

The Rev. Thomas Williams was well qualified to speak of the character of the Fijian.

His feelings are acute, but not lasting; his emotions easily roused, but transient; he can love truly, and hate deeply; he can sympathize with thorough sincerity, and feign with consummate skill; his fidelity and loyalty are strong and enduring, while his revenge never dies, but waits to avail itself of circumstances, or of the blackest treachery, to accomplish its purpose.

WILLIAMS: *Fiji and the Fijians.* 1870.

*

Intense and vengeful malignity strongly marks the Fijian character. When a person is offended, he seldom says anything, but places a stick or stone in such a position as to remind him continually of his grudge, until he has had revenge. Sometimes a man has hanging over his bed the dress of a murdered friend; or another will deprive himself of some favourite or even necessary food; while another will forego the pleasures of the dance; all being common ways of indicating sworn revenge. Sometimes a man is seen with the exact half of his head closely cropped, to which disfigurement another will add a long twist of hair hanging down the back; and thus they will appear until they have wreaked vengeance on those who slew their wives while fishing on the reef. From the ridge-pole of some chief's house, or a temple, a roll of tobacco is suspended; and there it must hang until taken down to be smoked over the dead body of some one of a hated tribe. A powerful savage, of sober aspect, is seen keeping profound silence in the village council. To ordinary inquiries he replies with a whistle. His son, the hero of the village, fell by a teacherous hand, and the father has vowed to abstain from the pleasures of conversation, until he opens his lips to revile the corpse of his son's murderer, or to bless the man who deprived it of life. Irritating songs are employed to excite the hatred of those who are likely to let their vengeance sleep. The youths of the place assemble before the house, and leletaka, or lament, that none revenge the death of their friend. The effect of such a song, framed so as to appeal to the most sensitive points of the Fijian's nature, is to awaken the malice and fury of those to whom it is addressed with all their original force, and vows of bloody retribution are made afresh.

WILLIAMS: *Fiji and the Fijians.* 1870.

The appearance and character of the Tongan, a Polynesian, was thus described by Captain Cook.

The natives of the Friendly Islands seldom exceed the common stature (though we have measured some, who were above six feet); but are very strong, and well made; especially as to their limbs. They are generally broad about the shoulders; and though the muscular disposition of the men, which seems a consequence of much action, rather conveys the appearance of strength than of beauty, there are several to be seen, who are really handsome. Their features are very various; insomuch, that it is scarcely possible to fix on any general likeness, by which to characterize them, unless it be a fullness at the point of the nose, which is very common. But, on the other hand, we met with hundreds of truly European faces, and many genuine Roman noses, amongst them. Their eyes and teeth are good; but the last neither so remarkably white, nor so well set as is often found amongst

Indian nations; though, to balance that, few of them have any un-common thickness about the lips, a defect as frequent as the other per-fection.

The women are not so much distinguished from the men by their features as by their general form, which is, for the most part, destitute of that strong fleshy firmness that appears in the latter. Though the features of some are so delicate, as not only to be a true index of their sex, but to lay claim to a considerable share of beauty and expression, the rule is, by no means, so general as in many other countries. But, at the same time, this is frequently the most exceptionable part; for the bodies and limbs of most of the females are well proportioned; and some, absolutely, perfect models of a beautiful figure. But the most remarkable distinction in the women, is the uncommon smallness and delicacy of their fingers, which may be put in competition with the finest in Europe.

The general colour is a cast deeper than the copper brown; but several of the men and women have a true olive complexion; and some of the last are even a great deal fairer; which is probably the effect of being less exposed to the sun, as a tendency to corpulence, in a few of the principal people, seems to be the consequence of a more indolent life. . . .

The graceful air and firm step with which these people walk, are not the least obvious proof of their personal accomplishments. They consider this as a thing so natural, or so necessary to be acquired, that nothing used to excite their laughter sooner, than to see us frequently stumbling upon the roots of trees, or other inequalities of the ground.

Their countenances very remarkably express the abundant mildness, or good-nature, which they possess; and are entirely free from that savage keenness which marks nations in a barbarous state. One would, indeed, be apt to fancy that they had been bred up under the severest restrictions, to acquire an aspect so settled, and such a command of their passions, as well as steadiness of conduct. But they are, at the same time, frank, cheerful, and good-humoured; though, sometimes, in the presence of their Chiefs, they put on a degree of gravity, and such a serious air as becomes stiff and awkward, and has an appearance of reserve.

Their peaceable disposition is sufficiently evinced, from the friendly reception all strangers have met with, who have visited them. Instead of offering to attack them openly, or clandestinely, as has been the case with most of the inhabitants of these seas, they have never appeared, in the smallest degree, hostile; but, on the contrary, like the most civi-lized people, have courted an intercourse with their visitors, by bartering, which is the only medium that unites all nations in a sort of friend-ship. They understand barter (which they call fukkatou) so perfectly, that, at first, we imagined they might have acquired this knowledge of it by commercial intercourse with the neighbouring islands; but we were afterward assured, that they had little or no traffic, except with Feejee, from which they get the red feathers, and the few other articles, mentioned before. Perhaps, no nation in the world traffic with more honesty and less distrust. We could always safely permit them to examine our goods, and to hand them about, one to another; and they put the same confidence in us. If either party repented of the bargain, the goods were re-exchanged with mutual consent and good-humour. Upon the whole, they seem possessed of many of the most excellent qualities that adorn the human mind; such as industry, ingenuity, perseverance, affability, and, perhaps other virtues which our short stay with them might prevent our observing.

COOK: *A Voyage to the Pacific Ocean.* 1776–80.

*

The Tonga maidens are remarkable for the possession of great per-sonal beauty. Their hair is straight and fine, and naturally of a dark colour, but the frequent use of lime-water and lime turns it red; yet they have black, expressive eyes; their oval faces are just tinged with olive; their busts and shoulders are well developed, their forms rounded and full, but not gross, and their limbs neatly turned. These are cer-tainly attractive charms, and when united to an intelligent expression of countenance, gaiety, but not frivolity of heart, frank and easy manners, and a true inbred modesty, almost always proof against temptation, surely entitle their possessors to an enviable distinction.

JENKINS: *Expeditions to the South Seas and the Pacific.* 1853.

In Tonga the men are tattooed; in Fiji the women.

Fijians account humorously for the Tongan practice of tattooing being confined to the men instead of the women. They say that the Tongan who first reported the custom to his countrymen, being anxious to state it correctly, repeated, in a sing-song tone, as he went along, "Tattoo the women, but not the men; tattoo the women, but not the men." By ill-luck he struck his foot violently against a stump in the path, and, in the confusion which followed, reversed the order of his message, singing, for the rest of his journey, "Tattoo the men, but not the women." And thus the Tongan chiefs heard the report;

and thus it came to pass that the smart of the qia tooth was inflicted on
the Tonga men, instead of their wives.

WILLIAMS: Fiji and the Fijians. 1890.

*In most of the islands women did the work, but in Tonga they occupied a
privileged position.*

The natives of Fiji, Hamoa, and the Sandwich Islands, who were
resident at Tonga, used to say that it was not a good practice of the
people of the latter place to let their women lead such easy lives; the
men, they said, had enough to do in matters of war, etc. and the
women ought therefore to be made to work hard and till the ground:
no, say the Tonga men, it is not *gnale faf'ine* (consistent with the
feminine character) to let them do hard work; women ought only to
do what is feminine: who loves a masculine woman? besides, men are
stronger, and therefore it is but proper that they should do the hard
labour.

MARTIN: An Account of the Natives of the Tonga Islands. 1818.

*The ferocity of the Solomon Islander was legendary, and his appearance
was, in European eyes, also against him.*

I can conceive of no more repulsive objects than were some of these
men; let a copper-coloured savage shave his head in parts; let him
gather up such of his crisp woolly hair as is not cut, into long, frizzly
tails, which will stand out like spokes from the boss of a wheel; let
him dye some of these white and some scarlet as his sweet fancy may
direct; let him smear his face with charcoal, relieving the monotony of
soot, however, with scarlet or yellow streaks; let his body be scaly like
a fish's, from skin disease, and yellow in parts from the wearing or
carrying of turmeric-coated mats; put a thin mat between his legs,
and a large round shell plate upon his chest; squeeze a dozen pearl shell
bangles upon the upper part of his arms, and hang a ring through his
nose and twenty in his ears, not forgetting to smear his big ugly mouth
with the red juice of the betl nut; let him carry always and everywhere
some twenty thick arrows, highly carved, tipped with poisoned human
bone, and painted red and white; add to this interesting bundle a long
red bow, and perhaps a richly-ornamented club;—and you have the
makings of a pretty considerable ruffian!

COOTE: The Western Pacific. 1883.

Though Woodford lived alone and in safety among them he had no illusions.
From my somewhat wide and varied experience of them, I am of

opinion that the first thought that animates a native upon the sight of a stranger is, "Will he kill me?" Having answered this to his own satisfaction, his next thought is, "Can I kill him?" the latter question being considerably influenced by the fear of future retribution to be apprehended from the friends of the stranger.

WOODFORD: *A Naturalist among the Head-Hunters.* 1890.

Robert Louis Stevenson lived for some time at Butaritari in the Gilbert Islands.

The men are of a marked Arabian cast of features, often bearded and mustached, often gaily dressed, some with bracelets and anklets, all stalking hidalgo-like, and accepting salutations with a haughty lip. The hair (with the dandies of either sex) is worn turban-wise in a frizzled bush; and like the daggers of the Japanese a pointed stick (used for a comb) is thrust gallantly among the curls. The women from this bush of hair look forth enticingly: the race cannot be compared with the Tahitian for female beauty; I doubt even if the average be high; but some of the prettiest girls, and one of the handsomest women I ever saw, were Gilbertines.

STEVENSON: *In the South Seas.* 1900.

★

Mrs. Stevenson had gone alone to the sea-side of the island after shells. I am very sure the proceeding was unsafe; and she soon perceived a man and woman watching her. Do what she would, her guardians held her steadily in view; and when the afternoon began to fall, and they thought she had stayed long enough, took her in charge, and by signs and broken English ordered her home. On the way the lady drew from her earring-hole a clay pipe, the husband lighted it, and it was handed to my unfortunate wife, who knew not how to refuse the incommodious favour; and when they were all come to our house, the pair sat down beside her on the floor, and improved the occasion with prayer. From that day they were our family friends, bringing thrice a day the beautiful island garlands of white flowers, visiting us any evening, and frequently carrying us down to their own maniap' in return, the woman leading Mrs. Stevenson by the hand like one child with another.

Ibid.

4. CANNIBALS AND HEADHUNTERS

Until the acceptance of Christianity, cannibalism flourished in Fiji. "It is interwoven in the elements of society," wrote the Rev. Thomas Williams. "It forms one of their pursuits, and is regarded by the masses as a refinement."

When the bodies of enemies are procured for the oven, the event is published by a peculiar beating of the drum, which alarmed me even before I was informed of its import. Soon after hearing it I saw two canoes steering for the island, while some one on board struck the water, at intervals, with a long pole, to denote that they had killed some one. When sufficiently near they began their fiendish war-dance, which was answered by the indecent dance of the women. On the boxed end of one of the canoes was a human corpse, which was cut adrift and tumbled into the water soon after the canoe touched land, where it was tossed to and fro by the rising and falling waves until the men had reported their exploit, when it was dragged ashore by a vine tied to the left hand. A crowd, chiefly females, surrounded the dead man, who was above the ordinary size, and expressed most unfeelingly their surprise and delight. "A man, truly! a ship! a land!" The warriors, having rested, put a vine round the other wrist of the bakolo—dead body designed for eating—and two of them dragged it, face downwards, to the town, the rest going before and performing the war-dance, which consists in jumping, brandishing of weapons, and two or three, in advance of the main body, running towards the town, throwing their clubs aloft, or firing muskets, while they assure those within of their capability to defend them. The following song was uttered in a wild monotone, finished with shrill yells.

> "Drag me gently. Drag me gently.
> For I am the champion of thy land.
> Give thanks! Give thanks! Give thanks!" etc.

On reaching the middle of the town, the body was thrown down before the chief, who directed the priest to offer it in due form to the war-god. Fire had been placed in the great oven, and the smoke rose above the old temple, as the body was again drawn to the shore to be cut up. The carver was a young man; but he seemed skilful. He used a piece of slit bamboo, with which, after having washed the body in the sea, he cut off the several members, joint by joint. He first made a long

349

deep gash down the abdomen, and then cut all round the neck down to the bone, and rapidly twisted off the head from the axis. The several parts were then folded in leaves and placed in the oven.

WILLIAMS: *Fiji and the Fijians.* 1870.

★

Cannibalism does not confine its selection to one sex, or a particular age. I have seen the grey-headed and children of both sexes devoted to the oven. I have laboured to make the murderers of females ashamed of themselves; and have heard their cowardly cruelty defended by the assertion that such victims were doubly good—because they ate well, and because of the distress it caused their husbands and friends. The heart, the thigh, and the arm above the elbow were considered the greatest dainties.

Ibid.

It was customary in eating human flesh to use wooden forks.

On another occasion Mr. Harding asked his cannibal acquaintances why they used forks for human flesh only.

They replied that human flesh when cooked emitted in the dark a peculiar halo which, according to their description, resembles a phosphorescent lustre or magnetic flame. The utensils or saturated wrappers containing it, or the hands of any one manipulating it, present the same appearance; and therefore it is that, being much afraid of this, they used the well-known "cannibal forks".

COOPER: *Coral Lands.* 1880.

★

I do not think the Fijians practised cannibalism, as a rule, for the mere indulgence of the appetite. I think the object was to strike terror into their enemies—to be considered fearless; and unquestionably cannibalism was held to be the very climax of revenge, just as at the present day, when a Fijian catches an enemy crawling about his head, he invariably exclaims, "You bit me, and now I eat you," and does so accordingly; or when a thorn pricks him, he picks it out of his flesh and eats it. A story is told of a chief who had slices cut out of a living man, as the poor wretch sat before him, and deliberately ate the pieces in his presence. This same chief, when I had him on board the *Paul Jones*, down in the cabin, admitted to me, very reluctantly, and in a low whisper, that he had done so to be spoken of throughout Fiji as a most terrible monster, whose anger was to be carefully avoided. It is said that Loti, who, I believe, became afterwards a good Christian, deliberately sent his wife to collect firewood to make an oven, and to get a piece of bamboo to be used as a knife, and then killed her with his own hands, and baked her with the materials she had herself innocently prepared. The man did this to become notorious, a ruling passion with the Fijians. Indeed, so subject are they to this passion for notoriety, that the only wonder is that there are no stories told of chiefs having eaten choice cuts from themselves.

PRITCHARD:
Polynesian Reminiscences; or, Life in the South Pacific Islands. 1866.

On the death of a chief, his wives were killed.

On being told on the morning of the 24th of August that the king was dead, and preparations were being made for his interment, I could scarcely credit the report. The ominous word *preparing* urged me to hasten, but my utmost speed failed to bring me to the king's house in time. It was evident that as far as concerned two women, I was too late. The effect of the scene was overwhelming. Scores of deliberate murderers, in the very act, surrounded me; yet there was no confusion and no noise, only an unearthly horrid stillness. Nature seemed to lend her aid to deepen the dread effect, there was not a breath stirring in the air, and the half-subdued light in the hall of death showed every object with unusual distinctness. All was motionless as sculpture, and a strange feeling came upon me, as though I myself was becoming a statue. To speak was impossible; I was unconscious that I breathed; and against my will I sank to the floor, assuming the cowering posture of those who were not actually engaged in murder. My arrival was during a hush, just at the crisis of death, and to that strange silence must be attributed my emotion; for I was but too familiar with murders of this kind. Occupying the centre of that large room were two groups on the floor; the middle figure of each group being held in a sitting posture by several females, and hidden by a large veil. On either side of each veiled figure were eight or ten strong men, one company hauling against the other on a white cord which was passed twice round the neck of the doomed one, who thus in a few minutes ceased to live. As my self-command was returning, the group farthest from me began to move; the men slackened their hold, and the attendant women removed the large covering, making it into a couch for the victim. As that veil was lifted, some of the men beheld the distorted features of a mother, whom they had helped to murder, and smiled with satisfaction as the corpse was laid out for decoration. Convulsive struggles on the part of the other poor creature near me showed that she still lived. She was a stout woman, and some of the executioners jocosely invited those who sat near to have pity and help them. At length the women said, "She is cold."

The fatal cord fell; and as the covering was raised, I saw dead the obedient wife and unwearied attendant of the old King. Leaving the women to adjust her hair, oil her body, cover her face with vermilion, and adorn her with flowers, I passed on to see the remains of the deceased Tui Cakau. To my astonishment, I found him alive! He was weak, but quite conscious, and whenever he coughed, placed his hand on his side as though in pain. Yet his chief wife and a male attendant were covering him with a thick coat of black powder, and tying round his arms and legs a number of white scarves, fastened in rosettes, with the long ends hanging down his sides. His head was turbaned in a scarlet handkerchief, secured by a chaplet of small white cowries, and he wore armlets of the same shells. On his neck was the ivory necklace, formed in long curved points. To complete his royal attire, according to Fijian ideas, he had on a large new masi, or large sulu, the train being wrapped in a number of loose folds at his feet. No one seemed to display real grief, which gave way to show and ceremony. The whole tragedy had the air of cruel mockery. It was a masquerading of grim death, a decking, as for the dance, of bodies which were meant for the grave. . . .

I came to the young king to ask for the life of the women, but now it seemed my duty to demand that of his father. Yet should I be successful, it would cause other murders on a future day. Perplexed in thought, with a deep gloom on my mind, feeling my blood curdle, and the "hair of my flesh to stand up," I approached the young king, whom I could only regard with abhorrence. He seemed greatly moved, put his arm round and embraced me, saying before I could speak, "See! the father of us two is dead." "Dead!" I exclaimed, in a tone of surprise—"dead! No!" "Yes," he answered; "his spirit is gone. You see his body move; but that it does unconsciously." Knowing that it would be useless to dispute the point, I went on to say the chief object of myself and my colleague was to beg them to "love us and prevent any more women from being strangled, as he could not by multiplying the dead render any benefit to his father." He replied, "There are only two, but they shall suffice. Were not you missionaries here we would make an end of all the women sitting around." The queen who pretended grief, cried, "Why is it that I am not strangled?" The king gave as a reason that there was no one present of sufficiently high rank to suffocate her.

Preparations were made for removing the bodies, and we retired.

In doing so, I noticed an interesting female, oiled, and dressed in a new liku, carrying a long bamboo, the top of which contained about a pint of water, which, as the bodies were carried out of one door, she poured on the threshold of another. The bodies of the women were placed on either end of a canoe, with the old king on the front deck attended by the queen and the mata, who with a fan kept the insects off him. The shell ornaments were then taken off his person, which was covered with cloth and mats, and the earth heaped upon him. He was heard to cough after a considerable quantity of earth had been thrown in the grave.

WILLIAMS: *Fiji and the Fijians.* 1870.

Human sacrifice also accompanied the erection of a chief's house or the launching of a chief's canoe. The following account, quoted by Miss Cumming, was given by an Englishman named Jackson who was stranded in Fiji in the 1840's.

A new house was about to be built for the chief, Tui Drekete, and the people assembled from all tributary villages to bring their offerings, and dance and make merry. A series of large holes were dug, to receive the main posts of the house; and as soon as these were reared, a number of wretched men were led to the spot, and one was compelled to descend into each hole, and therein, stand upright, with his arms clasped round it. The earth was then filled in, and the miserable victims were thus buried alive, deriving what comfort they might from the belief that the task thus assigned to them was one of much honour, as insuring stability to the chief's house. The same idea prevailed with respect to launching a chief's canoe, when the bodies of living men were substituted for ordinary rollers—a scene which Jackson also witnessed, and quotes to prove how cruelly the tributary tribes were treated by these Rewa chiefs, one of whom he accompanied to a neighbouring isle. They came to a place called Na ara Bale (meaning "to drag over", literally corresponding to our own Tarbert), a low, narrow isthmus, joining two islands together. By dragging the canoes across this half-mile of dry land, they were saved a long row round the island. On landing, they found the villagers entertaining the people of another village which had fallen under the displeasure of Rewa, and at the bidding of the chief these people allowed their guests to be surprised in the night, when forty were captured; and each being bound hand and foot to the stems of banana-trees, were then laid as rollers, face uppermost, along the path by which the canoes were to be dragged across the isthmus. The shrieks of the victims were drowned by the hauling songs of their captors, and, with one exception, all were crushed to death. One poor wretch lingered awhile in torture till the ovens were made ready, in which all were cooked, the guests of the previous day affording the feast for this.

CUMMING: *At Home in Fiji.* 1881.

The Solomons were bedevilled by head-hunting.

It is the custom in the eastern islands of the group to place out head-money for the head of any man who may have rendered himself obnoxious to any particular village. The money—a considerable amount of native shell-money—may be offered by the friends of a murdered man for the head of the murderer. Months, sometimes years, may elapse before the deed is accomplished and the money paid. The task is generally undertaken by a professional head-hunter, such as we met in the person of Mai, the second chief of the village of Sapuna, in the island of Santa Anna. To make a thorough examination of the home and surroundings of his victim, and to insinuate himself into that intimacy which friendship alone can give him, are necessary initiatory steps which only the cunning head-hunter can know how to carry to a successful issue. Time is of no moment. The means employed are slow, but the end is none the less secure; and when the opportunity arrives, it is the friend of months, if not of years, who gives the fatal blow.

GUPPY: *The Solomon Islands and Their Natives.* 1887.

5. HOMES AND OCCUPATIONS

Fijian house-builders were no mean craftsmen.

All the houses, whether of chief or vassal, are alike built on a foundation of stones several feet high. Thus the house is raised above the damp ground. Sometimes you enter by steps, rudely hewn from one log; and a wooden bowl of water invites the visitor to wash his feet before entering. We invariably take off our boots to avoid dirtying the nice clean mats. Every house consists of only one room, varying, of course, in size; but the largest must be limited to the length of one piece of timber, which is the ridge-pole, and with two other roughly hewn trees, laid lengthwise, supports the frame-work of rafters, whereon rests the heavy thatched roof, the whole sustained by upright trees, notched at the top, and all bound together with strongly knotted stems of some forest vine. The sides are supported, and doorways formed, by black pillars, about ten feet in height, made of the stems of beautiful tree-ferns, which here grow in such abundance that they are commonly used for making fences, also for edging graves.

In building a large house about a hundred of these pillars are required. Those forming the doorway are frequently bound with *sinnet* (which is a kind of coarse string), black, brown, or yellow, interwoven so as to form most elaborate patterns, extremely artistic in effect. Sometimes in churches, all the rafters are thus adorned, each being of a different design, telling of the patient care that has been lavished on their decoration. Sometimes, too, they are ornamented with pure white shells (the *Cyprea ovula*), strings of which are also wreathed round the projecting ends of the ridge-pole, and hang thence in long graceful festoons.

The walls, both of houses and churches, are generally formed of reeds, with a thick outer coating of dried leaves. You can fancy how readily such buildings burn on the smallest provocation; the only marvel is why fires are not far more numerous, considering the extreme carelessness with which the blazing bamboos, which act the part of candles, are carried about; to say nothing of the fireplaces, of which there are occasionally several in one house, and which are merely hollows sunk in the floor, with an edge of rough wood dividing them from the mats. One of these is generally in the centre of the house. Chimneys are unknown luxuries; so the smoke floats about at random, and settles in rich brown layers on the rafters, and on the household goods that rest thereon, which sometimes include an old war-club of curious form, which probably has made short work of many a foe-man's skull, or a long black spear, with three or four feet of most beautiful and intricate carving extending upward from the head.

There is generally a sort of scaffolding of rude posts and shelves above the fire, which is used for cooking, and here, through the thick blue wood-smoke you perceive various cooking-pots and earthen-ware jars. Carved wooden bowls of various form and size hang round the walls; some with curiously carved handles, of which you never see two alike, are used to contain oil; others are used in the manu-facture of the noxious national drink called *yangona* (elsewhere throughout the Pacific known as *kava*).

The large wooden bowls in which the yangona is prepared, and the small cocoa-nut shells in which it is served, both acquire a beautiful enamel, sometimes of a bluish colour, which is called the bloom, and gives great value to the bowl. A few wooden pillows—merely a stick or bamboo on two short legs—completed the scanty household in-ventory. There is no more furniture of any sort.

All round the fires lie the family and their friends on their mats, beneath which is spread a thick layer of soft dry grass.

We always occupy what I call the "company bedroom", for though the whole floor of the house is alike covered with mats, the best are reserved for the upper end, which is generally raised about a foot, forming a sort of dais for the use of the principal persons present, and often carpeted with a pile of fine mats. This is invariably given up to us, and here, as I told you, we hang up our mosquito-curtains, and with the help of a few mats and plaids quickly rig up our simple tents.

CUMMING: *At Home in Fiji.* 1881.

To protect themselves from head-hunters, Solomon Islanders sometimes had resort to tree houses.

The tree in which it was built was a magnificent one growing upon the cliff by the shore; all the lower branches were cleared away, and its peculiar appearance made it most conspicuous amongst the surround-ing palms and smaller growth. There was a cleared space around the foot of this giant, and from the branches hung a slender rattan-cane ladder. The ascent is certainly not a very enjoyable affair; the ladder seems of the very weakest, and swings about unpleasantly; the rounds, moreover, are merely bits of stick lashed on to a single cane rope, and afford practically no foot-hold to the booted European. On reaching

GIVUTU, SOLOMON ISLANDS

A COCOANUT ISLET IN THE SOLOMON ISLANDS

the top I was surprised to find a large well-built house, quite level, and fixed in among the branches with the greatest ingenuity. The floor is covered with mats and scrupulously clean. It is twenty-six feet long by eighteen wide, and the ridge-pole is ten feet from the floor. The strength and solidity of the whole structure is most remarkable, and I suppose at a pinch nearly all the inhabitants of the village might find refuge here. At either end of this house are pleasant balconies, one of which seemed literally to overhang the sea, which lay more than a hundred feet beneath. The height of the house from the ground is between seventy and eighty feet. Arrayed along the sides are numbers of small heaps of stones for defensive purposes. When a raid by the head-hunters is reported, the people all retire to this curious fortress, and drawing the thin ladder up after them, they can defy their enemies. If the invaders come near to try and cut down the tree (no light work, for the trunk is hard as iron), the besieged party pelt them with stones from above; and unless the enemy were armed with rifles, I should say these tree fortresses were quite impregnable.

COOTE: *The Western Pacific.* 1883.

In Tonga Captain Cook was impressed by the neatness of the villages.

The place we went to was a village, most delightfully situated on the bank of the inlet, where all, or most of the principal persons of the island reside; each having his house in the midst of a small plantation, with lesser houses, and offices for servants. These plantations are neatly fenced round; and, for the most part, have only one entrance. This is by a door, fastened, on the inside, by a prop of wood; so that a person has to knock, before he can get admittance. Public roads, and narrow lanes, lie between each plantation; so that no one trespasseth upon another. Great part of some of these inclosures is laid out in grass-plots, and planted with such things as seem more for ornament than use. But hardly any where without the kava plant, from which they made their favourite liquor. Every article of the vegetable produce of the island abounded in others of these plantations; but these, I observed, are not the residence of people of the first rank. There are some large houses near the public roads, with spacious smooth grass-plots before them, and uninclosed. These, I was told, belonged to the king; and, probably, they are the places where their public assemblies are held. It was to one of these houses, as I have already mentioned, that we were conducted, soon after our landing at this place.

COOK: *A Voyage to the Pacific Ocean.* 1776–80.

24

Woodford found that privacy was not among domestic arrangements in the Solomons.

The corner of a large house close to the landing-place was assigned to me during my stay, which I was to share with about a dozen men and boys, my corner being partitioned off by a piece of string; and though, whenever I was at home, an inquisitive mob of natives were constantly watching me and remarking to one another upon my every movement, no one ventured to intrude beyond the string or to touch any of my property.

In this corner I arranged my appliances for bird-skinning, and as I had brought some candles with me I was able to work at night, for the natives use no kind of lamp to light their houses after dark.

My food consisted of cooked yams, and fish was brought to me morning and evening.

My bed was a dirty pandanus-leaf mat spread upon some logs laid side by side upon the bare ground, and each of the other occupants of the house was similarly provided, the beds or bunks being ranged in a line down each side of the house, the feet of the sleepers almost meeting in the middle.

By the side of each sleeper was a small fire of wood (although the nights in the Solomons are very warm, and I never registered a lower night temperature at sea-level than 74° Fahr.). The smoke from these smouldering fires makes it extremely disagreeable to pass the night in native houses. But, from long experience, I have at length become somewhat accustomed to it.

The bunks are sometimes so horribly dirty that I have, on more than one occasion, when travelling with the natives in the bush, preferred to lie down among the white ashes of an old fire rather than upon the uncomfortable logs.

The house which I am describing was about fifteen feet wide by forty feet long. Simply a sloping roof of sago thatch.

At night the narrow window-like doorway was barricaded from the inside, and no one left the house till daylight. Sharp-pointed stakes are stuck obliquely in the ground outside to offer an obstacle to the approach of enemies in the dark.

As I sat in my corner I could see, by the light of my candle, the natives lolling in all sorts of easy and uneasy attitudes on their respective bunks.

Above each man's head, the handle stuck into the thatch, where it would be in a moment within reach of his hand in case of necessity, was his tomahawk, while his wicker-shield was close by. In racks above my head were dozens of spears, some of them only sharpened sticks, others elaborately decorated and carved and cruelly barbed with bones from the wing of the flying-fox.

There is another kind of spear that is highly valued by the natives of Guadalcanar. The head is made of a human thigh-bone, and so ingeniously carved and barbed in opposite directions that I should imagine a wound from one would almost certainly be fatal. The brittle heads of this kind of spear are kept carefully covered with a case of bamboo to preserve them from injury.

From end to end of the house, along the rafters, was a string of pigs' jawbones and a few turtles' heads, signs of former feats partaken of in the house. I counted up to two hundred pigs' jaws, but I looked in vain for human bones, which may be frequently seen strung with the pigs' jaws on some of the other islands.

WOODFORD: *A Naturalist among the Head-Hunters.* 1890.

Yam planting in Fiji was an occasion.

Crowded as the island is with houses, the chief has reserved to himself a small yam garden on the top of the hill, close to the Mission buildings. Here were collected some twenty or thirty Fijians, with the chief at their head. As an addition to the usual very scanty allowance of tapa, some had painted themselves with turmeric, to protect their skin from the sun, and also to signify that they were engaged in work. They all carried long staves pointed at one end; these they first laid aside while they chanted a song in honour of the chief, clapping their hands in rude accompaniment. Suddenly the song ceased, and half of the band seizing their staves, rushed to work. Forming into groups of three, they drove their staves fiercely into the ground, until the points nearly met, some shouting, some laughing, (if the horrid savage yells they uttered could be so called), some springing from the ground, and with one or both hands bringing the whole weight of their bodies to bear on the upper end of their staves. Meanwhile the rest of the party, sitting down, encouraged their brethren by looking on, and chanting at intervals, until the time came for them to change places. When the ground had been all dug over, it was formed into little mounds, in each of which the chief planted a seed-yam. The yam is the principal article of food in Fiji, and the proper time of planting is known by the ndrala-tree putting forth its beautiful crimson blossoms.

SMYTHE: *Ten Months in The Fiji Islands.* 1864.

Canoe building is an important occupation in all the islands.

A Fijian canoe is a very wonderful piece of naval architecture. The single canoes are composed of two pieces hollowed out of the trunk of a tree, and joined together in the centre with marvellous exactness and security considering the roughness of the Fijians' tools, and that they have nothing stronger than sinnet to bind the wood with. The small single canoes, some of which are only 10 ft. or 12 ft. long, are propelled by sculling, but the large ones carry an immense mat sail. A double canoe is built by placing two large single canoes side by side, and bridging over the middle third of the hulk with a deck twice its own width, and raised on a deep plank built edgeways on each gunwale. The canoe is balanced by a wooden frame or outrigger on one side, nearly as broad as the deck. All between the edge of the deck and the outrigger is open. The projecting ends of the canoe are boxed up, but the water washes in in the centre, and it is necessary when at sea to be constantly baling. In large canoes there is a house built on deck, with a sloping roof, under which the chief and the women of the party seek shelter in bad weather. The mat sail, which is very large in proportion to the canoe, is shaped something like a leg of mutton. It is hoisted on a mast by means of ropes, and when it is taken in the mast comes down with it, and is laid horizontally on the deck. The mast is stepped in a chock at one end of the deck, and in order to 'bout ship it is necessary to unstep it and carry it to the other end, for the canoes cannot turn round. This is a very awkward arrangement, and men are often knocked overboard in unstepping the mast and attempting to carry it on their shoulders. On the return journey the mast suddenly fell length ways across the deck among a cluster of Fijians, but fortunately without striking any of them. Had it fallen on a man's head it would have been sufficient to kill him. If the man who has charge of the sheet does not slack away at once, when a sudden gust of wind takes the sail, the thama, or outrigger, is raised in the air, and the canoe capsizes; and unless the steersmen are careful to keep the sail on the weather side, the canoe will be swamped by the wind driving the sail against the mast, and forcing the outrigger under the water. The canoe is steered by a long oar, and when the sail is not up it is propelled by vertical sculling, two men standing at one end of the deck and two at the other, throwing the full weight of their bodies on the sculls in a swinging motion from side to side. The extreme length of one of these canoes is about 100 ft. A canoe that length would have a deck 46 ft. long and 20 ft. wide. The mast would be 62 ft. high, the height from the keel to the house top 14 ft., and the draught of water 2 ft. Such a canoe would carry 100 persons and several tons of goods. The best of these canoes under a stiff breeze will travel over 10 miles an hour. The construction of a canoe 60 ft or 70 ft. long occupies several years, and the completion of one is the occasion of great public rejoicings. In the old heathen days they were launched upon the bodies of men used as rollers, and at every place which they visited upon their first voyage, fresh sacrifices took place, the victims being always eaten. The canoe builders are a hereditary caste, called "king's carpenters". These canoes, from their light draught of water, are well adapted to insular navigation, but they are not safe, for if a strong wind or heavy sea should suddenly arise, they become unmanageable, and are swamped. The natives never put to sea in them in bad weather, but they are often overtaken by it, and when out of swimming distance of the land, are drowned. It is said that there is a high point on Vanua Levu from which, with a good glass, native canoes may be seen capsized every day. The little canoes used for inside reef passages and on the rivers, are extremely dangerous. The smallest jerk is sufficient to upset them. They do not sink, however, when this occurs, and the natives will sometimes, while supporting themselves in the water, bale a canoe out and right it. The duties in connexion with the sailing of a canoe are not performed in a perfunctory manner. The sail is raised with a great shout; every manœuvre is executed with an accompaniment of laughter and singing, varied by playful addresses to the wind, while the scullers are also referred to in frequent expressions of thanks for their labours. Everyone exerts himself to make the whole affair a pleasure jaunt, and the labour is very much lightened by the jocoseness and good humour with which all the work is done.

BRITTON: *Fiji in* 1870.

There are more ways of catching fish in the Solomons than by hook and line.

Various devices are practised in the so-called gentle craft, such as kite-fishing and decoys. A small palm-leaf kite hovers astern of a canoe, kept up in a calm by the pace with which the canoe is travelling, while in a light breeze the fisherman need not add to his labours by paddling. From the tail of the kite, just bobbing along the surface of the sea, a ball of cobweb hangs. This is a deadly bait for the "Guard fish", in whose long, scissor-like jaws the glutinous morsel jams. When a suitable fish for the purpose has been caught by a hook and line, or other method, he is made to serve as a decoy. His jaw is bored below the teeth, and through the hole a fine line is threaded and made fast. The poor fish is now restored to his native element and swims about alongside the canoe. Other fish soon come to join their comrade, who, by skilful manœuvring on the part of the fisherman, are brought within reach of a large-mouthed landing net, in which, with a dexterous sweep, they are enclosed.

PENNY: *Ten Years in Melanesia.* 1887.

Both in Fiji and Tonga a fibre cloth was made.

This tapa is made from the bark of the paper mulberry. The strips of green bark are first thoroughly soaked in water. The different strips of the relaxed and softened fibres, now in a pulpy mass, are then extended in successive layers upon some hard and smooth surface, and beaten with a wooden mallet marked with the parallel indentations which are found imprinted on the cloth in its finished state. The material is hammered out in strips to the degree of thinness required, and when bleached and dried in the sun it is beautifully white. Sometimes it is stained with a vegetable juice a chocolate brown or bright yellow, and these coloured pieces are generally used for partitioning screens in the houses, while the white supplies the sulus in which the christianised natives take particular pride on Sundays, when they appear with many fathoms of it wrapped around their loins. The noise of the mallets employed in the manufacture can be heard at a great distance, as the wood is very hard, and when a number are at work together, the effect produced is very peculiar.

BRITTON: *Fiji in* 1870.

*

Another process which I have watched with considerable interest is that of the girls preparing mandrai, which is bread made of bananas and bread-fruit. A Fijian baker's oven is simply a pit lined with plantain leaves and filled with bananas or bread-fruit, on which the girls tread to compress them into a pulpy mass: this they then cover with a thick layer of green leaves and stones, and leave it to ferment, a process which begins about the third day. The indescribable stench which poisons the air for half-a-mile round on the day when these dreadful pits are opened is simply intolerable—at least to the uneducated nose of us, the papalangi (i.e., foreigners); but the Fijian inhales it with delight, therein scenting the bread and puddings in which he most delights.

These puddings are sometimes made on a gigantic scale, on the occasion of any great gathering of the tribes. One has been described to me as measuring twenty feet in circumference.

CUMMING: *At Home in Fiji.* 1881.

6. PLEASURES AND PASTIMES

Talking, feasting, singing and dancing fill the islands' lighter moments.

They employ themselves in conversation, not only at any time during the day, but also at night: if one wakes, and is not disposed to go to sleep again, he wakens his neighbour to have some talk: by and by, perhaps, they are all roused, and join in the conversation: it sometimes happens that the chief has ordered his cooks, in the evening, to bake a pig, or some fish, and bring it in hot in the middle of the night, with some yams: in this case the torches are again lighted, and they all get up to eat their share; after which they retire to their mats; the torches are put out; some go to sleep, and others, perhaps, talk till day-light.

MARTIN: *An Account of the Natives of the Tonga Islands.* 1818.

No ceremony in Fiji or Tonga was complete without its kava-drinking. The taste of kava (or yangona) must apparently be acquired since European accounts variously describe it as like "manganese and soapsuds" and "soapsuds seasoned with pepper".

Picture to yourself the deep shade of the house, its brown smoke-thatched rafters and dark thatch-roof, with a film of blue smoke rising from the fireplace at the far end, which is simply a square in the floor edged with stones, round which, on mats, lie the boatmen, and a group of natives with flowers coquettishly stuck in their hair, and very slight drapery of native cloth, and fringes of bright croton-leaves. A great wooden bowl, with four legs, is then brought in. It is beautifully polished from long use, and has a purple bloom like that on a grape. A rope is fastened to it, and the end of this is thrown towards the chief. The yangona-root is then brought in, scraped and cleaned, cut up into small pieces, and distributed to a select circle of young men to chew. The operation is not *quite* so nasty as might be supposed, as they repeatedly rinse their mouths with fresh water during the process, which occupies some time; while all the company sit round most solemnly, and some sing quaint *mékés* (i.e., choruses), very wild and characteristic. They are so old that many of them are incomprehensible even to the singers, who merely repeat the words in an unknown tongue, as they learnt them from their parents.

When the chewing process is complete, each man produces a lump of finely chewed white fibre. This is then deposited in a large wooden bowl, and one of the number is told off to pour water on the yangona, and wring it out through a piece of hybiscus fibre, which is like a piece of fine netting. A turbid yellowish fluid is thus produced, in taste resembling rhubarb and magnesia, flavoured with sal-volatile. It is handed round in cups made of the shell of large cocoa-nuts, the chief being the first to drink, while all the onlookers join in a very peculiar measured hand-clapping. When he has finished, they shout some exclamation in chorus, and clap hands in a different manner. Then all the others drink in regular order of precedence.

Though no one pretends to like the taste of yangona, its after-effects are said to be so pleasantly stimulating that a considerable number of white men drink it habitually, and even insist on having it prepared by chewing, which is a custom imported from Tonga, and one which has never been adopted in the interior of Fiji, where the old manner of grating the root is preferred. It certainly sounds less nasty, but connoisseurs declare with one voice that grated yangona is not comparable to that which has been chewed. The gentlemen all say that, sometimes when they have had a very long day of hard walking, they are thankful to the native who brings them this, the only stimulant which he has to offer, and that its effect is like sal-volatile. Confirmed drinkers acquire a craving for it. Its action is peculiar, inasmuch as drunkenness from this cause does not affect the brain, but paralyses the muscles, so that a man lies helpless on the ground, perfectly aware of all that is going on.

CUMMING: *At Home in Fiji.* 1881.

When missionaries went on tour, their visits were made public holidays, and people gathered in the village from all the surrounding countryside.

We sat under trees on the river-bank, facing the village green, and each town came up in turn in procession, all quaintly dressed up as if for a fancy ball, and marched slowly past us, every one carrying his offering in his mouth for greater security—a purse at once novel and self-acting; for, as both hands were often busy with spear and fan, it was a saving of trouble, and by no means disrespectful, just to spit out the coin on the mat spread to receive offerings. Some had quite a mouthful to give—three or four shillings. The latter was a sum much aimed at, as the donors of such large contributions had the pride of knowing that their names would appear in a printed list! an honour not wholly without attraction even in Fiji.

The town then divided into two companies. One acted as orchestra, sitting on the ground—some clapping hands, some striking the ground with short, resonant bamboos—all singing. The other company danced—the quaintest wildest dances you can conceive, with much pantomime and most graceful action. Every action and posture one sees in a good ballet are found here; and such pretty grouping with fans, spears, or clubs. Many of the figures are very intricate, and the rapidity of movement and flexibility of the whole body are something marvellous—it seems as if every muscle was in action, and all the postures are graceful. The dance gets wilder and more excited as it goes on, generally ending with an unearthly yell, in which all the spectators join.

They are all sitting round in every available corner, generally spreading a bit of plantain-leaf on the ground to keep their dress clean: for, of course, every one is attired in his very best—perhaps a kilt of English long-cloth (or, far more attractive in our eyes, native cloth of rich brown pattern). White native cloth is worn as a girdle, and hangs behind in large folds; wreaths of long hanging grass are worn round the arms and legs, as well as on the body. Some even powder their hair black, or else wear huge wigs of heathen days, and crowns of scarlet parrots' feathers.

Most have their faces painted with every variety of colour, in stripes, circles, and spots. Some are all scarlet, with black spectacles, or vice versa; some, of a very gaudy turn of mind, half blue and half scarlet. Some are painted half plain and half spotted, or striped like clowns. In short, fancy has free scope in devising grotesque patterns of every sort. Many are entirely blackened down to the waist, or perhaps have one side of the face and one shoulder dyed dark-red; but the commonest and ugliest freak of all is to paint only the nose bright scarlet, and the rest of the face dead black, and very hideous is the result.

The paint-box on these occasions is simple: red ochre supplies one shade, and the seeds of the vermilion-tree, so dull in the pod, but so brilliant when crushed, supply another. The nearest wood-fire yields black in abundance; while a dark-brown fungus is found on the bark of certain trees, and finds immense favour with many who cannot understand how infinitely more beautiful is the rich brown of their own silky skin, with its gloss of cocoa-nut oil. The gaudy blue is a recent addition to their stock—from English laundries; and an unusually vivid scarlet likewise tells occasionally of dealings with British traders.

On great festivals the family jewels are all displayed. They consist of necklaces of whales' teeth rudely fastened together with sinnet, or else most carefully cut into long, curved strips like miniature tusks, highly polished, and strung together in the form of a great collar, which is worn with the curved points turning outwards like a frill. The average length of each tooth is about six inches; but some necklaces, which are treasured as heirlooms, are nearly double this size, and all the teeth are beautifully regular. Their effect when worn by a chief in full dress is singularly picturesque, though scarcely so becoming as the large, curved boar's tooth, which sometimes forms an almost double circle, and is worn suspended from the neck, the white ivory gleaming against the rich brown skin.

The most artistic and uncommon ornament of a Fijian chief is a breast-plate from six to ten inches in diameter, made of polished whale's tooth, sliced and inlaid with pearly shell, all most beautifully joined together. These, like all native work, whether wood-carving or ivory, not only claim admiration, but fill me with wonder at the patient ingenuity which could possibly produce such results with the tools hitherto possessed by these people, to whom metals were un-known, whose axes and hatchets were made of smooth and beauti-fully polished greenstone (precisely similar to the celts of our fore-fathers, and how they made these is to me incomprehensible).

CUMMING: *At Home in Fiji.* 1881.

Dancing in the South Seas is a high accomplishment. Most graceful of the mékés, in Miss Cumming's experience, was one developed by the people of Rewa. It represented the breaking of waves on a coral reef.

The idea to be conveyed is that of the tide gradually rising on the reef, till at length there remains only a little coral isle, round which the angry breakers rage, flinging their white foam on every side. At first the dancers form in long lines and approach silently, to represent the quiet advance of the waves. After a while the lines break up into smaller companies, which advance with outspread hands and bodies bent forward, to represent rippling wavelets, the tiniest waves being represented by children. Quicker and quicker they come on, now advancing, now retreating, yet, like true waves, steadily progressing, and gradually closing on every side of the imaginary islet, round which they play or battle, after the manner of breakers, springing high in mid-air, and flinging their arms far above their heads to represent the action of spray. As they leap and toss their heads, the soft white masi or native cloth (which for greater effect they wear as a turban with long streamers, and also wind round the waist, thence it floats in long scarf-like ends) trembles and flutters in the breeze. The whole effect is most artistic, and the orchestra do their part by imitating the roar of the surf on the reef—a sound which to them has been a never-ceasing lullaby from the hour of their birth.

Ibid.

At festivities in Tonga, club-fighting, wrestling, and boxing were traditional features.

A man from one side runs over to the opposite party and sits down before it; he then makes a sign to know if any one will engage with him: the person who chooses to accept the challenge comes forward brandishing his club, when the two combatants proceed to the middle of the circle, each attended by one from his own party to assist as second. They next determine whether they shall fight after the Tonga or Hamoa fashion; the difference of which is, that the Hamoa custom allows a man to beat his antagonist after he is knocked down, as long as he perceives signs of motion: the Tonga mode, on the contrary, only allows him to flourish his club over his fallen foe, and the fight is at an end. This point being agreed on, the two champions for the applause of the multitude begin to engage. When they have finished, another party comes on in the same way. Sometimes there are three or four sets of combatants engaged at the same time.

MARTIN: *An Account of the Natives of the Tonga Islands.* 1818.

*

When any of them chooses to wrestle, he gets up from one side of the ring, and crosses the ground in a sort of measured pace, clapping smartly on the elbow joint of one arm, which is bent, and produces a hollow sound; that is reckoned the challenge. If no person comes out from the opposite side to engage him, he returns in the same manner, and sits down; but sometimes stands clapping in the midst of the ground, to provoke some one to come out. If an opponent appear, they come together with marks of the greatest good nature, generally smiling, and taking time to adjust the piece of cloth which is fastened round the waist. They then lay hold of each other by this girdle, with a hand on each side, and he who succeeds in drawing his antagonist to him immediately tries to lift him upon his breast, and throw him upon his back, and if he be able to turn round with him two or three times in that position, before he throws him, his dexterity never fails of procuring plaudits from the spectators. If they be more equally matched, they close soon, and endeavour to throw each other by entwining their legs, or lifting each other from the ground; in which struggles they shew a prodigious exertion of strength, every muscle, as it were, being ready to burst with straining. When one is thrown, he immediately quits the field; but the victor sits down for a few seconds, then gets up, and goes to the side he came from, who proclaim the victory aloud, in a sentence delivered slowly, and in a musical cadence. After sitting a short space, he rises again and challenges, when sometimes several antagonists make their appearance; but he has the privilege of choosing which of them he pleases, to wrestle with; and has likewise the preference of challenging again, if he should throw his adversary, until he himself be vanquished; and then the opposite side sing the song of victory in favour of their champion. It also often happens, that five or six rise from each side, and challenge together, in which case it is common to see three or four couples engaged on the field at once. But it is astonishing to see what temper they preserve in this exercise: for we observed no instances of their leaving the spot with the least displeasure in their countenances. When they find that they are so equally matched as not to be likely to throw each other, they leave off by mutual consent. And if the fall of one is not fair, or if it does not appear very clearly who has had the advantage, both sides sing the victory, and then they engage again; but no person who has been vanquished can engage with his conqueror a second time.

The boxers advance sideways, changing the side at every pace, with one arm stretched fully out before, the other behind; and holding a piece of cord in one hand, which they wrap firmly about it when they find an antagonist, or else have done so before they enter. This I imagine they do to prevent a dislocation of the hand or fingers. Their blows are directed chiefly to the head, but sometimes to the sides; and are dealt out with great activity. They shift sides, and box equally well with both hands. But one of their favourite and most dexterous blows is, to turn round on their heel just as they have struck their antagonist, and to give him another very smart one with the other hand, backward.

The boxing matches seldom last long; and the parties either leave off together, or one acknowledges his being beat.

MARTIN: *An Account of the Natives of the Tongo Islands.* 1818.

Robert Louis Stevenson witnessed an inter-Island singing and dancing contest which nearly ended in disaster.

Perceiving themselves worsted, the choir of Butaritari grew confused, blundered, and broke down; amid this hubbub of unfamiliar intervals I should not myself have recognised the slip, but the audience were quick to catch it, and to jeer. To crown all, the Makin company began a dance of truly superlative merit. I know not what it was about, I was too much absorbed to ask. In one act a part of the chorus, squealing in some strange falsetto, produced very much the effect of our orchestra; in another, the dancers, leaping like jumping-jacks, with arms extended, passed through and through each other's ranks with extra-

ordinary speed, neatness, and humour. A more laughable effect I never
saw; in any European theatre it would have brought the house down,
and the island audience roared with laughter and applause. This filled
up the measure for the rival company, and they forgot themselves
and decency. After each act or figure of the ballet, the performers
pause a moment standing, and the next is introduced by the clapping
of hands in triplets. Not until the end of the whole ballet do they sit
down, which is the signal for the rivals to stand up. But now all rules
were to be broken. During the interval following on this great
applause, the company of Butaritari leaped suddenly to their feet and
most unhandsomely began a performance of their own. It was strange
to see the men of Makin staring; I have seen a tenor in Europe stare
with the same blank dignity into a hissing theatre; but presently, to my
surprise, they sobered down, gave up the unsung remainder of their
ballet, resumed their seats, and suffered their ungallant adversaries to
go on and finish. Nothing would suffice. Again, at the first interval,
Butaritari unhandsomely cut in; Makin, irritated in turn, followed the
example; and the two companies of dancers remained permanently
standing, continuously clapping hands, and regularly cutting across
each other at each pause. I expected blows to begin with any moment;
and our position in the midst was highly unstrategical. But the Makin
people had a better thought; and upon a fresh interruption turned and
trooped out of the house. We followed them, first because these were
the artists, second because they were guests and had been scurvily ill-
used. A large proportion of our neighbours did the same, so that the
causeway was filled from end to end by the procession of deserters; and
the Butaritari choir was left to sing for its own pleasure in an empty
house, having gained the point and lost the audience. It was surely fortunate that there was no one drunk; but, drunk or sober, where else
would a scene so irritating have concluded without blows?

STEVENSON: *In the South Seas.* 1900.

In the Pacific, as in Africa, legends attribute dark skins to divine punishment.

Their Account of the Creation is that all men are descended from the same parents. The first born was the Fiji; but he misbehaved himself, and was black, with but little clothing. The next born was Tonga, who was not quite so bad, and was consequently whiter, and received more clothing. Papalagis, or white men, were born last, but did not sin, and were therefore quite white, and had many clothes.

COOPER: *Coral Lands.* 1880.

Tangaloa, god of arts and inventions in the Tongan mythology, drew up the islands out of the sea while fishing, and sent his sons to inhabit them. One killed the other and Tangoloa called the two families together. First he spoke to the family of the murdered man.

Tangaloa straightway ordered them thus: Put your canoes to sea, and sail to the east, to the great land which is there, and take up your abode there. Be your skins white like your minds, for your minds are pure; you shall be wise, making axes, and all riches whatsoever, and shall have large canoes. I will go myself and command the wind to blow from your land to Tonga; but they (the Tonga people) shall not be able to go to you with their bad canoes.

Tangaloa then spoke thus to the others: You shall be black, because your minds are bad, and shall be destitute; you shall not be wise in useful things, neither shall you go to the great land of your brothers; how can you go with your bad canoes? But your brothers shall come to Tonga, and trade with you as they please.

MARTIN: *An Account of the Natives of the Tonga Islands.* 1818.

The following tradition accounts for the universal spread of death:

When the first man, the father of the human race, was being buried, a god passed by this first grave, and asked what it meant. On being informed by those standing by that they had just buried their father, he said, "Do not inter him. Dig the body up again." "No," was the reply, "we cannot do that; he has been dead four days, and stinks." "Not so," said the god; "disinter him, and I promise you he shall live again." Heedless, however, of the promise of the god, these original sextons persisted in leaving their father's remains in the earth. Perceiving their perverseness, the god said, "By refusing compliance with my commands you have sealed your own destinies. Had you dug up your ancestor you would have found him alive, and yourselves also, as you passed from this world, should have been buried, as bananas are, for the space of four days, after which you should have been dug up, not rotten, but ripe. But now, as a punishment for your disobedience, you shall die and rot."

WILLIAMS: *Fiji and the Fijians.* 1870.

Tongans and Fijians both had legends telling of a large island where the gods lived.

This island is supposed to be much larger than all their own islands put together, to be well stocked with all kinds of useful and ornamental plants, always in a state of high perfection, and always bearing the richest fruits and the most beautiful flowers according to their respective natures; that when these fruits or flowers are plucked, others immediately occupy their place, and that the whole atmosphere is filled with the most delightful fragrance that the imagination can conceive, proceeding from these immortal plants; the island is also well stocked with the most beautiful birds of all imaginable kinds as well as with abundance of hogs, all of which are immortal unless they are killed to provide food for the hotooas or gods; but the moment a hog or bird is killed another living hog or bird immediately comes into existence to supply its place, the same as with the fruits and flowers, and this as far as they know or suppose, is the only mode of propagation of plants and animals. The island of Bolotoo is supposed to be so far off as to render it dangerous for their canoes to attempt going there, and it is supposed moreover, that even if they were to succeed in reaching so far, unless it happened to be the particular will of the gods, they would be sure to miss it. They give, however, an account of a Tonga canoe, which, on her return from the Fiji islands a long time ago, was driven by stress of weather to Bolotoo: ignorant of the place where they were, and being much in want of provisions—seeing the country abound in all sorts of fruit, the crew landed, and proceeded to pluck some bread fruit, but to their unspeakable astonishment, they could no more lay hold of it than if it were a shadow; they walked through the trunks of the trees, and passed through the substance of the houses, (which were built like those of Tonga), without feeling any resistance. They at length saw some of the hotooas, who passed through the substance of their bodies as if there were nothing there: the hotooas recommended them to go away immediately, as they had no proper food for them, and promised them a fair wind and a speedy passage.

MARTIN: *An Account of the Natives of the Tonga Islands.* 1818.

Fijian legend had it that bachelors never went to heaven.

It is said that the soul of a bachelor never gets to heaven, or Burotu rather. Lurking round Naithombothombo is Na Alewa Levu, the great woman, who watches every spirit that approaches, and as soon as she sees the soul of a man who never had a wife in all his life, she makes a spring at it, with the intention of annihilating it. In her flurry to crush the unfortunate being whom no souls of strangled wives accompany, she sometimes misses the object of her vengeance. But before the soul has time to rejoice at the escape, the fierce Nangananga confronts it. It is his special business to demolish those who escape the fury of the great Woman—and his vigilance is never at fault. More wily than his companion, he hides amongst the rocks around Naithombothombo, and as the poor soul passes forward, he springs from his lair, and hurls it against a large stone, smashing it to atoms—and the soul of the bachelor is totally annihilated!

PRITCHARD:
Polynesian Reminiscences; or, Life in the South Pacific Islands. 1866.

Once upon a time the Fijian island of Oneata was not only without mosquitoes, but was also blessed with an abundance of shellfish. But its ruler, a foolish god, visited the island of Kambara, where there were mosquitoes but no shellfish.

After they had eaten their fill, and when the kava-bowl was empty, the god of Oneata began to yawn; for he was tired and sleepy.

"Come with me, friend," said Tuwara. And he took him within the great mosquito curtain.

"What is this?" asked the Oneata god, in great surprise at the bigness thereof, and the beauty of the painting. "A wonderful piece of cloth is this! We have none such in my land. But why do you keep it thus hung up, Tuwara? What then, is its use?"

"Its use," answered the other, "its use, do you ask? It is a useful thing. It is useful as a—yes, as a screen to hide me, when I wish to sleep. Therefore do I keep it thus hung up in the midst of the house. And, moreover, it is very useful when the wind blows strong and cold. But let us sleep now, and in the morning I will show you the town."

Thus spake Tuwara, because he was ashamed of the mosquitoes; for he knew that there were none at Oneata; and he wanted to hide from his companion the thing which was the plague of his land. Wherefore he lied to him about the curtain.

Not long was it after darkness had closed in, before the house was full of mosquitoes, and the god of Oneata heard them buzzing in thousands outside the curtain, just as he was dozing off to sleep.

"What is that?" cried he. "What sweet sound is that?"

"What can I say to him now?" thought Tuwara in great perplexity; and not being able to think of anything, he pretended to be asleep, and answered only with a snore.

"Hi! Tuwara!" shouted the Oneata god, punching him into wakefulness. "Wake up, Tuwara, and tell me what sweet sounds are these."

"Eh? What? What's the matter?" said Tuwara with a yawn.

"What are those pleasant sounds? Truly a sweet and soothing note is that which I now hear."

"Pleasant sounds? Ah, yes—the buzzing. Oh, that's only the mosquitoes."

"And what are mosquitoes?" asked his companion.

"They are little insects that fly in the air by night and buzz. I keep them to sing me to sleep," said the artful Tuwara.

"A treasure indeed!" cried the other god. "Woe is me that there are none at Oneata. Give them to me, Tuwara."

"Give you my mosquitoes! I dare not, indeed. My people would never forgive me. They would hate me, and rebel. Wretched indeed should we be if there were no mosquitoes on Kambara."

"Well, then, give me some of them," pleaded his companion. "Give me some, and keep some yourself, that we may both have them."

"It is impossible," replied the cunning one. "They are a loving tribe. If I send even a few of them away, all the rest will leave me. Truly my soul is sore in that I must refuse you, Wakulikuli; but refuse you I must. And now let us sleep, for my word is spoken."

"No, no!" whined the foolish god, in a voice that was neighbour to crying: "refuse me not, I beseech you. Give me the mosquitoes, that I may take them to our land; and, when we hear their song in the night, we shall think of you, and say to our children, 'Great is the love of Tuwara'."

"That, indeed, is a tempting thought," said the Kambara god. "Glad should I be for you to hold us in loving remembrance. But what am I to say to my people? How can I appease their anger when they rage against me, saying, 'Our god has given away *for nothing* our dear mosquitoes?"' And his voice fell heavy on the words "for nothing."

"For nothing!" cried the other. "No, truly! All that I have is yours. Name anything that you saw in my land, and you shall have it; only let the insects be mine that sing this pleasant song."

"Well then—I do not ask for myself. Gladly would I give you freely anything that is mine; but my people, friend, my people! You know these children of men, and their ways, how covetous they are. And what is there in your land that would satisfy them? Of a truth I cannot think of anything at all. Ah, yes! There is the shellfish! That will do. That is the very thing for these people. Fill but their stomachs, and you can do anything with them. Give me the shellfish, friend, and my mosquitoes are yours."

"Willingly, willingly!" cried the other in an eager voice. "It's a bargain, Tuwara. And now let us lift up the curtain and let some of them in, that I may see them."

"Forbear!" cried Tuwara, starting up in a great fright, lest the mosquitoes should get at his companion and bite him, and he thereby repent of his bargain. "Forbear! Lift not the curtain, friend, lift it not! A modest tribe and a bashful are they; nor can they bear to be looked upon: therefore do they hide themselves by day, and it is in the darkness only that they sing their pleasant song."

"Wou! wou!" exclaimed the silly one. "Wonderful things do I hear! The curtain shall remain unlifted."

"And now, do let us sleep," said Tuwara; "for it is far into the night; and we will sail together in the morning, taking with us the mosquitoes."

How he got the mosquitoes together we do not know; but our fathers said he shut them all up in a big basket, which was lined inside, and covered with fine mats, through the plait whereof not even a little one could crawl. And, when this basket was carried on board the canoe, they hoisted the sail, and went out, through the passage, into the open sea, steering for Oneata.

Terribly seasick were they both: but neither of them cared so much for it this time; he of Oneata being cheered by the thought of his sweet singers; and Tuwara because he was now well rid of them, and moreover because of the shellfish; wherefore were they both content to suffer.

The sun was still high in the heavens when they furled their sail at Oneata; and the Oneata god leaped on shore, crying aloud, "Come hither, my people. Come hither, all of you, and see the good things

I have brought. Hand down the basket, Tuwara, that the hearts of my people may be glad."

"Not so!" answered the cunning Tuwara. "The mosquitoes are a loving folk, as I told you before; and if we were to let them go while I am in sight, they will not leave the canoe; for they love me, friend, they love me. Give me therefore the shellfish, and I will depart, leaving the great basket with you. And, if you are wise, you will not open it till I am beyond the reef, lest the mosquitoes should fly after me, and leave you."

"True!" quoth the foolish god. "True are your words, Tuwara. A wise god are you; for you think of everything. Come from the beach, from the sea, from the rocks, ye shellfish! Come! for your lord is calling!"

Then from the rocks, from the sea, from the beach, came the shellfish, crawling over the sand, a great multitude. And the Boat-builders threw them into the canoe, our fathers also helping, till it was full, and heaped high above the deck, and there was not one shellfish left on the land.

"Go now, Tuwara," cried his companion, "give me the basket and go; for the shellfish are all on board."

So Tuwara handed down the basket, while the Boat-builders hoisted the great sail, and soon the canoe was gliding swiftly away towards the passage; while the Oneata men crowded round the basket, asking their god all manner of eager questions as to its contents.

"It must be something wonderful," said they, "or our lord would never have parted with the shellfish."

"Wait and see," quoth the god, with a self-satisfied smile.

As soon as the canoe had cleared the reef, he untied the fastenings of the basket, and lifted the mat wherewith it was covered. "Here is our treasure," cried the foolish god.

Then uprose the mosquitoes in a cloud, fierce and angry; and Tuwara could hear the screams and yells of our fathers, as they smarted under the sharp bites of the savage insects.

"The god of Oneata's sweet singers have begun their song," said he, as soon as he could speak for laughing. "Many fools have I met with among the children of men, but never such a fool as the god of Oneata."

FISON: *Tales from Old Fiji.* 1904.

A Voyage to the Pacific Ocean. Performed under the Directions of
Captains Cook, Clerke, and Gore, in His Majesty's Ships the
Resolution and *Discovery,* in the years 1776, 1777, 1778, 1779 and
1780. Vol. I and II written by CAPTAIN JAMES COOK.

This was the third and last of Captain Cook's voyages in the South
Seas. Knowing that he was expected "to relate, as well as to execute,
its operations", he kept a full journal. In the first volume he tells of
three months spent in the Tonga group in 1777. His account of the
Tongans—the first detailed account—is highly complimentary. Their
countenances, he said, "very remarkably express the abundant mildness, or good nature, which they possess . . . they are, at the same time,
frank, cheerful and good-humoured." Their only defect, he added,
was a propensity to thieving. In evidence of his esteem he named the
group the Friendly Islands. His good opinion was not, alas, entirely
warranted. Had he but known it, his hosts planned to kill him and to
seize his ship (as later they seized the *Port au Prince*), and did not make
the attempt only because of differences among themselves. Cook's
disposition to be too confiding cost him his life at Hawaii later in the
voyage. But by then he could fairly claim that the southern hemisphere was "sufficiently explored, and a final end put to the searching
after a Southern continent."

JOHN MARTIN: *An Account of the Natives of the Tonga Islands.* Compiled and arranged from the extensive communications of Mr.
WILLIAM MARINER. 1818.

In his introduction the author, a doctor, says: "In the year 1811 I
accidentally heard that Mr. William Mariner, the bearer of a letter
from the East Indies to one of my connections in London, had been a
resident at the Friendly Islands during the space of four years; and, my
curiosity being strongly excited, I solicited his acquaintance." The
result was publication of this comprehensive account of the habits, be-
liefs and customs of the Tongans. Mariner had a remarkable story to
tell. At the age of thirteen he elected to join the crew of a private
sloop of war, the *Port au Prince*, commanded by a friend of his father.
The ship sailed in February, 1805, and after some profitable actions
against Spanish ships and the Spanish garrison at Conception, it an-
chored off Lifuka, Captain Cook's original Friendly Island. On the

1st December, 1806, when half the crew was on shore, the Tongans treacherously seized the ship, clubbing twenty-two of the crew to death. Fortunately for the youthful Mariner—he was then fifteen—the king took a liking to him and for the next four years he lived among the Tongans as one of themselves. In 1810, when returning from a fishing trip, he sighted a ship, but before his three companions would agree to pull towards it he had to stun one of them. After paddling all night the canoe reached the ship, a trading brig, and Mariner was taken on board.

J. S. JENKINS: *Recent Exploring Expeditions to the Pacific and the South Seas.* 1853.

Except that the author also wrote *The History of the War with Mexico*, I have no information about him.

MRS. SMYTHE: *Ten Months in the Fiji Islands.* 1864.

When, in 1859, Her Majesty's Government decided to send a special Commissioner to Fiji to inquire into the offer of cession made by Thakombau, the appointment fell to Colonel W. T. Smythe, of the Royal Artillery. With him went his wife. Her book provides a valuable supplement to the official report. The Commissioner advised against acceptance of the offer of cession, but lived to change his opinions.

W. T. PRITCHARD: *Polynesian Reminiscences, or Life in the South Pacific Islands.* 1866.

Pritchard's father, the Rev. George Pritchard, went to Tahiti in 1824 as a missionary, and later served with distinction as British Consul for a "district" which covered Tahiti, Samoa, Tonga and Fiji. In 1844, he was involved in an incident with the French, which caused some excitement at the time in London and Paris and ended with an apology from the French Government. But the chief result was to confirm French predominance in Tahiti and to cause Pritchard to make Samoa his official residence. Here he was joined in 1848 by his son, who had been born in Tahiti and spent ten years there before going to England to be educated. In 1857 Fiji was created a separate consular district, and the younger Pritchard appointed first consul. He arrived at a time when Thakombau was being hard pressed by the American Government to settle a claim for 43,000 dollars in compensation for loss and damage to property belonging to American citizens. In his dilemma, Thakombau made the famous offer to Pritchard to cede Fiji to Britain, and this offer Pritchard took to London. There followed the inquiry conducted by Colonel Smythe and the decision not to accept cession. Smythe's report included an implication that Pritchard had interfered unwarrantably in native affairs, and following an investigation Pritchard was dismissed, the allegation being also made that he had overdrawn from official funds. After trying vainly for some time to have the matter re-opened, Pritchard went to Mexico and disappeared during a journey from there to California. He was undoubtedly a vigorous and able man, and there was a body of contemporary opinion which considered that he had been gravely wronged.

THOMAS WILLIAMS: *Fiji and the Fijians.*
JAMES CALVERT: *Missionary Labours Among the Cannibals.* 1870.

These books by two famous pioneer missionaries were edited and published in a single volume. Calvert arrived in Fiji in 1839, four years after the first two European missionaries had been received, and Williams a year later. They were destined to spend seventeen and thirteen years respectively in the islands. Most of that time they resided in districts where cannibalism and other barbarous practices were rife, and where their own lives frequently hung in the balance. The spectacle of cannibal feasts caused Williams to write: "Such scenes stagger faith and chill charity." But the persistence and devotion of men like Calvert and Williams eventually converted Fiji to Christianity and brought about a transformation.

H. BRITTON: *Fiji in* 1870.

As special correspondent of a Melbourne newspaper, Britton spent nine weeks in the islands and his "letters" to the paper are reprinted in this volume.

J. H. DE RICCI: *Fiji: Our New Province in the South Seas.* 1875.
De Ricci was Fiji's first Attorney-General after the cession.

H. STONEHEWER COOPER: *Coral Islands.* 1880.

The author did a leisurely tour of the South Pacific in the late 'seventies, collected a great deal of information, met people like Thakombau and Ma'afu in Fiji, and put the information and his conclusions into *Coral Lands.* The conclusions added up to a plea that Britain should take a more active interest in the Pacific, both because of the trading possibilities and because the peoples of the islands were "worthy of our care".

C. F. GORDON CUMMING: *At Home in Fiji.* 1881.

First Governor of Fiji after the cession in 1874 was Sir Arthur Hamilton Gordon, son of the fourth Earl of Aberdeen. He arrived at Levuka in June, 1875, and was joined a few months later by Lady Gordon. With Lady Gordon came Miss Gordon Cumming, who had already written a book of travel called *From the Hebrides to the Himalayas*, dealing in particular with her eighteen months' residence in Ceylon. Without suggesting that she did for Fiji what Mary Kingsley did for West Africa, yet *At Home in Fiji* has something of Mary Kingsley's charm.

WALTER COOTE: *The Western Pacific.* 1883.

Coote was among those who sought to awaken British interest in the Western Pacific at a time when France and Germany were showing a disposition to make claims there. He wrote from personal knowledge of the islands.

H.B. GUPPY: *The Solomon Islands and Their Natives.* 1887.

When, in 1881, H.M.S. *Lark* was sent on a surveying mission to the Solomons, Guppy went as Surgeon. He combined his professional duties with observations on the anthropology, natural history, botany, geology and meteorology of the group, and his book is recognised as one of the most important written about the Solomons.

REV. ALFRED PENNY: *Ten Years in Melanesia.* 1887.

An account of missionary experiences in the Solomons, beginning not long after the murder of Bishop Patteson in 1871.

C. M. WOODFORD: *A Naturalist Among the Head-Hunters.* 1890.

Woodford paid three visits to the Solomon Islands in the late 'eighties, and spent much of the time living alone among the people. In view of their merited reputation for ferocity, this required courage to the point of foolhardiness, but he succeded in winning their confidence and was invited to live permanently with them. The secret, he said, was the "exercise of the greatest patience and good temper".

MRS. EDGEWORTH DAVID: *Funafuti.* 1899.

Mrs. David accompanied her husband on an expedition designed to throw light on the origin of coral reefs and atolls. Boring apparatus was taken to Funafuti in the Ellice group; the bore went down 600 feet but the results were inconclusive. Mrs. David describes her book as "an unscientific account of a scientific expedition".

ROBERT LOUIS STEVENSON: *In the South Seas.*   1900.

The part of Stevenson's book from which I quote relates to his residence at Butaritari and at Apemama in the Gilberts. It includes an entertaining character study of the King of Apemama, "solely conspicuous, the hero of song, the butt of gossip."

LORIMER FISON: *Tales from Old Fiji.*   1904.

A collection of legends based on information obtained from Taliaitupou, King of Lakemba, "a talkative old gentleman with a lively imagination".